JOHN RIGG was born and raised in Leeds, Yorkshir̲̅ University of Cambridge with a First Class degree in Ecṵ̲̅ṵ̲̅ṵ̲̅ṵ̲̅ṵ̲̅, a Ph.D. He has worked as an economic consultant in London and in the Senior Civil Service in Scotland.

His sporting career principally comprised playing rugby league at primary school, rugby union at secondary school and college and cricket to a reasonable club standard.

John's first book on sport – *An Ordinary Spectator: 50 Years of Watching Sport* – was published by SilverWood Books in 2012. This was followed by *Still An Ordinary Spectator: Five More Years of Watching Sport* in 2017. He has also written sport-related articles for *Backpass*, *Backspin*, *The Nightwatchman: Wisden Cricket Quarterly*, *The Rugby League Journal*, *Forty-20* and (co-authored with Richard Lewney) *The International Review of the Sociology of Sport*.

John's non-sporting articles have included those on economics/statistics for the *Scottish Economic Bulletin* and *Scottish Economic Statistics*. He has also written articles on family history for the *Cleveland Family History Journal* and his book – *The Line of 16: Searching for my children's great, great grandparents* – will be published in 2023.

John's fiction is written under the name of JR Alexander. The novels – *Shouting at the Window* (2020) and *On the Carousel* (2021) – are published by High Ridge Publishing and available on Kindle and other online platforms. *Long Forgotten Events* will be published in 2024.

He is married with two children and lives in Scotland.

Find out more about John and his writing at: www.anordinaryspectator.com and www.jralexanderauthor.com.

**Also by John Rigg**

*An Ordinary Spectator: 50 Years of Watching Sport*
*Still An Ordinary Spectator: Five More Years of Watching Sport*

# AN ORDINARY
# SPECTATOR
## RETURNS
### WATCHING SPORT AGAIN

## John Rigg

SilverWood

Published in 2023 by SilverWood Books

SilverWood Books Ltd
14 Small Street, Bristol, BS1 1DE, United Kingdom
www.silverwoodbooks.co.uk

ISBN 9781800422520 (paperback)
Also available as an ebook

British Library Cataloguing in Publication Data
A CIP catalogue record for this book is available from the British Library

Page design and typesetting by SilverWood Books

*This book is dedicated to Angela, Tom and Katie*

# Contents

# Preface

*The best laid schemes o' Mice an' Men*
*Gang aft agley.*

From *To a Mouse* (1785) by Robert Burns

The quote given above is an appropriate line with which to begin this book's introduction.

I had originally intended that, following the publication of *An Ordinary Spectator: 50 Years of Watching Sport* in 2012 and *Still An Ordinary Spectator: Five More Years of Watching Sport* in 2017, this third volume in the series would appear in 2022. This would have maintained the neat 5-year cycle in bringing together some of the various pieces of sports writing that I had published.

It was not to be, for which blame the Covid-19 pandemic. Given that the plan had been for much of the book's contents to have consisted of reflections on matches and events watched over that half-decade, an obvious difficulty presented itself when a 17-month hiatus – perhaps more than a hiatus, a chasm – was created within that time frame, when I did not see any live sport at all.

The solution was also obvious – to delay publication of this book for a year – and that is what I have done.

As it turned out, there have been unanticipated benefits in this approach. There were various pieces of writing produced between February 2020 and July 2021 that, whilst not commenting on contemporaneous sports events, were able to offer a more contemplative view of the impact of the pandemic, including a considered assessment of why I – or we – watch live sport in the first place. In addition, I was able to devote more attention than planned to the history of certain sports events, including international football and Test Match cricket and the Olympic Games. As a result, the book contains a wider range of sport-related content than I had initially envisaged.

It also covers a longer time period than I had originally planned. Indeed, on occasion, my time-frame has extended back several decades: for example, to describe a unique pre-First World War sporting career or to acknowledge a leading American sports journalist of the Inter-War period.

In addition, I have taken the opportunity to include a selection of those essays that commemorate some of the anniversaries of sports events that – at a personal level – have left a longstanding impression on me. These include my recollections of attending a particularly dramatic European Cup tie (30<sup>th</sup> anniversary), my astonishment at seeing the unexpected dismissal of Gary Sobers in a Headingley test match (50<sup>th</sup>) and my fascination in reading for the first time about the exploits of a Great Britain rugby league team on a tour of Australasia (60<sup>th</sup>). A separate – though related – essay marked the 100<sup>th</sup> anniversary of the birth of the person who introduced me not only to watching sport, but to appreciating and analysing it: my father, William (Bill) Rigg.

At one level, these historical references can be justified as simple exercises in nostalgia. There is nothing wrong with that, I think. The word is derived from the Greek *nostos* – a return home – and the recollection of the places/events/people of the past can be a legitimate and powerful source of pleasure as well as contemplative reflection. In addition, however, I will continue to argue (as in *An Ordinary Spectator* and *Still An Ordinary Spectator*) that it is the informed examination of the sports of the past that assists us in passing judgement on the participants in sport – players, coaches, administrators, spectators – in the modern era.

Having – hopefully – justified the range of essays presented in this volume, it remains the case that the core of the book – accounting for roughly half of the essays that follow – contains contemporary assessments of sports events that I had been to see. Its format follows logically, therefore, that adopted in *Still An Ordinary Spectator.*

Against this background, it can be seen that the subtitle of this volume – *Watching Sport Again* – can happily be interpreted in two mutually supportive ways. On the one hand, it is number three in a trilogy of publications that stretch over a decade. And, on the other, it captures the excitement and relief that I experienced on the resumption of watching live sport – in the flesh – after the long shutdown deemed necessary due to the pandemic.

As with the first two books, the majority of essays focus on four main sports – soccer, cricket, rugby league and rugby union – and were initially published as occasional blogs on www.anordinaryspectator.com/news-blog. They have been supplemented by my contributions to *The Rugby League Journal*, the *Forty-20* rugby league magazine, *Backpass* and *The Nightwatchman: Wisden Cricket Quarterly* as well as my reminiscence of a cricket match played over half a century ago that was published on the website of the Sporting Memories charity.

However, again in keeping with the previous publications, I have ventured into new areas: in this case, baseball, basketball, badminton, cycling, snooker, shinty and professional boxing. It will be evident that I have no problem with this type of eclecticism. The events covered in the pages that follow range from elite encounters – including Premier League football (from the Etihad Stadium in Manchester), Major League Baseball (from the Rogers Centre in Toronto) and World Championship Boxing (from the OVO Hydro arena in Glasgow) – through to the 4th tier of Scottish professional soccer (in Berwick), amateur rugby league (in Edinburgh) and the 8th tier of the divisional structure of the Rugby Football Union (in Leeds).

The elite contests have allowed me to renew my admiration for the skills of highly paid professionals at the top of their game: Kevin De Bruyne playing football for Manchester City and Belgium, Mohammed Amir striking with the new ball for Essex CCC, Jonny Lomax creating try-scoring opportunities for his colleagues at St Helens RLFC... But, as will be seen, there are also references in this volume to some of those further down the pecking order of sporting rewards and fame: Adam Endersby, a bustling prop forward for the York Acorn amateur rugby league side, the goal-kicking of Alex Jones of Roundhegians RFC, a goal scored by Lauren Wade of the Glasgow City women's football team... Each in their turn impressed with their effort and determination... and skill.

Looking over the contents of this volume, I am also struck by the number of times I have appreciated the efforts of not only the players, but also the match officials. At the time, these might have seemed little more than throw-away (though genuinely held) comments but, in their aggregate, they serve as a significant reminder of the importance of the referee's skills and integrity. Some of the officials were (or had been) at the top of their profession – Jerome Garces and Nigel Owens (rugby union), Robert Hicks (rugby league), Ovidiu Hategan (football) – but others were in charge of lower league encounters and a couple (covering amateur rugby league and shinty) are regrettably unnamed in the text that follows.

I have to confess that, at times, the narrative in this volume does appear to stray away from its main subject matter. As a result, the contents range from the calory content of a foot-long hot-dog in Toronto to the first performances (in Vienna in 1808) of Ludwig van Beethoven's 5th and 6th Symphonies. The (admittedly thin) sporting threads are revealed, however.

As with the second book, the articles and blogs presented in this volume are more or less unchanged from their original publication. The principal editing that I have undertaken, where appropriate, has again been to shift some of the quotations taken from *An Ordinary Spectator* or *Still An Ordinary Spectator* to the beginning of the article in order to assist in establishing the general context to the piece. I have also removed some of the direct references to the two books themselves. (As before, I have retained the present tense in which many of these pieces were written). In addition, a limited amount of post-event updating has been presented in the End Notes to the book. I hasten to add that this has not been to correct blatant errors or incorrect forecasts – or, at least, not often – but to satisfy any curiosity on what the outcome of certain events turned out to have been.

Blatant errors and incorrect forecasts? Surely not. Surely, after 60-plus years of watching sport, I could be classified as reasonably expert on what I was watching? In general, yes, I think (he says, modestly). But, in the pages that follow, there will be references that cut across that overall conclusion. In October 2017, I ventured that Kilmarnock FC, at the time bottom of the Scottish Premiership, would face "a long and gruelling journey through to spring" (they finished the season securely in 5$^{th}$ place in the 12-team league table); the following January, I confidently stated that West of Scotland FC (a rugby club, of course) were "comfortably clear" of their division's single relegation place (they were relegated); in November 2019, I went to a Hearts vs St Mirren match in the Premiership "expecting a low-scoring encounter" (it finished 5-2); and, following the first match of the 2020 season, I ventured that the players of Hull FC (another rugby club) "offered much promise for their new Super League campaign" (the coach lost his job the following month after a run of poor results). Such is sport, I suppose – never short of surprises.

In my defence, there have been occasions when the track record has been rather more favourable. To give one example, in *Still An Ordinary Spectator*, I referred to the Belarus versus Egypt football game – a group match in the 2012 Olympic Games – that I had attended at Hampden Park in Glasgow. In reporting Egypt's 3-1 win, I specifically noted the performance of a relatively unknown 19 year-old: "I was impressed by the speedy Mohammed Salah on the right wing". Fast forward a decade to the beginning of 2023 and Salah is generally regarded as one of the best players in the world, having scored 172 goals (and counting) in 279 appearances in all competitions for Liverpool FC.

The years pass and time moves on. In the concluding chapter of *An Ordinary Spectator*, I paid tribute to some of those whom I had watched on the field of play, but who were now deceased. Some had lived to their 70s or 80s (Freddie Trueman, Eric Ashton, Don Fox…), others had died at a much earlier age (Billy Bremner, Walter Payton, Graham Dilley...) Each departure had been shocking and saddening in its own way. Likewise, in *Still An Ordinary Spectator*, there were specific entries following the deaths of the former Yorkshire and England spin-bowler Don Wilson and of Harry Jepson, the respected President of the Leeds Rhinos RLFC (who, 50 years earlier, had refereed a rugby league match in which I had played at primary school).

It was inevitable that the theme would be continued in this volume: there are entries for the great Hunslet and Great Britain rugby league forward Geoff Gunney, the Ashes-winning England cricket captain Ray Illingworth and the wonderful Australian leg-spin bowler Shane Warne.

Yes, the years pass and those that graced the sporting stage long ago – or not so long ago – depart the scene. But the new names of the next generation are always coming through. In my entry on the first cricket match that I watched after the Covid-19 pandemic – a Yorkshire versus Surrey 50-over game at Scarborough in July 2021 – I note how impressed I had been with two young players, one from each side, who were previously entirely unfamiliar to me: Matthew Revis and Nico Reifer. It might be that either – or both – enjoys a long and successful career. Or that neither does. The Ordinary Spectator will look out for their progress with interest.

# Cricket

# A Cricket First

I was present at Headingley on Sunday when a piece of English cricket history was made. In a T20 match, Ross Whiteley of the Worcestershire Royals – a Yorkshireman, as it happens – struck 6 sixes in an over from the Yorkshire Vikings left-arm spin bowler, Karl Carver. It was the first time that this had occurred in a senior cricket match in England – Gary Sobers's famous achievement in a County Championship game in 1968 took place in Swansea – and only the fifth time anywhere, the last example being in 2007.

I hesitate to say that I could it coming. But I could – sort of – see it coming. At the beginning of the over – the 16th of the innings – Worcestershire required 98 to win from 30 deliveries, a near-impossible task, so some extraordinary striking was required. It was a good batting wicket with the shorter boundary favouring the left-hander's shots to the leg side. I knew that Whiteley is a renowned powerful hitter, who has a track record against Yorkshire – he hit 11 sixes in an innings of 91 not out on the same ground two years ago. Moreover, he had had a sighter with the last ball of Carver's previous over, which he also hit for six. (The unfortunate bowler was therefore dispatched over the ropes for 7 consecutive legitimate deliveries; he also bowled a wide, so that his fateful over cost 37 runs). When the second six landed in the Western Terrace, I did begin to wonder.

The Yorkshire crowd acknowledged the achievement with polite applause, no doubt whilst also doing the mental calculations as to whether their side's apparently impregnable match-winning position was about to be lost. (It wasn't. Whiteley was out in the next over and the home side went on to win by 37 runs). At the same time, there was undoubtedly a general feeling of sympathy for Carver; even from my distant perspective in the East Stand, it did seem that his shoulders visibly sagged as he walked away to his fielding position at the end of the over.

Earlier, David Willey had struck 118 from 55 deliveries – including 8 sixes – in Yorkshire's total of 233 for 6: the county's individual and team records in this form of the game. Willey and Whiteley are similar types of player: left-handed with aggressive stances at the wicket and the ability to hit cleanly, especially in the arc from long-off through to mid-wicket. Willey had warmed up for his innings by scoring 70 (from 38 deliveries) in Yorkshire's 29 run win over the Birmingham Bears on the previous Friday evening; only 6 sixes on that occasion, but some of them massive blows, including one that disappeared over the top of the Western Terrace and out of the ground.

There were 44 six-hits over the course of the two T20 matches and these accounted for over one-third of the total number of runs scored. This suggests that there isn't too much room for subtlety in this form of the game but, in fact, all is not lost. On Sunday, I was impressed by the range of shots played by Joe Clarke, the controlled slow bowling of Mitch Santner and Adil Rashid and the excellent "death" bowling of Steve Patterson. In both matches, the quality of the fielding and catching in the deep reflected the skill and athleticism of professional cricketers in the modern age.

And – within the broader landscape of bat versus ball and the pendulum's swings between the one and the other – I continue to be attracted to the fine detail. At the end of Carver's over, a number of Yorkshire's players went over to offer support. Likewise, when Ed Barnard finally took Willey's wicket, after the Worcestershire attack had been flayed around the ground, the bowler graciously shook his tormentor's hand as he departed for the pavilion. Good for him, I thought.

www.anordinaryspectator.com/news-blog July 2017

Rugby League

# The Wrong Ground –
# But a Good Game Nonetheless

A Saturday afternoon in Leeds presented me with the opportunity to take in some amateur rugby league. A look at the fixture list revealed that the Hunslet Club Parkside were playing at home to the Milford Marlins: second versus third (with the top three sides separated only by points difference) in the Kingstone Press National Conference League Division 1 (which is the second tier of the nationwide amateur game). A tight match in prospect, I thought.

A 45 minute walk from the centre of the city through post-industrial Hunslet – past the warehouses and the clutch repairers and the Grade II-listed gateposts of "Boyne Engine Works, 1858" in Jack Lane – took me to the Hunslet Club, where a well-attended children's gala was in full swing. From there, it was a short walk past some open ground to the main rugby pitches, where the two teams were warming up.

A glance at the scoreboard informed me of my location. I was at the home ground of the Hunslet Warriors, who were about to take on the Lock Lane club – in the same division as HCP and the Marlins.

Having effectively entered the Warriors' ground through the (unguarded) back entrance, I asked the man taking the gate money where Hunslet Club Parkside were playing. He patiently explained that their ground was about a quarter of a mile away, down a path through some trees, and asked if I was still heading that way. No, I thought: this is where I have ended up and so here I will remain. I duly paid my £1-50p entrance fee plus £1 for a neat programme.

It was a good game. Playing down the slope, Lock Lane – a famous amateur club, based in Castleford – started the brighter with their prop forwards making a lot of ground. A 10-0 lead quickly opened up and I did wonder whether a half-time change of scenery to the match down the road might be in order. But the Warriors then had a period of consistent possession, aided by some ill-discipline from their visitors, and went into a 12-10 lead. Lock Lane edged in front just before the interval: 16-12.

In the second half, with the slope to their advantage, the Warriors took control and the final score of 28-16 was about right on the balance of play. Having started the day fourth from bottom of the division – with three sides to be relegated at the end of the season – this was a timely result for the home side, although it turned out that two of the three sides currently at the foot of the table also won on Saturday.

It was a hard – but, as far as I could detect, fair – game. The players looked to be well coached – running strongly, tackling aggressively and moving the ball competently through the hands. Standing behind the barrier close to the touchline provided me with a close view of the physical – and verbal – confrontations between the players, but the young referee kept a good control and only needed to brandish one yellow card towards the end of the game. The Lock Lane full back left the field temporarily with a shiner of a black eye and one of his colleagues was (uncomfortably) carried off after sustaining a first-half leg injury. He seemed to recover, however, walking gingerly down the touchline and reassuring his mates behind the barrier that he would still be fit for their planned Saturday night out.

Not all the invective was directed at the opposition. When, following a play-the-ball, a Warrior passed the ball to one of his colleagues on the narrow short side – only for him to be heavily tackled – a plaintive cry rang out from the middle of the pitch: "Will you stop doing that f…..g move?" I thought this a bit harsh: both sets of half-backs varied the play well and both hookers also distributed effectively to their willing runners.

After the match, I took a different route back into Leeds, stopping off briefly for a pint in The Garden Gate public house – another building with Grade II listed status – which houses the Hunslet RLFC Heritage Room, the opening of which I was pleased to attend in October 2014.

Later, I sought out the result of the Hunslet Club Parkside/Milford Marlins game. 24-0 to the home side: as it turned out, not such a tight match after all.[1]

www.anordinaryspectator.com/news-blog July 2017

# Cricket

# Good Company and Chance Encounters

For such as me, traditionalists – or conservatives or old fogies (delete as appropriate) – of English cricket, it is a source of some concern that the England and Wales Cricket Board (ECB) have hollowed out the County Championship season so that, in Yorkshire's case, only one 4-day match is being played this year between the 6th July and 5th September. Of the 14 Championship fixtures (reduced from 16 last year), no fewer than 8 are being played before the end of May or from the beginning of September. The days of mid-summer are largely allocated to the powerful beast that is Twenty-20 cricket.

There was a certain inevitability, therefore, that George Farrow – a near(ish) neighbour (though resident in the wilds of Strathblane) – and I should plan to attend the four days of the Essex fixture at Scarborough. We had pencilled in the engagement some time ago, given George's allegiance to the visitors, and the decision had been notably prescient, as Essex had established a healthy (29 point) lead at the top of Division 1. Yorkshire started the match in 4th position, 38 points behind the leaders, though perhaps equally relevantly only 36 points above the Somerset side occupying the second relegation place (and having played one more game).

We were joined for the Monday's play – the second and, as it turned out, final day – by Andrew Carter, an old schoolfriend, whose co-presence following Yorkshire's fortunes was a nice throwback to many a yesterday. On the Tuesday evening, in the hotel, George and I had a drink with Dick Davies – the respected cricket correspondent of BBC Radio Essex – and his wife Sarah, the latter also an expert on her county's side.

Good company.

Amongst the other spectators (around 5½ thousand on both days), there was a supporting cast of new faces who became increasingly (and eerily) familiar. On the outward train journey from York to Scarborough, George and I fell into conversation with two Essex supporters (one living in Hove and the other a native of Dundee!) and a Yorkshire member from Redcar. The latter was pessimistic, not only about the form of the home side's batting line-up, but about the likely quality of the B&B to which the Hove man had committed. Towards the end of Sunday's play, we met a Derbyshire supporter and his elderly father in the Scarborough ground's tea room, whilst watching the closing overs and being fortified by the thick slices of a rather good fruit loaf. On the Monday afternoon, on the front row of the raised stand opposite the Scarborough ground's entrance, my neighbour to the left was a middle-aged man explaining the finer points of the game – in a locally prep-schooled accent (as I later learned) – to his wife.

The Redcar man's pessimism was (partly) justified. Yorkshire's batsmen couldn't cope with the speed and control – and general excellence – of the Pakistani left-arm pace bowler Mohammad Amir, who took 10 wickets in the match and was ably supported by Jamie Porter who claimed 7 victims. (It is a sign of trouble when, 40 minutes into a 4-day match, the score stands at 25 for 5). Yorkshire's totals of 113 and 150 all out rested heavily on an outstanding first innings 68 by Adam Lyth and an impressive 70 on the last afternoon by Jack Leaning. Aside from these two efforts, the runs scored in the 10 innings played by Yorkshire's top six batsmen totalled exactly 31.

By contrast, when Essex batted, all of the top six made double figures and, batting at number 6, the captain Ryan ten Doeschate scored a well-constructed 88 to earn his side a decisive first innings lead of 118. If Essex do win this year's County Championship – and their lead at the top of the table at the end of this round of fixtures has stretched to 41 points – they will undoubtedly look back on ten Doeschate's innings as one of the season's defining contributions. On this occasion, Essex duly knocked off the 33 runs required for victory for the loss of two second innings wickets.

It's a small world. As George and I walked to the ground down North Marine Drive on the second morning, we met the Hove-based Essex supporter and his mate. They had been suitably impressed by the welcome given by the Scarborough club (and by their B&B) as well as the performance of their side. Later in the evening, we also met the Derbyshire man and his father in the dining room of the hotel. The following morning – the game having finished and our plans now revised to take in a visit to Beverley Minister – we met the Hove man for a third time on our way to Scarborough railway station.

It poured with rain in Beverley and it was with some relief that we completed the short walk from the station to the Minster. The first people we met on entering the church were the pleasant prep-schooled man and his wife.

The visit to the Minster completed, George and I went for a long walk through the driving rain out to Beverley racecourse and then returned, about an hour later, to the centre of the town. There seemed to be about 25 tea rooms in which to find suitable refreshment and to dry out. We chose one on Ladygate where, seated at an upper-floor table, were Mr and Mrs Prep-School. Almost inevitably, after George and I had rested for another hour and decided to take the long sweep past the Minster on the way back to the station, we met the same couple coming in the opposite direction.

It goes without saying that, back at the hotel, the man from Derbyshire was sitting in the hotel lobby with his parents.

Perhaps these opportunities for acquaintance and re-acquaintance take place all the time and we simply don't notice them. (I had a similar experience with a neighbouring spectator at a Leeds Rhinos/Castleford Tigers Super League match in 2014, who on the following lunchtime sat down at the adjoining table in the café at Leeds City Art Gallery). It could be that the element of chance is not in the encounter itself, but in the ability to recognise it when it occurs.

For the county cricketers of Yorkshire and Essex, the opportunities for re-acquaintance are already mapped out.At present, the respective directions of travel are clearly evident: for one, the look over the shoulder to the relegation places; for the other the progress towards a Championship pennant. The final 4-day match of the season is Essex versus Yorkshire at Chelmsford.[2]

www.anordinaryspectator.com/news-blog August 2017

Rugby League

# Sevens Heaven

In an article published in the *Rugby League Journal* last Spring (*"The Yorkshire Cup in the 1960s"*, Issue 58), I stated that it had been through success in the 1965 County Cup competition that the name of Bradford Northern had resumed its standing amongst the trophy winners of rugby league. This followed the club's failure to complete its league fixture programme only two years earlier and its subsequent – spectacular – resurrection.

The statement is correct as far as the major honours are concerned, of course. But there is a caveat. Over a year earlier – in August 1964 – Bradford Northern won the Bass-Worthington Trophy for being the Yorkshire Seven-a-Side champions.

Sevens rugby was invented well before the "Great Split" of 1895. It is generally accepted that it was the brainchild of a Melrose butcher – Ned Haig – in 1883 and the popularity of the abbreviated form of the game in the Scottish Borders has run right through to the present day. The union code has always embraced the format – the famous Middlesex Sevens date from 1926 – and, of course, its World Rugby Sevens Series is now an annual season-long multi-million dollar competition taking place in 10 countries over 5 continents.

The rugby league authorities explored the possibilities between the wars. My dated (but still authoritative) copy of AN Gaulton's *The Encyclopaedia of Rugby League Football* (published in 1968) reported that "there was a handsome trophy at Odsal Stadium, Bradford, in the 1930s and the acknowledged Sevens Champions were Huddersfield… In post-war years Leeds and Wigan, in particular, have established annual events which are always well attended". The reference book also helpfully noted that "speed, positional skill, good handling and quick thinking are amongst the essentials for those participating".

And so to the "Yorkshire Seven-a-Side Rugby League Competition" of 1964. This was contested between 12 of the county's teams – Castleford, Doncaster, Hull KR and York were absent – at Headingley on a Friday evening in early August.

The competition rules stated that "each side will consist of seven players, the usual formation being three forwards and four backs". (In truth, it is difficult to see what other formation there could have been).

The timetable was ambitious: the first match didn't kick-off until 6 o'clock and the games were scheduled at 15 minute intervals, notwithstanding that the halves were 7 minutes each way with a minute for half-time. This urgency was exemplified in another of the competition rules, which stated that no extension of time was allowed for goalkicks if the final "bell" had indicated the end of a session of play.

Two aspects of the competition rules presaged their later adoption into the full version of rugby league. As noted, the match duration was taken out of the control of the referee: "time is checked by an independent time keeper who allows for injury time". In addition, there was the (restricted) possibility of substitution during a game: "selection may be made from eight players, but once a game has started substitution will only be allowed in case of injury up to half time".

Shortly after 9 o'clock, Bradford Northern were victorious in the final against Huddersfield, having earlier also defeated Dewsbury, Halifax and Leeds. It is reasonable to conclude that Huddersfield's cause in the final – when it was 10 minutes each way with a two minute interval – might have been somewhat handicapped by the fact that they had had only a 10 minute break after beating Hunslet in the previous round. On the other hand, Bradford had competed in four rounds to Huddersfield's three.

The 1964 competition was clearly judged to have been a success because, the following June, the Leeds club hosted the first of its "WD & HO Wills Invitation Sevens" competitions, this time on a slightly less hectic Saturday afternoon. Thereafter, the tournament was played each year until 1977, usually on the Whit Saturday or Monday, anything from two days to two weeks after the Championship Final.

My programme collection extends as far as 1970, after which I (now) assume that the competing claims of my club/college cricket commitments must have taken precedence. I am slightly biased, therefore, in asserting that the "Wills Sevens" of the late 1960s represent the zenith of rugby league sevens in this country.

Looking back, one of the most striking features of these tournaments was, of course, their pioneering status in bringing sponsorship money into the sport. In this respect, WD & HO Wills was a leading practitioner. Its origins dating back to Bristol in the 1780s, the company had built a reputation for the imaginative marketing of tobacco products, including (from the 1880s) the early use of cigarette cards for advertising. (Indeed, in the 1930s, the cards available for collection included Jim Brough of Leeds, Jim Sullivan of Wigan and George Nepia of New Zealand). By 1970, the sports sponsorship portfolio of Wills – "pacemakers in tobacco" according to that year's programme – extended across horse racing, show jumping, golf, tennis and power-boat racing as well as rugby league.

The commercial involvement of Wills does not seem to have affected the BBC's enthusiasm for providing national coverage, notwithstanding the Corporation's general nervousness about any association with product endorsement. The 1966 tournament programme specifically referred to the "several million viewers" who had watched the previous year's event (which had featured prominently on a *Bank Holiday Grandstand*) with particular thanks being given to "Mr Eddie Waring for helping us to organise the competition".

The "invitation" component of the Wills Sevens represented the attempt to involve as many as possible of the season's trophy winners or runners-up within the limited line-up of 8 teams taking part each year. These included Barrow (as Challenge Cup runners-up) and Oldham (as Lancashire Cup runners-up) in 1967, Leigh (as Floodlit Trophy winners) in 1970 and, interestingly, Workington Town in 1969 (as winners of a short-lived BBC Sevens competition). This selectivity meant that there was no place for my team – Hunslet – after their first round eliminations in 1965 and 1966.

The officials were chosen on the same basis. The 4 referees on the afternoon's panel in 1970 were those at the top of their profession – Eric Clay and Joe Manley through to Fred Lindop and Billy Thompson – who had covered the season's cup finals and international matches.

The winners of the inaugural Wills Sevens in 1965 were St Helens – captained by Alex Murphy – who defeated Castleford 13-7 in the final. Two years later, the honours went to Huddersfield, with Leeds being the runners-up. By this time, the length of a half was 7½ minutes – a punishing additional minute per match – although the goalkickers were now allowed their turn in the event of the post-try klaxon being sounded.

In the intervening year, the winners were Bradford Northern, who beat Leeds in the final by 13 points to 10. The Odsal club thus showed that their earlier success in the Bass-Worthington Trophy had not been a fluke, although, if I have interpreted the evidence from the respective tournament programmes correctly, only two members of the squad – Johnny Rae and Idwal Fisher – were double-medal winners. (A neat echo was provided in the person of Northern's coach – Gus Risman – who had also featured on a Wills cigarette card 30 years earlier).

For the remainder of the decade, the "Sevens Kings" were undoubtedly Salford, who won the competition for 3 years in a row from 1968, scoring a total of 170 points in 9 unbeaten matches. Their line-up in 1970 was illustrative of the pace and skill that made them such a glamorous side. It included Mike Coulman and Colin Dixon in the forwards and Paul Charlton and Maurice Richards in the backs, with David Watkins at the centre of things as the creator and goal-kicker.

Watkins was also the captain and official coach: I would not have been surprised if he had driven the team bus as well.

It did occur to me at the time that, in addition to the individual talent at their disposal for this particular competition, Salford probably had an advantage in having a high proportion of their players – including Watkins, Richards and Coulman – with top-level rugby union experience. As noted, the sevens format was not as common in rugby league as in union, and I deduced that, whilst it would of course have been in the different code, the union experience would have stood Salford in good stead when it came to pacing a match or, indeed, the tournament as a whole. The final of the tournament was still 10 minutes each way – with now only a minute allowed for the interval – which I would have imagined to have been a lifetime to the players in the heat of a late May or June afternoon.

I can draw on several memories of the Wills Sevens, both general and specific. At a general level, there is the fond recollection of what enjoyable events these competitions were. I can recall sitting in the North Stand at Headingley (with my dad and uncles) and being aware that in front of me was an array of talent from a number of different clubs, some of whom I would not normally see in the course of a league season. In the six years to 1970, 18 different teams were represented in the Wills Sevens; apart from Leeds as the host club, only Castleford took part in each of these years.

Whilst the sevens format obviously required players to have the attributes noted in AN Gaulton's reference book, it is clear that the Wills events found room for the range of skills evident in the 13-a-side game. My 1969 programme, carefully annotated to note the changes from the printed teams, confirms that that year's squads included flying wingers (John Atkinson, Bill Burgess), elusive half-backs (Keith Hepworth, Frank Parr), pacey forwards (Phil Lowe, Phil Cookson) and front-row specialists (Clive Dickinson and Colin Clarke).

Of course, the ranks of the top players would be depleted in those years in which the Great Britain tourists were engaged elsewhere. The 1966 competition took place when Britain were in Australia, preparing for the first test match two weeks later, so the likes of Berwyn Jones of Wakefield Trinity and Alan Hardisty of Castleford were justifiably excused from duty at Headingley. Likewise, for the World Cup in 1968 and the Australasia tour of 1970. However, such absences didn't seem to detract from the excitement and enjoyment of the occasions.

More specifically, I recall at the 1964 Bass-Worthington Trophy event being fascinated by the behaviour of the crowd. There was obviously a sizeable Leeds component but, in addition, I was struck by the way that certain sections of the crowd suddenly came to life in different parts of the ground when their teams appeared for their opening ties. These were the days before the prevalence of spectators' replica shirts, of course – and coloured scarves would not have been much in evidence on a summer's evening – so there was something quite dramatic about how the previously hidden allegiance of each section of Headingley was suddenly revealed when their favourites took to the stage.

The other specific memory is of David Watkins himself. I was absolutely captivated by his play in each of the years that I saw him. He was outstandingly brilliant, with his speed off the mark and his jinking side-steps and the perfect timing of his passing to release his speedy colleagues. He also seemed hugely confident in his abilities – as he was entitled to have been, as a former Wales and British Lions fly-half – and he was the dominant figure throughout each of the afternoons, as he orchestrated the Salford efforts. Even the way that he wore his rugby shirt, with the collar lifted up around the back and sides of his neck, seemed to add to Watkins's lustre.

The Wills Sevens may have constituted an end-of-season curtain-call, but they were taken seriously with professional pride and silverware at stake. The weather was generally good – and sometimes hot – and the season ended (as it had begun) in the optimistic brightness of early-evening sunshine, rather than (as these days) the dark of an October night.

They were different times, of course. Tobacco company sponsorship, ex-rugby union internationals, millions watching on television, the tournament programme for a shilling… And they were good times.

*The Rugby League Journal* Issue 60, Autumn 2017

# Baseball

# Let's Go Blue Jays

The Toronto Blue Jays baseball team plays at the Rogers Centre – popularly known by its original name of the SkyDome – next to the famous CN Tower. This downtown location meant that, for my family and me, it was only a short walk from our hotel for one of last week's matches against the Tampa Bay Rays. It was a safe walk too, provided that we respected the pedestrian traffic signals and avoided the automobiles, buses, streetcars, joggers and cyclists as we crossed Queens Quay West; some of the last group, in their dedicated lane, would undoubtedly give Chris Froome a run for his money.

It was our first baseball game, so why not start with the Major League, in which the Blue Jays are the sole Canadian team. They entered the match with a record of .483 (from 57 wins and 61 defeats so far this year), which placed them in fifth position (out of five) in the American League East. However, with one-third of the regular season still to play, there was still a chance of a wild-card place in the play-offs, if they could put together an impressive run from their 40-odd remaining fixtures. The Tampa Bay Rays were third in the same division with a record of 59-61 (or .492).

As the game progressed, the four baseball novices started to work out the narrative from the plethora of statistics that flashed out of the multi-coloured scoreboard – notably the numbers of balls, strikes and outs in each inning. On the far side, another board registered the mounting score. The Rays stretched out to a 6-1 lead, but a home run by the Blue Jays' Josh Donaldson cut the deficit to 6-4 by the completion of the latter's fifth inning – the bottom of the fifth, as we baseball experts call it (I think). It turned out that this was the final score, some impressive pitching in the closing stages by the Dominican Republic–born Alex Colome denying the Blue Jays hitters any chance of overturning the deficit.

It was a spectacle that assaulted all the senses. The sights of the action on the pitch and the general bustle in the crowd and the colour of the advertisements were complemented by the loud cheering of the Blue Jays fans whenever one of their hitters made it to first base or a catcher secured a skier in the outfield. The scoreboard's instruction to "Make Some Noise" did seem somewhat superfluous, as the roars of over 33,000 spectators echoed around the stands. Our taste buds were satisfied by the foot-long hot dogs covered in tomato – pronounced tomato – sauce, which (for two points of information) officially come in at 860 calories each and are disconcertingly difficult to eat when one is also holding a plastic glass of beer.

The SkyDome had the distinction of being the first sports stadium in the world with a retractable roof – open on this occasion, a warm summer's evening. High in the stands is the "Level of Excellence", which honours some of the key personnel in the Blue Jays' 40-year history; this select group includes not only former players but also the radio play-by-play announcer, Tom Cheek, who called every Blue Jay game from the team's inaugural fixture in April 1977 until the beginning of June 2004. Looking down from above the hitter's plate, "42 Jackie Robinson" recognises the shirt number that was retired by every Major League Baseball team in April 1997.

From our excellent vantage point – square to the wicket in cricket parlance, in the Field Level Bases – we got a sense of the speed of the pitchers, who hurled their missiles at up to 95 mph, as instantly recorded on the scoreboard. (I gather that over 100 mph is regularly attained in the Major League). We were also impressed by a couple of spectacular catches – even allowing for the giant mitt in the catching hand (my cricketing background betraying itself again) – and, of course, by the huge hits that produced the evening's three home runs. I also admired the speed and accuracy of the throwing from the outfielders and by the infield custodians of each base.

In terms of cricketing analogies, I must also refer to the capacity of both sports for producing some wonderfully obscure statistical facts. When the Rays' Steven Souza Jr went out to bat, the scoreboard stated that his first 25 home runs had all been struck against right-handed pitchers and that he was the first "righty" to have achieved this feat since 1961. *Test Match Special*, eat your heart out.

About half way through the game (which lasted for just under 3¼ hours), I took a walk round the stadium on the raised concourse. On one side were the beer stalls and fast-food vendors and merchandise outlets and rest rooms and, on the other, a clear view of the continuing action on the field of play. At one point, I struck up a conversation with a young cop and asked him if he expected any trouble on an evening such as this.

His answer was firmly in the negative: there might be the occasional drunk, but such a potential felon would usually see sense "when confronted by 6 or 7 of us". I thought back ruefully to the Carlisle United-Hartlepool United football match that I had attended last autumn, when a sizeable police presence had been required to marshal the respective tribes at a fourth-tier English soccer match. Admittedly, there were only a few Tampa Bay Rays fans at the Rogers Centre (though there were some), but that is hardly the point.

The policeman and I talked for a few minutes about Toronto and baseball (which he said he absolutely adored) and soccer (which he found a bit slow) and Niagara (which he hailed from and also loved). I wished him a quiet evening and we shook hands. It was a pleasure to meet him; he was a credit to his city.

The Blue Jays played two more fixtures at home to the Rays on the following two days, by which time we had moved on to test out (and confirm) the cop's enthusiastic promises of Niagara Falls and Niagara-on-the-Lake. The consecutive victories in these games duly raised the post-season play-off hopes. Unfortunately, the three games played over the following weekend – all against the Chicago Cubs at Wrigley Field – were lost, as was the next match against the Rays (in Tampa), so the prospects of post-season glory have promptly receded again. The Blue Jays' World Series titles of 1992 and 1993 edge a little further into the past.

But no matter. Our allegiances within the significant component of Americana that is Major League Baseball are secured. And we bought the tee-shirts – Let's Go Blue Jays.

www.anordinaryspectator.com/news-blog August 2017

# Rugby League

# The Wolfpack and the Cheesy Dog

Last Saturday, in order to get to the Allan A Lamport Stadium from downtown Toronto – a distance of just over two miles – I took the 504 streetcar along King Street heading directly west. I arrived early and went for a beer in the nearby Shoeless Joe's, where the Toronto Blue Jays were in action on the screens in the second of their weekend triple-header against the Chicago Cubs at Wrigley Field. However, the purpose of my journey was not televised Major League Baseball, but live rugby league in the (British) Kingstone Press League 1: Toronto Wolfpack vs Newcastle Thunder.

We do live in times that are, occasionally, slightly bewildering.

The division has now entered the Super Eights phase of the season, in which the top 8 sides play each other to decide (eventually) which two teams will be promoted to the Championship. As the points accumulated during the season are carried forward, Toronto Wolfpack are in a strong position, as they lead the table from Barrow and Whitehaven. For their part, Newcastle were in 7th position, with an outside chance of finishing in the top 5 and engaging in the final rounds of knock-out play-offs.

I suspected that the match might be somewhat one-sided. Toronto have recruited ambitiously in their playing and coaching staff – the former Great Britain coach, Brian Noble, is the Director of Rugby – and had lost only one (and drawn one) of their 18 league and Super Eight matches to date, averaging 57 points per game. And so it proved. The left-winger Liam Kay went over for the first of his three tries inside two minutes and the home side ended up scoring a total of nine tries in a 50-0 win.

(A curious statistical aside. I have seen Newcastle Thunder play three times: once here and twice in their previous guise as Gateshead Thunder against the Hunslet Hawks at the South Leeds Stadium. On each occasion, they have conceded exactly 50 points).

The outcome of the match not being in much doubt, I was more interested in the presentation of the game and the local response to it. It was all pleasingly encouraging. The Lamport Stadium has several tiers of elevated open seating, running the full length of both touchlines, which provide good views of the action: ideal for a warm and sunny afternoon such as this, less so if Toronto experiences one of its occasional summer thunderstorms. The row of concession stands populating the King Street end of the ground, behind the goalposts, was also heavily patronised throughout the afternoon.

The sizeable crowd – over 7,500, according to the Wolfpack's website – enjoyed the home side's dominance, the volume of cheering not seeming to diminish as the later tries were run in. Interestingly, many spectators stayed around in their small groups after the game had finished, remaining on the seating or at the edge of the pitch: it was a social gathering on a pleasant Saturday afternoon.

As at other sporting venues in North America, there were a plentiful number of beer-sellers doing the rounds up and down the terraces. Food and drink is a significant component of these events and so I treated myself to a Big Mamma's Cheesy Dog with tomato sauce from one of the fast-food stalls. It was as delicious as the name suggested.

The demographics of the crowd covered all ages with many family groups, a significant proportion of women and – it seemed to me – a plethora of Canadian accents, rather than those of casual visitors from Britain or the Antipodes. The loudest gasps were heard at the collisions between the respective prop forwards, perhaps not surprisingly as one of those wearing a Wolfpack shirt was the formidable Tongan, Fuifui Moimoi – a veteran of 10 seasons in the Australian Rugby League – who was typically aggressive both with the ball and in defence. (It struck me that Moimoi's clear emergence as a local cult hero was not unlike that attained by the similarly-sized Ian Van Bellen in the latter stages of his career at the newly-formed Fulham club in the 1980s).

I talked to one or two of my neighbours. Of the two young men on my right, one was familiar with rugby union in Canada – a well-established sport in some areas of the country – and seemed to be accurately explaining the rules of rugby league to his friend. He remained nervous about the Wolfpack's promotion prospects, quoting to me the narrow leads over Barrow and Whitehaven (2 and 4 points, respectively) in the league table. When I asked about the local media coverage, the second man acknowledged that rugby league was a "second tier" sport, but noted that soccer (through the Toronto FC) was succeeding in making its own inroads from a similarly low base. He made an interesting point about the need to keep the entry price at a competitive level, compared with soccer: the cost to me (as an adult with no discount for seniors) was $30 Canadian (about £20).

The middle-aged couple seated in front of me were attending for the first time with their young children. The father told me that his preferred sport was lacrosse and his awareness of the Wolfpack had been raised by press reports of some of the injuries that the players had sustained (which partly answered the question about the local media). He seemed to thoroughly enjoy his afternoon and, I'm sure, they will be repeat visitors.

If professional rugby league is to take root in Canada, Toronto seems to be the best place to start. It is a large, prosperous and cosmopolitan city with a liberal attitude to outside influences: we were informed on the city bus tour that one-half of its inhabitants were born outside Canada. The sport might also be able to take advantage of the growing concerns across North America – including amongst the parents of high school and college students – about the potential effects of head knocks incurred playing American Football on long-term health and wellbeing.

It is a summer sport, however, and the main challenge in raising general awareness of the local rugby league is undoubtedly the blanket media coverage given to baseball. The Toronto Blue Jays have regular season fixtures in Major League Baseball on 160 of the 183 days between 1st April and 30th September. That said, the local television station did report the Wolfpack's win in a single by-line on the screen, whilst Monday's *Toronto Star* gave all four of the weekend's Super Eights results and an updated league table. It might be expected that the local media coverage will increase when there is a larger domestic presence within the Wolfpack ranks: the 25-man squad listed for the Newcastle game had 18 players from the British Isles, 3 from Australia or the Pacific Islands and 4 from Canada or the USA.

The other major challenge will be on the playing field, of course. If and when the Wolfpack are promoted, they will incur much tougher challenges than those posed this season by the Gloucestershire All Golds and Hemel Hempstead Stags and, indeed, Newcastle Thunder. Next season's opponents should include the skilled (and grizzled) campaigners of Featherstone and Halifax and Batley. All being well, this enhanced competition – and the higher standard of rugby league on offer – will lead to the further progress of the Toronto Wolfpack club.

More immediately, I noted from the match programme (price $2 Canadian) that the Toronto Wolfpack have three home fixtures remaining in this year's Super Eights. Two of these are against Barrow and Whitehaven.

www.anordinaryspectator.com/news-blog August 2017

Rugby Union

# Virtutem Petamus – and Other Thoughts

When I entered Roundhay School in north Leeds as a first-year pupil over 50 years ago, the school uniform included a cap with a metallic badge on which was inscribed *virtutem petamus*: "We seek virtue". (The cap was a compulsory part of the uniform, on pain of detention, until the end of the fourth year). Part of the ritual/initiation/minor bullying (delete as appropriate) faced by a freshman was for his cap to be snatched from his head, usually by a second-year pupil, and dashed against something solid – a brick wall or the concrete playground – in order that it might be "christened".

The modern Roundhay School is a comprehensive providing "all-through education from 4-18" and its badge reads "Courtesy, Cooperation, Commitment". I can quite understand that these are virtues that any school would wish to inculcate amongst its pupils. However, I am also pleased to see that the original Latin motto survives in the crest of the Roundhegians Rugby Football Club, the home ground of which is on Chelwood Drive, a mile and a half away along Street Lane.

The Old Roundhegians club, established in 1928, moved into its present home in 1953. In common with the venues of many other rugby clubs – including Headingley and Bristol – it is called the Memorial Ground in honour of the old boys of the school who lost their lives in the World Wars. The grounds are neatly maintained, comprising two pitches that are framed by a combination of mature trees and suburban housing. The club became an open one in the early 1970s.

I played at the Memorial Ground on one occasion – for the Roundhay School 1st XV against the Old Roundhegians 2nd XV in October 1971. We won that day, partly due to my left-footed drop goal which – I shouldn't be surprised – might still be referred to with some awe in the local clubhouse. Health and safety regulations have put an end to this type of school/Old Boy fixture – quite rightly, given the latter's invariable dominance of size and weight, though not necessarily of speed and skill.

This season, Roundhegians RFC are playing in Yorkshire League Division 2 of the RFU North's structure: the 8<sup>th</sup> tier of club rugby in England (if my calculations are correct). On Saturday they were at home to Wetherby in their second league fixture of the year, the initial outing having resulted in a 15-38 defeat at Old Crossleyans.

The first 20 minutes took place in a torrential downpour, when the 'Hegians also had to contend with playing into a stiff breeze and dealing with the marked superiority of their opponents in the set scrums. They stuck to their task, however, and, by the time the rain stopped, had established a 14-0 lead thanks to some skilful handling in the difficult conditions. The right-wing Alex Miyambo scored two tries, both impressively converted from wide out by Alex Jones.

By midway through the second half the position had changed, as Wetherby, taking advantage of their scrummaging superiority, took a 15-14 lead, one of their scores being an emphatic pushover try. The decisive phase came when the 'Hegians managed to hold out against another short-range scrum, turn over possession and make their way downfield, where a penalty goal took them to the final 17-15 scoreline.

The handful of spectators – family, friends and support staff in the main – braved the inclement weather under a colourful array of large umbrellas, either on the raised grass banking along the touchline or on the balcony of the clubhouse. At this level, rugby is arguably a game for players and coaches, rather than spectators, but there was still much to admire in the commitment and organisation of both teams. Indeed, the game's final play was genuinely exciting, as, in search of the winning score, Wetherby worked the ball through several phases down the field from under their own posts to their opponents' 22 before possession was lost.

And, of course, the game had its informal moments. The touch judges being supplied by the respective clubs, it was not really a surprise to hear one of them – an otherwise consistently impartial assessor of when the ball was out of play – shouting "offside, ref" during a tense period of play. Later, he gave one of his own side a high-five when the player had followed up a long clearance kick to touch. I also liked the moment when, standing on the touchline, the home side's coach turned round in surprise to see that one of his players was standing next to him; I had previously watched the player make the long walk from the far side of the pitch and round the back of the goalposts to this near touchline, having been sin-binned for 10 minutes. The coach's response was to offer him a sweet from the packet he was consuming.

After the match, I caught the bus to Roundhay Park and walked down from the main entrance to the café next to Waterloo Lake for a cup of tea and a rather good flapjack. Another shower of rain came and went. I then walked back to the main arena and up the steps next to Hill 60. Somewhere in that imposing grass mound is the toy soldier that I lost – to my considerable distress – when I was about 6 or 7.

I have two competing impressions of the suburban landscape in this part of the city. On the one hand, it changes over time: the shop frontages are different and I try to recollect which stores were there before; the public house is demolished and replaced by a foodstore's car park; a road junction is altered with a plethora of new markings and lights. On the other hand, there is the continuity of that which is unchanged: the rugby club with its lush pitches, the location of the bus stops, the beauty and greenness of the park.

On balance, I would say that, over the period which I find myself contemplating – 50 plus years – it is the latter characteristic that generally prevails. Notwithstanding all that is new or unfamiliar, there is an overwhelming sense of that which was there before still remaining in place. Of course, with the people inhabiting that landscape, it is the opposite that applies. We are all just passing through and our presence – whether counted in decades or years or occasional half-days – is only transient, irrespective of whether or not we seek virtue.

www.anordinaryspectator.com/news-blog September 2017

Football

# Difficult Times at Rugby Park

It is not one of the braver predictions to forecast that Celtic will win the Ladbrokes Scottish Premiership this season. Aberdeen and Rangers are likely to contest the runners-up place, though the term had a slightly hollow ring to it last season, when Aberdeen finished 30 points behind Celtic. It is also reasonable to assume that the consistently well-organised St Johnstone team will end up fourth (or thereabouts), the position they have reached in each of the last three years.

For the other eight teams in the division – and although they would no doubt publicly set their sights higher – the first priority is to avoid either direct relegation through finishing last or ending up in the penultimate place and facing a hazardous play-off against one of the Championship teams. A finish in the top 6 – also achieved last season by Hearts and Partick Thistle – would represent a distinctly successful season.

That is not to say that, outside the Old Firm and Aberdeen, the Scottish Premiership clubs lack the ambition for winning trophies. Over the course of the last decade, the Scottish Cup has been won not only by St Johnstone, but also by Dundee United, Hearts, Inverness Caledonian Thistle and Hibernian and so the prospect of lifting some silverware is clearly realistic. But, as far as the league is concerned, the long, gruelling task of autumn and winter is to eke out as many points as possible in order to enter the spring with some optimism.

On Saturday, I went to see two of the likely also-rans – Kilmarnock and Ross County – battle it out at Rugby Park, where a cash payment of £15 bought me a senior's seat in the Frank Beattie Stand. On the opposite side of the ground, the front of the roof proudly referenced the home club's foundation – "Kilmarnock FC 1869" – four years before the formation of the Scottish Football Association, of which it was a founder member.

The further investment of £3 procured an impressive match programme which, in addition to the usual news and comments from the home team's perspective, included details of the 18 previous encounters between Kilmarnock and Ross County as well as career summaries of all the players in the visitors' squad. There was also a fascinating piece on a relatively obscure piece of Scottish football history: the "B" Division Supplementary Cup, which was contested between the second division teams in 5 of the 6 seasons from 1946-47 (although the 1949-50 final between Kilmarnock and Forfar was not held because the clubs could not agree on a suitable date).

Kilmarnock have not been in the second tier of Scottish football for 25 years, but this season is already shaping up to be something of a challenge. Prior to Saturday's match, they were bottom of the table with 3 draws and 4 defeats from their opening 7 fixtures. For their part, Ross County – two places and one point above them – had responded earlier in the week to what was obviously considered to be their disappointing start to the season by parting company with their manager, Jim McIntyre, and replacing him with the experienced Owen Coyle.

The 2-0 win for Ross County was thoroughly deserved. They had forced half a dozen corners and generally held the upper hand with some impressive passing play before a neat header from Craig Curran gave them the lead after 35 minutes. Just before half-time, another extended passing sequence resulted in the left-back Kenny van der Weg finding space in the penalty area to score the second. Kilmarnock brought on their talismanic centre-forward Kris Boyd for the second half and had a period of pressure midway through the period – aided by the bright sunshine streaming into the faces of the visiting defenders – but their opponents held on comfortably. There were perhaps 100 or so visiting supporters in the stand behind Scott Fox's goal, who no doubt enjoyed their journey back to Dingwall.

Ross County were anchored in midfield by the physical presence of Ross Draper and Jim O'Brien; they have streetwise campaigners in the lively Michael Gardyne and the captain Andrew Davies; Fox is an experienced goalkeeper and Curran led the forward line with energy and commitment. Interestingly, their starting line-up had five players with experience in the lower divisions of the Football League in England.

In some respects, Ross County reminded me of the Inverness Caledonian Thistle team that I had seen play at St Mirren in November 2014 on their way to winning that season's Scottish Cup – indeed Draper was a member of that side – though perhaps without the cutting edge provided on that occasion by the young Ryan Christie. I might check out this season's Cup odds when the fourth round draw is made.

For Kilmarnock, these are difficult times. The referee's half-time and full-time whistles were accompanied by crescendos of booing from a sizeable proportion of the home supporters in the main stand behind the dugout. As I left the ground, I did wonder what the immediate future might hold for the manager,

Lee McCulloch, and, sure enough, it was announced yesterday that he had lost his job.

A rearrangement in the fixture schedule means that, for McCulloch's replacement, the first 5 league games will be away from home, including trips to Rangers and Celtic. A long and gruelling journey through to spring is indeed in prospect for Kilmarnock FC.

www.anordinaryspectator.com/news-blog October 2017

Rugby Union

# A Tough Pool

The Glasgow Warriors have been drawn in a tough pool in this season's European Rugby Champions Cup. In addition to the Exeter Chiefs (the English champions), their section includes Leinster (three times winners of the competition in its previous guise as the Heineken Cup) and Montpellier (currently third in the Top 14 championship in France). For their part, Glasgow had begun the season by winning their first six matches in the Guinness PRO14 championship.

Having already lost at Exeter on the previous weekend, Glasgow met Leinster at Scotstoun on Saturday.

The game was played in proper rugby conditions with dampness in the air and a tricky, swirling wind. It was clear that attention to detail – a *sine qua non* for a professional player I would have thought – would be important. I could imagine the frustration of the Glasgow coaches, therefore, when the scrum half, Ali Price, kicked the ball directly into touch from just outside his 22 on the first play of the game. It was from this advantageous field position that a Johnny Sexton penalty kick opened the scoring for the visitors. Later in the first half, with Glasgow leading 10-3, a massive punt downfield by Stuart Hogg took the ball all the way over the Leinster deadball line. The resultant scrum, brought back to 10 yards from the Glasgow line, led to the first of Cian Healy's two close-range tries. On such fine margins are matches won and lost.

Healy was one of 5 British Lions who took the field for Leinster, two of the others also being prop forwards: Tadhg Furlong and Jack McGrath. They were instrumental in the Leinster forwards gaining the upper hand in the tight exchanges. For their part, Glasgow often looked dangerous when moving the ball swiftly to the wider channels, where Hogg could time his intrusions from full-back into the three-quarter line. I thought that the accuracy of their passing was not all it might be, however, and there was also the commonly-seen fault of the runners drifting across the pitch.

It all added up to a very interesting contest with both sides demonstrating skill as well as muscular strength. Stuart Hogg's try required him to chase a bouncing ball over the try line and touch it down before either he or it went over the deadball line. The way that he managed to keep his feet in bounds as he stretched forward reminded me of one of the fundamental skills of a wide receiver in the National Football League, where a catch for a touchdown in the end-zone requires that both feet touch the ground in the field of play.

From 3-10 down, Leinster took a lead of 24-10 mid-way through the second half. A penalty goal by Finn Russell and a well-worked try by Tommy Seymour – along with Hogg the Glasgow Lions on view – gave the home supporters some hope before Leinster's late surge extended the final margin to 34-18.

As expected, the game was somewhat feisty at times, but it was well handled by the referee. This was equally anticipated, as the man in charge was Jerome Garces of France, one of the world's best. (It was Garces who dismissed Sonny Bill Williams of New Zealand from the field during the Lions' Second Test in July). It was a pleasure to see him in action.

Garces was especially efficient in stopping the game immediately when players received head knocks: four players left the field for Head Injury Assessments (HIAs). In the cases of Ryan Wilson and Callum Gibbins, these appeared to involve concussive injuries, even to this non-medical expert sitting in the depths of the stand. There is undoubtedly a serious problem for rugby union concerning this issue and I shall return to it in a future blog.

Experience suggests that teams' performances in the early rounds of the European Rugby Champions Cup can be deceptive. I recall watching a hugely disappointing Bath side losing 10-37 to Glasgow on the same ground in October 2014; Bath went on to win the pool. Conversely, the apparently all-conquering Toulouse team that won their first four matches in the same group that year somehow failed to qualify for the quarter-finals. But, having lost their first two fixtures in this year's competition (and without the consolation of any bonus points), it must now be long odds on Glasgow reaching the next stage.

www.anordinaryspectator.com/news-blog October 2017

Football

# A Tradition Maintained

I turned up at the Etihad Stadium on Sunday knowing that Manchester City had made an impressive start to the 2017-18 season: maximum points from their 4 Champions League games to date, 9 wins (and one draw) out of 10 Premier League matches and safely through to the quarter-final of the Carabao (or League) Cup. In the Premier League, they were five points clear of second-placed Manchester United and nine points ahead of Arsenal in fifth spot. As Sunday's game was against Arsenal – and United were playing fourth-placed Chelsea – there was the possibility that City would put further daylight between themselves and their title rivals.

I had wondered what to expect. The latest (2017) estimates of *Forbes* magazine are that the Manchester City and Arsenal corporate entities each have a value of approximately $2 billion. They are global brands in a global market. City are owned by the Abu Dhabi United Group; Arsenal's major shareholders are an American sports tycoon and a Russian billionaire. The respective managers are a Spaniard (or, more accurately in the current political climate, a Catalan) and a Frenchman. Both clubs had spent over £50 million on single players during the last transfer window. In the starting XIs, City fielded four Englishmen and Arsenal none (though there was one Welshman).

The question in my mind was whether – for the home supporters on this occasion – there was still a local connection. Do the City faithful still have a sense of identification with a club that will mark its 125th anniversary in 2019: the club of Billy Meredith and Bert Trautmann and Colin Bell?

There was plenty of evidence to indicate that the ties between club and supporters are still very strong. In this regard, the appeal to tradition is clearly significant. It was no coincidence that my seat was actually in the Colin Bell Stand. Moreover, the player described by the MC as probably the greatest ever to wear a Manchester City shirt was present to take his place before the kick-off in a guard of honour for Sergio Agüero who, in the previous match against Napoli, had become the club's record goal-scorer. Agüero's total of 178 had taken him past the 78 year-old record of Eric Brook, whose daughter was on hand to make a pre-match presentation. She was accompanied by Mike Summerbee, a "club ambassador" and, of course, a colleague of Bell's in the great City side of the late 1960s. In turn, Summerbee's article in the match programme having made reference to Remembrance Day, a separate piece recognised some of the City players killed or wounded in the First World War trenches 100 years ago.

When Agüero scored his 179th goal – a soft penalty awarded five minutes after half-time to give his side a 2-0 lead – it looked as if the floodgates might open, given Arsenal's occasional tendency in recent years to concede large scores to sides at or near the top of the table. Instead – prompted by the Welshman, Aaron Ramsey – they enjoyed their best spell of the match and a goal by the lively substitute Alexandre Lacazette duly reduced the arrears. For the third City goal, the naked eye suggested that David Silva was at least three yards offside before setting up the tap-in for Gabriel Jesus: the later television replay indicated it was perhaps half a yard, but offside nonetheless. 3-1 was the final score.

Much is made of Manchester City's playing style: a passing game, built up from the goalkeeper and the back four, so that the skilful presence of Silva, Kevin De Bruyne and Leroy Sane can threaten in the final third of the pitch. De Bruyne was announced to have been the man-of-the-match – he had struck the first goal and posed a danger throughout the afternoon – though Silva must have run him close, as also Fernandinho. The last of these is generally less-heralded, I suspect, but is clearly a vital component of City's midfield machinery.

Earlier in the day, I had visited the National Football Museum in the city centre. I had been meaning to go for some time, partly because, when it had previously been located in Preston (as it was from 2001 to 2010), one of the trustees was the late Brian Booth, whom I got to know when I was a Scottish Executive civil servant and he was a non-executive director of the Glasgow-based Student Loans Company. Brian was a proud advocate of the Museum and its Lancastrian location.

The Museum, which is free to enter (and invites donations), is well worth a visit. For the traditionalists and historians amongst us, there is some fascinating older material, including a hand-written version of the Rules of Association Football (from 1863) and an England shirt from the first international football match (against Scotland in 1872). One should be prepared to be overwhelmed, however, as there is scarcely an aspect of (English) football history that does not seem to be covered. I'm not really sure if the exhibits need to include the shorn locks of Robbie Savage's hair or the pickled knee cartilage of Willie Cunningham, though I suppose one of John Motson's sheepskin overcoats just about qualifies.

The "sport-in-society" theme of these occasional blogs was certainly captured in some of the Museum's displays, not least the dreadful array of knives carried by some of the members of the 1980s football gangs. On a more uplifting note, I was taken by the small model of the old Wembley Stadium – sculpted out of concrete – the concrete itself having been rescued at the time of the demolition of the old Wembley Stadium.

The usual rules apply, I think. If one seeks to understand the current state of affairs of something – in this case, of football in general or a club such as Manchester City in particular – it is immensely useful to start with its history. Some traditions are maintained, others are re-interpreted, yet others are broken.

For the present, Manchester City go from strength to strength. By the close-of-play on Sunday, their lead at the top of the Premier League had stretched to eight points, courtesy of Chelsea's 1-0 win over Manchester United. There is still over two-thirds of the league season to run, of course, but it is looking ominous for the rest of the field.

As for Arsenal, the traditions of my personal relationship with the club have been maintained. I have seen them play three times – against Leeds United at Elland Road in 1971, against Manchester United at Highbury in 1985 and now against Manchester City at the Etihad Stadium in 2017. They have lost on all three occasions.

www.anordinaryspectator.com/news-blog November 2017

# Rugby League

# International Sevens Played in the Park

In *Memories Volume Two* of the "Rugby League Journal History Series" there is a brief – and fascinating – reference to a seven-a-side match between England and Australia in 1933. The game was played at Roundhay Park in Leeds, where "a huge crowd of some 50,000 saw the Aussies win this match 29-11…"

I must confess to have been somewhat taken aback. I was brought up on rugby league in Leeds and I went to the local school in Roundhay. But I had not previously been aware of this significant occasion. Clearly, further research was required to fill this gap in my knowledge.

The internet provided me with a wonderful source. The vast My Heritage site contains an electronic reproduction of an edition of the *Newcastle Morning Herald and Miners' Advocate* of Saturday, September 30th 1933. This distinguished Australian newspaper – the origins of which could be traced back to 1858 – was a 16 page broadsheet, densely packed with text and advertisements. On page 3, an article headed "The Kangaroos" had the bye-line: "H Sunderland Reviews the First Match".

The author of the piece was Harry Sunderland, of course, and the opening match of the 1933 tour had been against St Helens Recs, whom the Australians had beaten somewhat unconvincingly by 13 points to 9. However, the article – which extended to over 4000 words – covered a great deal of other ground, including the Roundhay Park event.

For *Journal* readers who might not be familiar with Roundhay Park, I should report – perhaps with some bias – that it is one of the great civic spaces of Britain, if not beyond. At its centre, one end of the vast open arena leads down to Waterloo Lake – constructed by soldiers returning from the Napoleonic Wars – whilst the grassy banking on the other sides includes the famous Hill 60, named to commemorate a First World War battle near Ypres. The location has hosted concerts by such as the Rolling Stones and Michael Jackson and, in my mind's eye, I can easily picture the scene with this vast crowd of spectators – Sunderland's article puts the figure at 80,000 – watching the rugby of over 80 years ago.

The England-Australia sevens match, whilst being a curtain-raiser to the tour proper, was also the centrepiece of an evening of civic entertainment to celebrate "Royal Visit Day": August 23rd 1933. (Sutherland's article was written on the 29th, but not published in Australia until a month later). King George V and Queen Mary had visited the city to perform the official opening of Leeds Civic Hall (not to be confused with the nineteenth century Leeds Town Hall). The Royal party did not attend the rugby, however; the guests-of-honour were the Lord Mayor and Lady Mayoress of Leeds, the former performing the ceremonial kick-off.

There are several lines that jump off the page in Harry Sunderland's description of the sevens encounter, but I was particular struck by his observation that the three members of the Australian pack "lined up and joined the passing as if they were backs". No lumbering giants these, but players who were fast and skilful as well as tough. He was also struck by the "glorious football" played by the winger Jack Why and the half-back Les Mead. Indeed, it was the overall speed of the Australian squad – led on this occasion by the hooker, Dan Dempsey – that seems to have been the decisive factor. According to Sunderland, only "Stanley Brogden, the Huddersfield flyer, and young Ivor Davies of Halifax" within the England team could match the pace of the tourists.

The local newspaper reports confirmed this assessment. The *Leeds Mercury* stated that the Australians' "natural style of fast backing-up and handling" had stood them in good stead, notwithstanding that they were playing seven-a-side for the first time. The "really splendid finishing" produced three tries for Why and two for Vic Hey as well as touchdowns by Frank O'Connor and Mead, who also kicked four goals.

The *Yorkshire Evening Post* attempted to place the match in some context. Whilst acknowledging that the result was "distinctly creditable to the tourists", it also pointedly noted that "the England side was hardly with the personnel as to readily deserve that title". This was an unstated reference, perhaps, to the fact that the team was comprised of players from only three clubs: Hunslet (who supplied four), Huddersfield (two) and Halifax. For the *Leeds Mercury*, George Todd of Hunslet and Brogden were England's best players, the latter showing "his fine pace in a long run for a try in which he completely outstripped all his pursuers".

In addition to providing lengthy journalistic interpretations of the Australians' tour for the readers back home, Harry Sunderland had another role. He was the tourists' co-manager! No doubt, this responsibility had already placed a heavy burden on him, following the death from meningitis of the centre-threequarter Ray Morris in Malta on the outward journey to Europe.

Sunderland was clearly wearing his managerial hat when he noted, in his article's opening reference to the Roundhay Park sevens, that the spectators had not had to pay an entrance fee. (One can almost hear him frustratingly calculating the foregone receipts). Elsewhere in the piece, he noted with some satisfaction the agreed amount that would be paid for the tour transport – 11d per mile for the estimated 3800 miles in a "beautifully upholstered 32-seater charabanc" – whilst also comparing, again with approval, the gate takings at the St Helens Recs game (£610) with those of the opening fixture against Rochdale Hornets on the previous tour in 1929 (£547).

Perhaps most extraordinary, however, was the way that he went into print about certain of his players, not least the winger, Fred Neumann, who in the match against the Recs "gave the most unimpressive display I have seen a winger give on an opening game in England". Likewise, Sunderland's verdict on Frank Dooner who "was sound, but did not reveal the intiative that is required from a tour five-eighth". (In the event, neither Neumann nor Doonar made the test team). On the other hand, he evidently had a marked respect for the forwards Syd Pearce and Mick Madsen, the latter being "a remarkable type… in manliness and honesty".

It is also clear that Sunderland had a huge affection for England and the English. He recalled the kindness he had received at Oldham Hospital, where he had been treated for "a split forehead" sustained when co-managing the Australians' previous visit four years earlier. He also wrote movingly of the welcome received by the touring party in St Helens, where a crowd of "thousands of caps and shawls" turned out hours before the match as the Australians entered a civic reception hosted by the mayor. His description of the post-match journey back to Ben Rhydding near Ilkley – "we set out over the moors with the sparkling lights of Bradford and Shipley glimmering at us like a sea of diamonds" – is one that (perhaps unjustly) is not replicated in many modern-day tourist guides.

Harry Sunderland hoped that the Australians' sevens win in Roundhay Park might be a positive augury for the later test series. In this, he was to be disappointed. Great Britain retained the Ashes, as narrow victories by 4-0 at Belle Vue, Manchester – courtesy of two Jim Sullivan penalty goals – 7-5 at Headingley and 19-16 at Station Road, Swinton, secured a 3-0 series win for the hosts. After winning their first 11 games, the Australians' overall record for the tour – which lasted from the end of August to New Year's Eve – was played 37, won 27, lost 10.

Of course, it was all a long time ago. 1933 was the year in which Hitler came to power in Germany, FDR unveiled the New Deal in the USA and England's cricketers completed the Bodyline tour of Australia. What relevant impressions can we take from this detour into the depths of rugby league sevens history?

Two in particular, I think – though these are confirmations rather than original thoughts. First, we are reminded – again – of the hugely rich historical capital that the sport of rugby league has accumulated and of the capacity of that history to generate surprises, even to someone reasonably well-versed in the details of the game's evolution. As mentioned, the Roundhay Park event of 1933 was something about which I was not previously aware. It was a thrill to look into the story and to relate it to the geography and interests of my own past.

Second, the event confirmed that, at certain key times, the administrators of the sport have been immensely bold and imaginative. This was one such era. They were not always successful: the failure of the London-based clubs in the 1930s is evidence of that. But the 1933 tourists were the first Australian side to play under floodlights; their itinerary included exhibition games in Ceylon (as it then was) and Egypt; the last match of the tour (a separate fixture against – and thrashing of – England in Paris) was the first rugby league international to be played in France; and, of course, it had been only four years earlier that the Challenge Cup final had first been taken from its northern home and contested at Wembley.

The successful custodianship of any sport – including ours – requires a combination of two competing elements: innovation and conservatism. It demands both a willingness to evolve in response to the broader changes in society as well as a respectful acknowledgement of the values and traditions of the past. It is a difficult trick to pull off.

*The Rugby League Journal* Issue 61, Winter 2017

# Health

# Concussion

In a recent blog on the Glasgow Warriors-Leinster game in the European Rugby Champions Cup ("*A Tough Pool*", 23rd October 2017), I noted that, during the course of the match, four players left the field for Head Injury Assessments (HIAs). One of these – the Glasgow captain, Ryan Wilson – departed the scene under some protest and had to be restrained by the medical staff from rejoining the action. Even for a non-expert such as me looking on from a distance, it was clear that he was not fully aware of his circumstances and was suffering from some form of concussion.

Events within the last fortnight or so seem to have confirmed that most high-profile rugby matches – of both codes – include similar incidents. In the Rugby League World Cup quarter-final between England and Papua New Guinea in Melbourne, the latter's star player, David Mead, received a heavy blow to the head after only a couple of minutes and took no further part in the match. England's Kevin Brown similarly received a head injury a few minutes before half-time; he was allowed to continue until the interval – during which time he moved sluggishly on to a pass and dropped the ball – but did not re-appear for the second half. On the same day, in the rugby union international at Murrayfield, the Scotland prop forward Zander Fagerson was concussed against New Zealand and obliged to miss the following week's match against Australia. In last Saturday's Wales-New Zealand game, it was clear from the television coverage that the Welsh scrum-half Rhys Webb had been dazed after being tackled and hitting his head on the turf; play continued for some time afterwards, with Webb apparently recovering his wits and participating again in the Welsh attack, before he was taken from the field at the next stoppage of play. In the same match, the New Zealand centre, Ryan Crotty, went off for a HIA after 20 minutes and did not return. And so on…

It is widely agreed that these incidents are important not only because of the immediate injuries incurred by players, but because of the possible long-term implications for health and well-being. Indeed, such links are becoming part of the conventional wisdom: *The Scotsman*'s obituary of David Shedden, who died in October at the age of 73 after a decade-long battle against an aggressive form of early-onset dementia, noted that, in addition to his 15 Scottish rugby caps in the 1970s, he had suffered from no fewer than a dozen concussions on the field of play.

In the period since the Glasgow-Leinster encounter, I have read *Truth Doesn't Have a Side: My Alarming Discovery about the Danger of Contact Sports* (2017) by Bennet Omalu.

Dr Omalu was the neuropathologist with the Allegheny County Medical Examiner's office in Pennsylvania who conducted an autopsy on Mike Webster, a former American Football player with the Pittsburgh Steelers, who had died in September 2002 at the age of 50. He became aware of Webster's post-career history of mental illness, memory loss, depression, disorientation and spontaneous anger episodes, but, initially, could not find the evidence of blunt force trauma on the brain that he had expected to see with the naked eye. Nor was the deterioration of Webster's brain consistent with the *dementia pugilistica* that is seen in punch-drunk boxers. Instead, "many [brain cells] had died and disappeared and many appeared like ghost cells… [There were] spaces in the substance of the brain… like a partially demolished building stripped of its windows".

Eventually, Dr Omalu concluded Webster's decline and demise were the result of the brain disease Chronic Traumatic Encephalopathy (CTE) and brought about by the repeated blows to the head (concussive and sub-concussive) that Webster had incurred playing his sport. The wearing of a helmet had been irrelevant, in Dr Omalu's view, because it had not prevented the brain bouncing around inside the player's skull and suffering impact on the skull's inner surfaces.

The fascination of Dr Omalu's book is not only in the medical detective story that he presents – with its references to tau tangles and amyloid plaques – but in the broader circumstances in which he conducted his research and then presented his findings. He was born in Biafra at the height of the civil war in 1960s Nigeria and had made his way to the USA on a medical scholarship. After publishing his conclusions on CTE, he was widely attacked as an outsider seeking to undermine the sport that plays a central role in defining American society and culture. Perhaps naively, he was shocked by the counter-response, notably by some of the NFL franchises and the National Football League itself.

A feature film of Dr Omalu's story, starring Will Smith, was released in 2015. Ironically, its title – *Concussion* – cuts across one of his central findings: that damage to the brain is done by repeated incidents of "mild" trauma as well as obvious concussions in which a player temporarily loses consciousness. "The fundamental issue is not concussions, but repeated blows to the head without or without concussions". And once that damage is done, it is permanent and irreparable: "the human brain does not have any reasonable capacity to regenerate itself".

I was interested in what the author had to say about rugby. Not surprisingly, he did not differentiate between the union and league codes, so one assumes that it is the former with which he is the more familiar. The references in the book are relatively brief, but still very clear: participation in other "high impact, high contact" sports, in which repeated blows to the head are prevalent, also increases the risks of CTE. Rugby is included in this list.

It is not only American Football and rugby, of course. With regard to soccer, there has been much media comment in the UK following the recent broadcast of the very good BBC documentary – *Alan Shearer: Dementia, Football and Me.* The medical researchers interviewed in that programme echoed an important point made by Dr Omalu: there is the potential for brain damage from repeated heading of the ball – as Shearer reckoned he used to do about 100 times a day in training – as well as from the clashes of players' heads. A poignant episode in the programme was Shearer's interview with his first manager, Chris Nichol – a robust and committed centre-half in his own 20-year playing career – who bravely admitted that his memory was "in trouble" and, on occasion, that he forgot where he lived.

It is clear that, across many sports involving physical contact, the authorities are increasingly conscious – if you'll pardon the pun – of the potential long-term dangers of head injury. In rugby union, the HIAs procedures have been tightened up, though many medical experts would argue that they do not go far enough. The Football Association announced last month (jointly with the Professional Footballers Association, PFA) that experts at the University of Glasgow had been commissioned to conduct research on the incidence of degenerative neurocognitive disease in ex-professional footballers. In the USA, in 2015, heading a ball was removed from the soccer played by under 11s and heading practice limited for 11-13 year olds. (Dr Omalu would extend this ban to under 18s, given that the brain is still maturing to that age). The NFL has banned helmet-first tackling and has established new protocols for dealing with concussed players.

Although these developments suggest that a clear direction of travel is evident, it is also the case that there is far from unanimity about the linkages between sport-related blows to the head and the long-term health of the brain. (Part of the problem faced by researchers is that, currently, CTE cannot be diagnosed until after death). The counter-argument was made, in a soccer context, in another interesting recent documentary – Sky Sports' *Concussion: The Impact of Sport* – in which it was noted that modern footballs are much lighter than the heavy rain-sodden leather balls of old and that, in any case, "there don't seem to be hundreds of Jeff Astle cases out there": a reference to the former West Bromwich Albion and England centre-forward, whose death in 2002 at the age of 59 was judged by the coroner to have been due to an industrial disease i.e. football-related. In turn, the short answer to that is that we simply don't know how may "Jeff Astle cases" there are – a point acknowledged by the PFA chief executive, Gordon Taylor, in the Shearer documentary. An important aim of the FA/PFA-commissioned research will be to determine whether the incidence of long-term brain disease amongst ex-professionals is statistically different to that within a control population on non-players.

Where do we go from here? I find it very difficult to forecast what the sports of rugby and football (soccer) might look like in 10 or 20 years time. However, I think we can be reasonably confident of a number of things. First, there will be continued further lobbying for significant rule changes in many sports by some branches of the medical profession. In addition, parents will continue to pay close attention to activities that affect the well-being of their children (and, in large numbers, will prevent participation in sports that they judge to be too risky). We can also be sure that the lawyers will be painstakingly examining whether sports authorities and clubs are meeting their duty of care towards the participants of those sports.

And, finally, we can be certain that – irrespective of the perceived risks – many people will wish to continue playing "high impact, high contact" sports.

www.anordinaryspectator.com/news-blog December 2017

Journalism

# A Prisoner of His Time?

*[Disclaimer: This blog contains historic quotations of an offensive nature, which are pertinent to the subject under discussion].*

It is a familiar (and unoriginal) theme within these occasional blogs and the books of sports spectating reminiscence that preceded them – *An Ordinary Spectator* and *Still An Ordinary Spectator* – that, in any given period, sport is a barometer of the broader society around it. This applies not only to the playing and watching of sport – with its rules, rewards, technologies and morals – but also to the reporting of it.

As further evidence to support this proposition, let me refer to *Farewell to Sport* by Paul Gallico (1897-1976), which was first published in 1938 and reprinted in paperback by First Nebraska in 2008. I purchased a copy in the excellent The Sport Gallery in the Distillery District of Toronto.

Gallico is well-known as the author of fiction, notably *The Snow Goose* and *The Poseidon Adventure*. However, he made his name as the sports editor of the *New York Daily News* for the 14 years from 1923. In 1937, he gave up this prominent – and highly paid – position to travel and to concentrate on his fiction. *Farewell to Sport* was a collection of essays written at this time which, as the title suggested, offered some reflections on the sports he was leaving behind.

Given the newspaper for which he was writing, it is not surprising that Gallico focused on sport in America, especially boxing, baseball and golf. The book contains one favourable reference to soccer – "one of the greatest of all spectator sports from the point of view of sustained action and wide-open play" – and nothing on rugby or cricket. Some of the essays straightforwardly capture the admiration – indeed, hero-worship – that the author had for three sportsmen in particular: the heavyweight boxing champion Jack Dempsey, the baseball star Babe Ruth and, especially, the golfer Bobby Jones. In each case, this was partly an acknowledgement of their exceptional sporting prowess; equally, however, it was a reflection of their respective characters and the way in which fame and adulation did not change them.

Gallico was no mean sportsman himself – a rower at Columbia University and, later, a fencer of some note – and he was one of the first sports journalists to engage directly with the stars on the field of play (a branch of journalism that spawned other well-known practitioners, notably George Plimpton). Most dramatically, he sparred with Jack Dempsey (for all of 97 seconds) until the inevitable stoppage: "I learned...that the fighter rarely, if ever, sees the punch that tumbles blackness over him like a mantle". I liked his description of a Dempsey training camp at Saratoga Springs: "...the grand, exciting, bawdy atmosphere. There were sparring partners with bent noses and twisted ears...boxing writers, handsome state troopers in their gray and purple uniforms, doubtful blondes...and blondes about whom there was no doubt at all". Gallico was at pains not to drift into sentimentally, however; he knew that prize-fighting was a tough sport and that an unhesitatingly vicious instinct was required for ultimate success. Dempsey was "a jungle animal [with] hatred in his eyes... He was utterly without mercy or pity".

Gallico also saw himself as a crusader. He railed against what he saw as the hypocrisy of the administrators of what were supposed to be amateur sports – athletics, tennis and, especially college (American) football – whose major events attracted vast crowds and gate receipts. He was brave in naming the shady characters associated with many of the boxing promotions, notably in the post-Dempsey era of heavyweights. And he felt himself a helpless onlooker at the inferior status conferred on black boxers, as reflected in their treatment by hotels and restaurants, including the members of a Golden Gloves team from New York that he managed in Chicago.

In the final essay – "The Next Fifty Years" – Gallico attempted to look into his crystal ball to the sporting environment of 1987. He was correct to argue that the records of his time would be eradicated, though, in most cases, he significantly underestimated the speed of progress. He wondered if the then world record for the mile (4 minutes 6.7 seconds held by Glenn Cunningham) might be reduced to about 4 minutes 3 seconds. (As we know, Roger Bannister took it below 4 minutes as early as 1954). Likewise, he reckoned that the high-jump record might be raised to 7 feet and that the pole-vaulters might reach 15 feet. (In 1987, world records were set in these events by Patrik Sjoberg and Sergey Bubka at 7 feet 11¼ inches and 19 feet 9¼ inches, respectively).

In this connection, it is worth noting that Gallico had views about the regimes that he thought likely to be producing the record-breakers of the future. He predicted that the stranglehold that the US had on track and field athletics was likely to be broken by "the new generation of youngsters, regimented and trained from infancy in Germany and Italy and other Fascist states [in which there was] the athletic and military training of youngsters under ten years of age, teaching them the fundamentals of sports and drill". His caveat to this forecast was chillingly prophetic: "The early sports training may make them a nation of athletes far surpassing anything that we have ever known before – or it may make them cannon-food".

So far so good. However, even allowing for the *Sports Illustrated* and other accolades (see below), Paul Gallico's sports writing has fallen out of favour with many present-day commentators due to the shadows of sexism and racism. The relevant examples jump off the page in *Farewell to Sport*.

Gallico undoubtedly admired the spirit and determination of the top-class sportswomen. But his overall attitude to the "muscle molls" was captured in a couple of sentences: "[T]hey are at best second-rate imitations of the gentlemen… A man has swum a hundred yards in fifty-two seconds. A girl takes one minute three seconds for the same distance, and so it goes. No matter how good they are, they can never be good enough, quite, to matter".

Gallico's descriptions of specific women's sports were dominated by his assessments of the participants' physical attributes. Hence, for example, the female track athletes were "flat-chested most of them, with close-cropped hair. Not much on looks either. Most of them had hard faces". By contrast, "what lovely legs and bodies those figure skaters have". *Farewell to Sport* contains many passages in this vein.

The examples of racism also cause unease for the modern reader. Whilst Gallico recognised that the formidable Joe Louis was a *bone fide* world heavyweight champion with his exquisite skill and thrilling efficiency – aided by his being "exceptionally well managed and handled by a hard and capable crowd of people of his own race: a lawyer, an ex-numbers man and an ex-convict" – he also made the curious assertion that Louis had been "carefully trained in the sly servility that the white man accepts as his due".

In many ways the most bizarre example relates to the sport of basketball in New York, which "for the past years Jewish players on the college teams… have had…all to themselves. [T]he reason…that it appeals to the Hebrew with his Oriental background is that the games places a premium on an alert, scheming mind and flashy trickiness, artful dodging and general smartaleckness". We should remember that *Farewell to Sport* was published in 1938: the year of *Kristallnacht* in Germany.

Eighty years on from *Farewell to Sport*, it is difficult to rationalise the many unacceptable (to us) forms of words that Gallico used. However, arguably, they partly reflected the milieu in which he was operating: the alpha-male world of competitive sports reporting on the East Coast of the 1920s and 1930s. He was writing for a mass audience which, at that time, clearly did not have anything like the social sensitivities that we take for granted in the 21st Century. In this sense, he was a prisoner of his time. He knew his market and he reported back on terms that were familiar to it.

*Farewell to Sport* was allocated a place in the "Top 100 Sports Books of All Time" by *Sports Illustrated* magazine in 2002. Justifiably so in my view – for two reasons – notwithstanding that it is in places a distinctly uncomfortable read.

First, there was Gallico's descriptive prowess, which – for modern readers – continues to provide an evocative picture of the good and the bad of the major American sports and their elite practitioners in the 1920s and 1930s. For example, on the positive side, his affection for baseball was clearly unbounded. A game could produce "half a dozen split-second races between a running man and a thrown ball, in which the hundredth part of a second is all the difference between success and failure, dozens of examples of skill triumphant, skill defeated, traps baited and snapped shut upon victims, human folly, and human cowardice, narrow escapes, heroes, villains, individual deeds that verge upon the miraculous..."

Similarly with individuals. The portrait Gallico painted of Babe Ruth consisted of a rich combination of fine details within the overall composite: "He was kneaded, rough-thumbed out of earth, a golem, a figurine that might have been made by a savage...with an unshapely body that features a tremendous, barrel-shaped torso that tapers down into too small legs and an amazingly fragile and delicate pair of ankles... His nose is flat and pushed in. Nobody did it for him; it grew that way".

On the downside, Gallico's assessment of the corruption of the heavyweight boxing scene that took Primo Carnera to the world championship title – "Pity the Poor Giant" – concluded dramatically: "He was just a big sucker whom the wise guys took and trimmed... All this took place in our country, Anno Domini 1930-1935".

Second, Gallico himself was aware that he was writing in a particular time and that what he observed on the sports field reflected the wider society around it. He noted more than once that the huge crowds for sports events – notably boxing – that had occurred during the prosperity of the 1920s had not been maintained with the onset of the Great Depression. Indeed, at one point, he also doubts the validity of his own hugely-rewarded profession at a time when many American families were in desperate straits: "[M]any of us felt a little silly, still writing in the flamboyant post-war style of highly paid professional and amateur athletes at a time when most people were wondering where their next pay-check or meal was coming from"

Gallico's linkage of sport to society extended from the economic to the cultural. I was struck by a key paragraph describing the crowd's reaction when the black American (Joe Louis) was knocked out by the white German (Max Schmeling) in Yankee Stadium, New York, in 1936. Notwithstanding that Louis was fighting on home soil, "...an even lustier and more joyous [yell] went up from the unpigmented spectators... The white brother is fickle and tires very quickly of seeing a Negro triumph too often".

It is in this context that the damning flaws in Paul Gallico's sportswriting should be considered by modern readers. Their very presence should be seen as part of the overall package – in other words, as complementary with the evocative (and acceptable) descriptive passages in not only contributing to our understanding of American sport in the inter-war period, but also providing a window on the broader social context in which that sport took place.

www.anordinaryspectator.com/news-blog December 2017

# Football

# Better Times at Rugby Park

In *Difficult Times at Rugby Park* (2nd October 2017), I reported on the Kilmarnock versus Ross County fixture in the Ladbrokes Scottish Premiership that I had attended on the last day of September. The visitors had deservedly won – 2-0 – and I remarked that they had reminded me of the Inverness Caledonian Thistle team that I had seen play at St Mirren in November 2014 on their way to winning that season's William Hill Scottish Cup. I made a note to check out the bookmakers' odds when the top-tier teams entered this season's competition in January.

For Kilmarnock, things had not looked so promising. The referee's half-time and full-time whistles had been accompanied by crescendos of booing from a sizeable proportion of the home supporters in the main stand. The manager – Lee McCulloch – had been relieved of his post the following day. I had concluded that "a long and gruelling journey through to Spring" was in prospect for the Ayrshire club.

But what do I know? In the subsequent 3½ months, Kilmarnock – under the new manager, the experienced Steve Clarke – have won 6 and drawn 5 of their 13 league fixtures and risen to sixth in the table. By contrast, Ross County have won only 2 games out of 14 and slipped to bottom place, three points behind the side above them, Partick Thistle.

As promised, I duly checked out the bookmakers' assessments prior to the 4th Round of the Scottish Cup – with the Premiership teams now included – being played this weekend. One of the fixtures was Kilmarnock versus Ross County at Rugby Park. Their odds on lifting the trophy this season were 33 to 1 and 40 to 1, respectively.

On Saturday, following a soup and sandwich in the internet café in King Street and a 20 minute walk to the ground along the icy pavements, I took my place in the same seat of the Frank Beattie Stand that I had occupied in September.

The seats along from me were taken by two middle-aged women with their young sons, one of whom – aged about 7 or 8 – was on my immediate right.

The atmosphere was much more supportive of the home team that it had been on my previous visit. The Kilmarnock support clearly included the boy next to me, whom I assumed to have been on a sugar-rich diet, as he anticipated the kick-off by repeatedly jumping up and down and clapping and shouting. His activity level then seemed to rise a couple of notches after the game had started. When his mother asked if he was disturbing me, I took the opportunity to suggest that they swap seats, which she kindly did. She asked me to let her know if she herself starting bouncing up and down; I then made a reciprocal request.

It was a close-fought match. Both sides were well-organised and sound in defence allowing few chances to be created; both were wasteful of possession at crucial times. Kilmarnock did hit the post in the first half and, after the interval, Ross County's best move of the match created the opportunity for an unopposed close-range header from Jason Naismith, which he duly guided wide of the goal. The game drifted towards what seemed to be its inevitable stalemated closure and a replay on Tuesday evening. "They played better against Rangers" – a recent 2-1 victory – said my neighbour.

And then, as so often happens with football matches, we had five minutes of drama at the end of the tie. In the 87th minute, the Kilmarnock midfielder, Rory McKenzie, attempted to reach a floated pass in the visitors' penalty area. In my line of sight, he was running away across the six-yard box with the Ross County player, Tim Chow, in attendance. McKenzie stumbled as the ball bounced away off his outstretched foot and went past the post. The referee, Bobby Madden, pointed to the penalty spot and issued a red card to Chow. The Kilmarnock substitute, Lee Erwin, converted the kick. The crowd – led by the woman to my right – roared its approval.

There was still time for the 10-man Ross County to mount a rescue attempt. The stadium clock had stopped at 90 minutes when, showing rather more urgency than hitherto to get the ball into the Kilmarnock penalty area, the visitors forced a corner. The incoming kick was headed on by County's goalkeeper, Aaron McCarey – pressed into service by the circumstances as an auxiliary (and unlikely) attacking weapon – and saved on the line by the sprawling Jamie MacDonald in the Kilmarnock goal. McCarey furiously protested to referee Madden that the ball had crossed the line; Madden responded by blowing the final whistle.

And so the revival of Kilmarnock FC continues. They have been drawn at home against a Highland League side – Brora Rangers – in the next round of the Cup. Compared with the occasion of my previous visit, these are better times at Rugby Park.

www.anordinaryspectator.com/news-blog January 2018

# Rugby Union

# A Keen Contest on a Dreich Afternoon

Scottish Rugby has announced a significant set of changes to the structure of club rugby from the 2019-20 season. There will be six semi-professional clubs in a tier below the two current fully professional outfits (the Glasgow Warriors and Edinburgh Rugby). Below the "Super Six", all the other clubs will participate in amateur leagues, at the head of which will be a 12-team Scottish Championship.

The principal aim of the changes is to smooth the pathway for players graduating from the leading Scottish club sides into the professional ranks – currently something of a chasm.

The existing clubs (or syndicates of clubs) have until 30th March to submit their bids to Scottish Rugby to become one of the new elite group. The franchises, which will be announced on 1st May, will run for five years at a time and there will be at least one Super Six team in each of Scottish Rugby's four regions.

The new system will face a number of challenges. For example, much will depend on whether Scottish Rugby can also negotiate with one or more of the other Unions for a suitable competition in which the Super Six could participate. (There would be little attraction in them just playing each other all the time). I wonder, also, about the extent to which the Glasgow Warriors and/or Edinburgh Rugby might use their Super Six "partners" as convenient teams in which to ensure that members of their own squads have the opportunity to gain playing time when not in the first team or returning from injury. (This issue is not dissimilar to that in rugby league, when Super League sides use the "dual registration" arrangements with lower league clubs to parachute in players for certain matches, thereby risking team morale and continuity within the recipient sides). And, not least, history suggests that the policing of the amateur status below the Super Six – indeed "wholly amateur", according to Scottish Rugby's press release last autumn – might be a combination of the difficult and the casual.

On Saturday, I went to watch Peebles visit West of Scotland at Burnbrae in the National League Division 2. This is the third tier of the present club hierarchy and so their respective positions of 5th and 9th in the league placed the two sides at 27th and 31st within the overall nationwide standings. We can probably assume that neither club will be one of the selected half dozen.

It was evident from the first scrum that West were in for a tough afternoon. Their forwards were shunted yards backwards at the set-piece: a pattern that was to repeat itself throughout the game. West's sources of possession were more productive from the line-out and from a continual stream of Peebles infringements at the breakdown, but they were not sufficient to stem the tide. Peebles ran in their first try after six minutes and, aided by a strong breeze on a damp afternoon, were 26-0 ahead at half-time.

West did not give up, however, and kept scrapping right to the end: literally so, as some fine handling in the match's last passage of play led to their second try and a reduction in the final deficit to 12-36. (This had been immediately preceded by an anguished cry by one of the Peebles players – which seemed to echo around the main stand – when one of his colleagues had kicked the ball down the middle of the pitch instead of safely out of play over the touchline to end the match: "What the f... are you doing?")

I enjoyed the afternoon. For part of the second half, I joined the handful of spectators on the banking behind the lower touchline, where the sharp gusts of a swirling wind would occasionally blow into our faces. We formed a small group of camp followers close to the action as the play moved back and forth down the field. I had a good view of the commitment of the players and of the many small-scale examples of their courage and skill.

It is unlikely that either Peebles or West of Scotland will move out of Division 2 this season. As one of the league's sides (Aberdeenshire) has dropped out, there is only one relegation place and West seem to be comfortably clear of the Whitecraigs side currently occupying 11th place,[3] whilst Peebles will probably fall short of the two promotion slots. As the new Scottish Championship will presumably be comprised of 12 sides drawn from next season's Premiership and National League Division 1, this means that both clubs would remain within the new National League structure at its inauguration in 2019.

Scottish Rugby has stated that it hopes the absence of player payments will allow Scottish Championship and National League clubs to build stronger community ties and invest in developing their infrastructures. In the cases of both West of Scotland and Peebles, it could be argued that the local ties are already strong, as given, for example, by the former's extensive commitment to providing facilities and coaching for "micro", "mini" and "midi" rugby – i.e. from pre-school to the Under 16s of Bearsden and Milngavie – on a Sunday morning.

I wonder, therefore, how much club rugby at this level – as revealed by the competitive action on the pitch – will be affected by Scottish Rugby's bold plans. Relatively little, perhaps. And for this casual spectator looking to attend a keenly contested match on a dreich afternoon, that would be no bad thing.

www.anordinaryspectator.com/news-blog January 2018

# Rugby Union

# Nationality

The 2018 Six Nations Championship began on Saturday with comfortable wins for Wales and England over Scotland and Italy, respectively, and a dramatic last-minute victory for Ireland in Paris. Over the next six weeks, there will be the familiar annual cocktail of drama, skill, hype, excitement and frustration for the supporters of the national teams.

One issue that had interested me for some time is the composition of those "national" sides. A couple of statistics. For last weekend's matches, 20 out of the 90 players in the six starting XVs were not born in the country they were representing. The same applied to 13 of the 48 players on the replacement benches. This meant that 33 out of the 138 players – 24% – were born outside their country's borders. (The same applied to 4 of the 6 head coaches). For 5 of the countries, the foreign births accounted for either 4 or 5 of the 23-man match-day squads; in the case of Scotland, the figure was 10, including 8 of the starting XV.

Of course, the circumstances surrounding the players' places of birth will have varied considerably and, for this reason, it must be emphasised that this is a very crude measure of national "attachment".

In many cases, the strength of the players' national and cultural identification cannot be in any doubt. For some, the place of birth simply reflects the (temporary) employment of one or both parents. For others, it was the family's location prior to the player's migration and full assimilation into his new environment. Hence, for example, Ross Moriarty of Wales was born on Merseyside at the time that his father, Paul, was playing professional rugby league for Widnes; George Biagi of Italy was born in Scotland to a Scots/Italian father and Scottish mother and went to school in Scotland, but attended university in Italy and stayed on in that country to play his first club rugby.

However, there are also other factors at play – and, as discussed below, it is some of these that have recently come under scrutiny, not least from World Rugby, rugby union's world governing body.

[As an aside, I shall simply note in passing that the qualifications issue is one that has also exercised the minds of the followers of other sports – both team and individual – for some time, ranging from the Ireland football team and the England cricket side to the East African-born middle-distance runners representing Middle Eastern countries].

The current eligibility criteria for playing international rugby union (apart from ability) are based on either the place of birth of the player (or his parent or grandparent) or a residency qualification of three years.

To some extent, the impact on eligibility of the residency qualification is linked to straightforward market forces. The Australian and New Zealand rugby unions have long benefited from the higher overall living standards that their countries offer to promising rugby players from the Pacific Islands. Similarly, in those cases where the visa requirements can be met, the wealth of English and French rugby clubs constitutes a powerful magnet to players from overseas. A prime example here is the case of the Auckland-born Denny Solomona, part of whose 3-year qualification period for England (it has turned out in retrospect) was spent playing rugby league for Castleford prior to his switch of codes with Sale; he was selected for the England rugby union side last year as soon as he was eligible.

Some countries have attempted to work within the existing rules to offset the advantages of size and wealth that the larger rugby-playing countries possess. Two complementary strategies have been followed. The first has been to spend resources systematically identifying young talented rugby players in other countries who would be eligible for selection via the parent or grandparent route. In Scotland – to give one example – an upgraded Scottish Qualified Programme was launched last autumn with agents in the rest of the UK, Europe, Japan, South Africa, Australia and New Zealand.

Second, when the ancestral route is absent, there is the option to identify so-called "project players" to qualify on residency. These players are offered contracts with regional professional sides in the hope or expectation that they will graduate to international level at the 3-year mark. It is noticeable that media discussions of overseas-born players in the Irish and Scottish professional teams often include reference to the countdown to their international eligibility.

At this point, the question should be asked: does any of this matter? After all, the rules are the same for everyone.

In my view, the main danger does not lie with the likely attitude of the players. There is no reason to view the on-field commitment to their respective causes of the 24% (as calculated above) to be any different to that of the other 76% representing their countries.

Rather, the potential risk is to the credibility of international rugby – and therefore to its status as a source of spectator interest and identification. At what point does the proportion of players born outside the country mean that it is not really the "national" team that is being represented. If one-in-four is roughly the currently starting point, is it two-in-four or three-in four, or what? At what stage does the England versus Scotland Calcutta Cup match cease to be the sport's equivalent of an England/Scotland soccer match and become analogous to the old-style Football League versus Scottish League contests? The latter were representative matches, whose teams were drawn from those (in theory of all nationalities) playing in England and Scotland, irrespective of their places of birth. The fixture dated from 1892, but was discontinued due to lack of spectator (and club) interest in 1976.

The issues surrounding international rugby player eligibility have been debated for some time. (I note in particular an excellent article by Sarah Mockford – "How rugby's eligibility rules must change" – in the August 2015 edition of *Rugby World*). And World Rugby has responded. In May 2017, it announced that the residency qualification period for international players would be extended from three to five years from the end of 2020, thus ensuring that players have a "genuine, close, credible and established link with the nation of representation". The same theme was picked up by the WR chairman, Bill Beaumont: the reform is an "important and necessary step to protecting the integrity and credibility of international rugby".

The change from three to five years is a significant one: it is a long time for someone to commit to a new country and develop their career in the hope of making an international squad other than that of the country in which they were born. It will also represent an increased financial commitment by the home union on those marquee players that have been identified.

However, it will also have the effect of raising the importance of the parent/grandparent route as a means of identifying potential talent. (Those involved with the Scottish Qualified Programme can expect an increased pressure to deliver results). On this point, my view is that the grandparent criterion should be abolished and that only the parental link should be retained. For many players, it must be difficult to justify an emotional or cultural link with an ancestor who was born perhaps 80 years earlier and whom one might not have met.

In the meantime, the 2018 Six Nations bandwagon moves on – this weekend to Dublin, Twickenham and Murrayfield.

www.anordinaryspectator.com/news-blog February 2018

Football

# 700-plus Years After Edward I – a Two-All Draw

The 2018 Calcutta Cup match was played on Saturday – Scotland versus England at Murrayfield. The annual rituals of national identification were presented: *Flower of Scotland*, swirling bagpipes, the red rose, *Swing Low, Sweet Chariot*… Scotland succeeded in sending their visitors homeward, tae think again: 25-13.

By the time the game kicked off (in the early evening), I was about to begin my return journey to Glasgow from a place with a history of far more serious – and bloody – conflict between the Scots and English. Over the centuries, Berwick-on-Tweed was the location of continual and bitter dispute – including sacking and massacre – the town changing hands more than a dozen times in the 400 years before it was finally retaken for England by the future Richard III in 1482.

Thankfully, the occasion of my visit was for more peaceful matters: Berwick Rangers versus Montrose in the Ladbrokes Scottish Professional League Division 2.

The later border tensions of the (first) Elizabethan era are revealed in the town's extensive defensive ramparts that date from that time, the restoration of which now provided an invigorating walk on a sunny, but chilly, day. I was following in good company. A plaque on the walk's route noted that LS Lowry had been a frequent visitor to Berwick and that one of his pen and pencil sketches – *Football Match* – captured an impromptu soccer game being played in one of the dry moats. Sure enough, when I reached the top of the rampart, I had a clear view of two teams battling it out on a pitch in the middle distance – red and yellow, as if Manchester United were playing Wolverhampton Wanderers – the shrill blasts of the referee's whistle and the cursing of frustrated players carried towards me on the stiff breeze coming off the sea.

After a quick lunch in a cafe near the Town Hall (1754-60) – a cheese and tomato toastie followed by a slice of a rather good toffee cake – I walked over Berwick Old Bridge (1610-24) and down the road to Shielfield Park. I paid my £7 senior's entrance fee and then a further £7 for a Berwick Rangers coffee mug in the club shop, fully recognising that this would not assist in my wife's current desire to rationalise our stock of kitchenware. The Berwick drinking vessel has thus been added to an eclectic list that includes Arsenal FC, the Washington Redskins and Melbourne Cricket Ground.

Montrose are having a good season. Prior to Saturday's match, they were 5 points clear at the top of the league – chasing the automatic promotion slot – albeit that they had played one game more than their nearest challengers, Peterhead. For them, this is unfamiliar territory: the club has been nestled in the fourth tier of Scottish football for over 20 years.

By contrast, Berwick began the day third from bottom of the 10-team division, although they were probably already sufficiently well clear of bottom-placed Cowdenbeath to be concerned about the end-of-season play-off match with the winner of either the Highland League or Lowland League to decide next year's league status. An away draw at Peterhead in the previous match had aided their cause.

Montrose's championship challenge has been assisted by their excellent away form, which has gathered in more league points than in their home fixtures. Before Saturday, 9 matches had been won out of 13 played with only 8 goals conceded. It was a surprise, therefore, that it was a pair of defensive lapses that twice allowed Berwick to draw level after Montrose had taken the lead.

After Berwick had conceded an early own goal, it was a defensive misjudgement between the Montrose centre backs and the goalkeeper Allan Fleming, when a high kick downfield was held up in the wind, that allowed the skilful Ousman See to nudge home the first equaliser. Then, midway through the second half, a Berwick free kick taken by Paul Willis from wide out on the left was allowed to pass through a crowd of players and into the far corner of the goal. At 2-2 with 25 minutes left, there was all to play for – and both teams did indeed search enthusiastically for the winner – but the score remained unchanged, the end result being a fair reflection of the afternoon's efforts. The nearest to a winning goal came from another (and closer) Willis free kick, which was splendidly saved by the acrobatic Fleming.

Just as at Murrayfield – indeed, just as at virtually any regularly held sporting event – the events at Shielfield Park provided all the participants with their own rituals and customs, to be drawn upon as they wished. The plastic cup of Bovril from the fast-food stall; the 50-50 half-time draw (a Mr Harrison won £126); the manager's reflections in the excellent match programme on the unjust defeat in the previous home game; the black and gold woolly hats; the announcement of the man-of-the match (Berwick's Darren Lavery); the reporting of the attendance (417)... It is the comfort of the familiar. I also noted that both managers shook the hands of all their respective players at the end of the game, that the stewarding was pleasantly low-key, and that the referee (Craig Charleston) had a sound match.

And so this was Berwick on a Saturday afternoon. A town of about 12,000, of whom a very small percentage had ventured out to watch their soccer team. A town with its cafes and pubs and hairdressers and charity shops…all seeking to keep themselves afloat in a challenging economic climate. A town with a history.

I think it's the sense of place and time that I always have difficulty putting into context. Above the steps leading down to the platforms at Berwick railway station is a large plaque marking the spot where, in 1292, Edward's I's arbitration in favour of John Balliol (rather than Robert the Bruce) in the contest for the Scottish crown was announced.

I walked down the steps towards the waiting room. The ruins of the castle were just a little way over to the left. It was 700-plus years later and I had just been to see a football match about a mile and a half down the road.[4]

www.anordinaryspectator.com/news-blog February 2018

Football

# Even Better Times at Rugby Park

I am not sure what the psychologists would make of this. On Saturday, despite not having any particular allegiance to either team, I was drawn to Rugby Park to watch the Ladbrokes Scottish Premiership match between Kilmarnock and Ross County. It was the third time I had seen these two sides play on this ground in 2017-18: see *"Difficult Times at Rugby Park"* (2nd October 2017) and *"Better Times at Rugby Park"* (22nd January 2018).

I can only put this down to a curious interest in the "journeys" – to use a term familiar to viewers of *Strictly Come Dancing* or *The X-Factor* – that the two sides have made over the course of the season.

In the autumn, Kilmarnock were bottom of the league, their then-manager (Lee McCulloch) was dismissed the day after the match and Ross County (who won 2-0) looked to be a well-organised side that might prosper under their new manager, Owen Coyle.

However, by the time of the 4th Round William Hill Scottish Cup tie in the New Year, it was Ross County who were propping up the league; by contrast, a run of Kilmarnock successes under the experienced Steve Clarke had taken the home side well clear of the relegation threat. The respective league fortunes were echoed in the cup-tie, when a debatable 87th minute penalty secured the victory for Kilmarnock.

In the period between these two Rugby Park fixtures, the sides had also met once in a league fixture at the Victoria Park ground in Dingwall: a 2-2 draw in mid-December. Within the narrow confines of this particular rivalry, therefore, last Saturday's match could have been considered the season's "decider".

At the start of play, Kilmarnock were in fifth place in the league table. Beaten only once in the 16 games played in all competitions since the beginning of December, their impressive recent record had included home victories over both Celtic and Rangers. The Scottish Cup run was also still in progress; next

Wednesday's replay against Aberdeen will decide the semi-final opponents for Motherwell.

By contrast, Ross County remained rooted in twelfth and last position, three points below the side above them. The club having parted company with Coyle following his unsuccessful five months in charge, joint-managers – Stuart Kettlewell and Steven Ferguson – had been appointed on an interim basis until the end of the season.

I am a creature of habit: a latte consumed on the train journey from Glasgow; a quick lunch in the internet café in King Street; a walk to the ground followed by the purchase of match programme and lottery ticket; a (now familiar) place taken in the Frank Beattie Stand. (I am still mystified as to how I managed to lose a pair of gloves during my own journey from the turnstile to my seat).

Until five minutes from the end of the match, the action on the pitch was as if set out in the pre-ordained script. A flowing move down the right brought Kilmarnock's opener from Lee Erwin after a quarter of an hour; the veteran Kris Boyd hammered in his 125th goal for the club within a minute of the second-half re-start (thereby taking him closer to the 128 that he registered in his periods at Rangers); with 15 minutes to play, the substitute – "birthday boy Eamonn Brophy", as introduced by the stadium announcer – scored a third almost immediately after having taken the field.

Kilmarnock were three goals up and cruising. The near-end-of-match announcements began: the man-of-the-match award (the home side's Rory McKenzie), the size of the crowd (4,001), the number of visiting supporters in the Chadwick Stand (103, generously applauded by home fans near me)…

Then, in the 86th minute, a complacent back-pass from the Kilmarnock midfield enabled Billy McKay to secure a goal for the visitors. Shortly afterwards, a run and cross down the left wing by the persistent Michael Gardyne brought a second for Alex Schalk. With the stadium clock showing 90 minutes played, it was announced that there would be three minutes of added time. The sudden nervousness in the home crowd – which had previously been enjoying their side's complete supremacy – was palpable.

There was to be no final sting in the tail, however. Kilmarnock duly secured the winning points and took another step towards consolidating their place in the top 6 (see below). Success against Aberdeen on Wednesday would bring a first Scottish Cup semi-final for over 20 years. These are even better times at Rugby Park.

The home point that Partick Thistle gained against Aberdeen on Saturday means that Ross County are now four points adrift at the bottom of the table. It will be a difficult task for joint managers Kettlewell and Ferguson to steer the side away from relegation at the end of the season's "journey". In this match (as in the cup-tie in January), Ross County had their fair share of possession, but did seem to lack the decisive cutting edge "in the final third" (to use the analyst's jargon). On the plus side, the squad has some experience – including a couple of members of the Inverness Caledonian Thistle team that I saw lift the Scottish Cup at Hampden Park three seasons ago – and also, clearly, some spirit. At 0-3 down with a few minutes left, away from home and playing into a lashing rain, other sides might have thrown in the towel.

There is a possible footnote to this season's Kilmarnock/Ross County saga. In the unlikely event that Kilmarnock were to slip back into the bottom 6 of the league table by the time of the Premiership's "split" in April (after which the teams in the top and bottom halves play only each other in the final 5 matches), they would meet Ross County again. Moreover, notwithstanding that Kilmarnock have had home advantage in two of three league meetings this year, there is no guarantee that Ross County would host that final game. (It would depend on how the other fixtures within the bottom group happened to fall). I might have to make another visit to Rugby Park before the end of the season.[5]

www.anordinaryspectator.com/news-blog March 2018

# Basketball

# Funding Priorities

*"[There was] something balletic in the speed and grace of these big men
and the skills that they possess… There would be the careful working of
a position and then a sudden flurry of fast action as the scoring play
was attempted and defended".*

[*An Ordinary Spectator*, page 213]

That Kieron Achara is a big man – 6 feet 9 inches and 240 pounds – is probably a help to him in his current occupation. He is a professional basketball player with the Glasgow Rocks, who compete in the top tier in the sport in the UK: the British Basketball League (BBL). Next month, he will captain Scotland in the men's basketball competition in the Commonwealth Games on the Gold Coast.

In Scotland, the principal BBL franchise has moved around somewhat since the establishment of the Edinburgh Rocks in 1998 with their base at Meadowbank. They were transformed into the Scottish Rocks on moving to Braehead in 2002 and then into the Glasgow Rocks on taking up residence at the city's Kelvin Hall in 2009. Since 2012, the Rocks' home has been the Emirates Arena in Glasgow's east end, which is where I saw them take on the Leicester Riders on Friday evening.

This was only my second-ever basketball match. Over 30 years ago, I took advantage of a free evening on a business trip to the US East Coast to watch the New York Knickerbockers play the Cleveland Cavaliers in the Madison Square Garden. One might as well start at the very top, I thought. My admiration for the speed and skills of the participants was recorded in *An Ordinary Spectator*, as noted above. I also reported that one of the Knicks – Patrick Ewing – was a mere 7 feet tall and that the match programme included an endorsement for a natural control hairspray by a New York rabbi!

Compared with other sports, basketball appears to be well down the pecking order in this country. Media coverage is limited – though I recently caught the two-hour coverage of a BBL match on the Free Sports satellite channel – as is, crucially, the central funding from UK Sport. I return to the latter point below.

To its credit, the BBL does attempt to ensure that, for domestic basketball players, there is a pathway to the top level so that the elite sides are not dominated by imports from overseas. There is a limit of three players from outside the European Union in a team's roster for the season with a maximum of five non-British players being allowed in any particular game.

The Leicester Riders fixture was a good one to choose. The visitors are on course to win the BBL Championship for the third consecutive year, having established a clear lead in the league table above the franchises in Newcastle and Glasgow. The Rocks' current third place – the position they finished in last season – is under some threat, the side having played more games than their nearest rivals, but they are easily on course to be one of the top eight (out of 12) sides that will contest the separate knock-out Play-Off tournament in May.

The tempo of the game was swift and upbeat and established by the relentless countdowns on the arena's electronic clock: the 10-minute quarters (with the last single minutes counted down to the tenth of a second); the one-minute time-outs (when the Glasgow Rockettes enthusiastically went through their routines in the centre of the arena); the 25-second limitation on a side's possession before it would attempt a shot at the basket.

The urgent rhythm was compounded by continual bursts of upbeat music – Status Quo's *Rocking All Over the World* and Van Halen's *Jump* being predictably prominent – and the speed with which, for both sides, defence would be transformed into attack when the opponents' assault was halted and possession regained. The Rocks' Nate Britt, for one, was impressively quick over the court, whilst the Riders' Pierre Hampton stood out with his skill and physicality.

That every second counts was emphatically confirmed in this match. Two penalty shots enabled the Riders to take the score to 80-77 with the clock ticking down to the end of the last minute. A final Rocks attack then saw Gareth Murray land a three-point basket from some distance. The ball passed through the net to a huge roar from the crowd – by now all on its feet – and, by the time I looked up at the clock again, it had counted down to 0.00. This was proper sports drama, of the type that has reeled me in over these many years.

The five minutes of overtime passed very quickly, even allowing for the tactical time-outs. At the close of play, it was the Riders who had edged home by 90-88: their ability to inch over the line perhaps indicative of being the league's leading team.

The visitors' success was all the more impressive, not only because they had only a handful of supporters in the crowd, but because the whole atmosphere was geared in support of the Rocks. This extended to the systematic stamping of the crowd's feet – prompted by the MC – as the Riders attempted a penalty throw at the basket and the subsequent playing of ironic duck quacks if the attempt were missed. It was not exactly Corinthian Casuals, though – I emphasise – it was not hostile, just orchestrated to be heavily biased, and I assume that this is the norm throughout the league. I also noted that the players shook hands with all their opponents (and with the referees) before the match – and did so warmly, not in the cursory manner usually seen before a soccer game.

It is clear that the Glasgow Rocks organisation is heavily involved in schools and community work. The match programme stated that the players had delivered roadshows in 87 schools in the current season. For the Riders match, the crowd in the arena was of all ages, including organised groups from three primary schools as well as teenagers, couples, families and office groups.

At half-time, a long queue of (mainly) youngsters formed on the court to take shots at the basket. Given the weight of the ball, it was not surprising that some struggled to reach half the height of the net – including a fully-attired Superman aged about seven – but others raised loud cheers from the crowd for their accurate throws. One young girl – probably aged about 11 or 12 with her ginger hair in a ponytail – addressed her shots with poise and calmness and nailed three out of four from the penalty line, each of her successes barely touching the rim of the basket.

Let us return to UK Sport, whose criteria for a sport's financial support are clearly set out on its website:

> "*The primary role of UK Sport is to strategically invest National Lottery and Exchequer income to maximise the performance of UK athletes in the Olympic and Paralympic Games and the global events which precede them*".

Hence, for example, the website reveals that sailing will receive over £25 million and equestrianism over £14 million in the run up to the 2020 Tokyo Olympics. By contrast, basketball will receive £630,000: the British men's and women's teams came 9th and 11th, respectively, in London in 2012 and neither qualified for Rio de Janeiro in 2016.

Of course, there have to be some criteria for the allocation of funding – and UK Sport is fully transparent on the course that it has decided – but this particular methodology is not without its critics. It places all its eggs in the basket of winning medals, rather than taking into account any broader impacts – economic, social, health – that a sport might have at the grassroots level. Thus, in the case of basketball, it does not take account of the low cost to the individual of taking part or its accessibility to potential participants in the major urban (and other) centres, where (again for example) options such as sailing and equestrianism might be less readily available.

It is a characteristic of modern democracies that there should be a continual debate about the allocation of public resources, the availability of which will always be limited. At the macro level, this involves big decisions: health or education or defence... etc? But the same principle applies throughout the hierarchy of public expenditure.

Hence, we should regularly ask: is the allocation of the (limited) public funds available for the support of sports participation and achievement the most appropriate that we can devise? I looked at the half-time queue on the court at the Emirates Arena on Friday evening – including the 7-year old Superman and the 12-year old girl with the ginger ponytail – and I did wonder if the current priorities were correct.

In the meantime, things move on. Good luck to Kieron Achara and Gareth Murray and their five Rocks colleagues representing Scotland in the Commonwealth Games. And to their other colleague, Kofi Josephs, and two of the Leicester Riders – Shane Walker and Andrew Thomson – who will be in the England squad for the first of their Pool B preliminary matches in Townsville on 5th April. That match is England versus Scotland.

www.anordinaryspectator.com/news-blog March 2018

# Cricket

# The Mist at the Boundary Edge

*[I woke up at four o'clock this morning from a dream…]*

I have been sitting on the wooden benches of the open terrace for some time now watching the players depart, down a slight slope, towards the far side of the ground. On the distant boundary edge, a mist seems to have descended, obscuring some of them from view.

The men are elderly, their progress slow and halting. A couple need some assistance.

When they had been in the middle – in my youth – they had been strong and robust. And skilful and determined. They had frequently argued amongst themselves, it is true – clashes of personality, as euphemistically described – but their collective will had prevailed. Six County Championships and two Gillette Cups in the 1960s.

Tony Nick is the first whom I can no longer see – taken before he had even reached his half century. Hour upon hour, he had bowled uphill or into the wind: the master of seam and length, his radar permanently fixed on the top of off stump.

Some time later, Freddie is the next to depart into the mist: gruff and opinionated, but with a cricketing brain as sharp as a tack. Phil and Don have walked off together, as you would expect the two great friends to do. One was short and round with the hands of a magician at first slip. The other, tall and angular, had followed in the path of the county's great left-armers.

Then, the captain. At once, both England's youngest test match player, to whom the game seemed to come so easily, and the hardened veteran – and I mean hard – with bruises to show from West Indian fast bowlers and county committees. In the field, Brian Close would take the blow at short leg, but woe betide you if you didn't catch the rebound.

John Hampshire is the most recent to have disappeared into the mist. The straight drive was his trademark: a wonderful synthesis of power and grace. How many times, from this seat here on the terrace, have I heard the crack of the rifle-shot as bat hit ball and then waited for the muffled echo to come back from the shadows of the Football Stand?

The remainder of the team continue to make their way slowly across the distant outfield. They are still clearly visible, praise be.

With affection, I recall their younger selves: Geoffrey's turned-up collar and immaculate straight bat; the cheery Dougie Padgett's ruddy face (and, later, his honest appraisal of my limited showing at the Indoor School); Ken Taylor's athletic fielding and his double life as a professional footballer; Jimmy Binks standing back to Fred behind the stumps. And Raymond, the off-spinning all-rounder and, later again, Ashes-winning captain: the cricketer on whom I modelled myself.

Of course, I realise that, fairly soon, I will have to leave my seat and start my own walk across the outfield and towards the mist. It's a journey that we all must make at some stage. Forgive me, however, if I delay awhile: I should like to cast my mind back and – with a smile of fond memory – take another look at this team in action in the middle.

www.anordinaryspectator.com/news-blog April 2018

# Cricket

# The Pensieve in the Attic

*[By way of a change, a blog on my (modest) playing –
rather than spectating – career...]*

We finally got round to clearing out the attic. A ruthless purge of the evidence of family life over 30-plus years: stair-gates, a baby bath, spare rolls of carpeting...

I knew what was in the bundle in the corner – wrapped in a couple of large black bin bags – as soon as it was unearthed from underneath a sack of kids' toys. I had tied up the straps of my cricket bag for the final time at the end of the 1985 season. I took it down to open up in the garage.

The only item of clothing was a pair of boots: freshly whitened, a stud missing on each sole and with marked signs of wear by my right toe. A memory was triggered: in the latter stages of my off-spinning days, I completely lost my rhythm and dragged my foot along the ground during the delivery stride.

All the rest was for batting. There were two sets of gloves: one an inner pair, the other (outer) pair with thick sausage fingers. Underneath these was a jock strap – who keeps a jock strap for 30 years? – and a plastic box. Next to them, my trusty thigh pad – home-made by my mother – with the longer upper strap to tie around my waist. I used to wear the pad high up, over my hip; a blow on the bone is considerably more painful than one on the fleshy part of the thigh. And resting on top of all this, three (?) pads: two an obvious pair – again newly whitened – the other a random spare.

Another memory. I always used to put the left pad on before the right. And – again always – with the buckles on the inside of the legs, so that they wouldn't be mistaken by an inattentive umpire for the outside edge of the bat.

That had been the extent of my protection. There was no helmet, of course.

My bat was inside its own soft protective sheath. I had obviously oiled it for a final time before storing it away because it stuck to the inside and was difficult to extract. (Does anybody still oil their bats these days?) A Gray Nicolls

GN100 Perimeter Weighted – a "Scoop" – with the vivid orange gouge on its back compensated for by the enhanced thickness of the edges.

Yet more recollections came. I thought about some of grounds on which I had played and the runs that the bat had supplied: a 100 on the Bank of England ground at Roehampton, a half-century for Saltaire CC in Roberts Park, a couple of scores in Cambridge on the flat tracks of the college grounds at Jesus and Trinity…

These were the exceptions, of course. The afternoons of triumph had been heavily outweighed by the failures elsewhere – a sketchy 9 here, a half-hour 3 there, a dodgy lbw on a green wicket in Guiseley… My last match was a second-ball duck at Weybridge: caught at second slip after I had hung my bat out at a wide one from a medium-paced trundler. I knew, as I trudged away to the pavilion, that that would be my final game of cricket.

In the garage, I looked again at the cricket bag and I realised what it really was. It was – in JK Rowling's magical world – a pensieve: the precious bowl in Professor Dumbledore's office in which an individual's distant memories can be located. The bag contained my stock of playing memories, some of which were now escaping…

The cricket bag and its contents survived the purge of the attic. In another 30 years, perhaps.

www.anordinaryspectator.com/news-blog May 2018

Rugby Union

# The Conductor of the Orchestra

Time flies. I am amazed to see that it is nearly 2½ years since I went to see the Glasgow Warriors play the Scarlets at Scotstoun Stadium in the group stage of the 2015-16 European Rugby Champions Cup.

On that occasion, my subsequent blog – "*What's in a Name?*" 14th December 2015 – did not go into detail about the Warriors' comfortable 43-6 win. Rather, its focus was on the name of the visitors, who had dropped the original Llanelli component several seasons earlier, notwithstanding its resonance across the rugby world. I was relieved to report that the team had been popularly known as the Scarlets long before the professional era started, when the modern branding managers were mere twinkles in their mothers' eyes.

Over the last 18 months, the Scarlets have prospered. They won last year's Guinness PRO12 competition by thrillingly defeating Munster in the final in Dublin. This season, they reached the semi-final of the European Cup before succumbing to Leinster.

For their part, Glasgow, whilst continuing to falter in the European arena, topped their half of this year's Guinness PRO14, which, bolstered by two South African sides, was split into two Conferences for the regular season. This gave the Warriors the twin benefits of home advantage for yesterday's semi-final (against the Scarlets) as well as a week off, when their opponents, who had come second in their Conference, had to defeat the Bloemfontein-based Cheetahs in a qualifying play-off.

Although there were sizeable pockets of Scarlets support, notably in Scotstoun's expanded temporary West Stand, the bulk of the 10,000 crowd was biased in favour of the home side. Not surprisingly, of course – biased and colourful and noisy. The middle-aged lady next to me, with husband and two children in tow, was to contribute significantly to the volume with some sustained shrieking throughout the match.

After the Scarlets had taken the field, they were kept waiting for almost two minutes before Ryan Wilson sprinted through the long corridor of flag-waving camp followers to lead his side on to the pitch. The crowd, prompted by the MC and with the knowledge of Glasgow's unbeaten PRO14 record at Scotstoun this season, roared with a combination of anticipation and intimidation as Finn Russell started the match with a high, hanging drop-kick.

The first minute provided a perfect microcosm of the game as a whole. Wilson made an illegal contact with the Scarlets winger, Tom Prydie, as the latter sought to take the kick-off. The penalty kick, close to the touch line, was then drilled 40 metres downfield by the visitors' fly-half, Rhys Patchell. At the ensuing lineout, the experienced Scarlets captain, Ken Owens, nailed the throw-in expertly to the athletic Tadhg Beirne and the Scarlets retained possession of the ball. They had kept their composure and weathered the initial storm.

Later, when I watched the recording of the match on television, I noted what the respected Sky Sports analyst, Ieuan Evans, had said in commentary about the Wilson infringement:

> "Well actually, it's not a bad penalty to give away. It shows an intent from Ryan Wilson... Very physical... Not prepared to allow any sort of space for the Scarlets and time to clear their decks".

With due respect to the expert, I wasn't so sure about this. In fact, I thought that it was a very poor penalty to give away. It meant that, rather than contesting for the ball on the opponents' 22 line, Glasgow were immediately forced back to a defensive position deep in their own half, the penalty award – by definition – having given the Scarlets "time to clear the decks". Three minutes later, after sustained Scarlets pressure, Patchell darted over from short range for the opening try. I suspect that, even at that point, some in the crowd had already begun to realise that the evening might not turn out as they had wished.

The Scarlets played the match at their tempo. On their line-out throw, the forwards would walk slowly to the mark, often keeping the Glasgow pack waiting in their turn, before there was a sudden flurry of activity and Owens unerringly hit his mark. In open play, it often seemed to be the opposite – unstructured, almost chaotic, and therefore risky – as the ball was kept alive and each player took responsibility for assessing the opportunities that might be available. Allied to this, however, was the consistent threat of the ball-handler being given two or three options by support runners taking different lines – an approach that Glasgow found difficult to contain. Their right-hand side defence was opened up twice more before the interval to produce tries for Gareth Davies and Rob Evans.

Patchell was the conductor of the orchestra. His initial kick for touch was only the first of a series of long pin-point punts from penalty awards, which gained huge amounts of ground without jeopardising the retention of possession for the Scarlets at the subsequent line-out. Benefiting from a swift and accurate service from Davies at scrum-half, Patchell was also dangerous in open play with his choice of running and passing options and his tactical kicking. It was no surprise when, a couple of minutes from the end of the game – by which time he had been replaced – he appeared on the large screen in the far corner of the ground: a deserved man-of-the-match.

Glasgow have been vulnerable all season to opponents deploying the driving maul from close-range line-outs: both the Exeter Chiefs and Leinster had success with this tactic during the European Champions Cup. The Scarlets, having done their homework, followed suit. Aided by Glasgow having a player in the sin-bin, the visiting forwards drove Owens over the line after 10 minutes of the second half to give their side, with Patchell's fourth conversion, a 28-3 lead.

Perhaps inevitably, some of the crowd began to look for scapegoats. A dropped pass by one of the Glasgow centres brought a heavy groan and then a wayward chip from Russell was scathingly reviewed by my neighbour – "Take him off", she yelled. However, the chief contender was the Irish referee, John Lacey, who, with one or two decisions – including (correctly) not allowing Glasgow tries claimed by George Horne and Jonny Gray – probably did not make himself the most popular man in the G14 postal district. I thought he had a good match, keeping a firm control and letting the play flow – and, not always the case with current referees, backing his own judgment with important decisions, rather than falling back on the comfort of a TMO referral.

Overall, however, the crowd stayed with their team and they were rewarded by two legitimate Glasgow tries in the last 20 minutes, when the usual army of replacements took the field and the Scarlets went off the boil. By this stage, the result was not in doubt and the Scarlets management team was probably already thinking ahead to the significant challenges that will be posed in next Saturday's final – another encounter with Leinster, we now know – in Dublin.

One final observation on the Scotstoun crowd. After 10 minutes, the Scarlets captain, John Barclay, was helped from the field with a leg injury to take no further part in the match. If he does not recover in time for the final, this will have been his last Scarlets appearance, as he has joined Edinburgh Rugby for next season.

Barclay's approach to the Main Stand was marked by a sustained round of loud applause, as the spectators paid proper tribute to a former Glasgow player, whose consistent excellence during five years in Llanelli had helped to restore him to the Scotland team (with its captaincy) after several seasons (perplexing to me) in the international wilderness. This season, Barclay has led his country to victories over Australia, France and England. It was sad to see him depart this particular stage in this manner, but also uplifting to see the crowd (literally) rise to the occasion.[6]

www.anordinaryspectator.com/news-blog May 2018

# Cricket

# Below Average

Since the introduction of the Gillette Cup in 1963, English cricket's abbreviated form has been contested by the First Class counties in various formats: 65 overs per side, 60 overs, 55 overs, 40 overs...

Under the present arrangements, there are two competitions: the T20 tournament (currently also known as the Vitality Blast), which has been running since 2003 and the 50-over Royal London One-Day Cup, which dates from 2014. In both cases, the 18 counties are divided into two groups (North and South) in order to decide which teams (8 in the T20 and 6 in the One-Day Cup) qualify for the knock-out stages.

Yorkshire CCC's record over the 55 years of one-day competitions can charitably be described as "below average". Of the 142 tournaments played to 2017, they have won just five: the 60-over Gillette Cup in 1965 and 1969, the 40-over John Player League in 1983 (when they were captained by the 51-year old Ray Illingworth), the 55-over Benson and Hedges Trophy in 1987 and the 50-over C&G Trophy in 2002. Of the other counties, only Derbyshire, Durham and Glamorgan have a lower haul, whilst, most painfully, the honours board at Lancashire registers no fewer than 17 one-day successes.

In many seasons, Yorkshire have promised much to start with, only to falter at a later stage, including the quarter- or semi-final. Last year, there was some controversy when, after success in the initial fixtures, it was announced that Yorkshire would not be able to host a home quarter-final in the NatWest T20 competition because Headingley was being prepared for a test match and Scarborough could not accommodate the required television cameras. In the event, Yorkshire solved the problem by winning only two of the last seven group matches and failing to qualify for the knock-out stage.

And so to another season, with hopes raised and optimism afresh. Last Friday, with a friend from Strathblane – George Farrow – I went along to Yorkshire's

One-Day Cup group match with Nottinghamshire at Headingley. Prior to the game, Yorkshire had won one match out of three in this year's competition.

It was the first time that George – a life-long Essex supporter – had been to Headingley. We took up our position in the East Stand Long Room with its honours board and second-hand bookstall and cricketing memorabilia and enticing bacon rolls. From our perspective out on to the ground, George will have got a sense of the vastness of the arena and – I hope – of its history: Don Bradman's two test match triple centuries, Hedley Verity's 10 for 10 against Nottinghamshire in 1932, Geoff Boycott's hundredth 100 in the 1977 test against Australia... We both got a good impression of the progress being made on the construction of the new Football Stand and the excellent views that will eventually be available behind the bowler's arm.

What we didn't get was any cricket. The drizzle intensified as we entered the ground and then came and went with unfortunate regularity until the umpires admitted defeat just after half past three and abandoned play for the day. As we left the ground, we bade our farewell to the wet and bedraggled lady in the hi-viz jacket who was supervising the exits from the car park. "You do look rather cold", suggested George, sympathetically. "Yes", she agreed ruefully, before taking a more optimistic line, "But I'll be warm soon".

Later, after a rather good fish and chip supper in one of the local restaurants, the route to our hotel took us past the extensive – and impressive – University of Leeds playing fields on Otley Road. A cricket match was under way behind the trees – a University 2nd XI match, we surmised – and so, just after nine o'clock, we sauntered up to the boundary edge to watch its conclusion.

Literally so, as it turned out. The first delivery we saw was swept behind square for four runs, at which point the players began shaking hands and walking off the ground towards the pavilion. The side batting second had successfully chased down their target of 164 with nearly 7 of their 20 overs to spare. All in all, therefore, it can be said that George and I did not see a great deal of cricketing action during this particular visit to Leeds. On the other hand, every delivery that we did see was struck to the boundary.

Friday's wash-out was not helpful to Yorkshire's bid to be placed in the top 3 of the North Group of this year's Royal London One-Day Cup and thereby qualify for the knock-out stages. However, their cause has been aided by yesterday's emphatic nine wicket win over Leicestershire in the same competition. There are only three more group matches left. Yorkshire will probably need to win all of them in order to reach the quarter-final.

Even if Yorkshire were to win both the T20 and 50-over competitions in 2018, their long-term mark would still be "below average", such has been the general paucity of their one-day results over half a century. It would make for an interesting season though and for most supporters – who somehow sustain an unlikely combination of optimism and fatalism – that would be good enough.[7]

www.anordinaryspectator.com/news-blog May 2018

Rugby League

# Geoff Gunney MBE [8]

*"…Hunslet's best known player… had toured Australasia with the Great Britain team in 1954 and had played in the 1957 Rugby League World Cup in Australia. Although he had been sought by bigger and wealthier clubs – notably Wigan – he had stayed loyal to Hunslet… At the time of my first visits to Parkside, he stood out as a big powerful man, equally adept at tackling and running, with a sledgehammer hand-off. When Hunslet were awarded a penalty, and if it was outside [Billy] Langton's range to the goalposts, Gunney took the punts into touch: big booming kicks, delivered with a slow run up and a graceful swing of the leg".*

[*An Ordinary Spectator*, page 10]

The entry in my *Lett's Schoolboys Diary* for Monday 28th March 1966 was typically succinct:

*"School. Went to see Hunslet 25 Batley 2. Got the autographs of Brian Gabbitas, Bernard Prior, Geoff Gunney and Ken Eyre. Bed 9.20".*

The diary will probably not be a hugely significant source for future historians, notwithstanding such entries as "Went to town. Bought *Five Go Down To The Sea*" (5th April) or "The number of threepenny bits that I have saved is now 67" (15th April). However, it does reveal what my 11-year old self thought were the important events of each day and there could have been no doubt that the rich haul of the autographs of four members of the Hunslet RLFC 1965 Challenge Cup final team fell into that category.

By this time, I was in my fifth season of supporting the team that my father had followed since he had been a boy. I was familiar with the career histories of all the players – not least Geoff Gunney, arguably Hunslet's greatest-ever. The reference in *An Ordinary Spectator*, noted above, recalls my initial impression of him after seeing my first games in the autumn of 1961.

Geoff Gunney made his debut for Hunslet in September 1951 and played in a total of 579 games for the club over 23 seasons, including the Championship Final against St Helens in 1959 and the Challenge Cup Final against Wigan at Wembley in 1965. He represented Great Britain on 11 occasions and also played 9 times for Yorkshire.

By the early 1970s, the Hunslet club was in disarray. The 1965 Wembley side had quickly broken up – through transfers, injuries and retirements – and the club finished bottom of the 30-team league in 1971 and 1972. The board of directors sold the Parkside ground – the home since 1888 – to a property development company and the club was wound up. The final home match, in April 1973, was poignantly described in Les Hoole and Mike Green's *The Parksiders: A Brief History of Hunslet RLFC, 1883-1973*:

> *"Geoff Gunney led his team on to the pitch for the last time. Despite a special effort, the young Hunslet side lost to York. Gunney was the last man to leave the field".*

Geoff Gunney's efforts for rugby league in Hunslet did not end there, however. He was a key figure in the reformation of the club as New Hunslet for the start of the 1973-74 season, being involved with coaching, fund-raising and securing the Elland Road Greyhound Stadium as a temporary home ground. (Indeed, he also played in a couple of the new club's matches in October 1973 – away to Workington Town and home to Doncaster – shortly before his 40th birthday).

The new club took root and, within four years, had been promoted to the league's First Division. The legacy has been carried through to the present Hunslet RLFC club at the South Leeds Stadium in Middleton.

Geoff Gunney was renowned as a gentleman on and off the pitch. In October 2014, I met him at the opening of the "Hunslet Rugby League Remembered" Heritage Room at the Garden Gate public house in South Leeds, to which I had been invited by Peter Todd, the then General Manager of the Hunslet Hawks RLFC. He was sitting at a table in one of the small bars when I made my nervous approach: "Hello. My name is John Rigg. My dad brought me to watch Hunslet play at Parkside when I was a small boy". "Hello, John" he replied, with a firm handshake and a warm smile. We chatted for a few precious minutes. It is a fond memory.

Both *An Ordinary Spectator* and *Still An Ordinary Spectator* contain several references to Geoff Gunney, including his powerful displays in matches against Wakefield Trinity in the Challenge Cup semi-final of 1965 and Castleford in that year's Yorkshire Cup, his shock dismissal in another encounter with Wakefield and our rather improbable joint membership of the Leeds Sports Council in 1973 (at a meeting of which I took the opportunity to discuss a Hunslet-Leeds match that had taken place a few days earlier).

There is one other Hunslet match to mention here. The last game of the 1970-71 season was an away fixture against Rochdale Hornets at the Athletic Grounds. The side, having floundered badly in the league and certain of finishing bottom of the table, was further depleted through injury and suspension. The lone survivor of the 1965 side, Gunney was easing towards retirement, having only played in four matches towards the tail-end of the season. However, at the age of 37 and following a 20 year career as a rampaging second-row forward, he offered to turn out at full-back. My father and I tuned into the early Saturday evening sports results fearing the worst.

The scores duly came on the screen. Hunslet had won 16-8. This was not a cup semi-final or final; it was a low-key league match played at the end of a traumatic season. I don't know why it was so difficult to hold back the emotions when I saw the result. (Later, I learned that a neat circle had been completed: Gunney had turned out with some distinction as a makeshift full-back for Great Britain on the Australasian tour of 1954).

Geoff Gunney died earlier this month at the age of 84. Another link with my youth and adolescence has been broken, prompting the now familiar response of pause and reflection. The poet AE Housman – a lad of Shropshire, rather than Yorkshire – captured it best, I think, when referring to his Land of Lost Content:

*"The happy highways where I went/And cannot come again".[9]*

As noted, Geoff Gunney's penultimate match was for Hunslet away at Workington Town. As it happens, that same fixture is in the schedule for next weekend. I had been vaguely wondering about going to the match, as I have not previously visited Derwent Park. Somehow, there now seems to be no excuse at all not to go.

Geoff Gunney MBE, 1933-2018. RIP.

www.anordinaryspectator.com/news-blog June 2018

Rugby League

# Oystercatchers and Blue Plaques

Not surprisingly, the FIFA World Cup is dominating the current sports news agenda, prompted by England's unexpected progress to Wednesday's semi-final against Croatia.

In the meantime, other sports continue on their season's journeys – and not just the headline events such as Wimbledon and international cricket. Yesterday – by way of the return train between Glasgow and Carlisle and the Stagecoach No 301 bus between Carlisle and Workington – I attended the Betfred League 1 rugby league match between Workington Town and Hunslet at Derwent Park.

Some background. Workington Town RLFC holds the distinction of being the club which has succeeded in winning both the Rugby League Championship (in 1951) and the Challenge Cup (1952) in the shortest time following its formation (1944). Their player-coach and captain was Gus Risman – one of the "greats" of the sport – who led them out at Wembley at the age of 41, 14 years after captaining Salford to victory at the same venue. In Workington's Challenge Cup victory, the Lance Todd Trophy winner was their loose forward, Billy Ivison, who played 385 matches for his sole club over 15 seasons.

The 1950s were boom years for rugby league in Cumberland. Workington also reached the Challenge Cup finals in 1955 and 1958 and the Championship final in 1958, whilst local rivals Whitehaven (formed three years later) defeated the Australian tourists in 1956 and were within five minutes of reaching Wembley the following year before succumbing to Leeds in a one-point Challenge Cup semi-final defeat.

The recent years have not been so kind. At the time of the formation of the Super League in 1995, considerable pressure was exerted by the league authorities to form a single Cumbrian "super club" (involving Workington, Whitehaven, Barrow and Carlisle), but this was resisted by the local interests (as were proposals for similar mergers elsewhere in the rugby league heartlands) and it was the unmerged Workington that took part in Super League's first season. Only two league matches were won, however, and, with demotion following, this was the last time that a Cumbrian side was placed at the sport's top table.

Following my visit to Barrow's Craven Park in March 2016, Derwent Park had remained one of only two that I had yet to visit – *of those that were still in use* – from the venues of the professional clubs (30 in total) that were in the Northern Rugby League when my father me took me to my first game in the early 1960s. (My attainment of the items on this particular bucket list is not quite as impressive as it sounds; as the caveat implies, many of those grounds were sold off or otherwise vacated before I had taken the opportunity to see a match at them). The Derwent Park box has now been ticked, however.

I am always interested in the history of the localities in which sports grounds are located and, as usual, Trevor Delaney's excellent (though obviously somewhat dated) *The Grounds of Rugby League* (1991) did not let me down. The Workington Town ground is at:

> *"The Cloffocks – the historic site of the Easter folk game of 'Uppies and Downies' and near to where a Viking sword has since been unearthed… Situated on the banks of the River Derwent, [it] is one rugby league ground where you are likely to find herons and cormorants within yards of the main gates… The present grandstand… stands on what was once a tidal estuary (The Saltings). Fishing boats are known to have tied up there before the First World War. The ground is built on eleven feet of ash and sundry rubble, the site being the former Council rubbish tip".*

Since 1970, Derwent Park has also been used for speedway; the Workington Comets compete in the Speedway Great Britain Championship. My expectation, therefore, was of a venue not dissimilar to that of Shielfield Park in Berwick, which I visited earlier this year (*"700-plus years after Edward I – a two-all draw"*, 26th February 2018) and where there is a corresponding marriage between speedway and soccer.

And this was what I found. Derwent Park has two long stands stretching down the touchlines, the main one of which has seating. The ends of the ground are open and, on this bright and sunny day, there were clear views from the stands into the middle distance and beyond: on one side, the wheeling towers of a wind farm that stretched away down the estuary; on the other, the solid presence of Workington's parish church, St Michael's, standing out against the blue sky.

In League 1, the side finishing at the top of the tree at the end of the regular season – the Bradford Bulls are currently most people's favourites – will gain automatic promotion to the Championship. The second promotion spot will be determined by play-offs involving the sides finishing between second and fifth.

However, the competitive nature of the upper half of the division is such that Newcastle Thunder (currently ninth) no doubt still harbour hopes of a top five finish. Every match counts. The Workington-Hunslet game was, therefore, a good one to choose. At the start of the weekend, with 11 matches to play, the sides were respectively placed fifth and third in the league table, the visitors having won seven games in succession.

The announcement of the Workington team revealed two players whom I expected to be key participants in the afternoon's events. I recalled that the prop forward Oliver Wilkes had played a powerful game for the Barrow Raiders in the Craven Park match a couple of years ago; more recently, I had also noted at first hand the cult-hero status that the experienced (and formidable) Tongan Fuifui Moi Moi had acquired during his period with the newly formed Toronto club ("The Wolfpack and the Cheesy Dog", 27th August 2017).

Hunslet had the better of the first half, prompted by the darting runs of Cain Southernwood and Jack Lee, and they led 14-4 at half-time. However, with both Wilkes and Moi Moi prominent, the greater strength of the Workington pack seemed to wear down their opponents and their dominant second half performance produced a 28-18 win. It was Wilkes's skilful offload in the tackle near the Hunslet line that led to an important try for the home side when the match was in the balance. By the end of the day's play, when all the scores had been settled across the league, Workington had moved up to fourth place in the table, whilst Hunslet had slipped to fifth.

After the match, I had a little time to spare before catching the bus back to Carlisle. I took the footbridge over the railway line and walked a short way along the path to a peaceful spot by the river. I couldn't see Trevor Delaney's herons or cormorants, but there was a flotilla of about a dozen swans on patrol, whilst overhead were four oystercatchers (I think, not being an expert) with their bright orange-red beaks and black and white plumage and incessant urgent chatter.

I also called in at St Michael's Church. The outer door was open and I was greeted in the porch by a member of the vestry, who was there for a meeting which was due to start a few minutes later. Without any prompting, he ushered me inside and gave me a short guided tour, proudly explaining how the church had been rebuilt following a serious fire in 1994. My host pointed out the figures of the "Northern Saints" high up on the walls and talked me through the narratives of the impressive stained glass windows. I mentioned that I had been at the rugby and had seen the church from my seat in the stand; when I told him the score, he said his son would have been pleased as he had gone along too. We shook hands at the end of a really pleasant exchange.

There was just time for me to stroll through the centre of Workington. The town was nearly deserted in the early Sunday evening sunshine and so I had no distractions when I took the photographs of the blue plaques commemorating Billy

Ivison and Gus Risman. It is good to see that they are given due prominence not only for their contributions to Workington Town, but also as significant figures in the history of Workington the town.

www.anordinaryspectator.com/news-blog July 2018

# Rugby League

# A Long Time Between Visits

In September 1965 when I was aged 10, I was taken by my father and my uncle Bob to the Fartown Ground in Huddersfield to watch the rugby league fixture with our team, Hunslet. During the match, Brian Gabbitas – the latter's stand-off and one of our favourite players – suffered a broken jaw. Dad saw the incident – a late and cowardly off-the-ball assault – and he told me later who did it. Gabbitas never played again. (The following week, I was on my travels again – this time with just my uncle, as my Dad couldn't get the time off work – to Lawkholme Lane in Keighley and another Hunslet defeat).

Huddersfield moved out of the Fartown ground in 1992 and, two years later, took up station in what is now called the John Smith's Stadium. On Thursday, I went there to watch the Super League match between the Huddersfield Giants and Wigan Warriors.

I took the train from Leeds and, on alighting at Huddersfield Station, made the short walk across the square to the George Hotel. It was there, in August 1895, that the representatives of 21 clubs met to confirm their resignation from the Rugby Football Union to form their own Northern Rugby Football Union. (At the meeting, Dewsbury decided not to secede; Stockport did so by telegraph).

Although the George Hotel is one of the most significant sites in British sporting history – the birthplace of Rugby League – it now presents a somewhat sorry picture. The Grade II-listed building, with its Italianate facade, built in 1851, was closed in 2013. The site security notice on the locked front door refers to the standard fare of hard hats, deep excavations and no unauthorised entry. The contents of the Rugby League Heritage Centre, which had been established in the hotel in 2005, were placed in storage and now await the arrival of the National Rugby League Museum, which is scheduled to open in Bradford in 2020.[10]

The match was of some significance. With three games left to play in the regular season, Huddersfield occupied eighth place in the league table – two points ahead of Leeds – with hopes of being in the "Super Eights" in the season's final phase, rather than having to compete in the "Qualifiers" (with three other Super League sides and four teams from the Championship) to decide the final four places in next year's Super League. For their part, Wigan were looking to consolidate their second place in the table, which would not only (by definition) secure a top-four position and a Super League semi-final berth, but also a home fixture for that match.

Huddersfield deserved their win. They overcame the setback of the officials seeming to miss an obvious knock-on in the build-up to an early Wigan try – after a month of World Cup viewing, I waited in vain for the VAR referral – and the temporary loss of their star winger Jermaine McGillvary following a head-high tackle. The initial 0-6 deficit had been transformed into a healthy 20-6 lead before Wigan scored their only other try (nonchalantly converted from the touchline by Sam Tomkins) two minutes from time: 20-12.

I was impressed by the Huddersfield half-backs – Lee Gaskell and Danny Brough – whose varied passing and attacking kicks were inadequately dealt with by the visitors; their respective contributions led to tries for Darnell McIntosh and Leroy Cudjoe. For their part, Wigan were let down by an uncharacteristically disjointed attack and some poor discipline, Huddersfield benefitting on more than one occasion from a penalty kick to relieve their lines. However, I wonder if the visitors might have had some consolation in the performance of Samy Kibula, an 18 year-old on his debut – 6 ft 3 ins, 18 stones – who made a couple of impressive runs, his powerful leg drive earning additional yards after apparently being held in the tackle.

Although this was a match of some importance for the reasons mentioned, played on a pleasant summer's evening in nice surroundings, the attendance was not huge: it was officially given as 5,264. The lady in the stand next to me said that it was about the norm, apart from the home fixture with the Catalan Dragons, which had been free entry and attracted over 9,000. (She was a sound judge: the average of Huddersfield's other 8 home league fixtures this season has been 5,356). For a key fixture in British rugby league's premier division, this struck me as slightly worrying.

As noted, in 1965, there had been a week between my visits to the rugby league grounds in Huddersfield and Keighley. This time, it was only a day. The Lawkholme Lane ground in Keighley has been called the Cougar Stadium since the re-branding of the club in 1991. On Friday, on my first visit for over half a century, I took in the Betfred League 1 encounter between the Keighley Cougars and Oldham Roughyeds.

I mentioned in the previous blog (*"Oystercatchers and Blue Plaques"*, 9th July 2018) that there are still probably nine clubs challenging for the two promotion places from League 1 to the Championship. Workington Town and Hunslet, covered there, are two of them. Friday's contestants were two others, although the hosts' current financial difficulties have recently forced them to release a couple of their key players; Oldham, in third place in the table at the start of the evening's proceedings, seemed to have the more realistic prospects.

It was a hard attritional game with the defences generally on top; there were only two tries, one to each side in the first half. Although Oldham held an 8-7 half-time lead, Keighley kept their defensive shape and their discipline and they were rewarded with four second half penalty goals to secure the 15-8 victory. The final whistle was greeted with great celebration by the local faithful: the majority of the 510 attendance, as Oldham's support probably numbered a couple of coachloads at most. (I noted that the visitors' supporters were mainly decked in their side's traditional colours of red and white – the strip I recall from a couple of tightly fought Challenge Cup ties with Hunslet in the 1960s – even though the team took the field in green).

The Danny Jones Stand at Cougar Park is not very deep and so, even though I was close to the back, I was near enough to the pitch when the play was in front of me to sense the full physical contact which the combatants experience. Rugby league is – and always has been – a game for the courageous. The players in this, the third tier of the professional sport in this country, might have lacked the speed or skills of those on show the previous evening at the John Smith Stadium, but there was no compromise in their determination and commitment.

After the game had finished and most of the crowd had begun to leave the ground, I went down and stood on the touchline. In the distance, the view of Rombalds Moor was disappearing in the fading light. One of the Keighley players – stocky and muscular – walked towards me on his way to the changing room. "Well done", I said quietly, realising as I did so that I could have been the William Hartnell character in Lindsay Anderson's classic film version of *This Sporting Life*. He gave me a proud smile, "Cheers, pal".

There is much discussion at present in the rugby league media and by various interested parties about the future of the sport. This has many sub-plots – the structure of Super League, the arrangements for promotion and relegation, the options for international expansion and competition, *et al* – all set against the new round of negotiations with television companies and other media outlets which will come around before too long.

Another such component concerns the future of the traditional clubs in the rugby league heartlands that for some time have been living from hand-to-mouth on average crowds of a few hundred or so. I have seen four of them in the last week (Workington Town, Hunslet, Keighley and Oldham) and there are others, for example Barrow and Whitehaven. How will be their futures be resolved, when the soft capital that they have in terms of history and community – evidenced on Friday in the neatly presented Hall of Fame I enjoyed visiting in the Keighley clubhouse at half-time – is matched with the cold hard disciplines of power structures and market forces?

In the meantime, I reflect on my second trip to Lawkholme Lane/Cougar Park, the home of Keighley RLFC, 52 years and 10 months after my first. It has indeed been a long time between visits.

www.anordinaryspectator.com/news-blog July 2018

# Football

# Millennium Square

In theory, I could claim to have been twice thwarted this season in my plans to watch Yorkshire CCC in action. First, persistent rain prevented any play in the Royal London One-Day 50-over match against Nottinghamshire at Headingley (as reported in *"Below Average"*, 28th May 2018). Then, it was decided that last Wednesday's scheduled fixture against Derbyshire in the Vitality Blast T20 on the same ground should be postponed until the end of the month in order to accommodate the desire of many (perhaps most) spectators (and players) to watch the England footballers contest the FIFA World Cup semi-final against Croatia.

I cannot tell a lie, however. I must confess that I was also in this category and would have taken my place in Wednesday's fanzone in the Millennium Square in Leeds even if the cricket had taken place. England's tally of three World Cup semi-finals in nearly 70 years of trying suggests that – in comparison with T20 cricket matches – these occasions do not come around very often.

And now the final has been played. The euphoria and disappointment will last for a while and then dissipate, perhaps slowly. The World Cup caravan will move on to Qatar in 2022.

The newspaper and television headlines about this year's World Cup "fever" seem to have been reporting on a readily observable phenomenon. It has taken many forms, one example of which was no doubt replicated throughout England. On the bus journey from Carlisle to Workington that I took to watch a rugby match recently (*"Oystercatchers and Blue Plaques"*, 9th July 2018), I lost count of the displays of bunting and the flag of St George that were displayed from houses and pubs and other buildings. One flag draped from an upstairs bedroom window of a two-storey house stretched down to block the sunlight from entering the living room below; another dwelling's garage doors had obviously been newly painted in the red and white; in one street, the decorations had been applied to several houses in a row, as if it were some sort of competition between neighbours. And this was suburban and semi-rural Cumbria – not a known hotbed of soccer passions – rather than the environs of Old Trafford or White Hart Lane.

Not everyone was caught up, of course. A few miles before Workington, two men – both in their 60s, I would guess – got on the bus and sat in the rows in front of me. One, wearing the slightly improbable combination of a Workington Town rugby shirt and a golden earring, had a conversation with the back of his friend's head as the latter looked forward from the seat in front. The conversation briefly strayed on to England's quarter-final win over Sweden the day before.

*"Did you watch the soccer?"*
*"First half. Then I switched off".*
*"£200,000 a week... Not £200,000 a month, mind...*
*£200,000 a week".*

That was it. The rest of the conversation was on rugby league matters: Wigan's recent narrow victory over Warrington; the acquisition by Hunslet (Workington's opponents that day) of two players from Keighley; the dismissal by the Leeds Rhinos of their head coach, Brian McDermott, who had overseen the winning of eight major trophies in eight years... *"It counts for nowt..."*

Even allowing for this minority – perhaps sizeable minority – view, I am left to wonder why it is that the World Cup gripped the nation's imagination, even more so than usual.

Part of the explanation must obviously lie in England's performance in reaching the semi-final, having defeated the might of Tunisia, Panama, Colombia (on penalties) and Sweden, even if the Second XI did lose to Belgium's reserves in the final group match. In itself, the victory in a penalty shoot-out – the first by England at a World Cup – must have helped to release the pressure gauge. The identification with the national team tapped in to the basic urge towards tribalism and the seeking of meaning through association, which we see every week during the club season.

It is clear, also, that football enthusiasts and non-football followers alike have been more willing to identify with this England team, in contrast with some of its predecessors, because of the more acceptable qualities they demonstrated off the pitch. The manager came across as a decent and honourable man; the squad appeared to lack the egotistical non-performers of previous campaigns; the recent entrants to the team (John Stones, Kieron Trippier, Jesse Lingard) played with some skill.

However, more general factors were also surely at play. With the exception of the story of the heroic rescue of the young Thai football team and their coach from their refuge in the flooded cave complex, the current news agenda, typically, has not been one to raise the spirits: blundering and self-centred British politicians floundering about Brexit; societal divisions exposed by a visit to this country of an (elected) US President; death from the Novichok nerve agent in Wiltshire. There was an urgent requirement for something to bring the country together and the exploits of the footballers – plus the heatwave – somehow managed to do this.

And so to the Millennium Square in Leeds on Wednesday evening.

The first thing to report is that the City Council had designated the fanzone as alcohol-free. We were therefore spared the beer showers that characterised some of the other zones across the country – to the apparent amusement of the television news presenters and soccer pundits watching from the comfort of their distant studios, though not necessarily much fun for all those caught directly underneath. The Leeds zone had a proper cross-section of England support: chanting youths, families of all ages, office parties, groups of young men of Asian descent draped under the St George's flag, Japanese tourists (?)... Leaning on the crash barrier next to me was a young woman of about 20: "Come on, England", she yelled enthusiastically. I was the one – possibly, the only one – wearing an England rugby shirt.

The minutes counted down to the kick-off. The screen relayed the pre-match views from the ITV studio: Ian Wright was his customary bundle of patriotic nerves, Lee Dixon worried about the space that Croatia might exploit down the flanks, Roy Keane looked as if he were slightly bored by the whole proceedings. Then, the first roar as the scene shifted to the players waiting in the tunnel and the camera focused on Harry Kane. For the national anthem, everyone seated on the wooden benches or the concrete floor stood up to join the rest of us in a full-throated rendition. (The Croatian anthem was greeted by the chanting youths with a flurry of gesticulation and half-hearted booing. They can't see or hear you, I thought, recognising as I did so that – of course – that would apply to all the sounds we were to make during the course of the evening).

Trippier converted his wonderful free-kick after five minutes. The huge roar engulfed the Square, the sound echoing back from the Leeds Civic Hall and the City Museum. We collectively raised our arms in triumph, then cheered again as the goal was replayed, this time admiring the skilful technique as well as the happy outcome.

We can reflect on the ifs and buts, but it doesn't change the match result. If Kane and Lingard had taken their clear-cut chances in the first quarter, England would have been 3-0 up at half time. As it was, I sensed that I was not the only one to detect that, from about the half-hour mark, Croatia were gaining the upper hand. In the second half, Luka Modric and Ivan Rakitic controlled the midfield, creating the space on the wings from which the Croatian full-backs could launch their attacks – Lee Dixon had been right – whilst England increasingly resorted to the traditional route of long hopeful punts downfield.

The occupants of the fanzone kicked every ball and made every challenge of this compelling match. Croatia equalised and then, almost immediately, hit the post. Ashley Young was replaced by Danny Rose. "That's four Yorkshiremen on the pitch now", I helpfully informed my young neighbour, who smiled politely. In extra time, Stones had a header cleared off the line before, at the other end, Jordan Pickford made a point-blank save. The substitutions of Raheem Sterling and Jordan Henderson were greeted with appreciative applause for their efforts.

Croatia scored their winning goal. The match ended. The England support dispersed quietly into the Leeds night.

Somewhere between the Millennium Square and the front of the Art Gallery on the nearby Headrow, I managed to misplace the Stade de France baseball cap that I had acquired during a family holiday in 1999. Two losses in one evening.

www.anordinaryspectator.com/news-blog July 2018

# Cycling

# Two Wheels Good – Part 1

This is the first occasion on which several sports are holding their European Championships in the same cities at the same time. These arrangements are currently being inaugurated in Berlin and Glasgow. The former has the athletics and "Glasgow" has everything else (though its catchment area has been liberally expanded for this purpose): golf (in Gleneagles), rowing and triathlon (both in the Strathclyde Country Park), swimming, diving (in Edinburgh) gymnastics and cycling.

On different occasions this week, various members of the family are accompanying me at a range of cycling events: yesterday evening's programme in the Sir Chris Hoy Velodrome, tomorrow's Men's and Women's Time Trials through the streets of Glasgow and East Dunbartonshire, the Men's and Women's Road Races on successive Sundays and Friday's qualifications races in the BMX events. We are currently part-way through the programme.

The Women's Road Race took place over 9 laps of a 14 kilometre circuit through the city, starting and finishing on Glasgow Green. The proximity of the long straight stretches of St Vincent Street (on the outward journey to Kelvingrove Park and the West End) and West George Street (on the return) meant that we could flit between the two without having to wait long for the caravan to pass. Both roads are also fairly steep – a regular feature of the course – so we had good views of the cyclists on both a demanding incline and a speedy descent. Elsewhere, we also took in the perspectives from the front of Queen Street Station, where the riders emerged from a chicane skirting the church of St George's Tron, and the pedestrian precinct in Buchanan Street, close to where the much-missed Borders Bookshop used to be.

The anticipation of seeing the riders pass by for the first time brings its own excitement. The preliminary vehicles come through – the race announcer with the Baptist's promise of the imminent coming, the safety vehicles, the police outriders, the mounted members of the press *et al* – and then there is the gentle whoosh as the *peloton* glides by, the softness of the sound brought about by a combination of the wheels on the road and the streamlined passage of the riders through the air in the canyon created by the city-centre office blocks. Then, more tour officials' cars and police motorcycles and the teams' support vehicles – Skoda seem to have cornered much of the market – with the spare bikes on the roofs: Denmark, Slovakia, Ireland...

A group of five riders broke away on the second circuit but, by the time of our Buchanan Street viewing on lap five, the young British rider Sophie Wright had established a lead of about 35 seconds over her nearest rival with the main group further behind by over a minute. The game can change quickly, however. By the time we had returned after a quick sandwich in Eat (on the seventh circuit), Wright had been reeled back in and her brave adventure thwarted. The race was won by the Italian, Marta Bastianelli, just ahead of the Dutch World Champion, Marianne Vos.

The Dutch featured prominently at the Velodrome on the Monday evening, winning two of the three gold medals and one of the bronzes up for grabs. We saw the last two (of the four) stages of the gruelling Women's Omnium event, in which the first two places were contested by the veteran Kirsten Wild and the local favourite, Katie Archibald from Bearsden.

Archibald brought about the loudest roars of the evening when she won the final sprint of the Elimination stage of the Omnium and a couple of the intermediate sprints in the 80-lap (and 20 kilometre) finale to the event, but Wild skilfully tracked her throughout the latter race and ensured that she extended the points lead that she had established in the earlier rounds. The Netherlands national anthem was then repeated as the powerful Jeffrey Hoogland won the final of the Men's Sprint by defeating the German, Stefan Botticher.

Indoor track cycling has its own captivating – almost mesmeric – qualities as the eye follows the riders around the circuit. It is also no place for the faint-hearted. Three of the Omnium riders took heavy tumbles during the course of the evening (one of them twice), but all got back on the horse and resumed their journeys. I was amazed that there weren't more crashes, given the speeds being reached and the continual jockeying for position. I thought of a murmuration of starlings soaring and diving: each member in control of her individual space whilst being part of the larger whole.

The spectators in the Velodrome, most of whom were obviously rooting for Archibald, were generous in their support. They acknowledged the courage of the riders who had taken a tumble and, later, dutifully stood (with only one or two exceptions) for the Russian anthem when Maria Shmeleva swept home in the Women's 500 metre Time Trial.

Of course, the Velodrome audience had – one assumes – chosen to be there. For the Women's Road Race, the spectators in Glasgow city centre would have comprised cycling enthusiasts, casual observers, Sunday shoppers and the rest. I suspected that most people would have been aware of the event, not least because of the various road closures and access limitations that it had necessitated.

Not everyone, however. As I was leaning on the barrier in Buchanan Street, I was approaching by an elderly man with a wispy beard and a couple of carrier bags.

"*What's happening here?*" he asked with a quizzical smile.

I explained the event – European Championships, Women's Road Race, fifth lap, leader coming through soon...

He smiled again.

"*Oh, that's good. At least it's not something political*".

www.anordinaryspectator.com/news-blog August 2018

Cycling

# Two Wheels Good – Part 2

My attendance at some sports events over the years has been based on a straightforward principle: the event was in the general vicinity of where I was living and there was no excuse not to go. Hitherto, the most extreme example occurred in April 2015, when I walked to the end of our street – literally – and crossed over the Auchenhowie Road to the Milngavie and Bearsden Sports Club, where I watched a couple of matches at the Western Wildcats Hockey Club.

For last Wednesday's Women's Time Trial at the 2018 European Cycling Championships, I did not even have to go that far, as the course actually included Auchenhowie Road, which I did not need to cross.

It was 9.30 in the morning. We were in a group of about 50 – adults in their cycling gear ("Newcastle West Cycling Club"), young children with their bikes and crash helmets (and parents), some elderly ladies, a keen photographer crouching on his haunches – together with the volunteer stewards and a couple of policemen.

The junction with Glasgow Road was a good spot from which to observe the race. It was a tight right-handed bend, which forced the cyclists to decelerate as they came up from Waitrose before speeding up again along another fast stretch. The light rain and dampened road added to the technical requirements. A couple of riders misjudged the turn and brushed their arms against the spectator barriers.

The 34 competitors had set off at one-minute intervals from the centre of Glasgow, but a number had already changed their places in the irregular procession before they reached us, just over one-third of the way along the 31 kilometre course. One of these was the winner of the event for the last two years – Ellen van Dijk of the Netherlands – who had been the last to depart. After we returned home, we learned that Van Dijk had completed the hat-trick, defeating her compatriot, Anna van der Breggen, by two seconds.

For the Men's Time Trial, after lunch, we had to walk about 100 yards further on to the Glasgow Road to observe the cyclists make their way towards the traffic lights at St Paul's Church and up the hill leading to Strathblane. (Their route was 45 kilometres). Although our phase of the race was greeted by pleasant sunshine and a light breeze, the local vagaries of the weather meant that the final run into Glasgow was met with squally rain. As with the morning's race, the defending champion held on to the title by a very narrow margin: Victor Campenaerts of Belgium was judged to have outpaced the Spaniard, Jonathan Castoviejo, by less than one second after more than 53 minutes of racing.

An obvious feature of the week's cycling at the Championships was the huge variety of events that were included. For example, although the participants in the Time Trials had their advisors in the support cars and their on-bike computers to inform them of their progress, I sense that it is essentially a solitary pursuit: the rider by himself/herself over a long haul, judging the conditions, sensing whether the speed is fast enough, coping with the pain, dealing with the inner demons...

Contrast that with BMX Cycling. On Friday, we took in the Qualifying rounds of that sport's European Championships at the Glasgow BMX Centre in Knightswood Park.

Previously, I had only caught glimpses of BMX racing on television, where it comes across as fast and frenetic and intimate, with the rider in a chaotic maelstrom with the other competitors. I can report that it comes across as exactly the same when viewed in the flesh, but also with its own requirements for skill and control and – in a slightly strange way – with its own elegance.

The stands were nicely full in the early afternoon sunshine and I was not surprised to see many young children – boys and girls – eagerly and attentively watching with their parents. The prospects for the sport look good, if these are the enthusiasts of the future (as well as the present), perhaps to the detriment of the numbers participating in older traditional ball games.

The course started with a precipitous 8 metre descent – I'm afraid that I wouldn't have got beyond that point, especially at the riders began by pedalling furiously on the way down to build up their momentum – and then ran over 400 metres of variable humps and bumps on four parallel straights bounded by three 180 degree curves. In these Qualifying rounds, the Men's heats (or *Motos*) comprised 3 series of ten races; the Women had 3 series of four.

The MC provided a running commentary from the side of the track, his enthusiasm consistently revealed. The British rider Kye Whyte won one of his heats having "*crept up like a tiger stalking his prey*". Later, another rider "*just got squashed at that corner a little bit*". However, I did think that, at times, the presentation was somewhat rushed; it would certainly have benefited from having individual introductions of the riders and their nationalities before their first appearances.

The races came thick and fast: 42 in an hour and 20 minutes, even with a lengthy hold-up after the rider representing Germany, Liam Webster, had taken a heavy fall. Indeed, one race started before the previous one had technically finished, as another faller had remounted his bike and was just completing the final straight when his pursuers were hurtling out of the start-gate. Incidentally, I was captivated – somewhat morbidly, I admit – by the start itself: the release of the gate following the dull tone of the hooter sounded as if the executioner had pulled the lever of the trapdoor.

Both the Men's and Women's World Champions – Sylvain Andre of France and Laura Smulders of the Netherlands – were present and both won their three Qualifying races, although the latter's younger sister, Merel, did seem to ease up when favourably placed against her in two of them. The following day, the elder Smulders retained her European title. In the Men's final, Andre finished third behind the tiger, Whyte, and Kyle Evans of Great Britain, who took the gold medal.

My appetite for the Men's Road Race around central Glasgow yesterday had been whetted by the Women's race on the previous weekend. (*"Two Wheels Good – Part 1"*, 7th August 2018). It was the same 14 kilometre course, though the men had to complete 16 laps rather than nine: the equivalent, I suppose, of their respective tennis counterparts playing 5- and 3-set matches at Wimbledon.

We took up positions at various vantage points throughout the city centre: Buchanan Street, St Vincent Street and West George Street (as the week before), the bend leading into the final straight at Glasgow Green, the bottom of the long sweep down the High Street, the short but steep incline of Montrose Street… It was at this last point, about half-way through the race, that we saw that the World Champion and pre-match favourite, Peter Sagan of Slovakia, was suffering from some sort of mechanical trouble and falling behind the *peloton*. He recovered to join its tail end, but did not last much longer, dropping out with six laps to go.

From the start of the race, a group of seven riders (later reduced to six) broke away from the main field; at one point they had a lead of over five minutes. After they had been reeled back in, another breakaway formed of ten riders. We viewed them at Charing Cross as they headed out to Kelvingrove Park and the West End for the last time. On their return, a few minutes later, there were only five: the result, it transpired, of a crash at the far end of the course. It was from this select group that Matteo Trentin of Italy was to win the final sprint for the line on the Green.

It was a gruelling race: nearly 6 hours in drizzly conditions on a wet surface. I would guess that considerably fewer than half the starters completed the course. Amongst the steadily reducing *peloton*, the grimacing faces were progressively darkened by their continuous exposure to the sprayed wet dirt of the city streets; on their final lap, they looked like miners emerging from their underground shift.

Behind them, the individual stragglers looked to any means to circumvent the rules and ease their passage; slipstreaming behind one of the support cars was not uncommon. I noted that, on two separate occasions, one of the riders from eastern Europe firmly grasped a water bottle being held out of the window of his support car (and did so for some time) as he struggled up a long ascent. "He's got a sticky bottle", exclaimed one of the stewards, sarcastically, "He's not even pedalling".

I knew it was against the rules, but – perhaps I am getting soft – I also sensed where my sympathies lay. The rider had negotiated over 200 kilometres on a dreich day on a demanding course; he was detached from the remainder of the field; his body would have been sore; and he was a long way from home. I cannot say that I would not have done the same.

www.anordinaryspectator.com/news-blog August 2018

# A Unique Sporting Career

The concurrence of the Rugby League and Association Football seasons for most of the 20th Century suggests that one would struggle to find players who had combined the oval ball with the spherical one at the professional level. However, there is one example from over a century ago which is quite remarkable.

David "Dai" Davies, born in Llanelli in 1880, was a teenage rugby prodigy. He was a member of his home town rugby union side that lost only one of its 31 matches under the captaincy of Owen Badger in the 1896-97 season, playing at half-back. He signed for Swinton (for £20) in 1899, playing his first match in a winning side at Widnes. (Badger had preceded him to Swinton, having signed for £75 in 1897, though he had subsequently returned to Wales).

Within a year, Davies was a member of a victorious Northern Rugby Football Union Challenge Cup final team. Swinton won the trophy on 28th April 1900 by defeating Salford 16-8 at the Fallowfield Stadium in Manchester, Davies himself scoring one of Swinton's four tries.

The following Monday's *Manchester Courier and Lancashire General Advertiser* reported that the final had been "a great struggle" on "a fine day of bright sunshine with a breezy coldness in the air". A "vast crowd of good-humoured and light-hearted sportsmen" – just under 18,000 paying spectators – had seen Davies score "a clever try", which had been the last of the match and taken Swinton to their unassailable lead. However, perhaps the key moment in the game had been in the first half when, after a "regrettable incident" of "rough play", the Salford forward William Brown was sent from the field.

In his authoritative *Rugby's Great Split: Class, Culture and the Origins of Rugby League Football* (1998), Tony Collins has reported that the Swinton players' winning bonuses ran to ten shillings in the first round, £1 in the subsequent rounds and £5 in the final. These were the rewards, therefore, for accounting for Eastmoor, Holbeck, Oldham, Broughton Rangers and Leeds Parish Church before the victory over Salford.

As ever, the contemporary newspaper reports enable us to place this major sporting occasion within its proper context. The dominant feature of this edition of the *Manchester Courier* was its detailed update on the progress of "The War" – the Second Boer War (1899-1902) – under a series of stirring sub-headings: "Fighting North of Bloemfontein", "Dalgety's Dramatic Stand", "The Flight of the Boers"…

Remarkably, Dai Davies changed sports in 1902 and played for the next seven years in goal for Bolton Wanderers. What prompted his shift in allegiance is not clear – especially as he is reported to have had no previous experience of soccer at all – though one suspects that household economics came into it. He married Annie Salt in 1902 and they were to have a son the following year Tony Collins notes that, in the early years of the century, rugby league was in a generally poor financial state, whilst soccer was enjoying a boom period.

Bolton were relegated to the Second Division at the end of Davies's first season, but they reached the FA Cup final in April 1904, when they were beaten by Manchester City. Another Welshman, Billy Meredith, scored the game's only goal. The *Bolton Evening News* reported that "Davies made one or two daring saves that at once made him popular… [though] he was helpless with Meredith's scoring shot".

As he guarded the Bolton goal, Davies must have had a clear awareness of the contrast in the size of the respective sports' premier events. The crowd at Crystal Palace was in excess of 61,000. Moreover, whereas the 1900 Challenge Cup had been presented to the winners by the wife of the President of the Northern Union, the guest of honour at the football showpiece was none other than the Prime Minister, Arthur Balfour.

It was also in 1904 that Dai Davies became a soccer international, playing for Wales against Scotland and Ireland in the British Championships. He followed this up with an appearance against England at the Racecourse Ground in Wrexham in 1908. The circumstances of the last of these were highly unusual for the time, as Davies, having only attended the match as a spectator, came on as a half-time substitute. The Welsh goalkeeper Leigh Roose was injured in the first half and Davies was allowed to fill in with the home side 0-4 down; the final score was 1-7. The *Manchester Courier* reported that, although he was beaten three times, he "brought off some capital saves".

The soccer databases reveal that Davies played 123 times for Bolton Wanderers between 1902 and 1909: contemporary reports state that he was a "tough individual" who had an "indifference to cuts and bruises". During this period, Bolton were the archetypal "yo-yo" side: promoted back to the First Division in 1905, relegated in 1908, promoted as Second Division champions in 1909. By the time of the next relegation in 1910, Davies had reverted back to rugby league, having re-signed for Swinton. He re-entered the team in a 0-16 defeat at home to Wigan on New Year's Day.

Davies had represented his adopted county of Lancashire three times in 1900-01 and his return to rugby league brought him further honours. In December 1910 – playing with his brother and Swinton club colleague, Dan – he scored a try for the Wales side that lost to England by 13-39 in Coventry. (The England-Wales fixture was an regular event in the pre-First World War period, the former winning 7 of the 9 fixtures between 1908 and 1914). In the same month, Davies captained Swinton in their first Lancashire Cup final, when they were narrowly beaten by Oldham in Broughton.

The *1901 Census of England and Wales* formally records the 20 year-old David Davies as a "fitter's labourer" resident as a boarder in a house in Swinton. However, for the corresponding entry 10 years later, his sporting prowess was given full rein: a "publican and professional footballer" living in Salford with his wife Annie, younger brother Garfield and 8 year-old son, also Garfield.

In September 1913, Davies was transferred on a player exchange to Leigh for whom he made his debut (again against Wigan) that month in a game that, according to the *Leigh Chronicle and Weekly District Advertiser*, "provided a series of sensations which kept 9,000 spectators at fever pitch". [An aside. The newspaper also provided a report on the reciprocal 'A'-team match between Wigan and Leigh, where the attendance was no less than 3,000].

Although Wigan – with "a very strong Colonial and South Wales element in their team" (i.e. 4 New Zealanders and 5 Welshmen) – won the match 25-14, the *Leigh Chronicle* was clearly impressed with the local side's new acquisition. Davies was "...a master of strategy... not only does he pass beautifully, but he has a tremendous kick with him". Interestingly, the match report also referred to Davies's build – which was sizeable for a half-back at 5 ft 11 ins and 13 stone – as being "very useful".

Unfortunately, Davies's career was brought to an end by injury not long afterwards. By the time of its end of season review in April 1914, the local newspaper had revised its opinion of the early-season player exchange: "Dai Davies... only played in about five matches. Leigh had the worst of the bargain by a long way".

Davies remained in Lancashire in later life. He died in Salford in June 1944 at the age of 64, two months after the death of his wife. They are buried in Swinton Cemetery.

Dai Davies was not only a dual international in rugby league and soccer, but also a participant in the two major Cup Finals in these sports. His was a unique and extraordinary sporting career, the high-level versatility of which – arguably – approaches those of his near-contemporaries Andrew Stoddart (1863-1915) and CB Fry (1872-1956).

Today, it is Stoddart and Fry who are much better known. Their attainments were indeed mightily impressive – the former a dual captain of England at cricket and rugby (before the Great Split of 1895); the latter variously England cricketer and footballer, FA Cup runner-up with Southampton FC (in 1902, two years before Davies's appearance in the final) and one-time world record holder for the long jump – and, unlike Davies, they duly have their column inches in the voluminous *Oxford Dictionary of National Biography*.

Of course, Dai Davies was operating in a different social milieu. By definition, his was not the world of the "Amateur" or the "Gentleman", but the hard-nosed professional. It is clear that, in terms of national recognition for sporting achievement in that environment, the bar was deemed to have been set much higher.

The details of Dai Davies's exploits are not lost, however. Some of the information presented here – rugby as well as football – comes from Gareth Davies and Ian Garland's excellent *Who's Who of Welsh International Soccer Players* (1991) and this has been supplemented by useful data sources such as Michael Joyce's *Football League Players Records, 1988 to 1939* (2004) and the splendid website of the Swinton Lions Supporters Trust (www.swintonlionsrlc.co.uk).

It is something of a detective exercise to put the complete picture together, however. Dai Davies's is a remarkable story of sporting achievement and it deserves to be better known.

www.anordinaryspectator.com/news-blog September 2018

Football

# Geographical Shifts

*"We went to the terraces that were situated in front of the Lowfields Road stand... I was immediately struck by how green the grass was and how boldly the whitewash and the goalmouth stood out...*

*...Once the match kicked off, I noticed that the spectators around me did not seem to have much patience with the Leeds [United] team's efforts. They were not interested in fancy routines or intricate manoeuvres. They wanted instant results. Specifically, they wanted the ball to be deposited in the Charlton net and, when Leeds eventually put it there, it triggered a paroxysm of unbridled celebration from everyone on the terrace. It was the only goal of the game, but it was sufficient to meet the demands of the local supporters".*

[*An Ordinary Spectator*, pp 103-104]

I was relatively late coming to live soccer. My father had given me my rugby league baptism (Hunslet vs Whitehaven) at the age of 6 in 1961 and taken me to watch Yorkshire play cricket (in the Roses match at Headingley) in 1966, but it was not until 1968 that I caught up with Leeds United at Elland Road. September 4th 1968 to be exact – 50 years ago today.

Dad had no real interest in soccer – and was certainly not a Leeds United supporter – and so it was with some friends after school that I attended a relatively low-key match: a second round Football League Cup tie with Charlton Athletic.

My main interest was in seeing the individual players and, unlike the major clubs' approach to the equivalent tournament today, there was little doubt that Leeds would field a near full-strength side. I duly made a mental note of the famous names – Bremner, Charlton, Hunter *et al* – that I was seeing for the first time, live and in the flesh.

In the book, I also recognised how the match programme (price one shilling) now registered as a historical record of the times. In particular, the Club Notes included a piece on how the arrangements for the second leg of Leeds's Inter Cities Fairs Cup final – the away tie with Ferencvaros of Hungary – which had been held over from the previous season, were somewhat uncertain because of "the Czecho-Slovakia-Russian political events of the last few weeks". (The Russian tanks had rolled into Czechoslovakia a fortnight earlier). The club was using all the available means "to ascertain the situation, by telephone and cable".

I will return to the Leeds/Charlton match programme below.

If I were to summarise my approach to watching soccer over half a century, I would describe it as opportunistic. I have not had the pleasure (or burden, delete as appropriate) of fervently supporting a particular side and so most of the games I have attended have been from a genuinely neutral perspective.

The venues have been determined by a variety of factors: where I happened to have been living (Cambridge United at the Abbey Stadium, Wimbledon at Plough Lane) or visiting (Ipswich Town at Portman Road) or just passing through (Leicester City at Filbert Street on the way back to Cambridge after playing cricket in Loughborough). There have also been the occasional sojourns on foreign holidays (for home fixtures of Bayern Munich, Hertha Berlin and Espanol in the respective Olympic Stadiums of Munich, Berlin and Barcelona). These days, I have an eclectic approach to day-trips from my Milngavie base, mainly to Scottish venues (Dumbarton, Stirling, Albion Rovers), but sometimes further afield (Carlisle, Newcastle, Berwick).

Looking back at the Leeds/Charlton match, one point that is of interest is the status of the two teams at the time. Leeds United were the current holders of the League Cup – their first major trophy – having defeated Arsenal at Wembley the previous Spring. The side would go on to lift the Football League Championship for the first time that season. Charlton Athletic came into the match as leaders of the old Second Division, though they were to finish third and outside the promotion places. In 2018-19, fifty years on, Leeds have been outside the top division for 15 years, whilst Charlton are now in League 1 (or League Division Three in old-speak).

More generally, half a century of promotion and relegation has produced its inevitable churn in the hierarchy of English football. Of the 22 teams in the 1968-69 First Division, 13 are in the 20-side Premier League of 2018-19, 7 in the Championship and two (Sunderland and Coventry City) in League 1. Further down the pyramid, the fates of the teams in the Third Division of 1968-69 vary from those now in the Premier League (AFC Bournemouth, Brighton and Hove Albion, Watford) to the 6 clubs that are no longer in the Football League at all.

The drop-outs are particularly revealing, I think, because their composition is an echo of the broader economic shifts in the country as a whole over the last five decades. Of the 92 teams in the Football League in 1968-69, 15 are no longer in these top four divisions and, of these, 12 were situated above the Wash-Severn line. Their replacements include only 6 sides from this large region, the remainder being found largely in the more affluent South East.

We can stay with this theme. Yorkshire has lost three clubs from the Football League of 50 years ago – Bradford Park Avenue, Halifax Town and York City – without replacement, whilst several of the other departures have been from geographically remote locations (from the rest of the League's perspective) such as Barrow, Workington, Darlington and Torquay. (The accession of Yeovil Town slightly redresses this point).

I make these observations without comment, as it could be argued that the "old" Football League was top-heavy with sides in the North of England and some sort of regional re-balancing was needed. Moreover, the arrangements for promotion and relegation to the League have been based on a meritocracy for many years, rather than the old system of election or re-election by the other member clubs.

Finally, back to the match programme for Leeds United vs Charlton Athletic in 1968. I mentioned in *An Ordinary Spectator* that stapled within it was the "Official Journal of the Football League" – the *Football League Review* – which I assumed to have been attached to all clubs' programmes in a given week. It looked worthy and dull and, at the time, I didn't read it.

I did look at it for this blog, however, and some of its contents are not a pleasant read. Quite apart from examples of casual sexism, there is one reference – in the "Opinion" column of Walter Pilkington of the *Lancashire Evening Post* – to the population of Bradford which is frankly grotesque.

I mention this not to make an obvious point about the social mores of a past age and the differences in what was/is considered acceptable then and now. Rather, it is to illustrate how difficult it is – from the perspective of today – for me to make sense of the occasion of my first exposure to live soccer 50 years ago.

On the one hand, much remains absolutely crystal clear, as if I had watched Leeds United play Charlton Athletic yesterday: the state of the pitch, having to continually jerk my head to get a line of sight from the shallow terrace, the passion of the crowd...

And yet, in other respects, it does seem such a long time ago.

www.anordinaryspectator.com/news-blog September 2018

# Hier Stehe Ich

There is a tenuous sporting connection to this blog, as discussed below.

My sister, Rosie, and I have recently spent several days in the Niedersachsen (Lower Saxony) *Land* of Germany visiting some of the places associated with our family history. Our grandfather, Alfred Edgar Niblett, was born in Osnabrück in 1888 to an English father, Charles James Niblett, and a German mother, whose maiden name was Anna Karoline Borstelmann.

It was a highly successful trip. I knew that Anna Karoline Borstelmann died in Ludwig Strasse in Osnabrück in 1938 at the age of 84. The city's cemetery authority had previously informed me that the street no longer exists, but, in a local bookshop, I came across a map of the Osnabrück tram system of 1906 on which the location was marked. It is now called Ludwig Baete Strasse (after a 20th Century writer and historian) and is a pleasant tree-lined street of post-Second World War housing.

In the small town of Elze, to the south of Hannover, we visited *die Peter und Paul-Kirche*, in which Charles and Anna had married in 1873. It was curiously empty on the Sunday lunchtime, apart from two middle-aged women – the organist and a singer – who held a long practice session, perhaps 40 minutes or so, for the time we were there. The melodic sounds resonated down from the balcony and around the clean white walls of the church's interior.

Outside, I found the statue of Martin Luther, erected in 1883 on the 400th anniversary of his birth, to be both powerful and moving. The inscription read: *Hier stehe ich. Ich kann nicht anders. Gott helfe mir. Amen!* ["Here, I stand. I can do no other. God help me. Amen!"]. This is reputed to have been Luther's statement to the Holy Roman Emperor, Charles V, at the formal hearing in Worms in 1521. In his monumental *A History of Christianity*, published in 2009, Diarmaid MacCulloch notes that the phrase was only attributed to Luther after his death by the editor of his collected works).

For the following day, we had hired an excellent local guide – Almuth Quehl – to show us around the village of Kirchwalsede and the town of Visselhoevede, including the two beautiful parish churches. At the former, Almuth had arranged for us to see some of the original church records. We started by finding the baptism record of Anna Margreta Marquardt – the mother of Anna Karoline Borstelmann's father, Johann Friedrich Borstelmann, (and my great (x3) grandmother) – in 1772. I felt the lump in my throat as I saw her name on the page: I just about held it together.

I have previously spent some time examining the comprehensive online database of Lutheran church records in Niedersachsen and was familiar with the long direct family line that goes back through the Marquadt, Lange, Dieckhof and Henke families to the baptism of Harm Henke in 1582. We looked up some of the other original records: the burial of Gert Dieckhof in 1713, the burial of Casten Henke in 1691, and so on.

An unexpected bonus was that the written records contained additional information. Even in the Lutheran church, the type of service was, to some extent, dependent on the amount spent by the worshippers. Hence, the burial of Anna Marie Henke in 1711 was accompanied by "a sermon from the pulpit". Elsewhere, the causes of death were given: the unfortunate Johann Lange died at the age of 56 three weeks before the Christmas of 1686 when a stone fell on him as he was digging a hole (presumably in the graveyard).

The baptism of Harm Henke in 1582 was, of course, relatively early in the history of the Protestant Church; it had been only two generations earlier that Luther had nailed his 95 Theses to the door of the Castle Church in Wittenberg. Or, to put it another way, it was six years before Philip of Spain sent his Armada into the English Channel. As I looked around the church in Kirchwalsede, its interior neatly decorated with flowers from a recent wedding, I was aware that, even though it had been modified and repaired many times over the centuries, this was still the space in which my great (x9) grandfather had lived and breathed. And it was now, in a different context to Luther, that here I stood.

On the Tuesday, our family researches completed for the time being, Rosie and I did the tourist run in Hannover. The bus tour took us past the Eriebnis Zoo and out to the Royal Gardens of Herrenhausen. Towards the end of the route we passed the HDI Arena – the home of the *Bundesliga 1* side, Hannover 96 – the street in front of which is called Robert Enke Strasse.

Robert Enke was a goalkeeper who played for Hannover 96 for five years from 2004. He also played for Benfica and Borussia Moenchengladbach, amongst other clubs, and won eight caps for Germany He took his own life in 2009 at the age of 32. (The excellent *A Life Too Short: the Tragedy of Robert Enke* by Ronald Reng, published in 2011, is a detailed and poignant biography).

After the bus tour, Rosie and I briefly went our separate ways and I paid my three euros to take the escalator to the top of the dome of the *Neues Rathaus* (the New Town Hall) for the views across the city and the surrounding plains. Then, in the late afternoon, I walked back to the football stadium, even though I knew that the gates were closed and access was not possible. (This was an obvious flaw in the schedule I had planned: Hannover 96 are at home to FC Nuremburg next Tuesday). As I returned to the hotel, I attempted to marshal the conflicting themes that the overall visit had generated in the back of my mind.

There is an obvious point about continuity and longevity, even amongst the turmoil and destruction that the centuries have brought to this part of the world. The *Rathaus* in Osnabrück, heavily damaged in the Second World War, has been repaired to the Late Gothic design of the 1512 original; it was where one of the treaties of the Peace of Westphalia was signed in 1648 to bring an end to the Thirty Years' War. In Bad Münder am Deister (where my great (x2) grandmother, Anna Perlasky, was born in 1827), the door of the imposing *Steinhof* is dated 1721 and names the family who owned the property at that time. Even in the *Marktkirche* in Hannover, also destroyed in the War and impressively rebuilt in red brick subsequently, the striking triptych at the altar dates from 1480.

The theme of continuity is also evident in the robustness of the family line in Niedersachsen, irrespective of whichever of the various armies – Swedish or Napoleonic or Hannoverian or Prussian – have marched through the territory to claim the land. The local inhabitants – farmers, shepherds, builders, *et al* – got on with their lives and raised their families and prayed to God and kept going from one generation to the next.

At the same time, I am conscious that there is also transience and fragility. In this respect, although I have mentioned the late goalkeeper of Hannover 96, I doubt that – on reflection – this is a blog about sport at all, not even tenuously. If it is, it is only a reflection of sport's peripheral place in the much grander scheme of things.

Rather, I might suggest that the blog is principally about connections and relationships and how, against the deep background of the long centuries, there is an inevitable impermanence to our being – whether 32 years for Robert Enke or 56 years for Johann Lange or 84 years for Anna Karoline Borstelmann. We all dip our hand in the flowing stream – some just a finger, others up to the wrist – and, in the rippling of the water, we leave the memories and traces for those that are left behind.

www.anordinaryspectator.com/news-blog September 2018

Rugby Union

# Another Tough Pool

Since the Glasgow Warriors returned to Scotstoun as their home ground in 2012, I have been fairly selective in the matches I have attended. Prior to last weekend, the total stood at six games (to add to the five matches I saw there during the Warriors' temporary residence in 1997). There had been a 50 per cent success rate: victories against the Llanelli Scarlets (in what was then the Guinness PRO12 competition), Bath Rugby and Racing 92 of Paris (at the Kilmarnock FC stadium because the Scotstoun pitch was unfit) and losses against Stade Toulousain and, last season, Leinster and the Scarlets (the latter in the semi final of the Guinness PRO14).

On Sunday, on a sunny autumnal afternoon, Glasgow played their first match – against Saracens FC – in the pool stages of this year's Heineken Champions Cup. The other teams in the pool are the Cardiff Blues and Lyon and so it is a formidable challenge to win the group and guarantee a place in the quarter-finals. It was the same story last year, when Glasgow were pitched in with Leinster – the competition's eventual winners – Exeter Chiefs and Montpellier and won only one game out of six. ("*A Tough Pool*", 23rd October 2017).

The last time I saw Saracens play was over 10 years ago, in January 2008, when, in another European pool match, they defeated Glasgow 23-16 at Firhill. On that occasion, there had been a classic "echo" in my sports spectating: the visitors' line-up had included Andy Farrell, whom I had seen 15 years earlier as an 18 year-old playing for the Great Britain rugby league team against New Zealand at Headingley.

Sunday's match also provided a sense of the times passing and the generations moving on. Somewhat quirkily, the fathers of both fly-halves – Adam Hastings and Owen Farrell – had captained British rugby sides on tours of New Zealand: Gavin Hastings led the British Lions on the 1993 tour, whilst Farrell *pere* was captain of the GB rugby league tourists in 1996.

104

In the decade since the Firhill meeting, Saracens have been one of the powerhouses of European rugby, winning what is now the Champions Cup twice and being runners-up once; they have also won the English Premiership four times. In 2017, the club provided half a dozen members of the British Lions tour party to New Zealand.

All six of the most recent Lions – including the younger Farrell – took the field on Sunday and, with hindsight, it was perhaps the experience of closing out tight matches that saw Saracens retain the 13-3 lead they had built up at half-time through a scoreless second half. The home side was in the fight throughout, however, roared on by its vociferous support. Perhaps the crucial period was in the frenetic five minutes or so leading up to half-time, when Glasgow were encamped on the visitors' try-line – aided by four penalty awards given in quick succession by the French referee, Matthieu Reynal – but unable to fashion the critical try. (Another official might have been less tolerant of the frequency of Saracens' infringements within 10 metres of their line and reached for a yellow card).

As the score suggests, it was a match in which the defences – both of which were well-organised and (to put it mildly) uncompromisingly robust – were on top. However, the sole (Saracens) try was beautifully worked; it followed a quick line-out on the half-way line, the rapid transfer of the ball, a couple of swift changes in the point of attack and the creation of a two-man overlap on the left-hand side of the field. Mike Rhodes, who played a fine game in the Saracens back row, touched down.

As ever in these closely contested, physical encounters, I looked for the moments of individual contribution. For the visitors, Alex Goode – in my view, consistently and mysteriously overlooked for the England full-back position over a long period – made a couple of thrillingly committed catches of the high ball, whilst, as expected, Maro Itoje combined his athletic presence in open play with a productive tally at the line-out. On the Glasgow side, the recruitment of the South African prop, Oli Kebble, has clearly enhanced the threat from their set scrum, which had the visitors' front-row under consistent pressure.

More generally, I also noted that – apart from retreating in the face of an ominous drive straight from the opening kick-off – the Glasgow forwards dealt impressively with the Saracens attempts at the driving maul. This was a marked contrast with last season, when the home side's vulnerability in this area was ruthlessly exposed by Leinster and the Scarlets, amongst others.

The weekend's away wins by Saracens and the Cardiff Blues (the latter in Lyon) have obviously put these two sides in joint pole position after the first round of Champions Cup pool matches. Moreover, Glasgow now have two successive away fixtures prior to Lyon visiting Scotstoun in mid-December. All is not yet lost, however, and there might yet be some twists before the quarter-final line-up is known. It is another tough pool.

In the meantime, Glasgow's success rate for my Scotstoun *sojourns* has fallen below 50 per cent.[11]

www.anordinaryspectator.com/news-blog October 2018

# Football

# Recreation Park

On Saturday, I resumed my occasional tour of the football grounds of Scotland. I looked for a match between two sides I had not seen before: Alloa Athletic versus Brechin City in the third round of the William Hill Scottish Cup fitted the bill.

On paper, the home side were the pre-match favourites, as their Championship status placed them a division above their League One visitors. The clubs had bypassed each other at the end of last season, when Alloa were promoted from League One through the play-offs and Brechin ended a torrid year in the Championship, having taken only four points from their 36 games. Some might have expected the latter to free-fall through League One this year, but the ship has been steadied; Brechin have won four league matches and are currently placed in mid-table.

Alloa were elected to the Scottish Football League in 1921. Brechin are relative newcomers, therefore, having first been admitted to the League in 1923 and with their current membership dating from 1954. The furthest progression that either club has made in the Scottish Cup has been to the quarter-final: three times in the case of Alloa, the most recent of which was 30 years ago, and once by Brechin in 2011. But Saturday's match was of some significance: success in the tie would mean a place in the fourth round draw and the prospect of a lucrative encounter with one of the major clubs from the Scottish Premiership.

Before the match, I took in a mini-tour of Alloa town centre: the choir of Christmas singers at the top of the High Street; the 14th Century Alloa Tower, a superb example of a Scottish tower house, restored in the 1980s (though unfortunately closed for the winter); Tobias Bauchop's House, the 1695 dwelling of the eponymous architect, in Kirkgate; and a branch of the Dnisi coffee house chain (for my first mince pie of the season). Entry to the ground was £9 for a senior with the excellent match programme a further £2: good value, I think.

Alloa Athletic have played at Recreation Park since 1895. Under a sponsorship deal, the ground has been called the Indodrill Stadium since 2014, but, with due acknowledge to the benefactors, my – admittedly external – preference is for the former name. It has echoes of other sports grounds that are – or were – the centres of communal attention: the rugby league venues at the Recreation Ground in Whitehaven or the Athletic Grounds at Rochdale Hornets, for example. Indeed, I was struck by the parallels with another rugby ground – Cougar Stadium in Keighley – which I visited in the summer ("*A Long Time Between Visits*", 15th July 2018): the main stand is long and narrow, providing a close view of the action on the pitch from the few rows of available seating; there is a busy main road running behind one end of the ground (in this case taking the local traffic to Clackmannan, rather than Bingley); and, looking out to the left, there is the impressive backdrop of the Ochil Hills, beyond which lies Strathallan and the ancient road to Perth (instead of the gentler rising slopes of Rombalds Moor, which separates Airedale from Wharfedale).

The home side's status of favourites was justified. Their pleasant passing game – orchestrated by the impressive Iain Flannigan in midfield – threatened the Brechin goal several times before Dario Zanatta fired a low shot into the net after half an hour. "Keep it moving" was the persistent instruction from the Alloa manager, Jim Goodwin, on the touchline. Alloa duly kept it moving and two further goals in quick succession around the hour mark sealed a comfortable 3-0 win. Brechin did not give up and their goalkeeper, Conor Brennan, made a couple of brave point-blank saves, but there was little to cheer the handful of supporters who had made the journey down the A90. The game was played in a competitive – but respectful – spirit and was efficiently refereed by Steven Reid.

And so it is Alloa Athletic who will take part in the fourth round of the Scottish Cup. The draw has indeed given them Premiership opposition, although it could have been more generous than an away fixture with St Mirren.[12]

For my part, at the game's conclusion, I had three-quarters of an hour to wait until the train that would take me back to Glasgow. Just enough time for another visit to the Dnisi café and my second mince pie of the season.

www.anordinaryspectator.com/news-blog November 2018

# Rugby Union/Rugby League

# The Double Lions – Part 1

As has been regularly – and justifiably – lamented in the *Rugby League Journal*, the convergence of the rugby league seasons in the two hemispheres since 1995 has taken its inevitable toll on the scheduling of major international tours. Combined with the decision to replace Great Britain representation with those of the individual home countries, this has meant that, prior to the visit scheduled for next year, the last GB team to travel Down Under did so for a Tri-Nations tournament in 2006.

In the meantime, rugby union's British Lions tours have gone from strength to strength – in part because of the vacuum created by their league counterparts. They are now on an (apparently) established four-year cycle to South Africa, Australia and New Zealand, accompanied by huge promotional hype, extensive media coverage and thousands of travelling supporters. (Note the caveat, however, to which I shall return in Part 2).

Tours of Australia and New Zealand by British rugby sides pre-date the "Great Split" of 1895. Seven years earlier, RL (Bob) Seddon of Swinton and Lancashire led a party of 20 players who were to contest 35 rugby matches (and 18 games of Australian Rules Football in Victoria). Tragically, Seddon drowned in the early part of the tour when sculling on the Hunter River.

There had been a further half-dozen tours by British rugby union teams before the first Northern Rugby Football Union tour of Australia and New Zealand in 1910, although these parties were usually far from representative of the available domestic talent. By contrast, the final composition of the 1910 NRFU squad captained by James Lomas of Salford was determined after trial matches in Leeds and Wigan.

For most of the century to follow, the respective lists of players selected for the union and league tours were predominantly – in the mathematician's term – non-overlapping sets. However, there have been some fascinating crossovers. In these two articles, I discuss 16 players who have represented the British Lions (union) – or their predecessors – and the British Lions/Great Britain (league), of whom 14 played in test matches in both codes.

I am aware of the sensitivities that have existed around labelling, particularly over the definition of "Lions" in the league context. For my purposes, I am interested in those who have represented Great Britain at rugby league either at home or overseas. This obviously includes those tourists who went Down Under in the period before the Second World War, when the Australian authorities (and press) often referred to the British teams as England. However, I have not included those who have played for England or Wales, but not GB, since the War.

Definitions on the union side are more easily dealt with, given that the Lions are only brought together for tours, although even this concept has been usurped on a couple of occasions. Rugby union's use of the Lions title officially dates from 1950, although it was used informally from the 1920s; since 2001, they have been known as the British and Irish Lions.

When I was undertaking my rugby league spectating apprenticeship in Leeds in the 1960s, I was aware that, across the Northern Rugby Football League as a whole, a few select players had played international rugby union, including for the British Lions. Indeed, this was precisely the background of two of the Headingley club's greatest-ever players.

Lewis Jones is one of only two British players to have featured on the winning side of a *test series* in Australasia *in both codes*. (The second player appears in the next article). As a 19 year-old union prodigy, Jones played in the two tests against Australia in 1950, both of which the Lions won. Indeed, in the first match in Brisbane, he dealt the "full hand" of try, drop goal, two conversions and two penalty goals. Earlier on the tour, when the Lions were in New Zealand, they lost the series against the All Blacks 0-3 (with one match drawn), Jones playing in the fourth test in Auckland.

Four years later, having switched to league, Jones kicked 25 goals in the 6 tests in Australia and New Zealand. This time, the series outcomes were reversed with the league Lions going down 1-2 to Australia, but then defeating New Zealand by the same margin. In the latter series, the deciding match was the third test in Auckland, when the full-back landed 3 goals in Great Britain's 12-6 victory.

On a personal note, I recall with pleasure that, as an 8 year-old, I managed to see Lewis Jones play towards the end of his Leeds career – in a match against Hunslet at Headingley in September 1963, which was won by the visitors. I remember that Jones did not have the most comfortable of games – this was his last season before emigrating to play and coach in Australia – and that some of the home supporters, with their short memories, were not forgiving of his mistakes.

However, even at my tender age, I had already committed various rugby league statistics to memory and I knew whom I was seeing: a justly famous rugby player, who had once kicked 10 goals in a test match in Australia and who was the holder of the record for the most points scored in a season (496 in 1956-57). Lewis Jones played 15 times for Great Britain between 1954 and 1957.

When the union British Lions won in their next series in Australia (again 2-0) in 1959, the fly-half was Bev Risman of Manchester and England. Unlike Lewis Jones, he did not take part in a winning series on an overseas tour in the league code, but he did have the distinction of being in British teams in both codes that defeated New Zealand in the southern hemisphere.

Risman played in two of the four tests against the 1959 All Blacks, including the 9-6 victory in the last game, when he scored the decisive third try. (In the first test, the Lions lost 17-18, despite scoring four tries to none, courtesy of an Otago referee and six penalty goals from the unerring boot of Don Clarke). In 1968, Risman captained the Great Britain rugby league side to a 38-14 win in the World Cup match against New Zealand in Sydney, landing 7 goals in the process, although this followed defeats in the earlier games against Australia and France. His five caps for GB all fell in the few months between February and June 1968.

It was during this same period, of course, that Risman played for Leeds in the Challenge Cup final against Wakefield Trinity at Wembley. The 50th anniversary of this historic match has been duly commemorated, not least in the BBC's excellent *Rugby League's Legendary Watersplash Final* documentary. I was reminded that, at the end of the game, as the distraught Don Fox prepared the leave the pitch surrounded by his Trinity teammates, it was Bev Risman who was the Leeds player to approach him with sympathy and respect. It is a touching scene.

Another player from the 1959 union Lions tour to make his mark in rugby league was Malcolm Price of Pontypool and Wales, who signed for Oldham in 1962. He played in five union tests against Australia and New Zealand on that tour (four in the centre and one at fly-half) and had the distinction of scoring four tries, a fair strike rate in those days.

Price had moved to Rochdale Hornets by the time that I saw him play for Great Britain in the first test against Australia at Headingley in 1967 – a 16-11 win that featured the try-scoring international debut of the young Roger Millward. Price also played in the third test at Station Road in Swinton, but his try was the only British score in the 3-11 defeat that saw the Australians retain the Ashes.

The passage of time allows us to see that the crossover of Lions from union to league has taken place in distinct phases, of which the 1950s (Jones, Risman and Price) is one example. Previously, the Inter-War period had provided a couple of marvellous career histories: those of Roy Kinnear and Jack Morley.

Roy Kinnear was the first player to tour with the union British Lions and later play for the Great Britain rugby league side. A centre three-quarter, he toured South Africa as a 20-year-old student in 1924. (The Passenger List on the *Edinburgh Castle* departing from Southampton shows that the Lions travelled First Class).

Rugby union historians point to this being the least successful tour that the Lions have undertaken, as several front-line players were unavailable, with only 9 of the 21 matches being won. However, Kinnear was good enough to play in all four tests in the losing series and, two years later, to win three caps in the strong Scotland team that shared the Five Nations Championship with Ireland.

After turning professional with Wigan, Roy Kinnear won his sole Great Britain cap in an 8-31 defeat against Australia in Hull in 1929. That was a few months after he had taken part in the first Challenge Cup final to be played at Wembley, when he scored one of Wigan's tries in their historic victory over Dewsbury.

Kinnear's career path was all the more extraordinary, given his background in Scotland. He was born in Edinburgh and his club team was Heriot's FP – the old boys' side for the former pupils of the George Heriot's School in that city and a highly unusual (if not unique) springboard for the journey into rugby league. The official history of Heriot's Rugby Club, published to commemorate the 125th anniversary in 2017, notes that: "There had been persistent rumours about Kinnear joining the professional game… and his loss was a severe blow… [T]he rugby club committee felt obliged to seek his resignation as a member of Heriot's, which was duly received".

Roy Kinnear was a Flight-Sergeant in the RAF during the Second World War; he collapsed and died at the age of 38 when taking part in an inter-services rugby match. Thankfully, the rift with his union club does not appear to have been permanent, as the official history also states that Kinnear "re-enters the Heriot's story some years later". Moreover, his son (also Roy Kinnear) was educated at George Heriot's, so clearly the family's links with the school and the city were not broken. (The younger Roy Kinnear became the well-known actor, the profession now pursued with distinction by his own son, Rory).

The first Double Lions tourist was the winger Jack Morley. A native of Newport, he first played rugby union for Wales as a 19 year-old against England in 1929, eventually winning 14 caps and scoring 5 international tries. On the tour of New Zealand in 1930, his last minute try in the first test in Dunedin secured a 6-3 win, the first ever by the Lions over the All Blacks. (The series was lost 1-3).

Two years later, Morley signed for Wigan, for whom he played almost 300 games over the remainder of the decade, including the Championship final victory over Salford in 1934. He toured Australia with Great Britain in 1936 and played in the first test in Sydney: an 8-24 loss, although the series was won by the tourists 2-1. In the return series the following year (also won by Great Britain by a 2-1 margin), Morley again played in the first test: a 5-4 victory at Headingley. He was therefore the first player to be on the winning side for both the union British Lions and the Great Britain rugby league team.

Morley qualified as a dentist during his time in Wigan and returned to Wales in that professional capacity. He died in Newport in 1972 at the age of 62.

Jack Morley was relatively slightly built – 5 ft 7ins and 11½ stone – and the excellent official website of Newport RFC (www.blackandambers.co.uk) states that he was "lightning fast with a swerve and change of pace". As this description suggests that he was not dissimilar to another (later) Double Lion, I shall jump forward to this most recent example.

Jason Robinson emulated Jack Morley's feat of playing in a winning British Lions rugby union side Down Under and having success with Great Britain at home. As the website implies, their respective careers for Wigan and Great Britain might have been separated by over 60 years, but they were clearly kindred spirits in their defence-splitting capabilities.

Robinson played in 12 tests for Great Britain between 1993 and 1999 – including victories over Australia at Wembley in 1994 and Old Trafford in 1997 – scoring 8 tries. His first test appearance (out of five) for the union Lions was also in a win against Australia – in Brisbane in 2001 – when he announced his arrival with a brilliant individual try. This was Robinson's only Lions success, however; the Australia series was lost 1-2 and the Lions were comprehensively beaten by the All Blacks on his next tour in 2005.

It was also in 2005 that Jason Robinson led his side out at the Millennium Stadium in Cardiff for the Six Nations Championship match against Wales. I was there and, as he took the field, I made a mental note in recognition of his journey from the Hunslet Boys Club rugby league team to the captaincy of the England rugby union side.

*The Rugby League Journal* Issue 65, Winter 2018

# Music

# Tie-less in Vienna

For many people, this time of year is one of reflection. After wondering where the last 12 months have actually gone, we think about the events that have happened during the year, the places we have been, the people we have met, the joys and sorrows we have experienced...

For some reason, the month of December is also conducive to thinking about previous Decembers. I'm not exactly sure why the month should be singled out in this way, rather than any of the other eleven. However, I was reminded of this a few days ago, when a radio announcer, on introducing the first movement of Beethoven's Sixth Symphony, remarked that the work's premiere had taken place one December.

The month features significantly in many of the recollections given in *An Ordinary Spectator*. For example, the second Tuesday in December was traditionally the date of the Varsity rugby match at Twickenham (though it has had a more flexible scheduling in recent years); had Blues been won for spectating, rather than playing, I would have been awarded half a dozen between 1974 and 1979 and another in 2010.

Similarly, the Boxing Day morning rugby league match at Headingley (in which Leeds RLFC played host to one of their local rivals) was a fixed point at which my father and I could catch up with my Uncle Vic and, in all probability, enjoy a *Groundhog Day*-like conversation about the matches of previous years over a post-game beer. In the book, I recall the occasion on which the Wakefield Trinity stand-off, David Topliss, shredded the Leeds defence (1976) and the year (1969) when the combined weight of the spectators trying to get into the ground smashed down the large wooden gate on the Kirkstall Road, which had been one of several entrances that were closed, and I was swept through by the surging crowd.

A look through my collection of match programmes confirms other December sporting events. Can it really be 41 years since I stood at the Gelderd

End of Elland Road and saw Leeds United beat both Manchester City and Everton within a few days of each other? Or 39 years since I watched two young girls jumping up and down near me on the terraces of the Abbey Stadium as The Jam's *Eton Rifles* was played over the loudspeakers before a Cambridge United/Queen's Park Rangers game? Or even 10 years since the Glasgow Warriors narrowly lost to Bath in a Heineken Cup group match at the Firhill Stadium in Partick? On that occasion, I recall, I had a perfect view from my vantage point in the Jackie Hubbard Stand of the visitors' winger – the 6 ft 7 ins Matt Banahan – scoring a try by leaping high for a cross-kick and catching the ball in two hands above his head before falling over the try line.

The radio announcer did not need to tell me that the Pastoral Symphony had been first performed in the month of December. I already knew that. Ten years ago on Saturday – on 22nd December 2008 – a few days after watching the Glasgow/Bath encounter, I was in Vienna for a concert to mark the 200th anniversary of that initial performance.

On 22nd December 1808, Beethoven directed an *Akademie* – a concert organised by a composer or musician at his own risk and for his own benefit – at the Theater an der Wien. The programme consisted entirely of works receiving their first public performances: the Sixth Symphony, the aria *Ah perfido!*, the Gloria movement of the Mass in C Major, the Fourth Piano Concerto, the Fifth Symphony, the Sanctus and Benedictus movements of the Mass in C Major, a solo piano improvisation, and the Choral Fantasy for piano, choir and orchestra.

200 years later to the day, in the same concert hall, this programme was repeated, with only minor modifications, in a performance by the Radio Symphony Orchestra of Vienna, directed by Bertrand de Billy, and the Arnold Schoenberg Choir. The soloists were the German soprano Annette Dasch and – greatly to my surprise, as he had not featured in the original promotion of the concert – the pianist Boris Berezovsky.

As the orchestra launched into the Sixth Symphony (which had also opened the original concert, with the Fifth Symphony coming later in the evening), my mind wrestled with a couple of thoughts. The first was the recognition of the sheer scale of the musical outpourings to which that Viennese audience had been exposed two centuries earlier. The power, beauty, subtlety, romance and drama of these new Beethoven works: all in a single evening. Surely, when hearing the opening bars of the Fifth Symphony for the first time, the hairs must have stood to attention on the back of the audience's collective neck.

And then the second thought: the reality of the original performance itself. The 1808 concert had been – in the words of the 2008 concert brochure – "*eine einzige Katastrophe*". The catalogue of disasters is succinctly captured in John Suchet and Darren Henly's *The Friendly Guide to Beethoven*: Vienna's most proficient musicians had been hired to appear at a competing concert, leaving only those that were second rate at best; the orchestra had had only one rehearsal; the inexperienced soprano fluffed her performance completely; the bird song in the second movement of the Sixth Symphony was greeted by audience laughter; Beethoven had to stop the Choral Fantasy and start again after a mistake by one of the performers; the concert hall was bitterly cold; and the programme, running to 4 hours, tried the patience of performers and audience alike. What disappointment and frustration must the composer have felt, as his reputation and emotions were put through the wringer.

The 2008 performance also ran to just under 4 hours, but this time – I am pleased to report – there was no catastrophe. Bertrand de Billy directed the orchestra with authority and calmness. Annette Dasch's *Ah perfido!* was clear and commanding. The Fifth Symphony's final movement – *allegro, presto* – was nothing less than thrilling. The excellence of the concert hall's acoustics was confirmed in the dramatic climax of the Choral Fantasy.

Perhaps inevitably, the star of the show was Boris Berezovsky. His performance was one of impressive contrasts, whether bringing his commanding physical presence to bear on the vibrant passages within both the Choral Fantasy and the Fourth Piano Concerto, or, within the latter's second movement, revealing a delicate sensitivity to hold both audience and orchestra in rapt attention. I also liked the way in which Berezovsky respected the general conservatism of the occasion – wearing a matching grey suit to complement the dress code of the orchestra and director – whilst also, by appearing tie-less, ensuring that he retained his own informal dynamism.

Beethoven and his premiered works survived that freezing cold night in December 1808, of course. The two symphonies and the piano concerto, in particular, are now core items in the classical repertoire. Accordingly, I thought at the time that it was perhaps slightly surprising that the 2008 concert had not seemed to seek a more "international" presentation. The concert brochure was entirely in German and, during the whole evening, the only concession to English was the standard request to switch off mobile phones before the performance started. There were no speeches or tributes to mark the event

On reflection, that was probably just my misinterpretation of the occasion. Beethoven's music does not need introductory speeches. The concert itself was the tribute to that evening – both wonderful and disastrous – of two centuries before. And the internationalisation of the occasion was reflected in the performers – the director born in France, the headline soloists born in Germany and Russia, and the soloists in the Choral Fantasy born in Germany, Poland and Romania.

I return to our seasonal reflections. This year, no doubt, they will guided by the recognition that we have acknowledged some major communal anniversaries: the end of the First World War and the extension of the franchise to (some) women (100 years); the assassinations of Martin Luther King Jr and Robert Kennedy (50 years); the Lockerbie bombing (30 years), and so on. We will also have remembered the more private dates of significance: in my case, the death of a great uncle on the day before the Battle of Amiens (100 years); a close relative's "big" birthday (60 years); a particular wedding anniversary (30 years).

And – inevitably and probably by accident – we will have recalled some of the events which, whilst perhaps trivial in themselves, provide perspective and context when remembering the staging posts of life. Sport plays a role here, along with music or theatre or a thousand other activities: my first Ashes test match at Headingley (50 years); a first visit to Twickenham for a rugby union international (40 years). And a routine rugby match in Partick followed by a concert in Vienna (10 years).

The years pass.

www.anordinaryspectator.com/news-blog December 2018

Football

# And The Football World Title Holders Are…

I have spent some time on a modest research exercise to work out who have been – and who now are – the holders of the Football World Title (FWT). I would be very surprised if this hasn't been done before, though I haven't previously come across the results of such an exercise.

The concept is the same as that of a world championship title in boxing. We begin with the very first soccer international – Scotland versus England at Hamilton Crescent in Partick in 1872 – and take the winners of that match to have been the inaugural FWT holders. That country retained the title until it was next beaten, at which point the new FWT holder was crowned.

The football historians will have spotted the immediate technical hitch. The first international was a draw: 0-0. However, this simply means that Scotland and England were the joint-FWT holders until their next meeting the following March, when England won 4-2 at the Kennington Oval.

In the long period up to the First World War, the FWT holders were always from the Home Nations. This is not too much of a surprise because, for most of this period, they didn't play anyone else. England and Scotland battled it out for the honour, with challenges from Wales and Ireland, until the latter defeated Scotland 2-0 in 1903. It was during the 19$^{th}$ century that the FWT was to remain in the same hands for the longest continuous period: Scotland were the holders for the eight years from March 1880.

There was a break in the series between 1914 and 1919, when no soccer internationals were played by the Home Nations. Interestingly, the FWT holders over this hiatus were Ireland, who had defeated England in February 1914 and then drawn with Scotland. Scotland regained the crown in March 1920.

The first overseas challenge for the FWT occurred in May 1909, when Switzerland were put in their place (9-0) by England. It was to be another 22 years – in May 1931 – before the FWT moved outside the British Isles for the first time, when Austria defeated Scotland 5-0. The genie was out of the bottle: the Austrians retained the title over 11 successful defences, scoring another 44 goals in the process, before losing 3-4 to England in December 1932.

Dealing with the outbreak of the Second World War has required an important executive decision to be made by the Board of Governors of the Football World Title – i.e. me. In September 1939, the FWT holders were Italy on the basis, not of their World Cup win in 1938, but their defeat of the previous FWT holders, Yugoslavia, in June 1939.

There were two options. The first – the Peacetime Route – was to have assumed that competition for the FWT was in abeyance until the secession of the War in Europe in May 1945, when Italy were deemed to have resumed the custodianship of the title.

However, this does not allow for the fact that, for many countries, international football continued throughout the War years. After Italy lost 1-3 to Switzerland in November 1939, the possession of the FWT can be traced through the various matches played between the Axis powers (Germany and Italy), the countries within their political orbit (including Hungary and Romania) and neutral countries (Switzerland and Sweden). Following this path – the Wartime Route – the holders of the FWT in May 1945 were Sweden.

The Board of Governors decided that the best solution to this dilemma was to allow for two competing claims to the throne – rather in the way that different boxing authorities might claim that "their" man is the true world champion.

The two Routes remained on different paths for over a decade after the end of the War. The Peacetime Route largely stayed in Europe and included ownership of the FWT by the great Hungarian side between October 1950 and defeat by West Germany in the World Cup Final of 1954, as well as temporary custodianship by smaller football nations such as Belgium and Norway. The only home nation to feature on this Route was Northern Ireland, who briefly held the Title (twice) during the 1958 World Cup thanks to their two victories over Czechoslovakia.

England re-emerged as FWT holders on three occasions via the Wartime Route, initially when they beat Switzerland in 1946. Critically, they had the Title at the time of their infamous defeat by the USA in the World Cup of 1950. Equally significantly, the Americans then lost their next group match to Chile, at which point this version of the FWT became the property of South America until Italy temporarily took back custodianship in 1956.

Although there were World Cup tournaments in 1950 and 1954, the way that the fixtures and the results fell meant that there was no re-unification of the two versions of the FWT until the following tournament in 1958. This occurred when Brazil (the Peacetime Route holders) beat Sweden (the Wartime Route holders) 5-2 in the final.

In the 60 years since re-unification, the chronology of matches has usually (though not always) meant that the World Cup winners have also taken on the mantle of FWT holders. This applied to England in 1966, for example, which means that the Scots' long-running claim to have been world champions following their win at Wembley in April 1967 can be supported (though they relinquished the FWT the following month by losing to the USSR).

The competition for the FWT has incorporated some famous international soccer matches down the years. In the case of England, the list also includes the "Battle of Highbury" against Italy in 1934 and the Euro 1996 clash with Scotland.

England last held the FWT in June 2000 – for three days between the defeat of Germany and the loss to Romania at that year's Euros. Scotland's most recent custodianship is similarly brief: four days between beating Georgia and losing to Italy in March 2007. In the post-War period, Wales have held the Title once, following their defeat of Italy in June 1988, though they also lost in their first defence (to Holland in a World Cup Qualifier).

The fact that the FWT can be won or lost in one-off matches means that there is an element of democratisation – or is it random quirkiness? – about the process. As a result, whilst the football heavyweights might have dominated its possession, the FWT has not been theirs alone: to return to the boxing analogy, think of James "Buster" Douglas knocking out Mike Tyson in 1990. Hence, for example, since the turn of the century, the FWT has been held (briefly) by Angola (in 2004), Turkey (2007) and South Korea (2013) amongst the middle or lower-ranking football nations.

I calculate that, by the end of 2018, there will have been a total of 951 FWT matches (with the Wartime Route, or 926 via the Peacetime Route) dating from that initial Scotland-England clash in 1872. The frequency of the contests has speeded up over time; whereas the first 100 games took over 36 years to complete and the second hundred another 20 years, the most recent century (to 900) took less than 7½ years to be reached. Indeed, due to the combination of the World Cup finals, UEFA Nations League matches and friendlies, 2018 saw the highest number of FWT matches in any single year – 18.

Clearly, the history of the FWT is ripe for analysis by the football statistician. 42 different countries have held the title via the Wartime Route (and 44 through the Peacetime Route). The country with the most successful title defences (via the Wartime Route) is Scotland with 86, all but 5 of which occurred before 1939. Next on the all-time list are England (75) and Brazil (60).

In the 60 years since the re-unification of the alternative Titles, the leaderboard looks somewhat different. Brazil have had 47 successful defences, followed by Spain (43) and Holland (42). England are in 13th place on this list with 14 successful defences and Scotland do not appear at all. The record for the longest run of consecutive successful defences is held by Spain with no fewer than 31 between November 2011 and June 2013.

Further statistical enquiry is no doubt possible: the leading goalscorer, for example, or the player with the most appearances or the team/player with the most red cards. We might be straying into nerdish territory here, however – or perhaps that ship has already sailed.

Finally, the Football World Title holders (at the beginning of 2019) are... the Netherlands.

Last year began with Peru in pole position before their loss to Denmark in the group stage of the World Cup and then the latter's subsequent defeat (on penalties in the round of the last 16) to Croatia. France's 4-2 win over Croatia in the final consolidated the winners of the World Cup with the holders of the Football World Title. However, following four subsequent successful defences, France lost 0-2 to the Netherlands in a Nations League match in November. The Dutch then drew 2-2 with Germany (courtesy of a last minute goal) and so entered the New Year as the Title holders.[13]

**Note on data**

The main source of data is the excellent online database at www.worldfootball. net, supplemented (in a couple of instances during the 1950s) by the internet records of individual countries and/or tournaments. All full international matches have been considered, including friendlies, with the exception of those played in Olympic Games, when there have been restrictions on the eligibility of players or squads. Where matches have been decided by a penalty shoot-out, these have been considered as wins and losses, rather than draws.

The responsibility for any errors is mine. The results presented here are given in good faith.

www.anordinaryspectator.com/news-blog January 2019

# Rugby League

# Cumbria versus Serbia

52 amateur teams competed this weekend in the first round of the 2019 Rugby League Challenge Cup. 13 of these sides will progress to the third round, when they will be joined by the 11 teams in League 1. Thereafter, the staggered entry of sides in the rugby league hierarchy will continue until the sixth round, when the top 8 teams in last year's Super League will join the party. The final – won last year by the Catalan Dragons – will be played at Wembley in August.

I could not resist attending one of yesterday's fixtures. Millom RLFC – which is generally acknowledged to be the oldest amateur rugby league club in the world, having been formed in 1873 – were pitted against Red Star Belgrade. I know that we live in times that do occasionally appear rather bizarre but, even so, this was a side from the southernmost tip of the old county of Cumberland doing battle with a team from Serbia in a cup competition that dates from 1897 and of which the current trophy-holders are based in France.

The leading experts on the history of rugby league in Cumberland/Cumbria are Harry Edgar (the editor of the *Rugby League Journal*) and Stephen Bowes (an Editorial Contributor to the *Journal*). As it happens, in the latest (Winter 2018) edition of the publication, there is a very interesting article about the region's various towns and villages – from Burgh by Sands in the north to Millom in the south – and the distinguished players that they have produced over the years. (I learned, for example, that the latter was the birthplace of Billy Eagers, who played 40 matches in the centre for the great Hunslet "All Four Cups" side of 1907-08). Millom are currently in the Third Division of the Kingstone Press National Conference League: the fourth tier of the sport at the amateur/community level.

The coverage of the Red Star Sports Society in Belgrade extends to no fewer than 30 different sports, ranging from taekwondo to water polo and karate to women's basketball. The largest and best-known member is, of course, the football club, which won the European Cup in 1991. The rugby league section was founded in 2006.

The history of the sport in Serbia dates back much further – to its introduction by the French Rugby XIII Federation in 1953. However, in the following decade, the Yugoslav authorities demanded that clubs switch to rugby union and it was not until 2001 that the sport was re-established with the formation of the Serbian Rugby League Federation. Red Star Belgrade were the dominant team in 2018, winning the "quadruple" of Serbia's Championship, Cup and Supercup together with the Balkan Super League.

It might be noted that Millom is not the easiest place to reach by public transport from Glasgow on a weekend. I spent the Saturday night in Lancaster and took the local trains on a bright and cold Sunday morning, changing at Barrow-in-Furness. It is an interesting route, crossing the Kent and Leven Viaducts over the estuaries (sandy and misleadingly enticing at low tide) to Morecambe Bay and Lancaster Sound, passing through Ulverston (the birthplace of Stan Laurel, as the promotion of the recently released film *Stan & Ollie* currently reminds us) and skirting the ruins of the 12th century Furness Abbey.

I watched the match from the terraces in the company of Harry and Stephen. We looked out on a welcoming scene: a healthy crowd ringed the touchlines and in-goal areas (supplemented by those looking over the low wall on Devonshire Road, who had declined to stump up the £3 entrance fee); the pitch was in excellent condition; and, in the middle distance, against the blue sky, there was Black Combe which, at just under 2,000 feet above sea level, is the dominant natural landmark in the locality.

The only slight downside was the very strong wind, which blew straight down the pitch and favoured Millom in the first half. They took full advantage – not least through two long-range penalty goals, rare occurrences in modern-day rugby league – to establish a 22-6 lead at the interval. The question was whether this was a big enough margin for the home side to defend when the gale was against them and the answer was quickly given, when they scored the opening try of the second half. The final score was 38-10.

Red Star Belgrade were not disgraced. As expected, they played with passion and commitment, notably when defending on several occasions near their own line, and they scored two neat tries of their own. The American centre three-quarter Jamil Robinson – one of only three non-Balkan-born players in the team – played a particularly impressive game with his forceful running and stout defence. However, they were vulnerable to the runs from acting half-back by the Millom hooker, Noah Robinson, and they struggled to complete any threatening passing moves, though the windy conditions certainly did not help in that respect.

As ever with my trips to towns being visited for the first time, I was interested in Millom's economic history. The relevant starting point is the 1850s, when the local discovery of iron ore led to the swift transformation of a collection of fishing villages into a major industrial centre. The new town was built in the 1860s and, by 1881, the Hodbarrow Mining Company was operating seven pits to feed the furnaces of the Millom Ironworks. (Stephen Bowes informed me that many of the incoming workers came from Cornwall and that some Cornish surnames are still to be found in the locality today).

The industry's decline, when it came, was just as swift: the Hodbarrow Mines and Millom Ironworks were closed in 1968 and the town's population fell by over one-third (to just over 7,000) in three years. Wikipedia reports that "Millom's economy is now mainly based around retail, services and tourism" – the standard cocktail in post-industrial localities – with the options of commuting to Barrow or Sellafield.

My walks to and from the ground from the railway station suggested a neat town that is proud of its industrial heritage. There is firm evidence for this in Market Square, where Colin Telfer's sculpture *The Scutcher* stands in front of the 1879 Clock Tower. A scutcher's task was to stop the heavy iron ore tubs by thrusting a metal bar through the wheels – it required a hard man to do a hard job – and the public display is a fine tribute.

Harry Edgar's *Journal* article emphasises the strong two-way connection between Cumbria and rugby league, of which, over many decades, the tough industrial environment was a key component. For over a century, the region has provided a plethora of outstanding players, many of whom – from Billy Eagers onwards – earned their honours with other teams outside the area. At the same time, the sport has been an integral part of the local culture, which – I fervently hope – will continue into the future.

The Millom club is certainly playing its part. Harry informed me that the current side is almost entirely made up of local lads, whilst a glance of the match programme revealed that the club runs no fewer than seven age-group teams from Under 18s down to Under 6s. I wonder if, in 20 years time, some of the latter group will be playing for the first team in the Rugby League Challenge Cup.

www.anordinaryspectator.com/news-blog January 2019

# Football

# Tests of Skill and Character

Four years ago this month, I attended the first leg of the tie between Glasgow Celtic and FC Internazionale Milano (Inter Milan, of course) in the last 32 of the UEFA Europa League. It was a rousing match (3-3) featuring a superb performance by the visitors' Kosovo-born Swiss international Xherdean Shaqiri (who is now with Liverpool). Inter Milan went on to win the second leg 1-0 a week later.

Yesterday evening, Celtic were again at home at the same stage of the competition against attractive opposition, this time Valencia CF.

The two sides had reached the last 32 by different routes. Celtic had failed to reach the group stage of the Champions League, having been beaten in a qualifying round by AEK Athens, and so they had had to go through the group stage of the Europa League (which they just managed to do). By contrast, Valencia had featured in the Champions League, but had only finished third in their group behind Juventus and Manchester United, thereby qualifying for what might be considered the consolation tournament.

Not that Spanish teams take this competition lightly. Since Valencia themselves won the then UEFA Cup in 2003-04, the UEFA Cup/Europa League has been won 8 times by teams from Spain – the current holders being Atletico Madrid – with the runners-up being provided on two other occasions. It was also in 2003-04 that Valencia – founded 100 years ago next month – won the last of their 6 La Liga titles, the manager at the time being Rafael Benitez (who is now plying his trade with Newcastle United). Valencia are currently in eighth place in the Spanish league table – in contrast with their hosts, whose six-point lead at the top of the Scottish Premiership suggests that they are firmly on course for an eighth successive title.

I had a good seat in the Lisbon Lions Stand. Below me and to the left, at the end of the Main Stand, was the group of 300 or so visiting supporters, their presence cordoned off by stewards and police. They (the fans, not the police) kept up a steady series of chants of support throughout the evening, to which their team responded in some style.

The remainder of the near 60,000 crowd seemed to be bedecked in green and white and, as I had expected, the atmosphere created as the minutes ticked down to kick-off was electric. It can only be a totally emotionless person who is not affected by the Celtic fans' passionate pre-match rendition of *You'll Never Walk Alone*. As ever, it would be a test of the skill and character of the visiting players – and officials – to perform to the best of their abilities. (As it turned out, the referee – Ovidiu Hategan of Romania – also had an excellent game).

I have to say that I sensed in the opening minutes that this was not going to be Celtic's night. It was noticeable that most of the early fouls were committed by Celtic players, not through any obvious desire to rough up the opposition, but because of the speed and skill with which Valencia passed the ball so as to manoeuvre themselves into threatening positions. By contrast, Celtic's tempo seemed – throughout the match – to be lower, even to the extent of being sluggish on a couple of the backpasses to the goalkeeper, Scott Bain, which forced him into hurried clearances.

I thought the best players in the first half were the young Frenchman Mouctar Diakhaby, a calm presence in the centre of the Valencia defence, and his captain, the midfielder Daniel Parejo. However, as the interval approached, Celtic forced a couple of attacks on the Valencia goal and the home supporters' hopes were increased. The twenty-something supporter next to me whispered to his chum: "I sense a goal before half time".

He was absolutely right, though perhaps not quite in the manner he had wished. A few seconds later, Parejo's defence-splitting pass paved the way for Denis Cheryshev's opening strike. I was surprised to read in the excellent match programme that Parejo has won only one cap for Spain and it was disappointing that he did not reappear for the second half. His replacement was another Frenchmen, Francis Coquelin, the combative midfielder battle-hardened after ten seasons with Arsenal.

Valencia scored again shortly after the re-start. As with the first goal, Celtic lost possession near their opponents' penalty area and, this time, Valencia broke quickly down the left-hand side before Cheryshev's accurate cross was steered home by Ruben Sobrino. It was no doubt at this point that the jubilant throng of Valencia supporters below me confirmed to themselves that their journey had been fully worthwhile.

In *Still An Ordinary Spectator*, I reported on another football match in the 2014-15 season – a fourth round William Hill Scottish Cup tie between St Mirren and Inverness Caledonian Thistle – and noted that, in the visitors' side, the 19 year-old Ryan Christie "was particularly impressive with his excellent close control and the vision for a penetrating pass with his cultured left foot… a player of rich promise".

This season, Christie has established himself in the Celtic team, scoring ten goals in the process, and I was interested to see how he would fare against this level of opponent. In truth, he and his colleagues in the Celtic midfield had a hard time against opponents who marked closely and, when in possession of the ball, surrendered it only with the greatest reluctance. Christie was replaced on the hour as part of a double substitution in which the Celtic manager, Brendan Rodgers, brought on two strikers. "They're going for it", said my neighbour on the other side, though I detected that his renewed optimism was somewhat guarded.

Rightly so, as it turned out. Valencia's defensive formation retained its shape and discipline and, as the Celtic errors mounted – a misplaced pass, a wasted cross – my neighbour took to bowing his head and running his fingers over his eyebrows: it was an individual's reflection of the general resignation that seemed to take hold of the Celtic support. "They were second best tonight", I ventured to him at the final whistle. "Miles behind" was his instant reply.

Celtic's last serious tilt at European silverware was the UEFA Cup final of 2002-03, when, with an attack led by Henrik Larsson, they lost to FC Porto 2-3 after extra time in Seville. Since then they have won the domestic league on eleven occasions. For their supporters – and no doubt, all associated with the club – the mismatch between domestic and continental success remains frustratingly wide.

Of course, all is not lost for Celtic in this tie. The second leg is to be played in Valencia next week and the 0-2 deficit could be overturned. I note, however, that Wikipedia describes the 55,000 capacity Mestalla Stadium as "renowned for its steep terracing and for being one of the most intimidating atmospheres in Europe". Another test of the visitors' skill and character.[14]

www.anordinaryspectator.com/news-blog February 2019

# The Double Lions – Part 2

*"[A]fter John Bevan had powered his way over to score a trademark try
in the corner, it looked as if the home side might fight back for a stirring victory.
Bevan certainly thought so, because, after scoring, he ran back down the length
of the touchline in front of the main stand – in which we were situated – with
his arm in the air and the crowd roused to a passion".*

[*An Ordinary Spectator*, page 147]

In the first article, in the previous edition of the *Rugby League Journal*, I noted half
a dozen rugby players who had acquired the status of Double Lions: Roy Kinnear
and Jack Morley in the Inter-War period, Lewis Jones, Bev Risman and Malcolm
Price in the 1950s/1960s and, most recently, Jason Robinson. The story of those
who reached the pinnacle in both codes continues...

I suspect that, for many readers of the *Journal*, it is the British Lions converts
to league of the late 1960s/early 1970s that represent the "Golden Generation".

The union Lions made three tours in quick succession (Australia and New
Zealand in 1966 and 1971 and South Africa in 1968) and, from these various
parties, no fewer than 10 players turned professional. Of these, six subsequently
played rugby league for Great Britain: David Watkins, Terry Price, Keri Jones,
Maurice Richards, Mike Coulman and John Bevan.

Watkins and Price – respectively from the Newport and Llanelli clubs –
toured in 1966, the latter as a replacement. The Lions won both tests in Australia,
including the second match by the record margin of 31-0, but lost all four
matches in the subsequent series against the All Blacks; Watkins played in all
six tests. Richards, Jones and Coulman were on the 1968 tour to South Africa,
when Richards played in three tests and Coulman one (the latter's appearance
cut short by injury). Again, however, the series was lost, this time by 0-3 with one
game drawn.

In the cases of two of these players – Keri Jones and Mike Coulman –
their Great Britain rugby league caps were won at home. Jones, previously a flying
winger for Cardiff and Wales and by then of Wigan, played twice – in the victories

over France and New Zealand – in the 1970 World Cup, which was held in England. Coulman's three international appearances were also against France and New Zealand (twice) a year later.

The other four players toured Australasia with the British Lions rugby league side. Terry Price was a member of the successful 1970 party, though his only test match was the first in the series, when Great Britain were soundly beaten 15-37 in Brisbane.

Watkins, Richards and Bevan toured in 1974. All three played in the test series against Australia, though none in the Great Britain side that won the second match in Sydney. However, Richards was one of four Salford players to feature in the second test victory over New Zealand – 17-8 in Christchurch – that contributed to Great Britain's 2-1 series win. Watkins also played for Great Britain at home in matches against France, New Zealand and Australia.

My youthful spectating days at Parkside watching Hunslet did not provide the opportunity for me to see the Salford contingent – Watkins, Richards and Coulman – as there were only a few inter-county fixtures in the league programme at that time and the two sides were not matched together. However, as I have reported previously in the *Journal* ("*Sevens Heaven*", Issue 60), I did marvel at their exploits at the end-of-season WD & HO Wills Sevens at Headingley. All three played in 1970, for example, when Salford won the competition for the third year in a row. There is no doubt that the respective rugby union hinterlands of these players greatly added to the glamour of that Salford side.

Terry Price I did see at Parkside in the late 1960s. Again, I have a very clear recollection, this time of Bradford Northern's tactic – highly effective under the four-tackle rule – of passing the ball back to the full-back on the last tackle and Price launching his massive punts downfield. I watched in awe as the ball spiralled away, high and handsome, over huge distances.

In the previous article, I mentioned that Lewis Jones was one of only two players who had been members of series-winning squads in both codes in the southern hemisphere. The other is John Bevan – in his case, twice in New Zealand.

Rugby union's 1971 British Lions side remains the only such team to have won a series against the All Blacks in nearly 120 years of trying. Bevan played in the first test, which the Lions won 9-3 in Dunedin. (The Lions were spoilt for choice on the wing on that tour and, in the other three tests, the places were taken by Gerald Davies and David Duckham). On his return three years later, Bevan played for rugby league's British Lions in two of the tests against the Kiwis, scoring three tries; the tourists won the series 2-1.

I have a fond memory of seeing Bevan touch down for Great Britain against Australia at Headingley in 1978. In the passage in *An Ordinary Spectator* given above, I noted how his try had given hope to the home support that the tourists might succumb in the deciding test of the Ashes series. I also reported that it was not to be: the Australians re-grouped and ran out winners by 23 points to 6.

The next wave of union and league Double Lions is found on the former's 1997 tour of South Africa. Of course, by that time, rugby union had been fully professionalised and the direction of travel was from Great Britain league to British Lions union. Six players on the tour had been union internationals before turning to league and then reverting back again, of whom three – Alan Tait, John Bentley and Allan Bateman – played in the test series having also previously represented Great Britain at rugby league.

Fran Cotton, the Lions manager and former England prop forward (and native of Wigan), had recognised in advance of the tour that the attacking skills, defensive expertise and all-round professionalism of the ex-league contingent would prove invaluable against the then rugby union World Cup holders – and so it proved, the series being won by two tests to one.

Alan Tait played in the first two tests of the series – both Lions victories – and, in doing so, matched the achievements of Lewis Jones, Bev Risman and John Bevan of being on a winning British side in a test match in the southern hemisphere in both codes. In 1990, he had played in both Great Britain's tests in Papua New Guinea, the second of which had been won by the convincing margin of 40 points to 8.

Tait's distinguished Great Britain record – 14 appearances with 6 tries – includes the 1992 World Cup final at Wembley, when the home side narrowly lost out to Australia by 6-10. His appearance as a substitute that day was matched by the former Bridgend and Wales rugby union international, John Devereux, whose only defeat this was in 8 games for Great Britain.

Devereux toured Australia with the union Lions in 1989 and New Zealand with their league counterparts in 1992 (when he featured, again as a substitute, in the 19-16 victory over the Kiwis in Auckland). Although he did not play in a test match on the union trip, he qualifies as a Double Lion under rather unusual circumstances, as he played for the British Lions – at Cardiff Arms Park in 1986 – against the Overseas Unions in a match to celebrate the centenary of the International Board. The home participants in that match are considered to be official British Lions.

I first saw John Bentley play rugby union for Yorkshire against Middlesex as a 20 year-old in the County Championship final of 1987: a wonderful occasion, in the closing stages of which Twickenham's West Stand rang out to "Ilkley Moor Bah't 'At" as the White Rose secured the trophy. Years later, I looked with interest in his autobiography to see what the player's recollection of the game had been. Not much was the answer: *"I was punched off the ball early on and played the rest of the match... in a daze"*.

After winning two caps for England, Bentley turned professional with Leeds in 1988 and played twice for Great Britain in France, in 1992 and 1994, whilst with the Halifax club. (His colleagues in the first game included Alan Tait and John Devereux). On his return to rugby union, his selection for the Lions tour to South Africa in 1997 was regarded with some surprise by many at the time, but it turned out to be soundly based. Bentley played on the wing in the second test in Durban, the victory in which secured the series for the tourists.

Allan Bateman's journey from union to league and back again was not dissimilar to Bentley's. The skilful centre three-quarter with Neath RFC played four times for Wales before signing for Warrington in 1990. His three league caps for Great Britain also comprised two matches against France as well as the 8-4 win over Australia (with fellow Double Lion, Jason Robinson) at Wembley in 1994. Both Bateman and Bentley played in the third test of the Lions' 1997 South Africa series – the former as a replacement – albeit this time on the losing side. One difference is that Bateman resumed his international career with Wales, ending up with 35 caps.

Looking at our group as a whole, I think three particular characteristics stand out. The first is the high proportion of Welshman – 10 in total with 4 Englishmen and 2 Scots. This is no surprise, of course, given the country's prodigious source of rugby talent over successive generations and the willingness of the union stars to take on the challenges (and receive the rewards) of league.

Second, there is a clear dominance of Lancashire clubs being the first destinations in league of the international union converts. Of the 15 players mentioned in these two articles who started out in union (Jason Robinson is excluded), only three – Lewis Jones, Terry Price and John Bentley – were initially signed by clubs east of the Pennines. Wigan and Salford signed three players, Warrington, Widnes and Leeds signed two, and Oldham, Leigh and Bradford Northern one each.

Finally, there is an overwhelming majority of players behind the scrum rather than in the forwards – 15 to 1 this time. This is probably to have been expected, given the inherent skills that were being brought across from the union code.

What we should not lose sight of, however, is the sheer all-round excellence of these rugby players, who managed to reach the pinnacle in both sports. Even in the backs, this often necessitated considerable adaptability and adjustment to meet the demanding requirements of the new code: for example, Bev Risman and David Watkins were the top union fly-halves of their eras, but found their greatest successes in league at full-back and centre, respectively.

In this context, it is perhaps Mike Coulman who really stands out: a prop forward for Moseley, England and the British Lions (in South Africa in 1968) and a prop/second row forward for Salford and Great Britain. Given the vastly different technical requirements demanded of tight forwards in the two codes, his was certainly some achievement.

Of course, for all the players, there would have been an awareness that there were many (within and outside the league game) who resented their status and/or the payments made to them and hoped that they would fail, or who regarded them as "targets" on the field.

Their responses are revealed in the record books, not only with their status as Double Lions, but, in most cases, their contributions to the sport of rugby league over long careers: the near-300 matches played by Jack Morley for Wigan in the 1930s, the thousands of points accumulated by Lewis Jones and David Watkins, the 300-plus tries in the 14-year career of Maurice Richards, and so on.

The planned tour for the Great Britain rugby league side Down Under later this year, following the 2018 series at home against New Zealand, undoubtedly constitutes good news. If it leads to the re-establishment of regular test series, home and away, with Australia and New Zealand – coupled with fixtures against Papua New Guinea and the Pacific Island countries – that would fill a gap that has been sadly present for far too long not only in the rugby league calendar, but in that of international sport as a whole.

And what of the future of rugby union's British Lions? Perhaps significantly, the current schedule for the tour of South Africa in 2021 contains only 8 matches over 33 days, compared with 10 matches in 41 days on the previous visit to that country in 2009 and 13 matches in 49 days in 1997.

The union code has its own set of interested parties and political agendas, not least the major English clubs, who wish to extend the length of the domestic season as well as retain a firm hold over their main assets (i.e. the players). If I were to consult my crystal ball, I would predict that, by the end of the 2020s – 2020 vision, indeed – the union version of a British Lions tour will also have been reduced to just the three test matches.

Will there be any Double Lions in the years to come? I wouldn't rule it out. Sonny Bill Williams has shown how a flexible career path can be followed that manages several changes between league and union. Of course, much would depend on the respective incentive structures available to the players, involving finance and sporting kudos.

In the meantime, it is good fun to look at the modern day participants in league and union and speculate on whose skill sets – with some fine tuning – might be good enough to meet the highest demands of both codes.

*The Rugby League Journal* Issue 66, Spring 2019

# Rugby Union

# The Grizzled European Campaigners

Before this season, over the 22-year period in which Scottish sides have competed in the premier European competition (for what is now the Heineken Champions Cup), Edinburgh Rugby had progressed from the pool stages to the quarter-finals on exactly two occasions. In 2003-04, they lost in that round away to Toulouse, whilst in 2011-12 they beat the same opponents – when I was part of the near-39,000 crowd at Murrayfield, Edinburgh's largest home attendance to date – before losing to Ulster in the semi-final.

In some years, Edinburgh have not even qualified for the Heineken/Champions Cup because of their low position in the previous season's PRO12 League (in which they competed with the Welsh and Irish regional/provincial sides), leaving their Glasgow Warriors rivals as Scotland's only representatives. Edinburgh had to settle for the second-tier European Challenge Cup (now called the Rugby Challenge Cup), in which they were runners-up to Gloucester in 2014-15.

All in all, this has added up to a performance over two decades on the European stage that can be charitably described as modest, given the significant resources ploughed into Edinburgh Rugby by the Scottish Rugby Union, especially on a series of high-profile coaches: Todd Blackadder, Andy Robinson, Alan Solomons *et al*.

The 2018-19 season has seen a notable upturn in Edinburgh's European fortunes under the former Leicester coach Richard Cockerill, who took over the reins at the beginning of last season. Edinburgh came top of a demanding Champions Cup pool – which also contained Montpellier, Toulon and Newcastle Falcons – winning five matches out of six. Their reward was a home quarter-final against Munster, which was played at Murrayfield yesterday.

The Irish provinces have an excellent record in the Heineken/Champions Cup. Leinster have won the competition four times, Munster twice and Ulster once and, between them, these sides have also been runners-up on three other occasions. Munster entered yesterday's encounter having reached at least the quarter-final stage no fewer than 18 times since 1998-99 and, whilst their more recent trophy win was in 2007-08, they have reached the semi-finals in four of the last six years. They have a deserved reputation as experienced and grizzled campaigners on the European front.

Munster's proud rugby traditions long pre-date the European competitions, of course. Inter-provincial matches have been played in Ireland since 1875, whilst Munster have been challenging touring sides since the first All Blacks visit of 1905. Since then, they have defeated Australia four times and, on a famous occasion in 1978, New Zealand once, thereby lowering the All Black colours almost 40 years before the Ireland national side first managed to do so.

Munster have contributed a total of 35 players to the British and Irish Lions over the years, the most recent – for the 2017 tour to New Zealand – being Conor Murray, CJ Stander and Peter O'Mahony (who captained the Lions in the first test). All three played yesterday, along with Keith Earls, a veteran of the 2009 tour to South Africa.

O'Mahony's appearance represented something of an echo for me, as I had previously seen him play for Ireland in a Six Nations Under 18 tournament that was held in Glasgow in 2007, on that occasion against England at the West of Scotland club's ground at Burnbrae. I remember him then as a hard, aggressive competitor who, packing down in the Number 8 position, would launch himself into the set scrums with what was effectively an (illegal) mini-charge. Even at that stage, it was not difficult to envisage him graduating through the Munster ranks.

Munster edged yesterday's game 17-13. It was a compelling match of (predictably) unremitting confrontation and physical intensity, in which the 36,000 crowd – at least half of whom wore the visitors' red – were fully absorbed. Edinburgh had the bulk of the territorial advantage and there were several occasions when Munster had to defend desperately on their own try line but, as the match progressed – and even when the home side took a 13-10 lead – I did wonder if Munster's years of accumulating their European *nous* might be of consequence.

All four Lions played significant roles. Stander and O'Mahony (again predictably) were at the heart of the Munster effort in repelling Edinburgh's determined forward drives, Earls revealed his alert rugby brain by taking a quick tap penalty to score the opening try (on Munster's first visit to the Edinburgh 22, after nearly 20 minutes) and it was Murray's half-break that created the opportunity from which, following some skilful handling, Earls scored his second try with 10 minutes remaining.

As that try gave Munster a two-point lead, the conversion attempt was clearly going to be crucial, as the resultant four-point margin would mean that Edinburgh would need to score a try, rather than a single penalty goal, to rescue the match. When the replacement fly-half Tyler Bleyendaal struck a majestic kick from the right-hand touchline, the Munster roar was the loudest of the afternoon. It was duly followed by a spirited rendition of *The Fields of Athenry*.

Edinburgh were still in the fight, of course. The replacements came on for the exhausted front-line combatants – who had been impressively led by the captain Stuart McInally – to supplement the dangerous attacking threat continually posed from full-back by Darcy Graham. The last home attack saw Munster having to defend through no fewer than 29 phases of play over 4½ minutes of uninterrupted action (as I registered later on watching my television recording) before an infringement occurred and the visitors' arms could be raised in weary triumph.

Earlier, before the match, I spent some time at the memorial to the Scottish international rugby players who have been killed in wartime, the first of whom was DB Monypenny in the Boer War. It takes the form of an elegant arch below which is a plaque with the names of the 46 fallen. A young steward came over and asked me if I recognised the best-known of those listed. I knew, of course, that he was referring to Eric Liddell, who won seven caps in 1922 and 1923 and died in a Japanese internment camp in China in 1945.

In return, I was able to point to the name of Roy Kinnear, who won three caps in 1926. Drawing on my recent article for the *Rugby League Journal*, I mentioned that he had been the father of the late Roy Kinnear and grandfather of Rory Kinnear, both distinguished actors. The older Roy Kinnear had turned professional and scored a try for Wigan in the first Challenge Cup final played at Wembley in 1929; he was serving in the RAF when died of a heart attack in 1942.

The memorial is set on a prominent site in the Murrayfield grounds, neatly shaded by a couple of trees, to the left of the main turnstiles on Roseburn Crescent. I was only a few yards from the main thoroughfare of incoming supporters on their way to the stands or the beer tents or fast food stalls, but it was strangely – and pleasantly – peaceful.

Rugby in Munster has a long and proud history. So does rugby in Scotland.

www.anordinaryspectator.com/news-blog March 2019

# Snooker

# Ebbs and Flows

The 2019 World Snooker Championship has reached the second-round stage. On Friday morning, I went to see the first session of the match between Stephen Maguire and James Cahill.

The Championship has been played at the Crucible Theatre in Sheffield since 1977 and the format of the tournament is now well-established. The 16 top-ranked players in the world are joined by 16 qualifiers to contest a straight knock-out competition in which the matches expand in length from the best-of-19 frames in the first round to the best-of-35 in the final.

Of course, the Championship was in place long before taking up its residency in South Yorkshire. The first tournament – in 1927 and then called the Professional Snooker Championship – was won by Joe Davis from a field of 10. Davis retained the title the following year and the year after that... and the year after that... through to 1946, when the Championship resumed after a hiatus in the war years. It has to be noted that the fields were generally in single figures – with, in a couple of years, Davis's victories being in one-off matches against a single challenger – but, even so, it was some feat for him to have held a world championship title for 20 years. Moreover, the matches themselves made the present-day finals look like short sprints: in 1946, Davis beat the Australian, Horace Lindrum, by 73 frames to 62 in a final that was the best-of-145.

In the 10 years after Joe Davis's retirement from world championship play, there was a familiar name as the tournament winner on 8 occasions: his brother Fred. Indeed, it is Fred Davis who provides snooker's link with the modern era, as he was one of the earliest competitors on the *Pot Black* television programme, when it was first aired by the BBC in 1969.

I recall the early years of *Pot Black* with some affection. It had a jaunty theme tune and a sympathetic commentator in Ted Lowe: did he really once say "for those of you watching in black and white, the pink is next to the green"?

The programme also benefited from the technicalities of its presentation at a time when the take-up of colour television was rapidly expanding: there was a neat fit for a snooker table on the television screen and the half-hour duration was ideal for a single frame. Although the extensive tv coverage of major tournaments did not begin until the following decade, it was *Pot Black* that took snooker out of the dark, slightly seedy, smoke-filled halls it had previously inhabited and on to the path that has led to the modern-day riches of the elite players with their agents and promoters.

By reaching the second round, Maguire was guaranteed prize money of at least £30,000. (I assume that this didn't apply to Cahill, who is the first amateur to have qualified for the final stages in the Crucible era). However, a subsequent quarter-final place would take the reward to at least £50,000 – the winner of the final will receive £500,000 – and so there was an obvious financial incentive for him and the other professionals to progress further, quite apart from the kudos of reaching the latter stages of the tournament.

The tournament's sponsors are Betfred who, no doubt like everyone else, had been somewhat surprised that Cahill had won his first-round match, given that his opponent had been the world's number one player, Ronnie O'Sullivan. The pre-match odds on O'Sullivan to win that contest had been 50 to 1 *on*.

The Crucible's bar and foyer area was dominated by the Betfred "shop", at which an array of screens relayed the betting options on various sporting events. In front of them, a man with a microphone shouted the odds on a bewildering selection of the session's (and the tournament's) possible outcomes: the number of century breaks, the quarter-final pairings, the Australian Neil Robertson becoming the overall champion... At one point, he took a break to throw some Betfred T-shirts – medium-sized, so I declined the opportunity to catch one – into the group of potential punters. The man announced that Cahill was 7 to 2 to beat Maguire: not particularly generous odds, I thought, even allowing for the amateur's first-round success, given that Maguire is a seasoned 15-year professional.

For the first three rounds of the tournament, two matches are played are adjacent tables, separated by a large screen. Not surprisingly, the screen had the sponsor's details in prominent display. I noticed that some of the signage had a Chinese script: a reflection, without question, of the sport's major growth in that country. Six of this year's 32 competitors were from China, five of whom came through the qualifying stage.

On the other side of the screen, Robertson was playing Shaun Murphy: two former world champions. A few seats in the auditorium provide views of both games, but most of the spectators focus on only one of the pairings, with the progress in the other being signalled by the rounds of applause or the groans accompanying a missed shot or, more practically, the totals instantly updated on the respective scoreboards. I was struck by the intimacy of the environment, not least the proximity of the two mobile cameramen at each table.

The spectators in both halves of the Crucible concentrated hard on the ever-changing arrangements of the coloured balls on their respective tables, respectful of the talents of the players and fully appreciative of their skills. On our side, there were a couple of shouts of "Come on, James", but otherwise a general lack of overt partisanship. (This was probably not surprising, given that most of the tickets had been sold before the session's participants were known). The applause that both Maguire and Cahill received on recording century breaks during the session was loud and genuine.

Maguire took a 2-0 lead, a break of 67 securing a tense first frame and one of 103, after an early fluked red, the second. I did wonder if a one-sided match was on the cards. However, Cahill recovered to 2-2 with a century of his own and, although Maguire took three frames in a row after the interval, Cahill won the closely fought final frame to end the session only 3-5 in arrears.

I can see why people get absorbed on a tournament such as this. The players' fortunes do not so much ebb and flow as pause and then accelerate as, following cautious safety play, an opportunity might be presented and seized and a frame-winning break compiled. In a closely fought match such as Maguire-Cahill, a player might lose two or three frame in a row virtually without potting a ball and then respond with a run of winning frames of his own. In the meantime, the match score mounts as one player or the other (or perhaps both) approaches the target needed: in the second round, the first to 13. In this year's tournament, four of the 16 first-round encounters were decided by scores of 10-9.

I had just over 24 hours in Sheffield which, despite my having been born and brought up in Leeds – only 30 miles to the north – is not a city I know well. One of the many useful maps attached to the city centre bus-stops pointed me to a tourist information site near to the Crucible. I went there to see if there were any bus tours and, when I thought I was somewhere in the right vicinity, I enquired about this of two young women smoking vapour cigarettes near a glass-fronted office building. It turned out that, not only were there no bus tours, there was no tourist office (at least on this site), as it had closed last year. My tour of the city was therefore conducted at random and on foot.

Looking back, I suppose that my time in Sheffield also had its ebbs and flows. On the downside, I managed to lose (permanently) my house keys through a hole in my jacket pocket; at the Crucible, I had a sharp exchange with the officious steward who was demanding (rather too brusquely, I thought) that we clear the bar and foyer area after the morning session so that the afternoon's spectators could be let in; on the way back to the hotel, a huge rainstorm overwhelmed my flimsy brolly. I acknowledge, of course, that none of these events can really be said to have been the fault of Sheffield and, for the record, I can report that the rest of the stewarding at the Crucible was exemplarily polite.

But there were far more pluses, quite apart from watching – and feeling that I was almost participating in – a top-class snooker event. For one thing, a nice little café in Norfolk Row, just round the corner from the Crucible, supplied a very passable orange-flavoured scone. Then on the way back to the hotel, I spent half an hour in the light and spacious Sheffield Cathedral, fortuitously timing my visit when the choir was rehearsing for its evening service. The colour and originality of the Lantern Tower – a 1960s restoration that belies the usual architectural horrors of that decade – is worth seeing.

By that time, the preparations were in hand, no doubt, for the evening session at the Crucible, where Stephen Maguire and James Cahill were to resume their contest. Both players won four frames and so the former took a 9-7 lead into yesterday afternoon's last session. The final outcome was a win for Maguire by the narrowest of margins: 13 frames to 12. Perhaps those pre-match odds on a Cahill victory were not so unrealistic, after all.[15]

www.anordinaryspectator.com/news-blog April 2019

Football

# Kings, Queens and Poets

Prior to yesterday's last round of the season's 36 league matches in the Ladbrokes Scottish Championship – the second tier of the country's professional football hierarchy – four teams (Falkirk, Alloa Athletic, Queen of the South and Partick Thistle) were scrambling to avoid relegation to League One. At the end of the day's play, the bottom-placed club would be relegated automatically, whilst the second-bottom would need to come through play-offs with three sides from League One in order to survive.

Falkirk began the day three points adrift and, therefore, needed to win their match (against the divisional champions, Ross County) and hope that the side immediately above them (Alloa) lost to third-placed Ayr United. In that event, Alloa would be related and Falkirk would go into the play-offs. Queen of the South were level on points with Alloa, but had a much better goal difference so, for them, a draw (against Partick) would prevent automatic relegation, but would mean the play-offs if Alloa were to win; likewise, a defeat would also lead to the play-offs, if Alloa were to draw. For their part, a win or a draw for Partick would bring safety, but a loss would take them to the play-offs if Alloa were to join Queen of the South as winners of their respective matches. (As ever with these possible end-of-season permutations, a cold towel and a stiff drink are essential).

When I was a young boy in Leeds studying the league tables before filling in my mother's football pools coupon – whilst, at the same time, coming to grips with the geography of Britain – I used to look at the names of several Scottish clubs with an air of some perplexity. Where, exactly, were the locations of Raith Rovers and Hibernian and St Johnstone and Third Lanark…? However, I was quite clear that the most romantic name of them all – alongside Heart of Midlothian – was that of Queen of the South. I subsequently learned that the club is based in Dumfries and, so, it was there that I ventured yesterday: Queen of the South versus Partick Thistle at Palmerston Park.

In preparing for my trip, I realised that I was completing a medieval link that I had commenced last year on the other side of the country. In "*700-plus years after Edward I – a two-all draw*" (26th February 2018) – my account of attending a match between Berwick Rangers and Montrose – I noted that, above the steps leading down to the platforms at Berwick railway station, there is a large plaque marking the spot where, in 1292, Edward the First's arbitration in favour of John Balliol (rather than Robert the Bruce) in the contest for the Scottish crown was announced.

It was in Dumfries in 1300 that Edward signed a (short-lived) armistice solicited by Pope Boniface VIII, following his (Edward's) latest invasion of Scotland. In the following years, the town remained central to the political events of Scotland culminating, in February 1306, with Bruce stabbing to death his rival for the Scottish crown, John "The Red" Comyn, at the high altar of the Greyfriars friary. Bruce was crowned Kings of Scots at Scone a few weeks later.

Before the match, I planned (and took) a short town-centre walking tour, courtesy of the information provided by the local tourist office. I walked up the High Street to the Greyfriars Kirk, which dates from 1868 and is roughly half a football pitch from the location of the original Franciscan friary at the top of Friars Vennel. On the other side of the road, a bronze plaque on the wall of an unoccupied shop marks the site of Comyn's murder. Inside the next shop – a branch of Greggs, no less – there is a neatly mounted display summarising the events of the period, whilst the interior walls contain a number of photographs and historical images. I made a short inspection, largely ignored by the local patrons, who tucked in to their sausage baps and vegan rolls and fizzy drinks.

Outside, in the centre of a half-pedestrianised traffic island, the statue of Robert Burns – a resident of Dumfries for five years until his death in 1796 – looks straight down the High Street. The selection of his verse on the plinth provides a neat – and well-chosen – summary of the poet's philosophies on life and humanity. I then walked down Friars Vennel and, after pausing briefly in a coffee shop, continued on to cross Devorgilla's Bridge – the oldest multi-spanned stone bridge in Scotland, dating from the 15th Century – and made my way to Palmerston Park. (The original timber bridge was commissioned by Lady Devorgilla of Galloway, the mother of John Balliol, in about 1280). Take a walk through the centre of any town or city in Britain and there is history everywhere you look.

Partick Thistle won the match in something of a canter. They started the game much more positively than their opponents and took the lead with a Lewis Mansell volley after 14 minutes. A second goal came after just before half-time and a second-half penalty secured a 3-0 victory to the huge acclaim of their 1500-plus travelling supporters (most of whom, it had seemed to me earlier, had been on the two-carriage train that ScotRail had thoughtfully provided for the 1¾ hour-long journey from Glasgow Central). Stuart Bannigan, the captain, had an influential role in midfield and the two centre-backs, Steven Anderson and Sean McGinty, kept a close eye on the prolific Queens centre-forward, Stephen Dobbie.

The 36 year-old Dobbie has scored 40 goals this season – only one behind the club record for a single year that has stood since 1932 – and I was interested to see him in action. However, apart from one early attempt that went outside a post and several nice pieces of linking play, he did not have an impact on the game, as Partick successfully cut off his supply lines.

The final score meant that the long run of disappointing results for the home team – only 2 wins in the 15 league matches since the middle of January – was continued. A Queens-supporting neighbour in the queue for the coach service back to Buchanan Street Bus Station – I had decided to eschew the potential delights of the return train journey – told me that it had been their worst home performance of the season, and he wondered how long the manager, Gary Naysmith, might remain in post.

The consolation for Dobbie – such as it is – is that he now has a couple of additional matches in which to break the goal-scoring record. At the end of the day's play, Alloa Athletic's draw at Ayr United meant that Queen of the South would have to line up against Montrose from League 1 on Tuesday evening in the first leg of the play-off semi-final. (Falkirk were relegated, despite beating Ross County. Partick Thistle's victory meant that they were safe, of course). I wondered if it had been with this next challenge in mind – the player having returned from injury for the Partick match – that Naysmith had taken Dobbie off with a few minutes to go. In the event, whilst Dobbie might feature against Montrose, Naysmith unfortunately won't. My source (who alighted from the coach in Moffat) had been correct in his speculation; the manager was relieved of his duties yesterday evening.[16]

In the course of my *sojourn* to watch Queen of the South, I learned that the name was coined not by Sir Walter Scott, as I had previously thought, but by a local poet, David Dunbar, who referred to the town of Dumfries as such when standing for Parliament in the General Election of 1857. The football club adopted the name on its formation in 1919. (It will be an anti-climactic end to Queen of the South's centenary season if it is marked by relegation). However, in the comfort of my coach seat on the journey back up the M74, as I thought back to the Devorgilla Bridge and the branch of Greggs and the friendly welcome by the stewards of Palmerston Park, it was some of the words of the other poet associated with the town of Dumfries – captured on the plinth of his statue – that came to mind.

****

*Man's inhumanity to man,*
*Makes countless thousands mourn!*

****

*Affliction's sons are brothers in distress;*
*A brother to relieve, how exquisite the bliss!*

Food and Drink

# Bacon Sandwiches

*"[W]e sat in the living room for an hour and chatted… The windows were open and a warm post-midnight breeze aired the room. We supplemented the discussion with Pimm's and lemonade and bacon sandwiches. A perfect coda to the evening".*

[*Still An Ordinary Spectator*, page 99]

My train journey back from Sheffield to Milngavie, after watching a session of the World Snooker Championship last month (*"Ebbs and Flows"*, 28th April 2019), took six hours. A delay to the East Midlands Trains service from Sheffield to Manchester Piccadilly meant that I missed the linking connection to Wigan North Western station and the scheduled Virgin Trains service to Glasgow Central. Even though I benefited from a different late-running train at Wigan, it was close to 11pm by the time I arrived home. The consolation was a home-made bacon sandwich, as I settled down to watch the snooker highlights on tv.

I am persuaded that there is a book to be written – probably under the category of "niche" – entitled: "Bacon Sandwiches in Their Sporting Context". This most obviously applies to the pre-match preparations for watching cricket, in which the "second breakfast" – as favoured by Pippin in JRR Tolkein's *The Lord of the Rings* – can be difficult to resist. I have a clear memory of the bacon sandwich I consumed (in 1999, believe it or not) in a café on the way from Haymarket Station to the Grange Cricket Club to watch, with friends, the Scotland versus New Zealand encounter in that year's World Cup. (New Zealand won by mid-afternoon). Likewise, the well-informed supporter of Yorkshire CCC will have been fully aware of the high quality of such offerings in the little café (long departed, sadly) just down the road from the St Michael's Lane entrance to the Headingley ground. (For the current Members of the Club, the pre-match supply in the long room of the East Stand provides a reasonable, though not fully compensatory, replacement).

In our household – as noted above – the favourite bacon sandwich recollection is of their consumption on returning home after an excellent evening's viewing of the 2014 Commonwealth Games swimming gala at the Tollcross International Swimming Centre in Glasgow.

It is now clear that the 2014 experience established an instant tradition to be followed on those (relatively rare) occasions when the whole family attends a sporting event together. Hence, it was agreed beforehand that the evening we were to spend at last year's European Cycling Championships at the Sir Chris Hoy Velodrome in Glasgow should conclude with exactly the same menu in exactly the same location, and it duly was.

And it's not just bacon sandwiches, of course. Looking back through *An Ordinary Spectator* and *Still An Ordinary Spectator* and the subsequent blogs, I am conscious of the many casual references to the various snacks that have featured in my catalogue of sports spectating.

A small sample reveals that these date from the "bag laden with sandwiches and pop" that I took on my primary school visit to Wembley for the Challenge Cup final of 1966 (Wigan vs St Helens) and the annual post-match drinks in the Original Oak in Headingley after the lunchtime Boxing Day rugby matches of the 1970s (usually Leeds vs Wakefield Trinity) through to the "hot dogs (three with tomato sauce, one without) and beers/cokes" that the family enjoyed whilst watching the college (American) football at the Alamodome in 2015 (University of Texas at San Antonio Roadrunners vs Louisiana Tech Bulldogs), my first mince pies of the 2018 Christmas season (Alloa Athletic vs Brechin City) and, most recently, the "orange-flavoured scone" that I consumed in the nice little café in Sheffield.

There are three points of interest to make here. The first is that I did not deliberately set out to compile a long culinary list when I started to report on my various spectating endeavours; the various food and drink items were incidental to the main themes of describing or recollecting the sporting actions. However – the second point – these items *were* duly registered: in other words, they must obviously have left some sort of an impression that I thought was worth recording as part of the overall spectating experience.

This leads to a more general conclusion, I think. It is not just the bacon sandwiches. And it is not just the other snacks of food and drink. It is the recognition that it is the full panoply of surrounding detail and minutiae that helps to provide the colour and warmth to the enjoyment of watching live sport. Of course, we watch the action on the pitch or in the arena – the runs, the tries, the fouls, *et al* – and we register the final scores and we record the winners and losers. But later – perhaps much later – as we look back, we might also, on occasion, recollect that surrounding detail.

More examples, from just recent years:

- The sponsorship of individual rugby players by a local working men's club and a local church (Dewsbury vs Halifax, 2015);

- In conversation, the neighbouring spectator's casual statement that his uncle had taken him to see Don Bradman's Australians in 1948 because his father had been killed in the War (Yorkshire vs Nottinghamshire, 2015);

- the blue ribbons on the lampposts outside the Brunton Park ground showing the height reached by the previous winter's floodwaters (Carlisle United vs Hartlepool United, 2016);

- Post-match, seeing the oystercatchers over the banks of the River Derwent (Workington Town vs Hunslet, 2018);

- The signage inside the respective sports arenas in Arabic (Manchester City vs Arsenal, 2017) and Chinese (World Snooker Championship, 2019).

… and the bacon sandwiches we consumed when we got home.

www.anordinaryspectator.com/news-blog May 2019

# Rugby Union

# Game Management

The Guinness PRO14 rugby competition is contested by sides from Scotland, Ireland and Wales, plus two from South Africa. During the season, the teams are allocated to one of two Conferences, although there are also a sizeable number of inter-Conference matches. A play-off system involving the top three sides from each Conference generates the tournament's finalists.

The final was played yesterday evening between the Glasgow Warriors and Leinster: quite appropriately, I thought, because these two teams had been the clear winners of their respective Conferences.

Glasgow had two possible advantages going into the match. First, the game was being played at Celtic Park and, therefore, was effectively a home fixture. Second, a fortnight ago, at the time when Glasgow had had a week off, Leinster had played in the fiercely-contested European Champions cup final against Saracens in Newcastle. I wondered how much of an emotional or physical cost might have resulted from the 10-20 defeat. (Glasgow had previously lost 27-56 to Saracens in that competition's quarter final).

I was pleased that the Glasgow team included Robert Harley at blind-side wing forward: a product of Douglas Academy in Milngavie, whom I had first seen play as a 17 year-old for the West of Scotland FC at Burnbrae. That was 11 years ago; Harley is the first player to have made more than 200 appearances for the Glasgow Warriors.

I could not help but consider the parallels and differences with the Edinburgh Rugby-Munster quarter-final tie in the Heineken Cup ("*The Grizzled European Campaigners*", 31st March 2019). On that occasion, I estimated that the travelling support had made up roughly half of the attendance at Murrayfield. Yesterday, by contrast, there was no doubt which side the majority of the 47,000-plus crowd was supporting and when, after 14 minutes – accompanied by the huge roars of "We are Warriors! We are Warriors" – the Glasgow forwards drove Matt

Fagerson over the Leinster try-line to take a 7-0 lead, I did wonder if it was to be their night. Unfortunately, straight from the kick-off, the Glasgow full-back Stuart Hogg had an attempted clearance charged down and the ball, spinning wickedly in the in-goal area to stay in play, was pounced upon by the impressive Garry Ringrose for the opening Leinster try.

The parallel with the Edinburgh-Munster encounter is that my previous (complimentary) description of the Munster side can undoubtedly also be applied (if not more so) to Leinster, whose list of honours includes winning (in their respective various guises) the European Champions Cup on four occasions and the Celtic League/PRO12/PRO14 title six times, including the "double" last year. They know how to win tight games and they won this one by 18 points to 15.

The visitors took a 15-10 lead into half-time thanks to a try by Cian Healy. The prop forward, with a low body angle and an unstoppable force, drove over the line after a series of close-range surges from his colleagues: a practiced manoeuvre which demands strength, technique and patience. It is not pretty, but it is very effective and it is a significant component of the Leinster armoury; at the beginning of last season, I had seen Healy score two such tries in a European Champions Cup group match against Glasgow at Scotstoun (*"A Tough Pool"*, 23rd October 2017).

After the interval, a Johnny Sexton penalty goal gave Leinster a two-score advantage. Thereafter, in a steady drizzle, most of the play took place in Glasgow's half of the field. This included the better part of five minutes when a scrum on the home side's try-line had to be re-set several times when one or other of the front-rows caved in. Towards the end of the game, after their full-back Rob Kearney had been sent to the sin-bin, there was a three-minute stretch in which the Leinster forwards crabbed back and forth across the Glasgow 22-line with a total of 26 individual "pick and go" routines – I counted them afterwards when watching the *Clwb Rygbi* recording of the match on the S4C channel – that produced a net gain of about three yards. "Game management" is the jargon phrase, I believe.

Then, four minutes from the end, in a rare attack, Glasgow made use of the extra man brought about by Kearney's absence to move the ball quickly and send the replacement hooker Grant Stewart to score in the corner. "We are Warriors!" roared out again as the crowd sensed a dramatic finish. It was to no avail, however; Leinster were again camped in the Glasgow half when the clock ran down.

At the end of the match, there was an inevitable delay whilst the presentation stage was set up on the pitch and the dignitaries took up their positions to make the various awards. The match officials, headed by the excellent referee Nigel Owens, received their momentos, followed by the Glasgow team. Then, the Leinster players went up in turn, each of their names announced individually as they did so. The Glasgow players, with their supporting group of coaches and camp followers, stood dutifully to one side, no doubt enduring the runners-up's usual cocktail of disconsolation and anti-climax and fervently wishing to leave the scene. On their left edge, as I looked, Robert Harley applauded each individual Leinster player as his name was called out.

www.anordinaryspectator.com/news-blog May 2019

# Rugby League

# "The Parksider"

When writing or broadcasting on a major theme, the eminent historian and museum director Neil MacGregor often introduces his overall subject by referring to a single physical object: for example, a coin or drinking vessel or hand tool. It is a highly effective way of enabling his audience to relate to the period in question.

I shall attempt something similar in this article by referring to the oldest match programme in my modest collection of sports memorabilia – the edition of "The Parksider" for the Hunslet versus Castleford game on 12th October 1946. In a previous contribution to the *Journal* ("*Match Programmes: Windows into the Past*", Issue No 47, Summer 2014), I noted that programmes were often significant social documents, providing insights on their times (in that article, the 1960s), and this particular example is no exception.

I am not exactly sure how the programme ended up in my possession. The most likely explanation is that it was passed down to me by my late father, whose support for his local Hunslet club had begun as a young boy at the beginning of the 1930s.

In the late 1940s, both Hunslet and Castleford were attempting to replicate their respective successes of the pre-Second World War period. In my dad's teenage years, Hunslet had won the Challenge Cup (defeating Widnes at Wembley in 1934) and the Championship in 1938 (winning the "All Leeds" final at Elland Road) as well as the Yorkshire League in 1932.

Castleford's Challenge Cup success had come in 1935, when Huddersfield were defeated in the final. (The third-round tie at home to Hunslet produced Wheldon Road's highest-ever attendance, officially registered as 25,449). They had also been Yorkshire League winners in 1933 and 1939 and Championship runners-up (to Salford) in the last season before the War.

"The Parksider" was neatly produced, its eight pages (at a cost of tuppence) providing the listing of both teams, a page of club news and a summary of the next month's fixtures for Hunslet's first and "A" teams. It was very much a home-club product, however: apart from their team sheet, Castleford were accorded only two lines of introduction. (The title of the programme remained when I attended my first match as a six-year old in 1961 and, indeed, was still in use when Hunslet played their last game at Parkside against York in 1973).

There were a total of 10 paid advertisements, including one for the sports shop in Leeds of the great Yorkshire batsman Herbert Sutcliffe and another for the "cabinet makers and upholsterers" Jack Walkington & Co of Bramley. There was also an invitation after the match to "call and see Les White at the Moor House Inn" on Dewsbury Road for "fine ales in good condition". (The Welsh hooker had been the only non-local in Hunslet's 1934 Wembley side and had also featured in the 1938 Championship success).

Walkington's name did not only appear in his business's advert, as the veteran captain of the 1934 and 1938 trophy-winning sides was also listed as the Hunslet full-back. He was to retire the following year with over 570 games under his belt. It is reasonable to claim that Jack Walkington – along with Albert Goldthorpe and Geoff Gunney – is one of the three greatest figures in the history of Hunslet RLFC.

There were three other survivors of Hunslet's pre-War Championship winning side in the pack: the two prop forwards Eddie Bennett and Sam Newbound and the second-rower Colin Stansfield. The line-up given in the programme also included Cyril Morrell (who had been a try-scorer in the Challenge Cup final) and Cyril Plenderleith, although neither were in the numbered final 13.

These experienced campaigners were complemented by the relative newcomers. The most prominent of these, recently returned from Royal Navy duty, was the scrum-half, Alf "Ginger" Burnell. Burnell was to give over a decade's service to the Hunslet club, appearing on over 370 occasions, and was a Great Britain tourist to Australasia in 1954, when he played in the series-deciding third test against New Zealand in Auckland.

Castleford also had a combination of the old and the new. Half a dozen players listed in their line-up (winger Reg Lloyd, centre Norman Guest and the forwards Patrick McManus, Jim Crossley, Charlie Staines and Eric Jones) had appeared for the club before the War. Indeed, the two veterans lining up at prop (McManus and Crossley) had been Challenge Cup winners 11 years previously.

In fact, although Reg Lloyd's name was given in the match programme, he was actually engaged elsewhere – playing for Wales against England at Station Road, Swinton, in the first match of the 1946-47 European Championship. One of his team-mates on that occasion, Tuss Griffiths, was missing from the Hunslet side and the pair enjoyed a productive afternoon, a Lloyd try helping the Welshmen to a 13-10 win in front of a crowd of over 20,000. (England were to win that season's tournament, however, thanks to a later victory in Swansea and narrow home and away wins over France).

Reg Lloyd was another who had played in a pre-War Challenge Cup final. As a 19 year-old – at the time, the youngest participant in the Wembley showpiece – he had scored Keighley's only try in their 1937 defeat by Widnes.

The social context in which the Hunslet-Castleford league fixture of 1946 was played is clearly illustrated on the back page of the programme, on which there is a list – 13 names in total – of "Hunslet Players serving in HM Forces". Although it had been 17 months since the Second World War had ended in Europe (and 14 in the Far East), the long process of the demobilisation of the Armed Forces was still under way, whilst British troops were also still engaged in several trouble-spots around the world, including the Middle East and South East Asia. All the professional rugby league clubs were to lose players to National Service for many years to come.

The list included the 20 year-old Ken Traill, whose career path was shortly to take him from Hunslet to great success with Bradford Northern and Great Britain. He was to be a fellow tourist of Alf Burnell's in 1954, having also toured Down Under with Ernest Ward's team four years earlier.

It is when I pick up the match programme that the sense of physical connection with the period – as skilfully employed by Neil MacGregor – is made. It is as if I am somehow touching the late 1940s. With a little imagination – albeit from the warmth and comfort of 70-plus years on – I can envisage the time of chronic shortages, cold winters and widespread hardship.

Another of the programme's advertisements – for a firm of commercial printers – referred to the efficient service that it had maintained throughout the years "through numerous difficulties, staff shortages, controls and regulations". This short phrase helps us to capture the severe economic conditions that, in October 1946, showed little sign of easing. Indeed, bread rationing – which had been avoided during the War – had been introduced the previous June, thereby adding to the long list of foodstuffs (along with other basics such as petrol, clothing and soap) for which coupons were required.

And yet it was also a time of hope. Hitler's Germany had been defeated. Families were being re-united. People could look forward with both optimism for the future and gratitude that they had survived the long ordeal of war. The policies promised by Clement Attlee's Government, which had been elected in July 1945 – including the nationalisation of key industries and the creation of a National Health Service – would lead, it was widely believed, to the New Jerusalem.

It was also a boom time for sports spectating. Freed from the wartime constraints on social gatherings, the crowds flocked back to the stadiums – as they also did to the cinemas and the dance halls – to enjoy the liberation and excitement of the communal event. Hunslet's ground was one such venue for celebration, as

Les Hoole and Mike Green evocatively described in the introduction to their 1989 booklet *Parkside Memories*: Parkside was "more than a rugby ground, it was a centre for sports of all kinds and provided a vibrant social scene". The 1946 match programme provides a physical embodiment of those times.

Of course, all these years later, we know what happened next. The immediate outcome of the match was a win for the visitors by 18 points to 10. The following Monday's *Yorkshire Post* reported that: "[t]he strong Castleford pack kept a tight grip on the scrummages and the men behind were quick to seize their chance". Langfield, Robinson, Guest and Staines were the Castleford try-scorers with full-back Geoff Briggs landing three goals. For Hunslet, Harold Buck, the speedy left-winger "scored a try that will be talked about for a long time, when he beat three men in a run from half way".

Castleford completed the "double" four weeks later with a 24-10 win at Wheldon Road. On the same day, the season's County Championship was decided when Yorkshire beat Lancashire 13-10 – at Parkside.

It transpired that the Hunslet-Castleford contests were between two middle-ranking teams in the 1946-47 Championship. Castleford were to finish in 13th place in the 28-team league, one place above their hosts. It did take longer than usual to determine these positions; the "Big Freeze" in the early months of 1947 meant that the season was not completed until June.

As we have seen, we can also follow the subsequent playing and coaching careers of the participants. For example, from the Castleford ranks, George Langfield – matched at scrum-half against Alf Burnell in the 1946 Parkside contest – went on to play for St Helens against Huddersfield in the Challenge Cup final of 1953 when, like Reg Lloyd before him, he was a try-scorer in a losing cause. Norman Guest, who made over 130 appearances for Castleford between 1938 and 1950, went on to play for Doncaster in their first four seasons in the league, notching up another century of matches before hanging up his boots in 1955.

On his retirement from playing, Jack Walkington coached the Hunslet team through to 1960, though it would not be until Fred Ward took over the reins that another trophy would be won, when the Yorkshire Cup was lifted in 1962. After his playing career ended, Ken Traill masterminded Wakefield Trinity's decade of success in the 1960s (though it would be remiss of me not to mention his side's defeat to Hunslet in the Challenge Cup semi final of 1965).

In other respects, the story is not so positive. The 1946 match programme's front page prominently lists the members of the Committee of the Hunslet Rugby Football Club. One of them, later to become chairman, was still in post to oversee the club's demise and liquidation – and the sale of Parkside to a property development company – nearly 30 years later.

And, finally, what of the presumed original purchaser of the programme? In October 1946, Bill Rigg was in his mid 20s, a qualified joiner, having been demobilised the previous Christmas from his RAF duties as a Leading Aircraftman. Marriage was three years away, when he made the permanent move from south Leeds to the leafier climes of Moortown in the north of the city. He was always a Hunslet man, however, right up to his death in 2004.

In common with the many millions coming to terms with the realities of post-Second World War Britain, my father worked hard and raised his family and created the circumstances from which the succeeding generations have benefited. The 1946 edition of "The Parksider" sits proudly in my programme collection as a reminder of his enthusiasm in passing on his love of the sport. Sometimes, we do indeed stand on the shoulders of giants.

*The Rugby League Journal* Issue 67, Summer 2019

# Cricket

# The Circle of Cricketing Life

Last summer – recalled now as one of unremitting sunshine and scorching temperatures – my friend George Farrow and I managed the impressive feat of attending a one-day cricket match at Headingley (Yorkshire vs Nottinghamshire in the Royal London One-Day Cup) that was washed out without a ball being bowled. This year, we decided to improve our chances of seeing some action by arranging to watch the first two days of Yorkshire's Specsavers County Championship game with Essex, which began on Monday on the same ground.

The general consensus amongst the cricket cognoscenti – and the online Yorkshire Members' Forum – is that Essex are one of the three counties that are most likely to lift this year's title (along with the champions, Surrey, and Somerset, who have already won the 2019 Royal London tournament). They have much the same squad as their championship-winning group of two years ago, though without the Pakistani fast-bowler Mohammed Amir and the experienced wicket-keeper James Foster. The Australian Peter Siddle has replaced Amir, whilst Essex have the bonus of the former England captain, Alastair Cook, being available for the whole summer following his retirement from test match cricket.

Cook ended his international career with the England records for the most tests (161), most consecutive tests (159, the world record), most tests as captain (59), most runs (12,472), most centuries (33) and most outfield catches (175). Equally importantly (if not more so) in an era when, for some, spiteful confrontation and perpetual aggression seemed to represent appropriate conduct on and off the cricket field – culminating in the shameful exposure and disgrace of the Australians' "sandpaper-gate" in South Africa – it strikes me that Cook has always combined dignity and modesty in a way that is wholly admirable. Other than on television, I had not seen him play before and I was looking forward to doing so,

Given that, since retiring from test cricket, Cook has been knighted, I was also interested to see how he would be designated on the match scorecard. "AN Cook" was the answer.

George and I saw a full day's play on Monday and the morning session on Tuesday, during which time Yorkshire compiled a first innings total of 390. As Essex then batted for 25 minutes before the rains came, I was pleased to be able to see Sir Alastair Cook walk out to open the innings. I was also able to see him walk back to the pavilion, as he was caught in the slips for two off the seventh delivery he received.

The evolution of the Yorkshire innings comprised all that is to like about first class cricket: an excellent knock by the opener Adam Lyth – who, in the neat description by Chris Waters in the following day's *Yorkshire Post,* provided "the usual cinema reel of exquisite cover drives" – before falling five runs short of his century; a mid-innings collapse in which four wickets fell for 28 runs; a neat consolidating partnership by Johnny Tattersall and Dom Bess in the late middle order; a sharp piece of fielding by Sam Cook (no relation) to run out Gary Ballance; the break put on the Yorkshire scoring by the off-spinner Simon Harmer, who received a meagre rewarded for his long bowling stint with a solitary wicket late in the day.

The Yorkshire supporters in the East Stand were fully engaged by the action: "No ball, umpire. Get a grip" shouted one, when Ravi Bopara appeared to overstep the crease in his delivery stride; "Good fielding" acknowledged another, when the sprawling Nick Browne – not the fastest of movers in the outfield – valiantly dived full-length in front of us to prevent a boundary.

A couple of the names were new to me. Will Fraine opened the batting on his Yorkshire first-class debut and seemed to ally a sound temperament with a solid technique; it was a surprise when he was bowled for 39. On the Essex side, Will Buttleman, a 19 year-old debutant wicket-keeper, was equally impressive, taking three catches and conceding only one bye in a Yorkshire innings that spanned 125 overs.

As with all sports, there is a circle of life to first-class cricket. Sir Alastair Cook is winding down his career (hopefully with another couple of seasons to come) after 13 years in the test match trenches. The other (near) veterans in this match included Siddle and Bopara at age 34, the 35 year-old Yorkshire captain Steve Patterson and the Essex skipper, Ryan ten Doeschate, who is 38. The hope must be that the game of first-class cricket – including the county championship – survives long enough in its present state for the likes of Fraine and Buttleman to have rewarding careers of similar longevity.

**Footnote**

The Yorkshire/Essex match ended today in a draw. With most sides now having completed 5 of their 14 fixtures, Somerset head the county championship table.[17]

www.anordinaryspectator.com/news-blog June 2019

# Horse-Racing

# In the Black

*"My careful study of the horses' and jockeys' form in the early races resulted in consistent losses to the friendly bookmaker taking my money through the small hatch at the end of the corridor behind our box... [F]inancial equilibrium was restored with successes in the last two races, for which my choices were based solely on the names of the horses".*

[*An Ordinary Spectator*, page 191]

Given that horseracing/equestrianism is the second most popular spectator sport in Britain (albeit a long way behind soccer), I am conscious that its general absence from my chronicles of sports-watching represents something of gap. The sole reference to horseracing in *An Ordinary Spectator* concerned an enjoyable office outing to Lingfield Park in Surrey in the 1980s, when – as noted above with the usual rationalisation of the (very) occasional gambler – I claimed to have finished the day breaking even. Last Friday, accompanied by my wife Angela, I sought to reduce this spectating deficit by attending the evening race meeting at Ayr.

The Ayr Racecourse website – www.ayr-racecourse.co.uk – informs us that the first organised horserace meeting in the town took place in 1771 with the move to the current site occurring in 1907. The establishment of the jumps circuit in 1950 meant that the course could hold both flat-racing and National Hunt meetings, the latter including (from 1966) the Scottish Grand National. A £20 million investment programme over the last dozen years or so has brought about a range of improvements to the course, which will host 32 days of racing this year.

Within horseracing, there is a hierarchy of rewards, the steep gradient of which parallels those seen in other professional sports. At Royal Ascot on Friday, the prize money for the winners of the 6 races – of which 4 were in the officially recognised Class 1 category – totalled in excess of £850,000. At Ayr, where the 7 races for the Tennent's Race Night were in Classes 4 to 6 – the winners received a total of just under £30,000 out of the overall prize money of £55,000.

However, I have to say that for this casual spectator at Ayr, these financial differences were irrelevant. The atmosphere was friendly and relaxed, the programme was administered efficiently (with an excellent course commentator) and the racing was competitive, with most of the winners getting home by half a length or less. Our view from the trackside marquee gave a panorama of the full course; it was a very pleasant location in which to spend a bright midsummer evening.

It turned out that my gambling strategy was to echo that employed at Lingfield Park all those years ago. After the first two bets on short-priced horses (based on a close reading of the *Racing Post*) had been frustrated by narrow defeats at the winning post, I reverted to selecting by name for the Coca Cola Handicap. How could I resist a wager on the sport-related Trautmann – presumably named after the former German prisoner-of-war who famously played on for Manchester City after breaking his neck in the 1956 FA Cup Final? The jockey – Alistair Rawlinson – rode a brilliant race, recovering from second-last at the turn into the straight to come through the field for a narrow win. Trautmann's odds of 6 to 1 put me into the black, where I was to remain for the rest of the evening thanks to the later investments on Suwaan (each-way in the Gordon's Pink Gin Handicap) and Mujassam (in the Magners Rose Handicap).

For the avoidance of doubt, I recognise that, on this occasion, the gambler's luck ran in my direction. On my next visit to the trackside, the success rate could well be nought from seven.

As ever with sports spectating – particularly with those sports with which I am less familiar – it is in the detail of the event that the clearest impressions are gained. On this occasion, there was much to take in: the ritual of the owners meeting the jockeys in the centre of the parade ring before the race; the thick wad of banknotes in the bookmaker's hand from which he paid out on Trautmann with a friendly "well done"; the pride in appearance taken by some of the spectators on their evening out (even though it was not a formal Ladies Night); the rumbling sound of hooves on turf as the horses passed the nearby winning post; the roar of triumph (by some) when the result of a photo finish was announced.

In the build-up to the two races that began at the end of the straight away to our left, rather than on the far side of the course, the respective fields passed directly in front of our marquee on their way to the start. Angela and I stood by the rail and watched in awed fascination as each horse and rider – a majestic combined presence – went by.

www.anordinaryspectator.com/news-blog June 2019

# Cricket

# Held in the Moment

It was 50 years ago this week – on 14<sup>th</sup> July 1969 to be precise – that my friend and I grabbed our rucksacks at the end of the schoolday and rushed down to the Oakwood Clock to catch the number 21 bus. In Harehills, we changed to the 44 that took us straight to the Headingley Cricket Ground.

In those days – incredible as it might seem now – the gates were opened for free at the tea time of a test match. And so, shortly after play had resumed following the break on the fourth day, we found ourselves standing by the low brick wall behind the shallow banking of packed Members' seating that ran from the "new" pavilion round towards the Old Pavilion and the Football Stand.

Initially requiring 303 to win in the fourth innings, the West Indies had reduced the target to below 100 with only three wickets down. It looked as if, in the last game of the three-match series, England would surrender their 1-0 lead.

The ground slopes down on that side of the arena; the spectator has a sense of looking up slightly to view the action. On the brighter early evenings – such as this – it can also be a strain looking towards the sun behind the Western Terrace. But we didn't care. Our view was perfect.

Hindsight suggests that the West Indies were not the side they had been on the previous tours: there was no Hall or Griffith, for example. But, again, that did not register with us. We were still watching the glamorous visitors from the Caribbean. And the next man in was Gary Sobers.

Basil Butcher had been something of a liability in the outfield. The radio commentators had said that his arm was "thrown out" and so he could only return the ball with a curious underarm whipping action. His batting seemed to more than compensate, however. We watched as he entered the 90s.

The England captain Ray Illingworth turned to one of his side's all-rounders – Barry Knight – to supplement the patient accuracy of Derek Underwood. I was intrigued by Knight's bowling action: a bouncy medium-paced approach to the crease that reached a climax with a huge leap that seemed to halt all his forward momentum prior to delivering the ball.

And then Underwood got Butcher out – caught behind by the wonderful Alan Knott. The crowd cheered. In came the great man.

Ten minutes (and four balls) later, out he went again – for nought. Bowled by Knight, off an inside edge, attempting a forceful back-foot shot. I watched – awestruck and open-mouthed – as Sobers trudged off the field.

The scorebook reveals that the West Indies innings collapsed. Clive Lloyd was out cheaply. The Underwood/Knott combination struck again to dismiss John Shepherd. Four wickets fell for nine runs. England won by 30 runs the following morning.

But, half a century later, it is not the final outcome of the test match that seems to matter. Rather, my overwhelming memory is captured in a single dominant tableau: Sobers has completed his elegant follow-through – but his wicket is broken behind him. I can close my eyes and see it now. I am held in the moment – captured and captivated.

I was 14 years old and all was well with the world.

www.anordinaryspectator.com/news-blog July 2019

# Shinty

# A Local Rivalry

In Scotland, the footprint for the locations of the 10 teams in the Premier Division of the sport of shinty – the Mowi Premiership – covers a large area across the north and west of the country: from Strathpeffer, a couple of miles from the mouth of the Cromarty Firth, to Tignabruaich in Argyll. However, the fiercest rivalry is between two near neighbours – Kingussie Camanachd Club and Newtonmore Camanachd Club – separated by a mere three miles in the Spey valley.

Kingussie gained an entry into the 2005 edition of the *Guinness World Records* as the world's most successful sports team, having won their league for 20 consecutive years. This run was later extended to include all of the first 12 seasons of the Premier Division, which was established in its present format in 1996. However, the tables have turned in recent years: Newtonmore have won 8 of the last 9 league titles and are the current champions. Moreover, Newtonmore are also the holders of the prestigious Tulloch Homes Camanachd Cup, the knock-out trophy which they have won a record 33 times and which they will defend next month in the 2019 final. (Kingussie were eliminated by Kyles Athletic at the quarter-final stage).

I have reported on the intensity of local sporting rivalries before, of course. *An Ordinary Spectator* offers reflections on Headingley versus Roundhay (rugby union) and Hull FC versus Hull Kingston Rovers (rugby league) for example, as well as (at a slightly wider level) Yorkshire versus Lancashire in different forms of cricket. On Friday evening, during a visit to the Highlands (with my wife, Angela), we took the opportunity to observe how this played out in Premier Division shinty when Kingussie (sitting at the top of the league) hosted Newtonmore (in fourth place, but with games in hand).

The Kingussie ground at The Dell is about half a mile out of town on the road to the ruined Ruthven Barracks, which were sacked by the retreating Jacobites after their defeat at Culloden in 1746. The arena comprises a flat, well-maintained pitch, bounded by trees on two sides, with a small grandstand on the popular side and an electronic scoreboard to the right of the tea-room behind one of the goals. Overlooking the venue is the 1600 foot Creag Bheag, which Angela and I walked up and over the following day on a route that then took us from Loch Gynack to the scattered remains of the former Raitts Township, where community life was brought to an end by the Highland Clearances of 200 years ago.

Not surprisingly, the combination of the battle for local bragging rights (as well as league points) and the warm early-evening weather generated a sizeable crowd: perhaps 500 or so. We stood in the shade towards one end of the pitch, where we had a good view of the whole expanse as well as a clear sight of the intricacies of the close-quarter play when the ball came into our vicinity.

Although shinty's playing area is much larger than that for rugby or soccer – pitches are usually 140-170 yards long – it was noticeable that the action shifted from one end to the other remarkably quickly, as the defensive players on both sides were adapt at striking the ball considerable distances in hurried circumstances. There were obvious overlaps with the skill-sets of not only golf and hockey, but also tennis: the re-starts when the ball went out of the play on the side lines took the form of a tricky double-handed overhead serve with the ball being struck by the toe-end of the stick.

What also came across very clearly was the full commitment of the players. It takes some bravery to compete for the ball, either in the air or on the ground, amidst the furious wielding and full-blooded swings of the sticks. Some of the players wore helmets, though not all. Early in the match I judged, in particular, that it would be very unlikely that I would ever volunteer for the position of goalkeeper: a decision that was emphatically confirmed later on.

The close matching of the two sides was evident. The play took the form of a series of close tussles, with very little time available to the player with the ball. Unlike in soccer, where a side might make a series of unchallenged passes, without gaining ground, in order to control the tempo of the game, there was no respite here. Likewise, unlike in rugby, where there can be a fluidity of movement through one side running or passing the ball through several phases of play, here there was a rapid turnover of possession between the sides.

I sensed that the individual players were familiar with their direct opponents. On some occasions, when there was a hold up in play, pairs of players seemed to engage in friendly conversation, as if enquiring about the health of their respective families. Seconds later, play having restarted, they would be crashing into each other without any holding back. I thought that the referee handled the game well. He seemed to pull up most of the obvious fouls, without detracting from the physical component of the encounter.

Kingussie had most of the early play and it was something of a surprise when, after 10 minutes, Newtonmore took the lead, a long-range shot being misjudged by the home goalkeeper. Kingussie's mobile forward line posed a continual threat, however, and, after the interval, two impressive strikes appeared to have secured their side the win. Then, in the third minute of added time, Kingussie carelessly lost possession in midfield and a final Newtonmore attack saw them squeeze home the equaliser to the delight of the visiting support. (Unfortunately, there was a lack of available team sheets with which to identify the players). The final score was 2-2.

After the final whistle sounded, Angela and I walked down the touchline towards the tea-room. When we reached the end of the pitch, we noticed that no-one else seemed to have moved very far and that the players were still out on the pitch. At first, I thought that this might have been analogous to watching the rugby league in Toronto, where the match is just part of an afternoon's socialising for the local spectators. However, it transpired that for this Kingussie-Newtonmore encounter – with the league points having been shared – there was to be a separate penalty shoot-out to decide the winners of the Sir Tommy MacPherson Memorial Trophy.

We had a close view of this from behind the goal (though safely to the side). The players took turns to blast the ball at the respective goalkeepers, the latter attired *sans* helmet or gloves. The outcome was decided when one of the Newtonmore penalty-takers fired his shot straight on to the Kingussie goalkeeper's fingers – a guaranteed fracture, I would have thought – and the ball stayed out of the net. The next Kingussie penalty was taken by the goalkeeper himself, who duly and emphatically dispatched his effort. When the final Newtonmore attempt sailed over the bar, high and handsome like an 8 iron, the cup was Kingussie's.

And so ended an enjoyable evening. I had not only added another sport to the list of those on which I have reported in book or blog, but I had also – to my reward – done so in the context of the local community in which it features so significantly. If there were any doubt about that, it was assuaged by the sight of the toddlers-- some aged no more than 3 or 4 – running on the pitch, complete with their sticks of appropriate size, at half-time and at the end of the game. Some will be participants in future Kingussie-Newtonmore encounters, no doubt.[18]

**Postscript**

The brief match report in today's edition of *The Scotsman* states that Kingussie's goalscorers were Ruaridh Anderson and James Falconer. The Newtonmore goals were scored by Fraser MacKintosh and Conor Jones.

www.anordinaryspectator.com/news-blog August 2019

Rugby League

# Imperious Saints

When I purchased my ticket (in February) for last Thursday's Leeds versus St Helens Super League encounter at Headingley, I had expected a close contest between two of rugby league's traditional heavyweights.

As it happens, the sides have had differing fortunes this season. Leeds have been in a struggle to avoid finishing in last place in the 12-team league table – with automatic relegation to the Championship – though a couple of recent victories have greatly aided their cause.

By contrast, St Helens have been the dominant side in 2019, having won the League Leaders Shield several weeks in advance of the Top 5 play-offs for the Super League title, which will begin next month. Indeed – remarkably – as things stood at the kick-off, the 14 point difference in the league table between St Helens and the teams in joint-second place (Warrington Wolves and Hull FC) was the same as that between Warrington/Hull and the bottom-placed team (London Broncos). In addition, St Helens have secured a place in next Saturday's Challenge Cup final (against Warrington) at Wembley.

In the build-up to the game, I had wondered if there might be an unfortunate echo of the Scotland-All Blacks match at Murrayfield in the group stage of the 2007 Rugby World Cup. (The £85 I invested for a seat at the end of the West Stand in the corner of the ground was, at that time, the most I had ever paid to see a sporting event). On that occasion, the Scottish team management took the game so seriously that they decided to field a near-second XV, so that the first-choice players could avoid injury and be ready for the crucial group encounter with Italy the following weekend. I thought that that had been an absolutely appalling decision. Not only was it an insult to the spectators that had paid considerable sums to watch the match – and mine was by no means the most expensive ticket – it was hugely disrespectful to the opposition and to the tournament itself. (New Zealand won the match 40-0, scoring six tries in the process). Whether coincidence or not, I have not paid to watch the Scotland rugby team since.

The question was, therefore: given that St Helens might wish to protect their key players from injury in advance of the significant matches to come, would they follow Scotland's lead and field a reserve team?

To their great credit, the answer was: no. Of the 17 players who represented St Helens in the Challenge Cup semi-final – and whom one might therefore suppose constituted the first-choice side – 11 played against Leeds. On the basis that some of the absentees had been unavailable through injury for the last couple of weeks, my assessment was that perhaps only two – the winger Tommy Makinson and the scrum-half Danny Richardson – were genuinely being shielded.

The risk of a mis-timed injury was illustrated mid-way through the first half when St Helens's French half-back Theo Fages was hurt in an unsuccessful attempt to prevent Ash Handley from scoring the first Leeds try and had to receive treatment on the pitch for several minutes. Thankfully, however, he recovered to play a full – and influential – part in the remainder of the match.

The first half was evenly contested with Leeds holding a 10-6 lead until a few minutes before half-time. At that point, St Helens pressed firmly down on the accelerator and the first of three tries by the impressive centre Kevin Naiqama signalling the start of a period of dominance through to the hour mark in which they registered 30 unanswered points. A couple of late Leeds tries gave the score-line an element of respectability for the home side – including a second for Handley to make him the league's joint-highest try-scorer this season, no mean feat in a side that has been generally struggling – but the final tally of 36-20 was an accurate reflection of St Helens's superiority. The headline to Peter Smith's report in the following day's *Yorkshire Evening Post* – "Imperious Saints canter to victory" – summed it up pretty well.

This was my first visit to the Headingley ground since the completion of its major overhaul. The two fine new stands running along the full lengths of the touchlines complement the Extentia Stand at the St Michael's Lane end of the ground, from which I had a full view of the proceedings. Only the triangular-shaped terrace for visiting supporters at the far end of the ground remains from the venue as it used to be. It is an attractive stadium and a worthy location for the Leeds club.

"All we need now is a team to match the surroundings", said the elderly man to my left as the sun was setting behind the St Helens support and the kick-off time approached. The subsequent events on the pitch confirmed his analysis of the current status of the Leeds team.

My view from a raised perspective behind the posts enabled me to appreciate fully the speed with which St Helens transferred the ball across the pitch and the options provided in the different running lines taken by the support players. At the heart of the action was the excellent Jonny Lomax – Fages's half-back partner – who invariably took the ball as third or fourth receiver from the play-the-ball and went through the repertoire of skills with his variations in passing and kicking and, occasionally, dummying the pass to run with the ball. His performance was a pleasure to watch as were, in their different ways, those of the aggressive prop forward Luke Thompson and the elusive Regan Grace on the left wing. "He's a good player, is that" said my neighbour in admiration, after Grace had skilfully side-stepped the covering defence and registered St Helens's opening try.

It's a theme I have explored before. The pleasure of watching top sportsmen at the top of their game.

www.anordinaryspectator.com/news-blog August 2019

# For Valour

Last year – in *"Below Average"* (28th May 2018) – I noted that Yorkshire CCC's record over the 55 years of one-day competitions could indeed charitably be described in those terms. Of the 142 tournaments – ranging from 60 overs to 20 overs per side – played to 2017, they had won just five with, of the other counties, only Derbyshire, Durham and Glamorgan having a lower haul. The completion of the 2018 season took the score to 5 out of 144.

Earlier this season, Yorkshire maintained their record by failing to progress out of the Group phase of the 50-over Royal London One-Day Cup (which was subsequently won by Somerset), thereby leaving the T20 tournament (the Vitality Blast) as the remaining vehicle for possible one-day success. However, prior to last Friday's fixture with the Durham Jets at Headingley, Yorkshire were placed bottom of the nine teams in the North Group in this competition, having won only 1 of the 9 matches to date (4 of which were completely rained off).

As only the top four sides qualify for the quarter-finals, they probably needed to win all 5 of the remaining Group matches (including the Durham game) in order to hold out any hope of reaching the knock-out stage.

It rained all day. The match didn't get near the starting blocks. The probability of Yorkshire reaching the next stage of this year's T20 tournament moved a little closer to zero.

This being Leeds, there is always a Plan B, of course. The inclement weather meant that I had a little more time than otherwise to visit a couple of the city's cultural attractions – the Leeds City Art Gallery and the Leeds City Museum – in each case to seek out one of the city's greatest sons.

The collection in the small Ziff Gallery in the Art Gallery includes three works by the Leeds-born artist, John Atkinson Grimshaw (1836-1893). One of them is a classical piece – *Iris* (1886) – but it is the other two to which I am repeatedly drawn. *Reflections on the Thames: Westminster* and *Nightfall Down the Thames* were both painted in 1880 and are part of the Atkinson Grimshaw *oeuvre* that focused on urban scenes at night-time. The former is a particularly haunting piece, I think, in which the "reflections" incorporate not only the lights of the moon and Westminster Bridge in the river's waters, but also – perhaps – the thoughts of the lonely woman plying her trade on the Embankment.

The Leeds City Museum in situated in the impressive building that was once the Mechanics' Institute in Millennium Square. At the entrance to "The Story of Leeds" Exhibition are the portraits of 20 or so famous people from the city, including the dual rugby international Jason Robinson, the snooker player Paul Hunter, the boxer Nicola Adams and the cyclist Beryl Burton. However, it was in a non-sporting context that I was making my visit.

Arthur Louis Aaron was born in 1922 and attended Roundhay School (which, as it happens, was also where I was educated many years later). He enlisted in the RAF in 1941 and was promoted to Flight Sergeant two years later. It was in August 1943 – 76 years ago this month – that the Stirling bomber, of which he was captain, came under heavy fire whilst on a mission over Italy. Several of the crew were killed, including the navigator, and Ft Sgt Aaron himself was badly injured, losing the use of an arm and part of his face. Nonetheless, he saved the remaining crew by directing the stricken plane towards North Africa and a landing in Algeria. He died shortly afterwards.

The posthumous Victoria Cross that was awarded to Ft Sgt Aaron is exhibited, along with his other medals, in "The Story of Leeds" together with a maquette to acknowledge his life and accomplishments and the letter written to his parents by Sir Arthur Harris, Commander-in-Chief of RAF Bomber Command.

On Friday, I sat for a little while in the café of the Leeds City Museum. Outside, the rain continued to pour down. I had been prevented by the elements from watching a cricket match. (On the same evening, several thousand Ed Sheeran fans would have been drenched when watching their idol perform at a concert in Roundhay Park). The Yorkshire cricketers – with an average age of 26 for the squad that had been announced for that evening's fixture – had been frustrated in their efforts to make progress in a one-day competition.

These were minor inconveniencies.

Flight Sergeant Arthur Louis Aaron VC DFM died at the age of 21.

www.anordinaryspectator.com/news-blog August 2019

Football

# Number One in the Rankings

Prior to yesterday's Scotland vs Belgium match at Hampden Park, the qualification tournament for the Euro 2020 Football Championships had reached the half-way stage. All six of the sides in Scotland's group had played 5 of their 10 matches.

In the qualifying table, Scotland were languishing in fourth place, some distance behind Belgium and Russia, who looked to be clear favourites to take the two automatically available places for the tournament's final stages. It appeared that Scotland's more realistic route to the finals might be via the play-offs of a separate four-team Nations League group (currently also comprising Norway, Serbia and Finland) for which they have already qualified. (In the event of one or more of these countries qualifying by the conventional route, they would be replaced in the Nations League group).

The mood music from the Scottish management seemed to recognise these realities. The talk was of taking something from the matches against Belgium and Russia (away next month) and putting in good performances, so that some momentum could be built up for the final three games (against San Marino, Cyprus and Kazakhstan) in advance of Scotland's participation in the Nations League group next March.

My trips to watch Scotland to play football are something of a rarity: the last occasion was a friendly match against Germany at Ibrox Stadium in March 1993. I was enticed to yesterday's encounter largely by the prospect of seeing Belgium: third-placed at the last World Cup in Russia, currently ranked as the world's number 1 team by FIFA and, for good measure, with a 100% record from their opening five games of Euro 2020.

I was also interested in how the Scottish supporters at the stadium would approach the game. Would it be with the traditionally raucous bravado of the tartaned hordes? Or would it reflect the pessimistic snatch of conversation that I overheard at the weekend (following Scotland's 1-2 defeat by Russia at Hampden on Friday evening): "…Belgium will probably go 6-0 up after 20 minutes and then bring on their substitutes…". The two perspectives are not mutually exclusive, of course.

And, indeed, it was both perspectives that were revealed.

The game was preceded by the crowd's passionate rendition of *Flower of Scotland*, movingly accompanied by the strains of a sole bagpiper. Scotland's players exploited this fervent atmosphere in the opening stages of the match, dominating possession and putting the Belgian defenders under continual pressure. Then, after eight minutes, in the visitors' first serious attack, Kevin De Bruyne broke free down the left-hand side and measured his pass perfectly for Romelu Lukaku to calmly shoot the ball past the Scottish goalkeeper, David Marshall. At that moment, I sensed that the home supporters recognised that their basic fears had been confirmed: it would be a long evening ahead.

The crowd attempted to rally their team and Scotland, as before, enjoyed a good share of possession until De Bruyne – on the right, this time – won the ball and delivered a penetrating pass across the goal which Thomas Vermaelen swept into the net. A short time later, a De Bruyne corner was headed home by Toby Alderweireld. It was not quite 6-0 after 20 minutes, but 3-0 just after the half-hour mark was decisive enough.

It will not have got unnoticed that the common theme in this description is Kevin De Bruyne of Manchester City. He is part of this so-called "Golden Generation" of Belgian footballers – which includes Lukaku (transferred this summer for £73 million from Manchester United to Juventus) and Eden Hazard (£88 million from Chelsea to Real Madrid, though absent yesterday through injury) – which is delivering to the hype. (The contrast with the unfulfilled English variant of a few years ago – Beckham, Lampard, Owen, Ferdinand *et al* – is palpable). In the first half, Scotland simply couldn't cope with De Bruyne's combination of speed, skill and awareness and, although he was less prominent after the interval, it was the same player's emphatic finish, following a neat pass by Lukaku, that resulted in the final scoreline of 4-0.

It is difficult to see the weaknesses in the Belgian set-up, because their overall excellence extends well beyond the headline players: the goalkeeper is Thibaut Courtois of Real Madrid, the defence dealt efficiently with Scotland's dangerous crosses into the penalty area and, in midfield, I was impressed with each of the telling contributions made by Youri Tielemans, Dries Mertens and Nacer Chadli. The fact that the Belgium starting XI was comprised of players drawn from 6 different leagues (with only Chadli playing in Belgium itself) did not affect their coherence and teamwork.

The Scottish manager, Steve Clarke, has more limited resources on which to draw. Four of his starting line-up play in the Championship (the second tier) in England and one of the substitutes, Johnny Russell, for Sporting Kansas City in the US Major Soccer League. It should be said that none of these players let him down yesterday and the goalkeeper, Marshall of Wigan Athletic, made a couple of the first-class saves in the second half to limit the overall damage on the scoreboard. Scotland looked most threatening from the direct runs at the Belgian defence of the left-back and captain, Andy Robertson.

The worrying signs surrounding the Scotland football team do not simply relate to the most recent results on the pitch. Yesterday's attendance – to see the number one-ranked team in the world, remember – was only just over 25,500: barely half the capacity of Hampden Park or, indeed, half the size of the attendance that Celtic might expect to draw for a routine home league match against Hamilton Academicals or Ross County.

There are probably several factors that account for this relatively low turnout. Perhaps it was due to the cumulative expense faced by spectators in attending two matches in four days (the game against Russia drew over 32,000) or their familiarity with Belgium's star players through seeing them on television (or their familiarity with the Belgium team, which also won 4-0 in a Hampden Park friendly in September last year).

However, I also wonder if it reflects a growing detachment between the country's casual football supporters and the national side as a result of Scotland's longstanding absence from dining at international soccer's top table: qualification for a major football tournament has not been achieved since the 1998 World Cup. This would be of some concern: these things can take a long time to repair.

On the other hand… Come March and two matches to win in the Nations League group in order to qualify for Euro 2020… Hampden Park's Tartan Army might still have a role to play.

www.anordinaryspectator.com/news-blog September 2019

Rugby League

# Elimination and Second Chances

The regular season of rugby league's Championship League 1 (the third tier) has been completed. The divisional champions – Whitehaven – having been promoted automatically into the Championship, the second promotion place will be determined through a series of play-offs involving the five teams finishing between second and sixth in the table.

Given that there were only 11 teams in the league, it does seem a rather generous provision to allow the middle-ranking side the chance to progress out of the division. Moreover, the play-off structure is not straightforward. In the jargon, it involves an "elimination final", a "qualifying final", two "semi-finals" and a "preliminary final" before the (final) "play-off final" is reached.

In fact, there is a meritocratic logic in the format. The higher places in the league table are rewarded by a later entry into the play-offs (for Oldham, the second-placed side) and/or second chances in the event of a first defeat (for Oldham and for Newcastle Thunder and Doncaster, who came third and fourth, respectively).

The elimination final was played at the South Leeds Stadium on Sunday between Hunslet (fifth) and Workington Town (sixth). For the loser of this match, there would be no second chance. The winner would remain in the competition but, at some stage, would need to win (away from home) at each of Oldham, Newcastle and Doncaster in order to secure promotion: a tall order.

I took my place in the stand after about a minute's play, just as the Workington team was walking back to its half of the field having already registered the game's first try. Hunslet's poor start apparently echoed a theme of their season, as they had won only 4 out of 12 matches at home (excluding the amateur opposition faced in the Challenge Cup), but 8 out of 10 games on their travels. On this occasion, they recovered well and, following two tries by the centre Tom Ashton, the home side had a 24-18 lead at the interval.

But it was the visitors who controlled much of the second half, their experienced forward pack containing three players in their mid to late 30s. One of these was the Tongan, Fuifui Moimoi, whom I had seen play for the Toronto Wolfpack against the Newcastle Thunder at the Allan A Lamport Stadium two years ago (*The Wolfpack and the Cheesy Dog*, 27th August 2017), when he was already well into the veteran stage of a career that has included 10 years at the highest level in Australia's NRL. On Sunday, he was employed – very effectively – in short stretches, his strong running with the ball helping to keep Workington on the front foot. It was a useful contribution from someone who will celebrate his 40th birthday next week.

Hunslet came close to adding to their score in the second half, but a combination of over-eagerness and careless errors near the Workington try-line – including, on one occasion, dropping the ball when actually over the line – prevented them from doing so. Workington completed a 32-24 victory in an entertaining match. (One point that struck me was the excellence of the two goalkickers – Joe Sanderson and Carl Forber – who, between them, were successful with 10 attempts out of 11, many from wide out near the touchline).

Their win has earned Workington a place in the next round of the play-offs at the weekend, when Fuifui Moimoi will be able to resume the battle with Newcastle Thunder that he enjoyed in downtown Toronto.

For Hunslet, defeat in last Sunday's "elimination final" does indeed mean elimination from this year's competitive action. Their 2019 season is over.

www.anordinaryspectator.com/news-blog September 2019

# Cricket

# In the Stars?

*Cassius*
*... Men at some time are masters of their fates.*
*The fault, dear Brutus, is not in our stars*
*But in ourselves...*

*Julius Caesar*, William Shakespeare, Act 1 Scene 2.

It is probably reasonable to assume that I am now unlikely to be selected to play test cricket for England. Quite apart from not having picked up a bat in anger for over 30 years, my age is now well beyond that of the oldest player to play test cricket – Wilfred Rhodes of Yorkshire and England – who was 52 years and 165 days on the final day of the England-West Indies test match in Kingston, Jamaica, in 1930.

I have consulted the "Births and Deaths: Test Cricketers" section of the *2019 Wisden Cricketers' Almanack* and other sources to examine whether it has been the Fates that somehow decreed that I would not be a test cricketer. Was there something in my name or place of birth or date of birth that somehow conspired against such an outcome? Was there something in the stars?

I think we can rule out place of birth. Given the contribution of God's Own County to test cricket over nearly 150 years, one can justifiably state that being born and brought up in its principal city of Leeds will not have presented an insurmountable handicap to receiving a good cricketing education. Whilst, if truth be told, Leeds has probably under-performed in terms of generating Yorkshire's international cricketers – compared with, say, the mining communities of South Yorkshire or the major West Riding nurseries such as Bradford and Huddersfield – the city's roll-call over the years does include the likes of the Honourable FS Jackson, Hedley Verity and Geoff Cope.

What about the surname? Do the gods conspire to prevent a Rigg from playing test cricket? Clearly not. Keith Rigg (1906-1995) played in 8 tests for Australia in the 1930s, scoring 401 runs at an average of 33 and with a top score of 127 against South Africa in 1931. My tentative researches suggest that his great grandparents were William and Louisa Rigg (nee Clark), who married in Newington, Surrey, in 1837 and subsequently emigrated to Australia, where they settled in Victoria. (I have not found any direct family link to my North Yorkshire ancestors).

If not the surname, perhaps the given names: John Alexander? Again, there are examples to indicate that these have also not been a barrier: Jameson and Maclean (4 tests for England and Australia, respectively, in the 1970s) and Rennie (4 for Zimbabwe in the 1990s). I think we can also reasonably add John Alexander Kennedy Cochran (1 for South Africa in 1930), though probably not Alexander John Bell (48 wickets in 16 tests for South Africa between 1929 and 1935).

John Jameson was an aggressive, hard-hitting batsman, who scored over 18,000 runs for Warwickshire between 1960 and 1976. I saw him play against Cambridge University at Fenner's in 1975, when I was on twelfth man duty for the students' side. For some reason, the first day's play started a couple of minutes before the scheduled time, when Jameson went out to bat with Dennis Amiss. The first ball was a gentle swinging full-toss from Dave Russell – a good bloke, as I recall – which Jameson sliced straight into the hands of cover point. I remember that, as he walked back to the pavilion, the expression of his face seemed (justifiably in the circumstances) to comprise a combination of fury and sheepishness, his mood probably not helped by the fact that the clock had not yet registered 11.30. (Later in the afternoon, I took the field for a few minutes when Peter Roebuck went off to answer a call of nature: my first – and only – appearance on a First Class cricket arena. Amiss hit one shot past me for a couple of runs on his way to scoring 123).

That leaves the timing of birth. Has my presence in Scorpio's part of the astrological charts – specifically, November 16th – been a factor in explaining my lack of test match prowess?

*Wisden* lists the dates of birth of the nearly 3000 cricketers who have reached test match level (from 1876 to January 2019). Other things equal, one would expect just over 8 to have been born on any given day of the year. The score for November 16th is below this average: 6. Of these, the best known (to me) are Waqar Younis (born 1971), who took 373 wickets for Pakistan in 87 test matches between 1989 and 2002 and the Huddersfield-born Chris Balderstone (1940-2000).

There is a wonderful description in Alec Stewart's autobiography of the formidable reverse-swing fast bowling of Waqar and his Pakistani colleague, Wasim Akram: "They were whizzbang bowlers… making the old ball go round corners at speed… the ultimate test for any batsman". This was certainly the case when I saw Waqar at Headingley in 1992: England collapsed from 270 for 1 to 320 all out and the last six batsmen registered exactly two runs off the bat (though England still managed to win on the fourth day).

Chris Balderstone is mentioned in *Still An Ordinary Spectator* in my account of a visit to Carlisle to watch a football match in October 2016. He had been "one of those talented all-round sportsmen who, before the overlap of the seasons, played two sports at a professional level: cricket in the summer and football in the winter". As a cricketer, Balderstone had considerable success with Leicestershire and played twice for England against the West Indian tourists of 1976. The Chris Balderstone Bar at Carlisle United's Brunton Park ground commemorates the footballer who, having played 117 times for Huddersfield Town, then appeared on 376 occasions for Carlisle United in the ten seasons to 1975.

It is Waqar Younis's long test career that contributes predominantly to the total of 120 test match appearances by the 6 cricketers born on November 16th. The average expected figure for any given day of the year (given that there were 2341 tests played to January 2019) is 141, so again our total is on the low side, though not excessively so.

The overall conclusion of this astrological musing must be that the answer to my non-test match appearance is not in the stars. Cassius was correct: the fault is in ourselves. In my case, this might be summarised as a vulnerability to being trapped leg-before-wicket to a fast straight delivery and/or the tendency to bowl too many long hops with my gentle off-spin.

A final observation, which might be of relevance to mothers-to-be hoping to give birth to a future test-playing cricketer. It seems that the likelihood of such an outcome is substantially above average if the delivery takes place on the 14th day of October.

Which – as it happens – is today's date.

www.anordinaryspectator.com/news-blog October 2019

# Football

# Lest We Forget

In "*Kings, Queens and Poets*" (5th May 2019), I mentioned that, when a young boy studying my mother's football pools coupons at our home in Leeds, I had thought that Heart of Midlothian and Queen of the South were the most romantic names of the clubs in Scotland. That particular blog reported on a visit to watch the latter in Dumfries in an end-of-term relegation battle in last season's Scottish Championship. On Saturday, I caught up with Hearts.

The Wikipedia entry for Hearts states that 16 players from the club enlisted *en masse* in a new volunteer battalion – later to become the 16th Royal Scots – raised by Sir George McCrae in November 1914. They were joined by hundreds of supporters as well as players from other clubs in the initial "Footballers Battalion" of the First World War. The seven first-team players who lost their lives in the conflict are commemorated at the McCrae's Battalion Great War Memorial in Contalmaison and the Heart of Midlothian War Memorial in Haymarket, Edinburgh.

I alighted at Haymarket Station on my way to Tynecastle Park to watch Hearts play St Mirren in the Ladbrokes Scottish Premiership. This was an appropriate weekend for me to see the home side play for the first time: it is 101 years ago today that the guns fell silent.

Hearts have played their home fixtures at this venue since 1886. It is a neat rectangular ground with a capacity of just over 20,000 following the completion of the newly built Main Stand two years ago. The size of the average home crowd – around 16,500 in this league season to date – means that it feels suitably full; on Saturday, the main gaps were in the Roseburn Stand to the right, where the 700 or so St Mirren supporters had not taken up their full allocation of seats.

Even this early in the season – for both teams, this was only the 12th of the 38 matches in the league programme – there was an air of relegation battle about the encounter. The two sides began the day locked together at the foot of the table – with the hosts in the higher place only on goal difference – both no doubt fearing the prospect of a long winter's struggle ahead. (The next two sides above them – St Johnstone and Hibernian – were meeting at the same time).

Hearts had already taken some action to address their poor start to the season by relieving the respected Craig Levein of his managerial responsibilities. This occurred 12 days ago, though the timing was somewhat curious as the side's next fixture had been the Betfred League Cup semi-final against Rangers at Hampden Park (which was subsequently lost). Austin MacPhee is holding the managerial reins for the time being. (Hibernian sacked Paul Heckingbottom as their manager last week).

The St Mirren manager, Jim Goodwin, is – for the time being anyway – probably on slightly safer ground, as he was only appointed last June. (He had been in charge of the Alloa Athletic side that I had seen play in a Scottish Cup fixture last autumn: "Recreation Park", 26th November 2018). Hitherto, his team had revealed a sound defence – only Celtic and Rangers had conceded fewer goals in the Premiership – but serious deficiencies in relation to their attacking prowess: only 5 goals had been registered in the league prior to Saturday's game. I was expecting a low scoring encounter.

But what do I know? There were five goals before half-time and the final score was 5-2 to Hearts. And it could have been more: both the respective goalkeepers – Joel Pereira and Vaclav Hladky – made outstanding diving saves in the closing minutes.

As the scoreline suggests, Hearts had the advantage of a more potent forward line. The man-of-the-match award went to Uche Ikpeazu – a powerful and skilful player – who had a fine game on the right-hand side of the attack. However, I thought that the afternoon's most influential participant was his partner, the experienced Steven Naismith, who swept in the first goal at a corner after six minutes and whose headed flick-on led to the Hearts second after St Mirren had equalised. It was also his weighted pass that provided the space in which Jake Mulraney, the Hearts substitute, could advance and curl his right-footed shot to Hladky's left for the final (and best) goal of the match. More generally, Naismith – who is one short of 50 caps for Scotland – was active throughout the match in cajoling/encouraging/berating/advising (delete as appropriate) his colleagues: it was a timely audition, should Hearts decide to take the player-manager route.

I was flanked in my seat in the Main Stand by two friendly Hearts season-ticket holders. The longstanding supporter to my left had made his regular journey from the Borders town of Lauder. He was concerned about the number of soft goals that Hearts had conceded this season, of which St Mirren's second – when a long punt upfield found the Hearts central defence totally absent, leaving Danny Mullen to calmly stroke the ball past Pereira – seemed to be a good example. Even at 4-2 up with 15 minutes to play, my neighbour was casting nervous glances at his watch, but he was able to relax a little after Mulraney's fine strike.

The conversation with the supporter on the other side revealed an impressive pedigree of sports-spectating, including rugby league in Leeds and soccer in Toronto. He was very knowledgeable about the Hearts players present and past: Jamie Walker is just back from a long injury break and Jake Mulraney is "incredibly fast", whilst Pasquale Bruno – an Italian who played for Hearts for two seasons in the 1990s (and who received loud cheers when he was introduced to the crowd at half-time) – had been a very physical and aggressive player. (Wikipedia somewhat coyly refers to Bruno's "occasional outrageous outbursts on the pitch, as well as his tendency to pick up cards").

The game ended. I shook hands with my neighbours as they departed. On the outside of the stadium, the Hearts badge shone brightly on the Main Stand in the darkness of the late autumn afternoon. The home supporters made their way contentedly down Gorgie Road. Elsewhere, Hibernian's 4-1 win at St Johnstone meant that it had been a double success for the Edinburgh clubs. They are now 8th and 9th in the league with Hamilton Academicals and the two Saints clubs below them. It is still tight, however, and the season's course is only one-third run.[19]

I read the impressive match programme on the train going home. The front cover displayed a field of poppies against a background of the stadium and under the heading "Lest We Forget". Inside, there was a notice complementing an announcement that had been made a couple of times during the afternoon. The annual Haymarket Remembrance Service – conducted by the Club Chaplain and attended by the first team, reserve team and members of the board – was to take place yesterday, beginning at 10.45am.

www.anordinaryspectator.com/news-blog November 2019

# Sport on Television

# Personality Tests

Prior to last Sunday's programme, it had been many years since I had watched the BBC's annual *Sports Personality of the Year*. In my youth and adolescence – when it was called the *Sports Review of the Year* – I considered it to be essential viewing. However, at some point, I realised that it had moved away from being a genuine review programme to one providing coverage of an awards ceremony. There were increased amounts of chat and padding, with many of the action shots being short clips presented in a sort of staccato fast-forward that was difficult (and annoying) to watch.

I recall it as a programme that was very predictable. In summarising the year's rugby league – to give one parochial example – the tribute invariably consisted simply of the two Challenge Cup final teams walking out at Wembley, that game's decisive try and footage of a punch-up between some (unnamed) players accompanied by Eddie Waring stating that someone might be going for an early bath. My father and I regarded this as a meagre reward for the significant number of hours of live sport that the code had provided (along with the horse racing) to the Saturday afternoon editions of *Grandstand* through the long winter months.

In most years, the programme's predictability was also reflected in the viewing public's choice (through a popular vote) for the Sports Personality of the Year. Not surprisingly, given the BBC's domination of sports presentation in the pre-satellite era – and the huge viewing figures that were attracted – there were clear winners in those years in which there were significant achievements in those sports with weighty coverage: for example, football (Bobby Moore in 1966), cricket (Ian Botham in 1981) and motor racing (Jackie Stewart in 1973). In addition, the BBC's Olympic Games coverage – and Britain's ability to conjure up some success even in the relative barren years – meant that gold medallists were regularly rewarded. Indeed, an Olympian came top of the poll in every such year between 1960 (David Broome) and 1984 (Jayne Torvill and Christopher Dean) and again between 2000 and 2008.

Not surprisingly, the method of voting has changed with the times. The original system of deciding the winner of the main prize via a free-for-all vote on postcard (over several weeks) has evolved into the current arrangement of a telephone/on-line vote (on the night of the ceremony) for the contenders on a pre-announced shortlist selected by an "expert panel". On Sunday, the contenders were Ben Stokes (cricket), Lewis Hamilton (motor racing), Dina Asher-Smith and Katarina Johnson-Thompson (athletics), Raheem Sterling (football) and Alun Wyn Jones (rugby union).

Although Stokes had been the clear favourite to win (due to his outstanding performances in the cricket World Cup final and the third Ashes test against Australia at Headingley), it was perhaps still some achievement for him to do so, given his sport's limited exposure on the non-satellite channels (and complete absence from the BBC). Moreover, prior to this year, cricket had provided only 4 winners since the programme started in 1954, compared with 18 in athletics; Andrew Flintoff was its last success in 2005.

Rather bizarrely, Gary Lineker – one of the (three) presenters – referred to Stokes as the "main award winner" before the voting had even started. I assume this was an inadvertent slip of the tongue rather than, as the conspiracy theorists have been quick to suggest on social media, evidence of an election "fix".

In its earlier incarnation, the *Sports Review of the Year* had 3 prizes of offer, the others being for the Team of the Year and the Overseas Sports Personality of the Year. This list now extends to 9, including the Helen Rollason Award for "outstanding achievement in the face of adversity" (this year given to Doddie Weir, the former Scottish rugby union international, who is battling motor neurone disease).

This year's Team of the Year award must have been quite difficult to decide, given the respective successes of Liverpool FC (Champions League), the England cricket team (World Cup) and the Wales rugby union team (Grand Slam winners) and the performance of the England rugby union side (World Cup runners-up). The current edition of the *Radio Times* suggests that the England Women's football team "must be strong contenders"; this for a side that failed to reach the final of the World Cup and which, following its semi-final defeat to the USA, won only one of its next six matches.

The prize was given to the England cricketers: a worthy choice though, had foreign teams been eligible, my selection would have another rugby union side – Japan – for its unexpectedly exhilarating play in the group stages of the World Cup, when they accounted for both Ireland and Scotland.

The choice of Overseas Personality (now called the World Sports Personality) was the Kenyan marathon runner, Eliud Kipchoge, who became the first man to complete the distance in under two hours (in Vienna in November).

This would not have been my choice. Whilst there is no doubt about the extraordinary levels of endurance and stamina that were needed to achieve this feat – I cannot imagine what is required to run at an average pace of 13 mph for two hours – I am not convinced that its attainment meets the criteria of a sporting contest. Kipchoge benefited from pace-makers (in vehicles and teams of runners) and a type of footwear that (I understand) is subject to some controversy. The International Association of Athletics Federations' (IAAF) official world marathon record remains at the 2 hours 1 minute 39 seconds set in Berlin in 2018 – by Eliud Kipchoge.

For what it's worth, my selection would have been either the Australian batsman Steve Smith for his Bradman-esque scoring feats in this year's Ashes series – which more or less guaranteed his side would retain the urn (notwithstanding Stokes's efforts at Headingley) – or the brilliant American gymnast Simone Biles, who extended her record of World Championships successes with a breath-taking repertoire of apparently gravity-defying routines. (In the programme, Biles received one brief name-check and Smith was not mentioned at all).

I shan't list all the award winners, except to note that the year's "Greatest Sporting Moment" was judged to have been the last-ball run-out that gave the England cricket team their World Cup final win over New Zealand. Three prizes for the cricketers, then. I wonder if the broadcaster noticed the irony of this, though Lineker did refer lamely to "live cricket" – he could have said "any cricket" – "returning to the BBC next year with the Hundred" competition.

The *Sports Personality of the Year* programme has a tasteful "In Memoriam" sequence – which I do not recall being present in my earlier watching – which, like its counterparts at the Oscars or the BAFTAs, causes us to reflect on the loss of some of the prominent participants of previous times. It was appropriate to remember the likes of Gordon Banks, Niki Lauda and Bob Willis. The programme's producers also did well to extend this coverage to include non-players such as the journalist Hugh McIlvanney and to remember that it not only the long-retired who have passed on. Sport itself produces casualties in active competition: in the last 12 months, these have included the American boxer Patrick Day at the age of 27 (who was included in the roll-call) and the Belgian cyclist Antoine Demoitie (aged 25).

Returning to my earlier (parochial) theme, the programme's rugby league coverage comprised half a dozen photographs in the "In Memoriam" sequence and a total of seven seconds of action (three tries in the Super League Grand Final and the men's and women's Challenge Cup finals) in one of the breathless round-ups of the year's events. But there were no references to punch-ups or early baths.

In general, I think *Sports Personality of the Year* was more or less what I had expected. It covered a glitzy sports awards ceremony with contributions from dancers, high profile pop singers (Lewis Capaldi and Emili Sandé), royalty (the Princess Royal) and, coming from Aberdeen, a local-born sporting hero (Denis Law). It was a flagship BBC presentation and, therefore, had a recurrent undertone of worthiness, its collateral themes including racism, physical disability, mental health and social deprivation. But that's fine. This is society – and sport is part of society.

www.anordinaryspectator.com/news-blog December 2019

Football

# Degrees of Latitude

In the current season's fixture lists of the Scottish Professional Football League (SPFL), the League 2 encounter between Annan Athletic (54.99 degrees north) and Elgin City (57.65 degrees) represents the one with the widest latitudinal difference between the respective teams' home grounds. The position would change if Elgin were to play Stranraer (54.90 degrees) but, for this season at least, the latter are plying their trade in League 1. (My reference source obviously prefers the decimal presentation, rather than the traditional one of degrees, minutes and seconds).

This is probably taking us into pub quiz territory, but it is interesting (perhaps) to note that the furthest north of the football clubs in England (in the top four divisions) – Newcastle United, 55.00 degrees – is closer to the North Pole than is the southernmost one in Scotland (Stranraer). In England, the latitudinal gap between north and south – 4.61 degrees from Newcastle's St James's Park to the Home Park ground of Plymouth Argyle – is larger than the 2.75 degrees in Scotland.

So much for the somewhat nerdish rationale for going to watch Annan Athletic play Elgin City at the Galabank riverside stadium yesterday.

In League 2, the divisional winners will gain automatic promotion and, as things currently stand, this looks to be a straight shoot-out between Cove Rangers and Edinburgh City, who have a commanding lead at the top of the table. The teams finishing between second and fourth will play off with the second-bottom League 1 side for the second promotion place. Prior to yesterday's game, Annan were fourth and Elgin were sixth, so there was certainly something to play for.

The day was one of grey skies, persistent – occasionally heavy – rain and a gusty wind. After a two-hour train ride from Glasgow, the first sight that greeted me on alighting at Annan was the ruined Central Hotel, with its broken and boarded windows and burned out interior: a sorry introduction to the town. The large sandstone Victorian buildings – many of which are now guesthouses – on the adjacent St John's Road give an indication of a once more prosperous era.

The rain having eased slightly, I took a short walk through the town to take in a riverside view of the three-arched Annan Bridge (designed by Robert Stevenson in the 1820s), the Town Hall (1878) with its bulbous clock tower fronted by a statue of Robert the Bruce and the remains of the Mote of Annan, the twelfth century motte and bailey castle that was the seat of the de Brus family until they moved this further north to Lochmaben Castle. A broad trench separates the mote itself from the base court and I walked up the muddy path to the top of the latter. The site has a commanding position next to the nearby river and, with a little imagination, it is not difficult to envisage being located at the centre of the medieval stronghold.

I was safely under cover in the Galabank ground's main stand when the match kicked off and the next heavy downpour began, the rain driving into the faces of the Elgin defenders. Although the early stages of the match were evenly contested, it soon became clear that the visitors had the more efficient passing game as they looked to exploit the pace down the flanks of the left winger, Connor O'Keefe, and the overlapping runs of the right back, Rory MacEwan. The latter, in particular, was composed on the ball and accurate with his passing and looked to be a player of some promise. By contrast, Annan relied largely on pumping the ball forward to their tall centre forward, Russell Currie.

As half-time approached, it looked to have been Currie who had created the opening period's best chance when, after a smart turn and a strong run, he unleashed a powerful shot that was well saved by the Elgin goalkeeper, Thomas McHale. However, just before the interval, another neat Elgin passing move produced an opportunity for Kane Hester to run through and stroke the ball into the Annan net. The keen home supporters seated nearby – including the middle-aged man in his team's sweatshirt and woolly hat and the stocky 20-something lad next to me who was kicking every ball and making every tackle – perhaps sensed that this was not going to be their afternoon.

And that turned out to be the case. With the wind at their backs during another long and heavy downpour, Elgin dominated the second half and registered three more goals to win the match 4-0. The result moves them up to fifth place in the league table and, although Annan are still fourth, I would suggest that it is Elgin who are the more likely contenders for the promotion play-offs.[20]

The hospitality at the Annan club was friendly. I took shelter in the clubhouse before the match and retired there afterwards for a pint before making my way back to the station. The MC at the game thanked the crowd – 211 in total – for attending in such miserable weather and hoped that they would support their local team at next week's fixture at home to Stirling Albion. I have no doubt that the Annan-kitted man and his younger colleague will be there.

On the train, I chatted briefly to an Elgin City supporter. He was about my age and readily identifiable in his scarf with its thick black and white stripes. He was intending to rush from Central Station up to the Buchanan Street bus station to catch the coach to Edinburgh, where he lived. "Every home match is a marathon", he said. They are of a kind, these supporters of lower league football clubs – keen, loyal, admirable, slightly mad – in whichever league their team plays.

Towards the end of the match, the scoring having been completed, another neighbour in the stand had speculated on what his own preference might be: a 4-0 win followed by a return journey of several hours; or a 0-4 loss and a half-mile walk home for his tea. I suspect that the Elgin City supporters would have emphatically opted for the former. They had had a good day.

And so had I. I had visited a town that I had not been to before and watched two unfamiliar football teams. And, at the remains of the Mote of Annan, I had inhabited the space from which the de Brus family – the Lords of Annandale – had overseen their domain over seven centuries ago.

www.anordinaryspectator.com/news-blog January 2020

Rugby Union/Rugby League

# From RM Kinnear to the Super 6

This season the Scottish Rugby Union (SRU) has introduced a new competition – the Super 6 – for elite clubs. As the name suggests, franchises have been given (for 5 years) to half a dozen clubs to play in their own league at a semi-professional level. The principal aim is to create a "pathway" for players to progress from the highest level of amateur club rugby in Scotland (the Premiership) to the two full-time professional teams in Glasgow and Edinburgh. At the end of the regular season, when the sides will have played each other twice, a play-off phase will decide the competition's overall winners.

It is probably reasonable to state that the administration of club rugby in Scotland has traditionally tended towards the conservative. Accordingly, the new structure has not been without its critics, not least because three of the six selected clubs are in Edinburgh and none in Glasgow. On Saturday, I watched two of them in action, when Heriot's Rugby played the Boroughmuir Bears.

The scrutiny of my collection of match programmes revealed that the last occasions on which I had seen these teams in action (in their previous guises) had been as long ago as November 2009 (Boroughmuir RFC) and October 2010 (Heriot's FP) on their respective visits to the Burnbrae ground in Milngavie to play West of Scotland. Unfortunately, since then, the West club's star has been on the wane; it now competes in National League Division 3, the fourth tier in the Scottish hierarchy (excluding the Super 6 level).

My contact with Heriot's had been more recent, however. In 2018, when preparing a couple of articles for the *Rugby League Journal* on players who had played for both the British Lions (rugby union) and Great Britain (rugby league) – "Double Lions", of whom there have only ever been 16 in total – I contacted the Administration and Events Manager, Shona Whyte, to enquire about the club's perspective on RM (Roy Muir) Kinnear, who won 3 caps for Scotland nearly a century ago.

Roy Kinnear had an extraordinary rugby career. After playing for the British Lions in South Africa (as a 20 year-old in 1924) and Scotland (in 1926), he turned professional with the Wigan rugby league club. He subsequently played in the first Challenge Cup final to be held at Wembley (against Dewsbury in 1929, when he scored a try) and for Great Britain in a test match against Australia at Hull in the same year. He was the first "Double Lion".

Ms Whyte had pointed me in the direction of the official history of the Heriot's Rugby Club, published to commemorate the 125th anniversary in 2017, which noted of Kinnear that: "[H]is loss was a severe blow… [T]he rugby club committee felt obliged to seek his resignation as a member of Heriot's, which was duly received". Thankfully, the rift does not appear to have been permanent, as the official history also states that Kinnear "re-enters the Heriot's story some years later".

Roy Kinnear died at the age of 38 in 1942 when he collapsed during a Services rugby match. He is commemorated on the War Memorial at Murrayfield, alongside other Scottish international rugby players (including Eric Liddell). His son, also Roy Kinnear, was a distinguished actor, as is his grandson, Rory Kinnear.

Heriot's and Boroughmuir entered Saturday's contest having had mixed fortunes in the Super 6 to date. The former had won 5 of their 7 matches to stand in third place (behind the Ayrshire Bulls on points difference) with the third Edinburgh side, Watsonians, leading the table. By contrast, the visitors had won only one of their games – at home to Heriot's, as it happened, last November.

The walk from Waverley Station to the Heriot's sports fields at Goldenacre took me through Edinburgh's New Town, the first part of which was set out by James Craig in the 1760s. The names of the streets echo with the confirmation of Hanoverian hegemony in the post-Culloden era: George Street, Queen Street, Cumberland Street, Great King Street… At the ground, from the concrete terrace behind the posts at one end, there is a fine view of the city skyline in the middle distance: Arthur's Seat, the tower of the Balmoral Hotel, the Scott Monument… On this side of town are the playing fields of the famous public schools including, just down the road, the Edinburgh Academical club's ground at Raeburn Place, where the first rugby international – Scotland versus England – was played in March 1871.

On this particular playing field, Heriot's were too strong for Boroughmuir. The opening try was scored after only a couple of minutes and quickly followed by two more. The visitors' most threatening period of play, when the score was 3-15 against them, saw Boroughmuir mount a prolonged attack on the Heriot's line, but a loose pass was intercepted and the hosts were able to break quickly downfield. Their fourth try was scored shortly afterwards. The final score was 53-10.

I am not able to judge whether this Super 6 contest satisfied the SRU's objective of providing a stepping stone on the pathway from amateur to professional rugby. It was clear, however, that both sides had an open style of play that made for an entertaining contest. The Heriot's half backs – Andrew Simmers and Ross Jones – were particularly adept at providing the swift transfer of the ball to their outside backs, whilst the Number 8 forward, Jason Hill, was at the forefront of securing a steady stream of possession.

During the second half, as Heriot's racked up the points and the earlier accuracy of the teams' play was disrupted by the wholesale introduction of new players from the respective replacement benches, I took a walk down the far touchline. On the adjacent pitch, another Heriot's team was engaged in a match that seemed to be more closely contested. I fell into conversation with a gentleman from Biggar, who informed me that this was the Heriot's Blues 2$^{nd}$ XV – effectively the third team – who were playing Hawick's 2$^{nd}$ XV. Meanwhile, he said, the Heriot's Blues 1$^{st}$ XV was playing in a Scottish Cup tie away at Gala RFC.

During the course of our chat, I mentioned that I was intending to visit Leeds next weekend to take in a couple of games at the start of the new Super League season, noting that the Castleford Tigers and Leeds Rhinos were two of the sides on my watch list. More or less spontaneously, the man offered his views on the coaching abilities of Gary Mercer – the New Zealander who was a former player and/or coach with both those clubs – who had also held the reins at the Biggar rugby union club for three seasons. Such are the interweaving strands of the rugby spectating network.

My other conversation at Heriot's was with Shona Whyte. I introduced myself to her at half-time, in the ground floor room of the impressive two-storey clubhouse, when the final tidying up after a clearly well-patronised pre-match luncheon was taking place. She mentioned that perhaps three or four players in the Heriot's team had attended the school, but that it was generally difficult to retain playing contacts with ex-pupils once they had left the area for university or other reasons. I thanked her again for the assistance she had given me on the *Journal* article.

On display in both the sizeable rooms in the clubhouse is a plethora of items commemorating the history of the Heriot's rugby club: trophies, jerseys, programmes, and so on. It is an impressive collection. The team photographs of the George Heriot's School First XV date back to before the First World War, whilst those of each year's Heriot's FP team are all meticulously named and dated. Each of the club's former international players has his individual picture on the wall. RM Kinnear duly takes his place in this proud line-up.

For those charged with managing the current entity that is Heriot's Rugby, there is a double-edged challenge: to respect the traditions of the club that have evolved over a century and a quarter; and to deal with the requirements of the next phase of the professional era, with its sponsorship and social media and pathways. Tradition and professionalism: a tension that Roy Kinnear would have fully appreciated.

www.anordinaryspectator.com/news-blog January 2020

# Rugby Union

# Arresting Decline

The Yorkshire Carnegie rugby side are *en route* to being relegated from the Greene King IPA Championship – the second tier of the club hierarchy in England – at the end of this season. Prior to last Friday's home match with Nottingham Rugby, they had registered only one point in the league table, having played 10 of their 22 scheduled fixtures. As the bottom side will go down – and the next-placed sides, Nottingham and the Bedford Blues, had 17 points – it is clear that their fate is close to being sealed.

The club's difficulties began before the season started with budget cut-backs, the move to part-time contracts, player and coaching departures and the resignation from the Board of the Executive President, Sir Ian McGeechan. As the mid-season approached, the union and league representatives of the parent club – Yorkshire Carnegie are based at Headingley, the home of the Leeds Rhinos RLFC – made public their various accusations and counter-accusations, providing further evidence that all was not well (if not in the state of Denmark, then at least in the LS6 postcode). Last month Joe Ford, who had taken on the player-coach role in August, became the latest to leave the club. Phil Davies, the former Wales international, has returned as Director of Rugby, having previously held the post for the 10 years to 2006.

Friday's game followed the expected pattern. Nottingham had already made one clean break through the middle of the Yorkshire Carnegie defence before their next effort led to a try for the left-wing Jack Spittle after five minutes. Shortly afterwards, a set-play move from an attacking line-out – involving the swift movement of the ball from left to right and then a change in the point of attack with an inside pass – produced another huge gap in the Yorkshire Carnegie defence from which Spittle again profited. Worse was to follow for the home side a few minutes later, when the identical set-play generated an identical outcome. It has to be said that succumbing twice to the same (fairly routine) attacking move reflected poorly on the home side's on-field organisation.

Yorkshire Carnegie did have some possession in the first half, but they found it much more difficult to generate any forward momentum; the Nottingham defence was accurate and aggressive. After the interval, Yorkshire Carnegie had the further disadvantage of being overwhelmed in the set scrum which, allied to Nottingham's 100% return from their own line-out throws, made for a consistent flow of one-way traffic. The final score in the visitors' favour was 62-10.

I'm not sure if there was a formal man-of-the-match award but, had there been, I assume it would have gone to Spittle, who ended the match with five tries. The most spectacular was his fourth, which began with a Yorkshire Carnegie penalty kick to touch which was tapped back into play by a Nottingham player. Spittle retrieved the ball behind his own try line and set off down his wing in front of the South Stand outmanoeuvring and then outpacing the Yorkshire Carnegie tacklers before touching down at the far end.

Over the years, I have seen some fine tries scored by some wonderful wing three-quarters sprinting down that touchline, beginning with Alan Smith and John Atkinson in the great Leeds rugby league team of the 1960s. The efforts of those two players were always accompanied by roars of encouragement from their (hugely biased) supporters crammed together on the adjacent terracing. By contrast, on this occasion, the backdrop to Spittle's effort was an empty stand, as the spectating areas – catering for a few hundred, at most – were restricted to the comfortable padded seats in the North Stand or the lower terracing behind the posts at what used to be called the St Michael's Lane end.

For those involved with the Yorkshire Carnegie club, there might seem to be little in the way of immediate consolation. However, one vignette did suggest otherwise. In the dying minutes of the match, when Nottingham were again pummelling at the home side's try line, it looked as if one of their sturdy replacement forwards was about to barrel his way over for a score under the posts. He was halted by a brave last-ditch tackle by a couple of the young Yorkshire Carnegie defenders – I did not catch which ones – and the attack was repulsed. Their side may have conceded 10 tries, but they were doing their level best to prevent number 11. Their side might effectively be in the wrong league, but they were keeping going.

As with most sporting league structures, the rugby union club hierarchy is a flawed meritocracy. Whilst the differences in resources mean that it is not a "level playing field" – even within any given tier – there are rewards for success and penalties for failure. For Yorkshire Carnegie in its current state, it is the latter which is of potential concern – and not only for this season. Evidence suggests that there is the risk that a season of chronically poor results can lead to a process of decline that is cumulative and long-lasting.

To give one example, Manchester Rugby Club was in the Championship (then called the National Division 1) as recently as the 2008-09 season. It won only two of its 30 league fixtures in that campaign and none at all in the next two years, as it underwent a total of 5 consecutive relegations to the South Lancs/Cheshire league, the 7th tier in the system. At that point (in 2013-14) things were stabilised and, following a subsequent promotion and relegation, the club remains at the same level (in what is now the Lancashire/Cheshire 1 Division).

In the circumstances faced by clubs in such precipitate decline, there is no respect for tradition. Manchester is the oldest club in continual existence in England (having been established in 1860) and the provider of 60 international players in its history (including 9 in the post-war period).

The Yorkshire Carnegie club effectively dates from 1992 when the Headingley and Roundhay clubs were merged to form Leeds RUFC. (Its most recent re-branding dates from 2014). It has had some modest success, including Premiership status in 8 of the seasons between 2002 and 2011 and winning the RFU's national knock-out trophy (the PowerGen Cup) in 2005. However, it is a cliched truism that, when one medium-sized rugby club merges with another medium-sized rugby club, the end result is a medium-sized rugby club.

I remember the Headingley and Roundhay clubs – formed in 1878 and 1924, respectively – as vibrant entities with close community links and established relationships with local schools and, especially, a fierce rivalry. But they are long gone. Let us hope that Phil Davies and his staff manage to arrest the decline of Yorkshire Carnegie by avoiding a Manchester-type free-fall and, in the years ahead, continuing to provide the city of Leeds with – at least – a medium-sized rugby union club.[21]

www.anordinaryspectator.com/news-blog February 2020

An Ordinary Spectator
Top: Allan A Lamport Stadium, Toronto, 2017
Bottom: Shielfield Park, Berwick, 2019

Match programmes as social documents
Top: "The Parksider", Hunslet versus Castleford, 1946
Middle: The first London Marathon, 1981
Bottom: Glasgow Rangers vs Leeds United, 1992

The arena
Top: The Etihad Stadium, Manchester, 2017
Middle: Millom RLFC, Cumbria, 2019
Bottom: Scarborough CC – my favourite cricket ground – 2021

Before and After – Shinty in the Highlands, 2019
Top: Pre-match presentations
Bottom: The final score between the local rivals

Local Heroes – 1
Top: Robert Enke, Hannover
Middle: Gus Risman, Workington
Bottom: The Scottish Rugby Union War
Memorial, Murrayfield

Local Heroes – 2
Top: Robert Burns, Dumfries
Middle: Colin Telfer's "The Scrutcher", Millom
Bottom: The Black Prince in Leeds City Square during the 2018 World Cup

Souvenirs
Top: Olympic rings, Moscow, 1980
Bottom: Coffee mugs from near and far

The author at the Morley Book Festival, 2018

# Rugby Union

# "Let's Keep It Up, Otley"

In the hierarchy of English club rugby, the division below the Premiership and the Championship – i.e. the third tier – is now called the National League 1. Below that, logically enough, is the National League 2, which is divided into North and South sections. On Saturday, the day after the Yorkshire Carnegie/Nottingham Rugby match in the Championship (*"Arresting Decline"*, 5th February 2020), I went to watch the lower league's northern encounter between Otley RUFC and Caldy RFC.

The Otley club was founded in 1865 and – I was surprised to learn from Wikipedia – actually played rugby league for 6 seasons from 1900. It reverted back to rugby union in 1907 and moved to its current Cross Green ground in 1921. There are plans afoot for a new stadium a little way along the main road to Pool.

It had been over half a century since I had watched a rugby match on this ground: the Yorkshire Cup final between Roundhay and Wakefield on a Monday evening in April 1969. I recall that that had been – as with all matches between the leading Yorkshire clubs – an intensely ferocious affair. However, what set the match apart – not only as a rugby union game, but for any sporting contest at that time – was that it was settled in sudden-death extra time. The Wakefield full-back, a large bearded player called Chris Parkes, kicked a long-range penalty goal to give his side the trophy.

Since then, my only other visit to the sports fields at Cross Green had been to the adjacent Otley CC in 1974, when I played for a season in the First XI of the North Leeds CC in the Airedale and Wharfedale Cricket League. Our hosts had a strong side and they won the title that year. However, if my memory is correct, the record books will show that, in the North Leeds innings, I took part in a (rather slow) half-century opening stand. (I appreciate that this is something of a minor aside but, for me, this was a rare success in a season of generally low scores).

Such are my rather tenuous connections with the sports teams of Otley.

There are 16 teams in the National League 2 North, of which three will be relegated at the end of the season. This is promising to be a close-run affair. Prior to Saturday's round of matches – when most clubs had 10 fixtures remaining – the bottom club Scunthorpe were well adrift (with 6 league points) and the next bottom (Preston Grasshoppers, 29 points) nearly so. However, there were only 9 points separating the 14th placed team (Luctonians with 43) from the side in 6th place (Sheffield Tigers with 52). Otley also had 43 points, narrowly above Luctonians on points difference. There are 4 points for a win, plus the scope for bonus points.

For Caldy, the season is shaping up in a different way. Having won all 19 of their league matches to date and with a 12-point lead at the top of the table – and a game in hand on their nearest rivals, Fylde – the Wirral-based side have their sights firmly set on securing the single automatic promotion place back to the National League 1 following their relegation last season. It looked a tall order for Otley, therefore, not least because Caldy had notched up a half century of points in the reverse fixture in October.

Otley had much of the early possession and the centre, Gavin Stead, made good progress with a couple of threatening runs. The Caldy defence was well organised, however, and when their turn came to attack, some swift and accurate passing enabled the left-wing, Ben Jones, to score in the corner. (It was turning into a good weekend for wearers of the number 11 shirt; his counterpart, Jack Spittle, had scored five tries for Nottingham Rugby against Yorkshire Carnegie the evening before).

Unlike the facilities at Headingley, those at Cross Green have a more "traditional" feel; the seating in the stand comprises wooden benches painted black and white (in contrast with the padded seats of the former's North Stand). However, they constituted a perfectly serviceable vantage point, not least in giving some respite from a cold, blustery wind. The Otley club also offered an impressive match programme and an informative – though not exactly unbiased – MC to keep us up to date with the game's progress. When – after Caldy had run up a 17-0 lead – the home side scored their first try, it was confirmed that it had been "after a superb bit of play". "Let's keep it up, Otley" was the immediate follow-up.

The half-time score of 17-7 remained unchanged until mid-way through the second half when back-to-back Caldy tries stretched out the score-line to one that was somewhat unfair to the home side. When both sides made the customary changes from their respective replacement benches, two of the Otley entrants wore the same number shirt. We were informed that the departing players had been "replaced by two Number 18s. I don't think anyone spotted that". "Oh, yes, we did" came the murmured chorus in reply. Otley's persistent efforts as the final whistle approached were rewarded with their second try, through Owen Dudman, which left the final tally at 31-12 in Caldy's favour.

The MC was magnanimous in his post-match announcement and, whilst his assessment of the season's likely outcome is slightly premature, I would be surprised if it is not also accurate: "Well played, Caldy. We wish you all the best next season after your promotion". He followed this, nicely, with "Well played, Otley".[22]

The Otley clubhouse is somewhat less grand than the previous one I had been in – at the Heriot's Rugby ground at Goldenacre in Edinburgh the week before (*"From RM Kinnear to the Super 6"*, 27th January 2020) – but it serves the same functions: a communal meeting place, a place of refreshment, the location for the memorabilia of the club's proud history. (It was on this ground, in 1979, that a Northern Division team led by Bill Beaumont registered a famous win over the All Blacks). On one of the shelves – alongside the collection of jerseys and match programmes and photographs – was an England cap that Arthur Gray of Otley RUFC had won in 1947, when he played three times for his country.

The first rugby (league) match in which I ever played was in Leeds for the Chapel Allerton Primary School against Alwoodley Primary School "B" team in 1965. I played at centre three-quarter and got punched on the nose for my trouble. In the review of the school matches for the Green Post edition of the *Yorkshire Evening Post*, I was reported as having provided "sound support" for our full-back and captain, Martin Gray. Martin – a good lad and a fine all-round games player in his own right – came from a distinguished rugby heritage: his father was Arthur Gray.

Did I mention that my connections with the sports teams of Otley were rather tenuous?

www.anordinaryspectator.com/news-blog February 2020

Rugby League

# The Return of Sonny Bill

The upward trajectory of the Toronto Wolfpack rugby league club – which has hitherto involved three seasons in the lower leagues – has now taken it into the Betfred Super League, the premier division of the game in Britain. I sense that views on this within the sport are divided: some welcome the broadening of rugby league's horizons and the other opportunities that might be presented in North America; others would prefer to consolidate within the traditional heartlands of the north of England and – I suspect, at the extreme – would be quite content for Wigan to play St Helens or Warrington every other week. I am firmly in the former camp.

The Toronto climate being what it is, the club is obliged to play the first few matches of the new season away from their base at the Lamport Stadium. Their first match in Toronto will not be until the visit of Hull FC in the middle of April. The opening fixture – last Sunday – was against the Castleford Tigers at Headingley as part of a double-header that also saw the Leeds Rhinos take on Hull (afterwards, not at the same time!).

As if the entry of a Canada-based team into a British sporting competition were not newsworthy enough, the Toronto Wolfpack club has raised the promotional stakes several further notches through the high-profile signing of the former All Blacks rugby union player, Sonny Bill Williams.

SBW started – in rugby league – in 2004 at the age of 18 with the Canterbury Bulldogs in Australia's National Rugby League. Four years later, he moved on France to play rugby union for Toulon. Since 2010, he has played for various union sides, mainly in New Zealand though also in Japan, interspersed with two seasons back in the NRL with the Sydney Roosters. His international appearances for New Zealand have been at both league (World Cup runner-up) and union (twice a World Cup winner). In addition, he has fought in (and won) 7 bouts of professional boxing (including for the New Zealand heavyweight title).

At the age of 34, it is reasonable to assume that SBW is approaching the end of his distinguished career: 16 years in professional rugby will have taken its toll and he has been far from injury-free during that time. Nonetheless, his acquisition by Toronto is a major coup – albeit an expensive one – which is generally recognised to have given a major shot in the arm not only to the Super League entrants, but to the sport as a whole. It is certainly one of the reasons I turned up at Headingley on Sunday.

Toronto took the field to polite applause from the near-capacity crowd. In their match-day squad, they fielded 5 players who had featured in the corresponding group for the League 1 encounter against Newcastle Thunder that I had seen at the Lamport Stadium in August 2017 and it was one of these – the winger, Liam Kay – who registered their first Super League points with an early try following a neat kick through by Hakim Miloudi. Miloudi – along with his fellow centre three-quarter Ricky Leutele – had a strong game and was rewarded with a long-range interception try late in the match. Another of the survivors from the Newcastle game – the Australian Blake Wallace – played soundly at full-back.

However, Toronto were generally second-best to Castleford, whose strong-running forwards provided the creative platform for the half-backs Jake Trueman and Danny Richardson to exploit. Castleford were also sharper around the play-the-ball, where the experienced Paul McShane ensured a strong momentum to the play. Toronto relied heavily on the distributional skills of the former St Helens veteran Jon Wilkin, but he was closely targeted by the Castleford defenders and several of his passes were rushed and misdirected. It was one of these, during another promising Toronto attack following Kay's try, that was picked off by the Castleford winger, Greg Eden, for an 80 metre run to the try-line.

Sonny Bill Williams made his keenly anticipated entrance from the replacements bench after 25 minutes. His first contribution to the match was to drop a pass. Thereafter, he had a generally quiet game, attempting without success to create something from his characteristic overloads in the tackle. He moved into midfield to play a more central role after Wilkin had been substituted but, by then, Castleford were coasting on their 22-4 half-time lead and the result of the match was not in doubt. The final score of 28-10 was a fair reflection of the play. One senses that more will be required from both SBW and Wilkin if Toronto are to hold their own at this level.

In the second game, the Leeds Rhinos were overwhelmed by Hull FC by 30 points to 4. The visitors have invested heavily in some big, powerful forwards and, on the evidence of this first game, it looks to have been money well spent. Leeds found it difficult to contain the powerful surges of Manu Ma'u and Andre Savelio, in particular; the home side's creative efforts, by contrast, tended to be far too lateral. Hull also have some firepower in their three-quarters, as shown by the winger Ratu Naulago who, after collecting a high kick on his own 22 line, displayed a potent combination of dexterity, power and speed in making the break for the opening score by Carlos Tuimavave. I suspect that, in due course, that try will come to be seen as one of the best of the season on this ground.

In the second half, Ash Handley's neatly taken try on Leeds's left-wing was little more than consolation, as his side was trailing by 24 points at the time. The latter stages were played in a heavy downpour, which seemed to serve as an appropriate metaphor for Leeds's disappointing start to the league season. By contrast, the Hull players – prompted by Marc Sneyd's accurate kicking game – revelled in the conditions and offered much promise for their new Super League campaign.

www.anordinaryspectator.com/news-blog February 2020

# Rugby League

# A Classic Encounter Re-visited

It is likely that a poll of the readers of the *Rugby League Journal* would offer a number of alternatives for the choice of the most memorable Challenge Cup final in the period from the end of the Second World War to the closure of Wembley Stadium for redevelopment in 1999. For many, this would naturally depend on their club allegiance, especially when the spoils of victory went to the underdog – for example, Featherstone Rovers in 1983 or Sheffield Eagles in 1998.

For many neutrals, however, it is a fair bet that the votes would be cast for either the Hunslet-Wigan match of 1965 or the Hull-Wigan encounter in 1985. In this article, I will examine the former and pose a question. Does its historical reputation as a – perhaps *the* – classic Wembley final stand up to scrutiny 55 years after the event?

That reputation was established in the immediate aftermath of the match. In his report for *The Guardian* the following Monday, Harold Mather wrote that he had seen "eighty minutes of excellent, fast, open football… a final which will surely live long in the memory". *The Times* stated that it had been "one of the best Rugby Cup finals [sic] seen at Wembley, one in which the ball was constantly on the move".

The emerging rugby league literature echoed this perspective. In the "Great Post-War Games" chapter of his *The Rugby League Game* (1967), Keith Macklin noted "the dramatic greatness of this game… magnificently thrilling… tremendous end-to-end stuff [with a] palpitating second half". Nearly 40 years later – in *Play to Win: Rugby League Heroes* (2005) – Maurice Bamford reflected the conventional wisdom when he stated that the match "has gone down in history as the best under the old unlimited tackle rule".

It might be argued that the counter-argument – that the Hunslet-Wigan final was an undistinguished encounter – is something of a straw man. However, this revisionist interpretation has been given, most notably in Dave Hadfield's *Up and Over: A Trek Through Rugby League Land* (2004) by the broadcaster and former international Phil Clarke, whose father – the Wigan hooker, Colin Clarke – played in the match and is reported as having thought it "slow and useless".

At the time of the 1965 final, I was already a veteran of four seasons of support for Hunslet, my father's team – and I had attended the 8-0 semi-final win over Wakefield Trinity at Headingley with my dad and uncles – but there had been little prospect of me going to the final. The London trip was for the grown-ups, not 10 year-olds. Instead – and I have a strong memory of this – I watched the match, alone, on the small television set at my grandparents' house in Leeds.

The following month, in mid-June, I was able to watch it again as BBC1 re-arranged its usual Sunday afternoon schedule to show a 50 minute highlights programme introduced by Eddie Waring – no doubt to the disappointment of some of the regular watchers of the cancelled *Z Cars*. This in itself was a clear indication, of course, that the match had been considered out of the ordinary.

Over half a century later, we can watch Hunslet play Wigan in the 1965 Challenge Cup final as often as we like, courtesy of the DVD reproduction of the original BBC coverage. The footage is far from perfect – a grainy black and white from a single camera angle – but it does enable us to see the actual events again, rather than rely on the biases of memory. What does the evidence reveal?

The pre-match expectations of the match were not of a classic for two reasons. First, there was the nature of Hunslet's semi-final win, which had been based on the dominant performance of their forward pack: the props Dennis Hartley and Ken Eyre, hooker Bernard Prior, second rows Geoff Gunney and Bill Ramsey, and loose-forward and captain Fred Ward. The *Yorkshire Evening Post* had gone so far as to draw comparisons with the "Terrible Six" of the club's 1907-08 "All Four Cups" season. A similarly pragmatic approach was expected from the Yorkshire side at Wembley.

Second, there was the wide divergence in the two sides' league form. Wigan had finished second in the league – beaten to the League Leaders' trophy by St Helens – whilst Hunslet, having been in the top six for much of the campaign, had faded to 14th. (Both sides had lost their first round Top 16 play-off games). When allied to Wigan's cup final experience – this was their fifth Wembley appearance in eight years – this meant that there were some fears of a one-sided encounter.

These fears were probably not assuaged when the Hunslet scrum-half, Alan Marchant, sent the opening kick-off out of play on the full and Laurie Gilfedder launched the resultant penalty kick comfortably over the bar from the half-way line. Parity was quickly restored, however, when the reliable Billy Langton replied with a long kick of his own three minutes later. (My dad told me afterwards that, when he saw the flags go up for the Langton penalty, he knew it was going to be a great game).

Wigan were never behind. They moved out to increasingly comfortable leads (5-2, 12-4, 20-9), but Hunslet kept pegging them back (5-4, 12-9, 20-16) until time ran out with the Central Park side holding their four-point advantage.

When re-examining matches of the past, the modern viewer must start by recognising that, as with all great sports, rugby league has evolved over time. The rules have been altered, tactics have changed, players have become fitter… and so on. However – as the *Journal* consistently argues – the fact that something differs from what it was in the past does not necessarily mean that it is better. We can only consider the evidence in front of us when mindful of the variations in context between then and now.

Hence – an obvious point – we must remember that some of the basic rules of rugby league were markedly different in the mid 1960s. Most significantly, at the time of the Hunslet-Wigan game, the offside line at the play-the-ball was only three yards. This meant that the centre of the field was severely congested and that there were no easy gains for the acting half-backs or first receivers to enjoy. Every yard had to be fought for.

Likewise, the scrums were – to put it mildly – "contested". In this match, there was no blatantly illegitimate feeding by the scrum halves; instead, there was a series of almighty wrestles in which the respective open-side props – Danny Gardiner and Dennis Hartley – sought to manoeuvre their hookers into favourable striking positions. Of the hookers, Prior edged Clarke in the scrums – 10 to 8 – with both men enjoying several wins against the head.

The 1965 Challenge Cup final was the last to be played under the "unlimited tackle" rule. Ironically, watching the game again, I wasn't really struck that this was much of an issue, as both sides had regular sequences in possession. (The rule's only real significance was when Wigan held possession for 19 tackles over the last three minutes of the game. "Wigan have got the ball. And they'll know what to do with it", said Eddie Waring. And they did).

It was noticeable that, at most of the play-the-balls, the defending player would look to strike for the ball, on every single occasion without success. There were only two tactical kicks in broken play during the whole game.

The gaps in the defensive line were to be found on the margins of the forward play. The outstanding player here was Brian Gabbitas, the Hunslet stand-off, whose speed off the mark and quick side-steps proved consistently damaging for his opponents. He contributed to what is, for me, the highlight of the match: Geoff Shelton's try just before half-time. About 40 yards out, Gabbitas drew two Wigan tacklers on to him to create the space in which the speeding Shelton could burst through the defensive line and, without apparently decelerating, swerve round the full-back, Ray Ashby, and win the race for the line. It was an absolutely majestic try and, seeing it again, I jumped off the sofa in delight, as I had all those years earlier at my grandparents' house.

For his part, Ashby played a prominent role in Wigan's attack. His presence as the extra man as the back division swiftly transferred the ball to the wings consistently enabled his side to make substantial territorial gains. It was his break down the middle of the pitch that presented the graceful Trevor Lake with the opportunity to make the long sprint for his second try.

The play was not without its faults: at various times, all four wingers were guilty of being shepherded into touch when in possession; both sides missed touch with penalty kicks, Hunslet three times in succession; there were dropped passes at vital moments.

But these blemishes were outweighed by the many examples of skill and courage evident throughout the match. Watching the game again, I was reminded of the scorching runs to the line made by Gilfedder and the Welsh winger, John Griffiths, for their respective second half tries, the three brilliant breaks made after the interval by the 21 year-old Ramsey in the Hunslet second row and the devastating finishing skills of Lake, the season's leading try-scorer.

And, not least, there was the heroic defence of full-back Langton, firstly after half an hour, when a textbook tackle halted a rampaging Billy Boston on Wigan's right wing a few yards short of the Hunslet try-line, and later, in the second half, when his last ditch effort grounded Keith Holden, whose subsequent double-movement under the posts was penalised by the referee, Joe Manley. Gabbitas and Ashby were worthy joint-winners of the Lance Todd Trophy, but Langton must have run them very close.

I think there are a number of reasons why the pundits have reviewed the 1965 Challenge Cup final so favourably. Hunslet's refusal to be shaken off on the scoreboard was certainly one; indeed, for much of the game, they held a noticeable territorial advantage. However, as Eddie Waring perceptively remarked, after absorbing these periods of pressure, Wigan took their chances ruthlessly when play switched to the other end of the pitch.

There was no let up in the action. In contrast with the modern game, there was no "wrestle" on the floor in the tackle; the proximity of the defensive line meant that players often remained upright when halted, enabling the play-the-balls to be made relatively quickly. After an infringement, the scrums were usually convened without too much delay. And the men with the "magic sponge" only came on to the pitch perhaps half a dozen times, notwithstanding some heavy collisions, which clearly left some players the worse for wear. (Near the end of the game, the sight of a groggy Bernard Prior collapsing to the ground and then getting up again to rejoin the action makes for uncomfortable viewing).

Moreover, the intensity of the action did not diminish, despite the fact that substitutes were only allowed up to half-time and none were used; the same 26 players were on the field throughout. There were noticeably fewer scrums in the second half when, as the players' levels of energy were depleted, the spaces opened up for the "end-to-end" action identified by Keith Macklin. As the match entered the final 10 minutes, Waring summed up what he was watching: "It's exciting and it's tough and it's good".

It was a fair description. As was the commentator's later observation about the Princess Alexandra, as she presented the trophy to Eric Ashton: "She's a bonny lass". They were, indeed, different times.

The ethos of the *Rugby League Journal* – "for fans who don't want to forget" – presents a quarterly challenge for contributor and reader alike. As the years (and decades) pass, our memories of the sport as we think it was – its players and teams and matches – are at risk of distortion by the potential biases in our recollection. In writing or reading about rugby league as it used to be – and our enjoyment of those times – we need to be continually on our guard against interpreting the past with the type of uncritical hype that undermines the presentation of so much of modern-day sport.

We are fortunate that a number of selected games from the past – admittedly, only a few – are available to us on DVD. I am pleased to confirm that – in the case of the Hunslet-Wigan Challenge Cup final of 1965 – the evidence suggests that our glowing memories are fully justified.

*The Rugby League Journal* Issue 70, Spring 2020

Sport: Economic Impact

# The Coronavirus: Economics, Questions and Priorities

The reports on the spread of the coronavirus – and the various measures being taken to contain it – are dominating the news agendas across the world.

Perhaps not surprisingly, a disproportionate amount of the media coverage has related to the impact on spectator sports. Of course, it is the case that the scale of the disruption to major events – which yesterday alone included announcements on the postponements of the Masters' golf tournament and the first four races in the Grand Prix season, the abandonment of England's cricket tour of Sri Lanka and a temporary halt to the Premier League and other soccer schedules in England and Scotland – is unprecedented in the post-Second World War period. Whilst most societal activity takes place outside the sporting arena, the presentation of the virus's impact on sport does assist – if we needed assisting – in emphasising the overall magnitude of the challenges currently faced by all governments and civic societies.

When watching the news coverage, I was reminded of some research with which I was involved – in my former role as an economic consultant – over 30 years ago. In 1985, my colleague Richard Lewney and I were commissioned by the Sports Council to estimate "The Economic Impact and Importance of Sport in the UK". Our independent report[23] was generally well received in both academic and policy-making circles and led to further investigations of the economic impact of sport in two local areas (Bracknell and the Wirral, as it happens) as well as in Northern Ireland and Wales. We also collaborated with the Sports Council in being the lead partner in a Council of Europe-funded programme of research across several countries. (There is a curious satisfaction in seeing the publication of a journal article in Finnish).

Our analytical framework was based on the system of National Income Accounting, which enabled us to examine not only the first-round effects of sport-related spending (for example, by consumers on admission charges, clothing and footwear, equipment, and so on), but also the backward linkages and "multiplier" effects of this expenditure throughout the economy. Our findings included that, at that time, over 370,000 jobs were sport-related in the UK and the value-added exceeded that created in a number of traditionally important sectors of industry, including motor vehicles/parts and drink/tobacco.

Three decades on, I would expect that the economic impact of sport in the UK is now proportionately greater than the estimate that Richard and I made in the 1980s. This reflects a range of social and economic factors. The former includes significant changes in lifestyle patterns, such as the increased popularity of running and cycling, the growth in spending on sport-related casual clothing and the huge expansion of sport's media coverage in the satellite age.

More generally, even allowing for a couple of recessionary periods, 30 years of more or less uninterrupted economic growth has meant that, on average, people have more disposable income on which to spend on service-based activities. Moreover, it is the case that – for much sport-related spectating activity, in particular – the real price of attendance has increased: that is, the cost has risen faster than the general rise in the price level. (I noted an illustration of this in *An Ordinary Spectator*, when I reported that, between 1994 and 2012, the nominal price of a balcony ticket in the Football Stand for the Headingley test match rose from £27 to £65 i.e. by 141%. As the increase in the All Items Consumer Price Index – the CPI – over the same period was 48%, the real price increase was 63%).

And so we know the sport's role in overall economic activity is significant. What, then, about the impact of the coronavirus on sport's finances?

This can be considered in the same way as examining the effect of the virus on other areas of economic activity, including those such as travel and tourism which are being severely affected. The reduction – in some cases, collapse – of demand for sports spectating and/or participation will obviously adversely affect the income of sport-related businesses (whether Premier League football club or local gym) and they, in turn, will reduce their own spending to the suppliers of the goods and services that they would normally purchase. Such are the multiplier effects down through the supply chain. The employees of those businesses are also likely to cut their expenditures, either because their personal incomes have fallen or, even if not, due to the enhanced "precautionary" motive for saving for an uncertain future.

From this, a number of key questions emerge. For how long will the halt to sports events continue? Will sports businesses (and their suppliers) be able to survive through this period of low or non-existent cash-flow? And what will the post-virus sporting landscape look like? The last of these questions relates to the issue of whether the lost sports events have been postponed (as, for example, in the case of the London Marathon from April to October) – in which case the finances of sport will make a quicker recovery – or cancelled altogether.

It is the prospect of outright cancellation that is focusing (some) minds on the political jockeying-for-position that this will generate. Yesterday, when interviewed, the Celtic FC manager Neil Lennon wasted no time in stating that, under these circumstances, his club – with their 13-point lead at the top of the Scottish Premiership – should be awarded the championship.

Meanwhile, Jurgen Klopp, the manager of Liverpool FC (which is leading the Premier League by 19 points) released his message to the club's supporters on social media. It did not refer to the league table at all and ended with the following appeal:

> *"It would be entirely wrong to speak about anything other than advising people to follow expert advice and look after themselves and each other.*
>
> *The message from the team to our supporters is only about your well-being. Put your health first. Don't take any risk. Think about the vulnerable in our society and act where possible with compassion for them.*
>
> *Please look after yourselves and look out for each other".*

It is clear that, in the current circumstances, the social fabric is being tested, the death rate is higher than it otherwise would have been and the future is uncertain. To his great credit, Mr Klopp recognises that some of the interests of those engaged in the sporting environment need to be placed in their proper perspective.

Some things are more important than others.

www.anordinaryspectator.com/news-blog March 2020

# Cricket

## The Football Stand

*[Today is Easter Sunday: a day of joy and hope and expectation.*

*It should also have been the start of the 2020 County Championship cricket season: the scheduled Division One fixtures were Lancashire vs Kent, Somerset vs Warwickshire and Yorkshire vs Gloucestershire. The coronavirus put paid to that some time ago, of course.*

*However, to mark the occasion – and to register a reminder that better times will, one day, return – I offer some reflections on a change in the landscape at the Headingley (correction, Emerald Headingley) cricket ground].*

The old Football Stand has gone. Inaugurated at a match in May 1933, when the great Bill Bowes took 12 wickets in Yorkshire's innings victory over Kent, it has now been demolished and replaced by a modern steeply-banked structure. Last August, I made my annual pilgrimage from Scotland to Headingley – for a T20 match against the Durham Jets – in order to take in the fresh new perspective from behind the bowler's arm.

Strictly speaking, it was not the Football Stand in the first place. It was the Rugby Stand, as it is the oval-balled games – both league and union – that are played on the pitch on the other side. But the Football Stand was the name by which it was generally known.

It was on the rugby side that I first took my seat in Headingley's dual-facing facility. The Yorkshire Cup final of 1962: Hunslet 12 Hull Kingston Rovers 2. Over the years, I saw Reg Gasnier and Ellery Hanley and Kevin Sinfield *et al*. On my most recent trip to Leeds – only just over a couple of months ago, but in what now seems to have been a different era – I watched games in both codes: *"Arresting Decline"* (5th February 2020) and *"The Return of Sonny Bill"* (7th February 2020). But let us focus here on the north-facing side of the stand.

On my first visit to watch the cricket at Headingley – for the Roses match of 1966 – the Football Stand was out of bounds for the likes of me. I was not a Member of Yorkshire CCC and, therefore – with my Dad – I watched the play from the vast array of the Western Terrace. We chose our wooden bench with care, obviously favouring one that had been recently restored with new timber, rather than an alternative that was damp and rotten and populated by those sinister-looking little red spiders. I looked across with a pang of envy when the Members let out a collective groan as Geoff Pullar nudged tentatively forward and narrowly missed another of Freddie Trueman's outswingers. Yorkshire won by 10 wickets on the second day.

Eventually, we graduated to take our rightful places in the stand. From the mid-1980s, after my father had retired, we would attend the second and third days of the test match, the first of which was always viewed from the lower stalls and the latter from high up in the balcony. The single exception was the West Indies test in 2000, when, in a change of routine, we booked the first two days. That was perfectly judged, of course: England duly won on the second day – Andrew Caddick completing the rout by taking four wickets in an over – and the young Michael Vaughan was man-of-the-match.

Other clear memories remain: Merv Hughes – hitherto known more for his moustache than his batting – sharing an improbable century stand with Steve Waugh in 1989; Graham Gooch's batting masterclass against the West Indies in 1991; Hansie Cronje bowled first ball by Phil deFreitas in 1994; Ricky Ponting's first test century in 1997; Sachin Tendulkar and Sourav Ganguly flailing England to all parts in 2002 (the last test I attended with my father before he was claimed by mesothelioma)…

In truth, however, I shall not miss the Football Stand. The seats were cramped and the level of comfort was poor, to say the least. In the balcony, the threats from either wasps or pigeons were persistent. (One year, one of the latter took particular exception to an unfortunate man situated a couple of rows in front of us and to our left, who twice received direct bombing hits). In its later years, viewed from the other end of the ground – where the "coconut shy" and the poplar trees had once been – the stand looked tired and past its best.

The replacement is named, inevitably, in line with the ground's sponsors: the Emerald Group. The Football Stand is dead. Long live the Emerald Stand at Emerald Headingley.

For those not entirely familiar with the brand, the Emerald Group's website states that it is "a specialist global search and selection company focused on supplying high calibre services across the financial services industry". Boldly emblazoned on the front of the Emerald Stand are the motifs that underpin the company's approach to business: "Bringing research to life", "Championing fresh thinking", "Equipping decision makers" and "Making an impact". That tells us a lot, I think.

Mind you, I still haven't viewed any cricket from the Emerald Stand. As I reported in "*For Valour*" (19th August 2019), Yorkshire's match with Durham was rained off without a ball bowled.[24]

www.anordinaryspectator.com/news-blog April 2020

# The Coronavirus Provides a Reminder

*"Sport is drama and conflict. Sport is the battle for honour and honours.
And an important part of the enjoyment in watching sport is to see the
resolution of that battle and its effects on the winners and losers".*

[*An Ordinary Spectator*, page 358]

For those of us who take an interest in watching sport, it is always worthwhile
to recognise that there are others for whom the whole concept is ridiculous – or,
indeed, abhorrent. The standard comments of disdain are familiar: "grown men
hitting a ball into a hole with a stick…", "overpaid prima donnas kicking a pig's
bladder…", and so on.

I was conscious of all this when, in the final chapter of *An Ordinary
Spectator*, I attempted to summarise the reasons why I had been continually drawn
to watching live sport, in the flesh, over a period of half a century.

My conclusions were perhaps not that surprising: admiration at seeing
elite performers at the top of their game; recognition of personal qualities such as
leadership and courage; the scope for drama, in which the arena is the stage for
the performing players; the sense of tradition and continuity attached to much
sporting activity; the signals that sport sends as a barometer for society as a whole;
and, not least, the role of sport in contributing to my self-identity and my sense of
place in the world.

At this time, when the coronavirus is taking such a heavy toll on human
life (as of yesterday, almost a quarter of a million deaths reported across the world,
including more than 28,000 in the UK), it might seem irrelevant – if not insensitive
– to concern oneself with matters sporting. But the effects of the virus are not only
in terms of premature mortality rates; they are also be found in virtually every
aspect of our lives that, until only two short months ago, we had been taking for
granted. Like most people, I suspect, I have found it extremely difficult to make
sense of it all: to think clearly about what it means for us now and what it will
mean in the future.

It is in this context – and to persuade myself that I remain capable of some sort of detached and rational analysis – that I have been reflecting on the huge disruption that the coronavirus has brought to the holding of all sports events, large and small. In effect, I have been encouraged to revisit the question of what it is that watching sport brings to our everyday lives. In doing so, I now recognise that the answer is to be found in themes that are far wider than the mainly sport-related ones that I had previously identified.

As before, I must also acknowledge that any consideration of this issue is bound to be heavily influenced by one's particular circumstances – age, upbringing, location, and so on. However, I shall attempt to complement the personal perspective with a more general assessment of what it is that watching sport provides for us as a whole. What, indeed, is it that the coronavirus has reminded us that we are missing?

The subject matter is hugely wide-ranging, of course, and, over time, I am sure that the area will generate a rich seam of research for sociologists and psychologists and that many learned academic papers and books will result. For the present, at this stage of sport's shutdown – it is now 7 weeks since the postponement of all professional football in the UK – let me offer some initial views by identifying half a dozen key points.

The obvious place at which to start is to recognise that watching sport takes up some of our time: it occupies some of the precious minutes (or hours) between waking up in the morning and going to bed at night. When this use of time is suddenly (and completely) taken away, we struggle (at least at first) to find a replacement. (In the current circumstances, this point also clearly applies to other leisure activities – going to the theatre, watching a concert, going to the pub *et al* – and the effect is magnified a thousand-fold when all these activities are removed at the same time).

The media picked up on this very quickly. Perhaps unreasonably quickly. One of the football correspondents of *The Scotsman* – under the heading "We're kicking our heels without football" – stated that "it feels like we have woken up in a post-apocalyptic wasteland". And this was on March 16th, the first Monday after the country's soccer programme (including the previous day's Rangers-Celtic match) had been postponed.

Of course, watching sport is more than simply a time-filler. There are occasions when we persuade ourselves – perhaps erroneously – that it is a worthwhile activity in its own right. We consider that it has a merit of its own so that, when we take our place in the stand or on the terrace, we are with the virtuous. It is part of our response when we seek to address Rudyard Kipling's query whether we "can fill the unforgiving minute with sixty seconds' worth of distance run".[25]

In the present circumstances, given the lack of sports-spectating options, the logical follow-up has been to consider how else we might spend our time.

It was no accident that the impressively quirky White Rose Forum – an online discussion group for followers of Yorkshire cricket – quickly developed a thread listing the activities that its members were intending to pursue in the absence of watching any matches: cooking with exotic sauces, learning the guitar, completing the novel (writing, not reading), improving basic German language skills… (The last two were mine incidentally). An interesting question for a later date will be the extent to which, in turn, the eventual resumption of sports watching will replace these activities as we revert back to "normal": largely, but not wholly, I expect.

A related point is that watching sport helps to provide a structure to our lives. Much of sports spectating has a rhythm or a cycle to it: the fortnightly home soccer match, the first day of the County Championship season, the Boxing Day rugby match, and so on. Allied to the events that we turn up to watch at first hand are those that we might not see in the flesh (or even on television), but which we register as having a place at a certain time in the calendar: the Boat Race, the London Marathon, the Grand National…

I suspect that the planning of our schedules – daily/weekly/monthly/annual – around these regular events is done largely subconsciously. They constitute an unseen sketchpad on which we can place our own specific entries. In my case, earlier this year, I had some enjoyment in planning the contents of a spectating timetable that lasted from the spring into the autumn: a women's football match in Glasgow, some cricket at Old Trafford, a Euro 2020 match at Hampden Park, an Ashes rugby league test in Leeds. These events were staging-posts for the year, around which I could fit in the important (non-sporting) occasions with family and friends: the holiday in Spain, the West End theatre trip, the annual visit to the parents' grave. Without these irregular markers, the future stretches ahead, shapeless and empty.

A further feature of sport spectating – again obvious – is that it provides us with social contact. For many, this takes the form of membership of an identifiable group – for example, as a football club's supporter in a replica shirt or as part of the "Barmy Army" of England cricket fans bewildering the locals in Bridgetown or Columbo.

However, even when we are watching an event by ourselves, we are also part of a communal audience – perhaps in a crowd of 60,000, perhaps with the other man and his dog – simultaneously observing the activity in front of us (though not necessarily seeing the same thing). This provides the opportunity for the type of interaction – in a conversation or a debate or a stadium's roar – which we (occasionally at least) seek as social animals.

In both *An Ordinary Spectator* and *Still An Ordinary Spectator* and in the subsequent blogs, I have regularly reported on the fleeting connections that I have made with strangers during the course of my sports spectating: the elderly man at a Yorkshire-Nottinghamshire cricket match at Headingley who told me that his father had been killed in the Second World War; the season-ticket holder at Tyneside worried about the Hearts team's defensive frailties; the young lady named Stephanie in San Antonio, Texas, who came to my rescue after I had been to a high school American Football match and missed the last bus into town… How else but through watching sport would we have entered each other's lives at those particular places at those particular times and, for a brief period at least, mutually enriched them?

And if not with strangers, then with family and friends. In *An Ordinary Spectator*, I refer to some of the friends – from adolescence and college and work – with whom I have shared the spectating experience over these many years. Post-working life, there have been additional and welcome members of the cast list. Perhaps most poignantly, the feedback to that book confirmed the hugely significant role that watching sport had provided in the bonding of family members – fathers and sons, uncles and nephews, older siblings and younger upstarts – on the terrace or in the stand. My story is no different: the book begins with me (as a 6 year-old boy) sitting on my father's shoulders at a rugby match in south Leeds and his presence is a regular feature in the narrative right through to the final page.

The contact is with places as well as people. In *Still An Ordinary Spectator*, I noted HG Bissinger's brilliant line in *Friday Night Lights*, when he describes the outcome of a visit to a high school football game in Marshall, Texas, by a delegation of Russians who had been visiting a nearby US Air Force base: "[T] hey don't understand a lick of [American] football, but… their understanding of America by the end of the game will be absolute whether they realise it or not".

I like to think that I do understand more than a lick about football but, even so, there can be no doubt that my understanding of America (and Texas in particular) was enhanced after my evenings watching the high school football at the Alamo Stadium and the college football in the Alamodome (which are different venues) in San Antonio. Just as my understanding of local communities was enhanced after watching the FC Union Berlin (association) football team at the wonderfully named *Stadion an der Alten Forsterei* (Stadium Near the Old Forester's House) in east Berlin or the Westport St Patrick's Gaelic Football team in County Mayo. Prior to the lockdown, as I have continued my occasional tour of the soccer grounds of Scotland, I would have been remiss not to have spent some time walking the streets of the relevant towns and getting a sense of place. How else would I have seen the buildings and sites that capture the history of Alloa or Annan or Dumfries?

Finally, I refer back to a conclusion in *An Ordinary Spectator* – reproduced above – that I (we?) watch sport because it provides drama: "Sport *is* drama and conflict…". I also noted that the duration of the drama can take many forms: the long build-up to the event, perhaps weeks or months; the length of the contest itself, whether over 80 minutes or 4 days, or – as illustrated by the dozen "nano-dramas" that I identified in that volume – a mere split-second of action.

I now think that there is another dimension to this. The drama of sport is not only performed in front of us. It takes place within us. It generates a set of questions about ourselves that we may or may not choose to answer. How would we have responded in that given situation? Would we have taken that steepling catch? Would we have scored that penalty kick? Could we have made that try-saving tackle? From the safety of beyond the touchline or the boundary rope, we can ask ourselves these questions and – after we have invariably answered positively – we can take pleasure in the success that we have vicariously achieved.

Jurgen Klopp, the manager of Liverpool FC – whom I have quoted with admiration relatively recently ("*The Coronavirus: Economics, Questions and Priorities*", 14th March 2020) – has stated that the halting of sports events is "a reminder that sport is the most important of the least important things". It is an impressive line, I think: one which assists in cutting the ground from under the "hitting a ball with a stick" and "pig's bladder" advocates.

And so, following Mr Klopp's lead – and addressing the question with which I began – of what do I think that the coronavirus has provided a reminder? In summary: that watching sports enables us to use up some of the time at our disposal; that it contributes to providing a structure to our lives; that it facilitates individual and communal contacts; that it encourages respect for local places and cultures; that it satisfies the need for drama; that it allows us to role-play, if only in our own minds.

It strikes me that, as we sit in our respective domains of self-isolation – perhaps worrying about our future physical and mental wellbeing – that is a fairly formidable catalogue: "the most important of the least important", indeed.

A final, final thought. We will select from that catalogue again. At some stage in the future, we will watch the white-coated figures walk out to the middle of the ground and place the bails on top of the stumps. The batsman will take his guard and the bowler will mark out his run-up. And the umpire will shout: "Play"…

www.anordinaryspectator.com/news-blog May 2020

Politics

# Losing the Changing Room

The English language has many examples of phrases taken from the sporting arena and used in a more general context. In the game of cricket "showing a straight bat" is a good technique to be employed when playing "on a sticky wicket"; in common usage, it refers to dealing with tricky matters in a manner that is determined and correct. If someone "bowls us a googly" (a leg-spinner's delivery that turns in from the off side), we need to be on our guard against something that is unexpected.

Likewise, on the green baize table, we are "snookered" when we do not have a direct shot with the cue ball to any of the reds or colours we are allowed to hit without hitting one of the other balls and incurring a penalty; in everyday life, it means being faced with a range of choices, none of which are welcomed. "Par for the course" and "the ball's in their court" – exported from golf and tennis, respectively – have similarly generalised interpretations. And so on.

Sometimes, the direction of causality goes the other way: a term that apparently has everyday usage (though it might not make much sense when taken literally) is applied in the sporting environment. Hence, in soccer, when teams "park the bus", it means that they form a heavily manned defensive shield in front of their goal at the expense of undertaking any attacking play.

In the same sport, one often hears of managers or coaches "losing the changing room". Of course, this does not mean that they have physically mislaid the changing area! Rather, it refers to the occasions when the players – usually a cabal of the most senior – have lost confidence in some aspect of the manager's leadership (perhaps his tactics or his motivational skills or his team selection) with this subsequently being reflected in the displays and results on the pitch.

Which brings us to the Prime Minister, Mr Boris Johnson.

For the last two days, the lead story across the media has related to Mr Johnson's chief adviser, Mr Dominic Cummings, who, with his family – his wife and 4 year-old son – drove 260 miles from London to Durham in the early period of lockdown at the end of March. Mr Cummings's wife is reported to have been showing symptoms of having the coronavirus at the time of the journey.

Mr Johnson has recently received some criticism for the alleged vagueness in his presentation of the guidance on the 1ˢᵗ Stage of the relaxation of lockdown. However, in his first tv address to the nation on 24ᵗʰ March and in his letter to all UK households, his statement was unequivocal: "We are giving one simple instruction – you *must* [his emphasis] stay at home". The accompanying guidance leaflet from the UK Government stated that: "Anyone who has… symptoms must stay at home until the symptoms have ended, and in all cases for at least seven days. Everyone else in the household must stay at home for at least 14 days after the first person's symptoms appear, even if they themselves do not have symptoms".

Mr Cummings' defence has been that he was looking to provide childcare for his son and that he had he done nothing unlawful. Of course, one can understand his desire to do the best for his family and, I suspect, very few people are in a position to know whether Mr Cummings had any access to childcare arrangements nearer to his London home. But we all wish to do the best for our families and I do wonder what the implications would have been if 27½ million other households across the UK had decided in March that making a 260 mile journey was the most appropriate way of doing this.

This is a fast-moving story and, at the time of posting (8.30pm on Sunday evening), Mr Cummings had not resigned from his post. However, we can let those events take their course. My interest is more in the implications for Mr Johnson.

To date, the Prime Minister has stood by his chief adviser and not dismissed him. Whatever happens to Mr Cummings in the next few days or weeks, the Prime Minister's clear preferences in this matter have been revealed. The key question now – as I see it – is this: what will be the impact on Mr Johnson's standing in the country?

To date, the UK public has kept to the guidance on the coronavirus lockdown remarkably well. I suspect that a key factor here was the news reporting of the Prime Minister's own serious exposure to the virus. However, it is clear that patience with respect to the economic impact of the lockdown is now running thin, with more questions being asked about the apparent (though over-simplified) trade-off between the damage to the economy and the increased mortality rate. As we have noted, the shift from full lockdown to the minor relaxation of Stage 1 has not been straightforward to deliver or understand; this will probably also be the case in the further sets of transitional arrangements that we are promised in order to move into Stages 2, 3 and 4.

It is highly unfortunate, therefore – to say the least – that, for many people, the lesson from this weekend will have been very straightforward: there has been one rule for the inner circle of No. 10 Downing Street and one rule for the rest. Against this background, it will be inevitable that the Prime Minister's desired route through the next Stages (which is already expected to be difficult) will now be even trickier to deliver than otherwise might have been the case.

I wonder, when future historians look back on this episode, they might consider the past couple of days as the time when, in attempting to deal with the coronavirus, the Prime Minister lost the country.

The time when the manager lost the changing room.

www.anordinaryspectator.com/news-blog May 2020

# Cricket

# The Rest of the World

It was 50 years ago today – 17th June 1970 – that the first day's play took place in the unprecedented five-match "test" series between England and the Rest of the World (ROW). The series had been arranged at short notice following the cancellation of the planned tour of England by South Africa – then the leading test match side.

Unusually for the time, this first day was a Wednesday, rather than a Thursday. The following day was designated a "rest day" as it was when a General Election was being held. (The Conservatives, led by Edward Heath, brought an end to the 6-year period in office of Harold Wilson's Labour Government).

The ROW team for the first match at Lord's included 4 South Africans: Barry Richards, Eddie Barlow, Graeme Pollock and Mike Procter. This formidable quartet was assisted by 4 West Indians (including the captain, Gary Sobers) and one player each from Australia, Pakistan and India. Sobers and Barlow scored centuries in a ROW innings win.

I have two strong memories of the series. The first is attending each day of the fourth match at Headingley and watching from my customary seat – at square leg, roughly two-thirds of the way back – on the Western Terrace. The star performer was Barlow, though this time it was with the ball, as he took 12 wickets in the match, including 4 in 5 deliveries (with a hat-trick) in England's first innings. Sobers made another century as the ROW won a tight game by two wickets to take a winning 3-1 lead in the series, which was duly converted to 4-1 in the final match at the Oval.

After all this time, I can recall the young Chris Old running up the hill from the Football Stand and bowling out Clive Lloyd in the ROW's first innings. Lloyd remained in his defensive position at the crease for a while, as if he had only played and missed, at which point Old pointed to the off bail on the ground and (politely I'm sure) informed the batsman that he had been dismissed. How is it that these fleeting images remain in one's mind after half a century?

My other recollection is of recording each delivery of the Oval match in one of my *Compactum* scoring books, courtesy of the intermittent BBC television coverage and/or the exhaustive ball-by-ball commentary of *Test Match Special* on Radio 3. This game was characterised by the high-quality batting of Pollock and his colleague Rohan Kanhai in the ROW side and Geoff Boycott in England's second innings, all of whom registered three figures. At the other extreme, Brian Luckhurst of Kent – Boycott's opening partner – registered a "pair", his stumps twice routed by in-swinging yorkers from the ferociously quick Procter.

Hindsight suggests that the 1970 ROW side was one of the most powerful cricket teams ever assembled: to be ranked, perhaps, alongside Warwick Armstrong's Australian tourists of 1921, Don Bradman's "Invincibles" of 1948 or the formidable West Indian sides of the 1980s captained by Clive Lloyd and Viv Richards. The margin of their series win was no surprise. However, the competition did England no harm. Ray Illingworth (by then of Leicestershire) retained the captaincy for the subsequent tour of Australia and it was the core of England's team in the ROW series – Basil d'Oliveira, Alan Knott, John Snow *et al* – that won the Ashes 2-0. (Illingworth remains one of three successful Yorkshire-born captains to Australia, the others being Len Hutton and James Cook).

For the 15 year-old perched on his seat on the Western Terrace or listening to John Arlott and EW Swanton on the radio in the small dining room of his parents' home, the 1970 England-ROW series was an unbridled joy. The best players in the world – who received far less media exposure than their counterparts today – were performing right in front of him. Moreover, these were hard-fought matches – contested, as far as I could see, as keenly as if it had been the originally planned England-South Africa series – not friendly knockabouts.

In preparing this short piece, I checked the scoring details in my 1971 edition of the *Playfair Cricket Annual* (price: 20p). The publication referred to the games as test matches. But the quotation marks I used in the opening paragraph were not accidental. The International Cricket Council (ICC) later ruled that the series had not warranted the highest status, but had been merely "first class". Accordingly, the runs, wickets and catches (and one stumping, by Farokh Engineer) of the players have not counted towards their test career records.

For one player in particular, this turned out to be especially bad news. Alan Jones – a prolific batsman for Glamorgan – opened the batting for England on that first day at Lord's. He made 5 and 0 in the match – another double victim of Mike Procter – and did not play for England again. Not only were his runs in that game expunged from the test match records, but so was his entire test match playing career.

(Note for future pub quiz reference: Alan Jones holds the record for scoring the most runs in first-class cricket – over 36,000 – without winning a test cap. His Glamorgan colleague, Don Shepherd, holds the corresponding bowling record with his 2,200-plus wickets).

### Postscript

The perils of blog posting. On the very morning that this particular blog was posted, the England and Wales Cricket Board (ECB) announced that Alan Jones would be awarded an England cap to mark his appearance in the first match of the 1970 series against the Rest of the World.

www.anordinaryspectator.com/news-blog June 2020

# Sport on Television

# Soul Limbo

It is no surprise that it has been the elite sports events that have been the first back on to our television screens as the coronavirus lockdown conditions are eased. The satellite broadcasters require new and live "content" to fill their airtime – there are limits to the reliance on old footage for even the most dedicated sports enthusiast – whilst the sports authorities urgently need to fulfil their part of the various bargains that generate millions (or, in the case of soccer, billions) of pounds for their coffers. In addition, there is a range of other interests to satisfy, including advertisers and bookmakers not to mention those who actually play or watch sport.

In Britain, the resumption of live broadcasting effectively began at the end of May with the National Rugby League in Australia and this was quickly followed by the top-level football leagues in Europe, beginning with the *Bundesliga* and the Premier League. The two codes of domestic rugby are scheduled to resume next month with matches in the Super League (rugby league) and Premiership Rugby and PRO14 (rugby union). All these are behind closed doors as far as live spectators are concerned, of course; we look on with both admiration and envy at the apparent success in dealing with the virus in New Zealand, where the re-introduction of the Super Rugby Aotearoa competition has been accompanied by large crowds in the stadiums.

I shall focus here on the BBC's television coverage of the test match series between England and the West Indies, which began on Wednesday in Southampton. This constitutes a daily hour-long highlights package, as the full day's play remains pay-for-view. It is the BBC's first such coverage for over 20 years, so there is an intriguing comparison to be made with the (generally excellent) highlights programmes that have been provided during that period by Channel 4 and Channel 5. In terms of the cricket itself, there is a further point of interest in terms of the perceived effect (as seen through the filter of television) on this highest form of the game – the test match – of the absence of spectators in the ground. After two days, what are the initial conclusions?

For those of us with long(ish) memories, the BBC's presentation got off to a good start as Booker T and the MGs' classic *Soul Limbo* was retained as the opening theme tune: we were temporarily transported back to the days of Richie Benaud and Jim Laker. I also thought that Isa Guha was a personable and engaging presenter, though she has a high standard to maintain in filling Mark Nicholas's shoes.

The historical references were noted, but not overplayed. We learned that Ben Stokes was the 81st person to captain the England cricket team, whilst Michael Vaughan reported that England's top 4 batting line-up was its least experienced since 1989. (Separately, on the online White Rose Forum of Yorkshire CCC members and supporters, it was of greater relevance that, with Joe Root's absence, the county was not providing a member of the England team for the first time since 2012. There was some consolation, however, in that the two umpires were Richard Illingworth and Richard Kettleborough – natives of Bradford and Sheffield, respectively – from the ICC's elite international panel).

The BBC's coverage was less insightful in terms of the pre- and post-match interviews with the players taking part, which contained the rollcall of bland clichés to which we have now become accustomed; likewise the short recorded interviews that were inserted into the action, but didn't really add anything.

But I must inevitably come back to Benaud, whose general approach to broadcasting has been usually summarised as: "Don't speak unless you can add to the picture." Regrettably, it is a dictum almost universally forgotten by modern-day television commentators across all sports, so it was no surprise that its absence also applied here. Sometimes – if only for two or three consecutive deliveries – the pictures really can speak for themselves.

This being England in July, the inevitable happened and – after the months of anticipation for the resumption of cricket in the country – rain truncated the first day's play to 17 overs. After England lost a wicket in the second over, Rory Burns and Joe Denly did well to negotiate some threatening bowling from the West Indies seam attack and take the score to 35 before the elements finally closed in at tea-time. I sensed that this was, indeed, "proper" test match cricket: a hard-fought contest between bat and ball.

There was more of the same on the second day. Although 7 of England's top 8 batsmen reached double figures, none made 50 and the team limped to a total of just over 200. After the hostile Shannon Gabriel had taken the first three wickets, the West Indies' impressive captain Jason Holder took centre stage, his analysis of 6 for 42 being a career best. At 57 for 1 at the close of the second day, the West Indies were perhaps the better placed, but – weather permitting – a close encounter was in prospect for the remainder of the game.

The sense of watching a competitive test match is aided, I think, in that, for the most part, the camera's view is predominantly focused on that area of the pitch running from the final part of the bowler's run-up through to the wicket-keeper; that there are no spectators in the stands does not register until the ball is hit off the square. [An aside: I quite like the fact that, when the ball is hit to the boundary, the fielder has to go and collect it himself – as any club cricketer would probably have to do – rather than wait for a member of the ground-staff to throw it back].

At the same time, the unprecedented circumstances in which the match is taking place dominated the highlights coverage: when Isa Guha interviewed Michael Vaughan and Carlos Brathwaite before play started on the first day, they seemed to be standing ten feet apart, let alone six; the ground-staff running on and off the field with the covers were properly attired in their face masks; there was a silence held before the game in memory of the victims of the virus (and also, in tribute to the great West Indies batsman, Everton Weekes, who died last week at the age of 95); and – the dominant news item – the players and coaching staff of both teams were shown "taking the knee" before the match began, with the West Indians also wearing single black gloves in upraised fists.

These are complex and rapidly changing times. And, as usual, the observers of sport also see the wider society around them – a recurrent theme in these occasional blogs.

Amongst all this, test match cricket has resumed. We can pick up a newspaper this morning and read the match report. But we still know that, in the conduct of our lives in general, the "old normal" has gone – and that the "new normal" (whatever that is) lies a long way across the sea. Navigating our way through the present turbulent waters to the security of that distant shore is not easy. We – all of us – need help in finding a safe passage.

www.anordinaryspectator.com/news-blog July 2020

# Citius, Altius, Fortius – Part 1: Mexico City 1968

Today should have been the first day of the athletics events at the 2020 Summer Olympic Games in Tokyo. We must now be patient in waiting for that particular extravaganza, of course: the current plans – coronavirus permitting – have put things on hold for 12 months.

In *An Ordinary Spectator*, I described my visits to the Olympic Stadiums in Munich (in 1975), Moscow (1980) and Barcelona (2005). (I should have added Melbourne – in 1987 – to that list). I followed this up in *Still An Ordinary Spectator* by noting trips to the stadiums in Berlin (in 2014) and London (2016). None of these visits were for the Games themselves: Munich, Barcelona and Berlin were to watch football matches and London for a rugby league international. In the case of Moscow, I simply walked in off the street – this was a month after the city had completed hosting the Games – and sat alone (and untroubled) in a seat in one of the open stands. I enjoyed the same casual access to the Melbourne Cricket Ground seven years later.

I have only ever been to two Olympic events, both of them soccer matches in 2012 when Hampden Park in Glasgow hosted some of the group matches of the football tournaments and my sports spectating itinerary took in Belarus versus Egypt (men) and France versus Sweden (women). Both were enjoyable occasions, as I recall.

In a recent blog – "*The Rest of the World*", 17th June 2020 – I mentioned how thrilled I had been, as a 15 year-old, to watch some of the world's best cricketers take part in the 1970 "test" match series between England and the Rest of the World, either on television or (for one of the matches) in the flesh at Headingley. It is perhaps not surprising that it is from the impressionable teenage years that there remain many of the strongest memories of sports spectating. In this essay and the one that follows, therefore, I shall reflect on the two Summer Olympic Games that took place during this period of my life: Mexico City in 1968 and

Munich in 1972. (A third blog will recall my visit to Moscow in 1980).

It is perhaps relevant to note that it is from these times that the modern politicisation of the Olympic Games really took hold. This was not a new phenomenon, of course – the Berlin Games of 1936 were testimony to that – but it is probably the case that the Tokyo Games of 1964 were the last to enjoy the post-war innocence that had been a characteristic of the Olympiads from 1948 onwards.

The 1968 Summer Olympics were prefaced – a few weeks earlier – by the Mexican military authorities' massacre of students and other protesters against the Games in Mexico City's Plaza de las Tres Cultura; Wikipedia refers to the death toll as "an indeterminant number, in the hundreds". Fifty-plus years on, the most powerful image of the Games themselves is probably that of the Black Power salutes at a medal ceremony by the American athletes, Tommie Smith and John Carlos. (As far as I am aware, it has gone largely unremarked that it was the salute given by Smith and Carlos – the single raised fist in a tight-fitting black glove – that was exactly replicated by the West Indies cricket team prior to this month's test matches against England at Southampton and Old Trafford. See "*Soul Limbo*", 10th July 2020).

I shall focus here on my recollections of a few of the sporting achievements from the athletics arena in 1968. At least, I think they are my recollections from seeing the events at the time – on television, of course, and in black and white – rather than in any subsequent repeat showings. For the purposes of this blog, however, I must confess to having supplemented the memory bank by also checking out the wealth of material now available on YouTube.

## \*    Men's 400 metres hurdles final

Great Britain's only gold medal on the athletics track in Mexico City was won by David Hemery. The YouTube excerpt captures my memory of his brilliant performance – a stunning combination of grace, power and technique – which yielded a new world record. Unfortunately, it also includes the crass television commentary by David Coleman as Hemery sprinted down the final straight: "*It's Hemery, Great Britain. It's Hemery. Great Britain* [with a gasp in the voice]… *David Hemery wins for Great Britain. In second place is Hennige* [Gerhard Hennige of West Germany]. *And who cares who's third? It doesn't matter*".

Well, we cared actually, David, because it did matter. In third place – and therefore a bronze medal winner in the Olympic Games – was the Yorkshireman, John Sherwood, running for Great Britain.

## \*    Women's 400 metres final

Lillian Board was the Golden Girl of British athletics in the late 1960s: talented, attractive and successful. She was the favourite to win the single-lap race in Mexico

City, even though she was unfavourably placed on the inside lane in the final.

Jarvis Scott of the USA went into a commanding lead down the back straight – *"She's really going for the gold"*, proclaimed Coleman helpfully – but, as the runners came off the final bend, it was Board who had edged to the front and had looked to have paced her race to perfection. It was in the last 30 metres or so that she faded and was beaten into second place. *"And Lillian Board is struggling. Lillian Board is struggling. And she's lost it"*, shouted Coleman into his microphone as she crossed the line. The winner was a French athlete – Colette Besson – whose name has stuck in the back of my mind ever since.

My recollection is that there was a general sense of anti-climax in the media reporting of Lillian Board's race – almost one of failure – as if following Coleman's lead. I thought at the time how unjust this was. Like John Sherwood, she was an Olympic medallist: how could that simply be dismissed?

Lillian Board was diagnosed with colorectal cancer in September 1970. She died three months later at the age of 22.

\* **Men's long jump final**

The men's long jump in Mexico City was a keenly anticipated event. The field included the gold medal winner at the previous Games in Tokyo (Lynn Davies of Great Britain) and the joint world record holders (Ralph Boston of the USA and Igor Ter-Ovanesyan of the Soviet Union, who had set the mark at 27 ft 4¾ins).

The event was effectively over after another American, Bob Beamon, had taken his first jump. Beamon simply bypassed the 28 feet range in setting the new world's best, which was eventually recorded at 29 ft 2½ ins. It took the officials some time to confirm the distance, as they had to do this manually with a tape measure, the optical device that had been installed for the event apparently having not been designed to measure a jump of such length.

The footage of Beamon's leap remains astonishing viewing: the driving rhythm of his arms and shoulders on the runway, the stretching of the neck to keep his head upright and his eyes looking forward, the acceleration of his sprint to reach its maximum speed as his foot hit the departure board, the synchronised sweep of the arms in mid-air, the two kangaroo jumps forward after his initial landing, the final bounce upwards into a standing position prior to exiting the sand pit...

The Olympic record for the men's long jump still dates from 1968 (though the world record was eclipsed in 1991 by another American, Mike Powell). At the time – and subsequently – much was made of the favourable effect that Mexico City's high altitude might have on explosive events such as the short sprints and the long jump. I ignore all that. Instead, I prefer to picture Bob Beamon sprinting from left to right across the television screen and jumping into history.

\*    **Men's high jump final**

I was fairly hopeless at the high jump at school. In our PE classes – a couple of times a year, if the weather were conducive – we might venture across the rugby field to the high jump pit, where we would attempt our versions of the "straddle" technique. This involved a diagonal approach to the barrier – an iron bar – before taking off from the inside leg, thrusting up with the arms to rotate the torso and clear the bar horizontally, and landing on the side of the body. At least, I think this was how it was supposed to be done. For me, it was an engagement invariably marked by painfully clattering into the bar and landing in a solid bed of damp sand.

Dick Fosbury of the USA introduced the world to the "Fosbury Flop" at the Mexico Games. He had been developing the technique for some time, but this was its theatrical premier in front of a global audience.

Fosbury also had a diagonal approach but at the end of it, instead of facing the bar and propelling himself upwards with his arms and legs, he turned the other way and arched his back as he pushed off from the ground and, like a worm climbing over a pencil, contorted his body so that all its parts cleared the hurdle, the last of which – with a final kick – were his legs. Has there ever been a more radical – indeed, revolutionary – change in an athletics technique?

And yet? Check out the YouTube footage of the action from the 1896 Olympic games in Athens. There are a few seconds of film of the high jump which, at that time, did not permit any run-up to the bar at all, but rather simply comprised a leap upwards from a standing position. One of the competitors is clearly seen to half-turn his body and clear the hurdle backwards.

Wikipedia reports that, by the time of the next Olympiad in Munich in 1972, 28 of the 40 competitors in the high jump were employing Dick Fosbury's new technique, although the winner at those Games – the Estonian Jüri Tarmak, representing the Soviet Union – was an old-fashioned straddler. He was the last of his kind to win Olympic gold.

It did occur to me, when seeing Dick Fosbury attempt the high jump in 1968, that a necessary condition for the Flop was to have the sort of soft-landing area that was the standard at major athletics events by that time. Or, to put at another way, the technique could not have been attempted at the school's high jump pit. One's first attempt would have been the last, complete with broken neck or fractured skull.

In *"Citius, Altius, Fortius: Part 2"* – to follow – my recollections of the athletics events in the Munich Games of 1972.

www.anordinaryspectator.com/news-blog July 2020

Olympic Games

# Citius, Altius, Fortius – Part 2: Munich 1972

The previous blog – *"Citius, Altius, Fortius – Part 1"* (31st July) – was published on the day that the programme of athletics events was due to have started at the 2020 Summer Olympic Games in Tokyo and referred to some of the athletics highlights that I recall from the 1968 Games in Mexico City. In this follow-up – on the day that the athletics schedule was due to have been completed in Japan – I move the story on to the Munich Games of 1972.

These were the two Olympiads that took place during my teenage years when – I would argue – memories of sporting achievements are particularly susceptible to being firmly lodged in the back of one's mind. As before, my recollections are of the black-and-white images that I viewed on television at the time supplemented – if this is not cheating too much – by the library of footage that is now available on YouTube.

(In passing, it might be noted that the YouTube collection of Olympic action includes a limited amount of material that dates all the way back to the first modern Games in Athens in 1896. It will no doubt hurt most modern sensibilities that the unofficial events in the next Games in Paris in 1900 included shooting – that is, shooting live pigeons. The film of those events appears to have been lost, fortunately. For the record, Leon de Lunden of Belgium and Donald Mackintosh of Australia were the winners).

Nearly half a century on, the Olympic Games of 1972 are chiefly remembered for the deaths of 11 Israeli athletes and coaches at the hands of Palestinian terrorists. I remember being told about the attack on the Olympic village when I turned up at school for a pre-season 1st XV rugby training session. I also recall the following week's cover of *The Economist* magazine: the famous photograph of a masked terrorist looking out over the balcony of the athletes' apartment with the journal's prescient heading *"He and his kind will be among us for the rest of our lives"*.

I focus here on three athletics events.

## * Women's pentathlon

There were 14 track and field events contested by women in Munich. (The longest distance race was the 1,500 metres, newly introduced). Of the available gold medals, 6 were claimed by East Germany, 4 by West Germany and 3 by the Soviet Union. The other – in the pentathlon – was won by Mary Peters of Great Britain and Northern Ireland.

As with David Hemery in the men's 400 metres hurdles event of 1968, this was GB & NI's only gold medal in athletics and, not surprisingly, it was the focus of the BBC's television coverage. My recollection is of the tension in the moments before the times for the last event (the 200 metres) were announced, as it was clear that whoever won the overall event had done so by the narrowest of margins. It turned out that Peters's cumulative score of 4801 points (a new world record) was just 10 points higher – the equivalent of a tenth of a second in the final race – than that of the runner-up, Heide Rosendhal of West Germany (who had already won the women's long jump and would later add another gold in the sprint relay).

Mary Peters's background was from the NI component of GB & NI. Although she was born in Lancashire, she had moved with her family to Northern Ireland at the age of 11. She ended up representing NI at every Commonwealth Games between 1958 (when she was 19) and 1974.

The Northern Ireland of 1972 was a sorry place. The official records show that it was the worst year for casualties in "The Troubles" with 479 deaths (including 130 British soldiers) and 4,876 injuries. It would probably have been no surprise to Peters – a Protestant competing (and winning) for GB & NI – that she would receive the death threats that were duly made to the BBC. I cannot imagine the distress that these calls would have caused, particularly as, to add to this combustible mix – the very next day after her success – the Palestinian terrorists invaded the Israeli compound and confirmed that there were no boundaries of Olympic decency and respect for human life that could not be crossed.

Mary Peters insisted that she would return to Belfast, where she was greeted by her fans at the airport and paraded through the streets. She has remained a resident of Northern Ireland ever since. For reasons that go far beyond the limitations of mere athletic excellence, I think her Olympic gold is amongst the greatest achievements in British sport.


## * Men's 10,000 metres final

Finland produced some very impressive long-distance runners in the early 1970s, thereby extending its reputation for success in these events that had been firmly established in the inter-war period. In 1971, I recall watching the final of the European Championships 10,000 metres race on television, when the domestic interest focused on the British runner, David Bedford. Bedford was leading with about 300 metres to go, but then seemed to tread water as two sprint finishers – the Finn Juha Väätäinen (the eventual winner in front of his home Helsinki crowd) and Jürgen Haase of East Germany – swept past him. It was an astonishing piece of athletics drama: these men might have just run over 6 miles (at a fair lick), but they then accelerated through the gears as if they were top-of-the-range sports cars.

Väätäinen's compatriot, Lasse Virén, won the gold medals in both the 5,000 and 10,000 metres finals in Munich (and went on the repeat the feat four years later at the Montreal Games). The main recollection I have from 1972 is of Virén taking a heavy fall about half-way through the 10,000 metres race and being stranded on the track 30 metres or so behind his leading rivals.

This is perhaps slightly unfair but, at this point, one is tempted to fast-forward to the Los Angeles Olympics of 1984, when the American favourite, Mary Decker, tripped and fell during the women's 3,000 metres. (She had clipped the heels of the South African-born Zola Budd, who was representing Great Britain). Whereas Decker remained prone of the ground bemoaning her misfortune, Virén sprung to his feet, dusted himself off and chased after the leading pack, to which he attached himself again within about 150 metres. He took the lead on the penultimate lap and, after holding off the challenge of Emiel Puttemans – the Belgian runner who came second – won the race comfortably by about ten metres.

Wikipedia's entry for Lasse Virén includes a fascinating reference to "bend (curve) mathematics". It's not exactly rocket science, but it is clever nonetheless. Virén ran almost all the bends near the inner edge of the first lane, thereby sparing himself tens of metres compared with his main rivals. (Think about how much the "stagger" is between individual lanes in a 400 metre race). It has been estimated that, in the 10,000 metres race in Munich, this gave him an advantage of about 50 metres over Puttemans, the latter having run many of the bends wide on the outer edge of the first lane or sometimes in the second lane.


\*      **Men's marathon**

The Olympic marathon runners have attracted popular attention since the event appeared in Athens in 1896. There is dramatic footage on YouTube of the Italian, Dorando Pietri, in a state of some distress from exhaustion and dehydration, coming home first in London in 1908, only to be later disqualified as he had been helped over the line by officials; the great Czech runner Emil Zátopek combined his 1952 win in Helsinki with wins in the 5,000 and 10,000 metres finals; the Ethiopian Abebe Bikila famously won in Rome in 1960 running in bare feet (although he did wear running shoes when he took the gold medal again in Tokyo four years later)…

In Munich, the marathon was won by America's Frank Shorter (who had actually been born in Germany). He must have had a shock in the closing stages when, certain that he had the lead, he entered the stadium to a chorus of boos and saw that there was another runner in front of him; it turned out that the crowd was simply venting its displeasure at the uninvited intervention of a student hoaxer, who had entered the race near its conclusion.

The significance of the 1972 event is that Shorter's success is widely acknowledged to have kick-started (pardon the pun) the jogging boom in the United States. By 1976, when Shorter took the silver medal at the Montreal Games, the New York Marathon had over 1,500 finishers, compared with 259 in 1974 and 55 in 1970.

Other cities took up the baton for hosting marathons, including London in 1981, which I remember watching from a vantage point in Poplar High Street at about the 16-mile mark. In the glossy official programme for that event, it was noted that a further 25 marathons were scheduled across the UK over the remainder of that year – from Aberdeen to the Isle of Wight – and over 200 in the US.

The running business is now a global multi-billion dollar industry. Accordingly, it is reasonable to argue that Frank Shorter turned out to be one of the most significant of modern Olympians in terms of his impact on general societal trends. (On the other hand, within the boundaries of his own individual sport, that accolade would undoubtedly belong elsewhere: to Dick Fosbury, whose introduction of the high jump "Flop" at the 1968 Olympics in Mexico City I mentioned last time).

One final thought about the Munich Games of 1972. It is of interest to note that the terrorist massacre of the Israelis halted the Games for a couple of days, but did not lead to their cancellation. I wonder what would happen if – heaven forbid – a similar outrage were to happen again? Would the Games be postponed – or cancelled – in the global wave of horror of the circumstances and empathy for the victims? Or would the powerful alliance of infrastructural, media and sporting interests result in only a temporary halt to the proceedings – as happened then – especially if it were married to the type of defiant "the terrorists won't win" determination that saw many New Yorkers turn up for work in Manhattan on the day after 9/11. I can't be sure of the answer – and I certainly hope that I never find out – but I think I know what it would be.

www.anordinaryspectator.com/news-blog August 2020

# Women's Football

# Unfinished Business at Petershill Park

When the coronavirus brought a premature end to the 2019-20 Scottish Premiership season in March, Celtic FC (with 8 games still to play) held a 13-point lead at the top of the table, albeit with their nearest challengers, Rangers, having a match in hand (and two further Old Firm games to play). As far as I am aware, most neutral observers agree that, under these circumstances, the decision of the SPFL Board to award the championship title to Celtic was the correct one, notwithstanding the mathematical possibility that the outcome of a fully completed season might have turned out differently.

This provided Celtic with their 9th consecutive championship success, equalling the feat of Jock Stein's teams of the 1960s/1970s. For their part, Rangers won the title for 9 years in a row up to (and including) the 1996-97 campaign. It is a fairly safe prediction that, in the 2020-21 season, Celtic's bid to take the unbroken run into an unprecedented double figures – and Rangers' attempt to stop them – will dominate the Scottish football headlines.

Against this background, it is interesting to note that there is another Glasgow-based football side with an even longer run of domestic championship success: the Glasgow City women's team has won the Scottish Women's Premier League for the last 13 seasons (up to and including 2019).

Traditionally, the SWPL has run over the calendar year and the 2020 season had only just kicked off when the virus brought matters to a halt. The early indications were that Glasgow City might have some serious competition: the Celtic women's team defeated them 2-1 in the opening league fixture in February. However, this campaign, which was initially put on hold after that first game, has now been declared null and void by Scottish Women's Football. All being well, the 2020-21 season will run from October to May with a condensed League Cup competition in May and June 2021.

In the meantime, the Glasgow City side has had interests elsewhere: in Europe. Their championship success of 2018 took them into the UEFA Women's Champions League for 2019-20. In this, they progressed to the last 8, defeating FK Chertanovo Moscow and Brøndby IF, the latter on penalties last October.

Glasgow City's quarter-final tie against VfL Wolfsburg had originally been scheduled as a conventional two-legged affair in March. The cancellation of the first game at Petershill Park in Springburn was an early victim of the coronavirus in the sports spectating itinerary that I had planned for the spring and summer of this year. (The refund of my £14 ticket was made with impressive efficiency by the club manager, Laura Montgomery).

After a long delay, the Women's Champions League has now resumed and the Glasgow City-VfL Wolfsburg quarter-final was played yesterday evening in the Anoeta Stadium in San Sebastian. (All the matches in this round, the semi-finals and the final are currently taking place in a mini-tournament in Bilbao and San Sebastian as one-off games behind closed doors). I took advantage of BBC Alba's coverage to see how things turned out.

It is relevant to note, I think, that, apart from Glasgow City, all this year's Women's Champions League quarter-finalists have formal associations with their men's counterparts – Arsenal, Barcelona, Paris St Germain, *et al* – with the advantages of technical support, use of facilities and access to sponsorship that these provide. Wolfsburg – similarly positioned – have a fine record in the competition, having won it twice and been runners-up on two other occasions in the last eight years. I was aware, therefore, that Glasgow City were facing a stern challenge in yesterday's match. (The club's only previous quarter-final appearance was a 0-7 aggregate loss to PSG in 2015).

The challenge turned out to be more than stern. Wolfsburg scored their first goal after 15 minutes and a second four minutes later. Two further scores just before half-time gave them a 4-0 interval lead. After the break, the goals kept coming at regular intervals to yield a final tally in favour of the German side of 9-1.

Glasgow City kept going until the end; their heads certainly did not drop. In the second half, Lauren Wade scored arguably the goal of the game with a spectacular shot from the corner of the penalty area, Leanne Crichton hit the cross-bar and Krystyna Freda sent a shot narrowly wide with the goalkeeper beaten. But, even allowing for the lack of match sharpness from this being Glasgow City's first competitive outing for 6 months, there could be no doubting that – both collectively and individually – Wolfsburg were in a different league.

The Wolfsburg side had an enviable combination of athleticism and skill. They moved the ball out of defence with confidence, attacked strongly down both flanks, maintained a high quality in their deliveries into the penalty area – notably from Svenja Huth on the right-hand side – and, when possession was lost, were quick to swarm round the Glasgow City player in order to win it back.

The Danish striker Pernille Harder led the way, her four goals comprising two headers and shots from the edge of the penalty area with left and then right foot. She was denied a fifth (and best) goal – a shot on the turn from distance – by the cross-bar. I was also impressed by the commanding presence in the centre of midfield of Ingrid Syrstad Engen – the scorer of two first-half goals – and the neat footwork and distribution of Huth.[26]

And so Glasgow City's 2019-20 European campaign, which began in Moscow last September, has come to an end. Of course, the football tides do not cease and the club's ebb and flow of transfer activity has seen four new signings – including the South African national captain, Janine van Wyk, who made her competitive debut yesterday – announced in the last couple of months. The new season – domestic and European – awaits. I hope that, at some point in its course, I can complete some unfinished business and take in a match at Petershill Park.

www.anordinaryspectator.com/news-blog August 2020

# Citius, Altius, Fortius – Part 3: Moscow 1980

*"In Moscow, during some of the spare time which we had been allocated to visit a large* beriozka... *I took the opportunity to wander off alone and walk down to the Lenin Stadium, which I entered and in which I sat for about quarter of an hour.*

*I made a mental note of the interior of the stadium: the tartan track, the generally spartan seating, the posher orange and red-backed seats on the far side, the flag poles, the bowl for the Olympic torch, the green football pitch in the centre and the big screens at each end.*

*... late in the afternoon, with the sun going down at the point directly behind one of the large square blocks of floodlights. It was a pleasant and personal little detour. The entry in my diary of the trip records that I was feeling quite exalted when I left the stadium, walked past the large statue of Lenin and headed down the main boulevard back towards the* beriozka".

[*An Ordinary Spectator*, page 168]

In 1980, I was one of a party of students on a "cultural exchange" to the Soviet Union organised by the National Union of Students. It was actually my second trip. Two years earlier, I had visited Minsk, Smolensk and Moscow. This time, the itinerary comprised Moscow, Riga and Leningrad (which is now St Petersburg once again, of course).

On neither occasion was there any need for me to have any particular left-wing sympathies – or, indeed, any political interests at all – in order to be selected for the respective tour parties. I simply responded to the advertisements in a student newspaper and, a few weeks later, joined the companies of 15 or so others who were curious about what they might find – or, more accurately, be shown – behind the Iron Curtain.

During the first visit, our group found itself in a cavernous and largely empty sports hall in Minsk watching some of the group-stage matches in the 1978 Women's World Volleyball Championships: Belgium vs Tunisia, Mexico vs Holland and Yugoslavia vs Italy. It had been our collective decision, part of the way through the second game, that we were *ersatz* Dutchmen and that we would suddenly start to cheer wildly whenever Holland won a point. I'm sure that this was instrumental in enabling our new-found heroines to level the score at two sets all, though it wasn't sufficient to take them to victory.

In this blog, I wish to recall something from my return visit to Moscow in 1980. My diary of the trip for Wednesday 10th September 1980 – 40 years ago to the day – records the entry (reproduced above) for when I had some spare time to myself one late afternoon.

It was exactly four decades ago and I can remember it very clearly. What surprised me at the time – and continues to do so in retrospect – is that I was allowed to enter the stadium and take my seat in the stand without any hindrance. I don't doubt that I was being observed by someone, from somewhere, but there was no hint of an official coming to tell me to vacate the premises. (I enjoyed exactly the same type of unencumbered access to the Melbourne Cricket Ground – which had been the main venue for the 1956 Summer Olympics – when I visited that city in 1987).

As I sat in the Lenin Stadium, I was aware that, only a few weeks earlier, it had been the venue of some dramatic athletics events which had brought gold medals for Allan Wells (100 metres), Steve Ovett (800 metres), Sebastian Coe (1,500 metres) and Daley Thompson (decathlon). Elsewhere, there had been Olympic success for Duncan Goodhew in the swimming pool.

In some respects, it was strange that there had been any British athletes there at all. In the aftermath of the Soviet invasion of Afghanistan in December 1979, the USA had led a boycott of the Games, which had been supported by 65 other nations, including Canada and West Germany. However, the UK was not amongst them. The Conservative Government, which had been elected with Margaret Thatcher as Prime Minister for the first time in 1979, supported the boycott, but left any final decision over participation to the National Olympic Committee and the individual athletes. In the event, the Games were boycotted by the British associations governing equestrianism, hockey and yachting.

In September 1980 – and for some time afterwards – the Cold War remained a central feature of global geopolitics. The old guard Soviet leadership – headed by Leonid Brezhnev – was still in place; two months later the USA would elect a new right-wing president in Ronald Reagan; the Soviet Union would lead a boycott of the Los Angeles Olympic Games by 14 Eastern Bloc countries in 1984; the fall of the Berlin Wall was nine years away...

The Lenin Stadium, which had been built in 1956, was extensively renovated in 1996 with, amongst other things, a roof being added. It had been renamed as the Luzhniki Stadium four years earlier. However, this structure was itself demolished and rebuilt in 2017, in time for Russia hosting the soccer World Cup the following year.

Today, I doubt that the casual visitor to the Grand Sports Arena of the Luzhniki Olympic Complex – to give it its full title – would be able to walk in off the street and take a seat in the stand. The security-conscious times in which we live would put paid to that. And that's before one acknowledges being a Western visitor amid the general tension in East-West relations that never really seems to go away.

However, one cheering fact revealed in the stadium's Wikipedia entry is that parts of the cover and the façade wall of the old structure were retained in the latest design, thus ensuring that not all of the 1980 Lenin Stadium has been lost.

For my part, I also have something from that time. The *beriozka* I mentioned at the beginning of my diary entry was a store in which good quality items could only be purchased with western currency. On my visit, I bought an elegant wooden letter-rack, complete with Olympic rings, which – 40 years on – retains its place in my study.

www.anordinaryspectator.com/news-blog September 2020

# Cricket

# The 1954 Vintage – Part 1

*"Clarke, notwithstanding an ungainly bowling action, exemplified the menace that surrounded so many West Indian fast bowlers of the time. In his thoughtful autobiography, Playing for Keeps, Alec Stewart described Clarke as the fastest and most intimidating bowler he played with or against. I clearly detected his threat, at the time, from the safety of the spectators' seats".*

[*An Ordinary Spectator*, page 133]

Next month, when I join the ranks of the UK's state pensioners, I shall post a blog on some of the thoughts that occur to this sports spectator on reaching that particular milestone on life's journey. Here, I preface those remarks with a cricket-specific exercise.

A trawl through the list of the 3,000-plus dates of birth of test cricketers listed in the *2020 Wisden Cricketers' Almanack* has presented me with the opportunity to select a test team entirely born in my year of birth – 1954.

The squad from which to choose is not large – 27 in total, including some who played only one or two matches – but I have to say that the First XI is not a bad side: 439 caps, 41 centuries and 347 wickets (though the last of these figures is somewhat skewed by one contribution, of which more below).

Although the representation comes from five different countries, it must be acknowledged that the contribution from the Sub-continent (with only one player selected from India) is disappointing. The lack of available players is partly explained by Sri Lanka's relatively late entry into test cricket (in 1981) and this factor obviously accounts for the absences of representatives from Zimbabwe and Bangladesh as well as Ireland and Afghanistan. I was also seriously constrained by my chosen age cohort being affected by the absence of South Africa from the test cricket arena during their peak playing years.

Being from my generation, I like my top order batsmen to be relied upon to give a solid foundation to the innings: none of this flashy stuff. Whilst Geoff Boycott fails to qualify (by 14 years), it can safely be said that a top-three of John

Wright, John Dyson and Chris Tavaré more than adequately meets this criterion. Wright scored 12 centuries in 82 tests, whilst Dyson and Tavaré have similar records: two centuries apiece in 30 and 31 appearances, respectively. One of John Dyson's hundreds – which I witnessed – was registered in the first innings of the Botham/Willis test at Headingley in 1981. Until the English pair's heroics on the last two days, this looked to have been the defining contribution of the match.

But it is at the other end of the batting order that the team's real strength is to be found. The opening bowlers are two West Indians, Michael Holding and Sylvester Clarke: a frighteningly formidable combination (though I don't envy the captain's task in telling one of them that he will have to bowl uphill).

Holding took no fewer than 249 test wickets in only 60 matches. I first saw him play in the Lord's test of 1976, when he opened the bowling with Andy Roberts. This was in the days when Mike Brearley, the England captain, was experimenting with a rudimentary skull-cap to give his head some protection: a virtually unheard-of development at the time. With the benefit of hindsight, it seems incredible that, until then, a soft cloth cap or a sunhat had provided the only defence against the 90-plus mph missiles that had been hurled at batsmen through the decades.

I was surprised to learn that Clarke played in only 11 tests, his appearances limited by the rich choice of fast bowlers available to the West Indian selectors in this era as well as his test match banishment for taking part in unauthorised "rebel" tours of South Africa. The quotation given above described my impressions on seeing him play for Surrey against Yorkshire in a Gillette Cup semi-final at the Oval in 1980.

The 1954 Test XI has a four-man bowling attack. The supporting seamer's role is filled by Arnie Sidebottom: a veteran of one test match and the obligatory Yorkshireman in the side. (If and when I get round to selecting my 1954 XI of English professional footballers, Sidebottom would again be a contender, given his 20 appearances for Manchester United between 1973 and 1975 and his subsequent career at Huddersfield Town and Halifax Town).

The choice of spin bowler rests between the Australians Ray Bright and Trevor Hohns and the West Indian Derick Parry. The first of these is selected on the basis of the length of his test career (with 53 wickets in 25 matches), the variation that his slow left-arm bowling would provide and his ability as a stock bowler when the opening pair need a rest.

It was Bright, of course, who nearly scuppered Boycott's glorious day at Headingley in 1977 – when the local hero made his 100th First Class century in a test match against Australia (which I also witnessed) – his passionate appeal for a catch by the wicket-keeper Rod Marsh down the leg-side being turned down by the umpire. The incident was also recollected in *An Ordinary Spectator*:

*"Bright's body language suggested he was less than impressed when the decision went against him; he snatched his sunhat from the umpire in disgust. The crowd on the Western Terrace jeered. We were square to the wicket, of course, and in no position to judge the validity of the appeal. But we knew it was not out: it couldn't possibly be. The fates had decreed otherwise. From my own perspective, I thought that Bright was a scruffy cricketer – with an appearance not unlike that of the Richard Dreyfus character in Jaws and an ungainly bowling action – and certainly not the man to disturb the natural course of events on this particular day".*

After the solid – if not stolid – foundations laid by the first three in the order, the heart of the batting line-up takes on a more flamboyant appearance through Allan Lamb and Kim Hughes with Yashpal Sharma getting the selector's nod for the last batting place over Australia's Peter Toohey and Faoud Bacchus of the West Indies. There is plenty of experience here with a total of 25 centuries in 186 tests.

Although I saw Lamb play several times for England, the reference to him in *An Ordinary Spectator* is from the Benson and Hedges Cup Final at Lord's in 1987, when Yorkshire defeated Northamptonshire. My father and I watched the game from a packed Mound Stand, two rows back from the boundary edge. I noted that after Lamb had been dismissed for a low score – edging a wide delivery from Paul Jarvis through to David Bairstow behind the stumps – my dad had been really impressed that he had walked off without waiting for the umpire to raise his finger. (Arnie Sidebottom was at the crease when, with the scores level, Jim Love blocked the last ball of the game to give Yorkshire the victory on the basis of having lost fewer wickets).

Hughes is the obvious choice as captain of the 1954 XI, I think, notwithstanding his experience as being another veteran (along with Bright again and Dyson) of the 1981 Headingley test match, which was one of the 28 occasions on which he led Australia. Wright, who captained New Zealand in 14 tests, would be his deputy.

That just leaves the wicket-keeper. The role is taken by Steve Rixon, who played 13 times for Australia between 1977 and 1984 taking 42 catches and making 5 stumpings.

The selection is not without its flaws. The batting line-up lacks a consistently heavy scorer – no-one in the side averaged 40 in tests – although having Yashpal Sharma at number 6 does provide a useful supplement to the top order. Perhaps most significantly, there was no obvious candidate to fit the bill as all-rounder and provide the ballast in the middle-order. As a result, Sidebottom is due to bat at number 7 and Rixon at 8, which might be at least one place too high in each case. The lack of an all-rounder also places a significant burden on Sidebottom and

Bright in their support of the main strike bowlers, Clarke and Holding. Overall, however, it looks to be a side of resilience and character and it will fight its corner.

On a broader historical note, it is perhaps not surprising that the 1954 cohort feature in some of the major developments in the cricket world during the last half century. For example, at the end of the 1970s, Bright and Holding took part in the World Series Cricket competitions organised by Kerry Packer as did two other 1954-born test players, Richard Austin of the West Indies and Taslim Arif of Pakistan.

Then, in the following decade, no fewer than five of the players in my 1954 Test XI took part in "rebel" tours of South Africa during the period before that country was admitted back into the test match fold: Clarke, Dyson, Rixon, Sidebottom and Hughes (who captained the Australian sides in two series in the mid-1980s). These squads also included four others born in 1954 who, as noted, didn't make the final XI: Austin, Bacchus, Parry and Hohns.

It is also interesting that, following the completion of their playing careers, three players – Wright, Dyson and Rixon – have held senior coaching positions with one or more of the test-playing nations.

So these are my contemporaries in the 1954 vintage (or were in the case of Sylvester Clarke and Richard Austin, who died in 1999 and 2015, respectively). I am in good company. Bring on the 1955 XI.

*The 1954 Test Team: JG Wright (New Zealand), J Dyson (Australia), CJ Tavare (England), AJ Lamb (England), KJ Hughes (Australia, captain), Yashpal Sharma (India), A Sidebottom (England), SJ Rixon (Australia, wicket-keeper), RJ Bright (Australia), ST Clarke (West Indies), MA Holding (West Indies), PM Toohey (Australia, 12th man).*

www.anordinaryspectator.com/news-blog October 2020

# Rugby Union/Rugby League

# Risks and Probable Outcomes

Two major rugby finals were played on Saturday: league's Challenge Cup final between the Leeds Rhinos and Salford Red Devils at Wembley and union's Heineken Champions League final between the Exeter Chiefs and Racing 92 at the Ashton Gate ground in Bristol.

There were several similarities: both were shown on terrestrial television (respectively, the BBC with 9 presenters/commentators/analysts) and Channel 4 with 8 – whatever happened to Ray French or Bill McLaren commentating with only Alex Murphy or Bill Beaumont in support?); both were played in stadiums that were eerily spectator-free as a result of the coronavirus restrictions; and both entered the last 10 minutes with the game evenly poised (16-16 at Wembley and 28-27 to Exeter at Bristol).

It is the contrast in game management in their respective final stages that is particularly interesting.

At Wembley, once Ash Handley had scored his second try to draw Leeds level (and Rhyse Martin had missed the touchline conversion), it was distinctly possible that the next score would determine the winners of the Challenge Cup. Moreover, it was also highly likely that that score would be a drop goal – as Jonathan Davies, one of the BBC's commentators, anticipated as early as the 70th minute (though he annoyingly used the Australian term "field goal").

Sure enough, Leeds twice manoeuvred themselves into position for Luke Gale – their drop goal expert – to make attempts at the extra point. His first effort (a minute or so after Davies had raised the possibility) went narrowly wide, but his second – perfectly struck with 4 minutes to go – sailed through the posts to give his side the decisive 17-16 lead.

The Salford defenders had known what was coming and on both occasions they made valiant attempts to charge the kick down. However, as their captain Lee Mossop acknowledged afterwards, the physical exertions of the game had taken their toll and Gale, knowing exactly how much time and space he had at his disposal, was able to successfully execute a well-rehearsed routine.

At Bristol, in a match in which the Parisian side had never held the lead, a penalty goal reduced their arrears to that single point after 64 minutes. That remained the position when Racing had possession within the Exeter 22 for a full five minutes from the 70th minute onwards, including a run of 19 successive phases, several of which were right in front of the Exeter posts. During this period, the Racing forwards took it upon themselves to make individual thrusts for the try-line in the hope that supporting colleagues would drive them over, before recycling the ball to launch another attempt; their fly-half and playmaker, Finn Russell, touched the ball once.

One wonders at what point Russell might have realised that the forwards' strategy was not yielding results against the impressively disciplined and organised Exeter goal-line defence. Why did he not take up a position a few yards deeper and demand the ball in order to attempt the easiest of drop kicks that, with the three points on offer, would have given his side a 30-28 lead? Indeed, the longer Racing's unsuccessful siege of the try line went on, the better the drop-kick option would have been, as the running down of the clock would have reduced the time available for Exeter to make a counter-strike on the scoreboard. (This approach is one with which all the great American Football quarterbacks have been familiar over the years – from Joe Namath to Tom Brady – namely, the timing of their team's winning field goal (sic) with the clock ticking down to its final few seconds).

Ultimately, game management at a time like this is a question of assessing the risks and probable outcomes of the alternative actions that are available – usually when in a state of physical and mental exhaustion. I would judge that the probability of Russell succeeding with the drop goal from 15 yards in front of the posts would have been close to 100%. The probability of Racing retaining possession through multiple phases before crossing the Exeter try-line might also have been high – and Exeter did have a player in the sin-bin for this period of play – but, crucially, not as high as the alternative. There was always a risk that possession would be lost or an infringement incurred – as did finally happen after the 19th phase. A penalty awarded to Exeter took them to the security of the half-way line with their lead intact.

It might be argued that this discussion is irrelevant because another subsequent penalty was awarded to Exeter to take the final score to 31-27. I think we can discount this. The psychology of the game would have been completely different if Racing had taken the lead – for the first time in the match – with only 5 minutes to go. And the last penalty was given away in a desperate attempt by a Racing player to regain possession, which wouldn't have been needed if his side's noses had been in front.

A final point. Neither Miles Harrison – the lead Channel 4 commentator – nor any of his army of supporting colleagues made any reference to the drop-goal option during this decisive period of play.

The assessment of risks and probable outcomes. Where else have I been hearing about that recently?

www.anordinaryspectator.com/news-blog October 2020

Sport: General

# The 1954 Vintage – Part 2

*"The average age of the Cambridge rugby side in my first term was, not surprisingly, two or three years older than me. The majority were, like me, undergraduates, though obviously further advanced in their courses…*

*But [it] was only those two or three years. These players were not far away from being a team of my contemporaries doing battle with mature club sides… If I had been of the required standard – which, of course, I was nowhere near – it would have been me out there on the pitch as well".*

[*An Ordinary Spectator*, page 117]

Earlier this week, I qualified for the New State Pension. The age for men of my generation had drifted slightly – it is now 66 – but I have got there in the end. Henceforth, the UK taxpayer will generously contribute to my (taxable) income by just under £171 per week.

I have mentioned previously (*"In The Stars?"*, 14th October 2019) that Wilfred Rhodes is the oldest cricketer ever to play for England (aged 52 in 1930). The corresponding achievement in rugby union is that of Fred Gilbert (aged 39 in 1923) and in football Stanley Matthews (42 in 1957). In rugby league, Gus Risman led Workington Town to success in the Challenge Cup final of 1952 at the age of 41.

The ages of the oldest winners of Men's and Ladies' Singles titles at Wimbledon are 41 and 37 (Arthur Gore and Charlotte Cooper Sterry in 1909 and 1908, respectively, though Serena Williams will beat the latter record if she wins an eighth title). The oldest cyclist to take part in the *Tour de France* is from the same era: Henri Paret was 50 when he competed in 1904. In the Open Championship, the oldest winner is – appropriately enough – Old Tom Morris, who was the advanced age of 46 when he took the title in 1867. Like countless others, I was willing the 59 year-old Tom Watson to shatter this record at Turnberry in 2009; he was the runner-up.

I have left all these ages behind.

So far, so predictable. We have a good idea of the age-groups in which high-level sporting prowess is at its peak and after which it diminishes. However, all is not yet lost as far as my potential sporting success is concerned. If I brush up my shooting skills and win a medal at the Olympic Games in either Tokyo next year or Paris in 2024, I would still be younger that the 72 year-old Oscar Swahn, a Swede who won a silver medal in the "sports shooting" event at the 1920 Olympics in Antwerp.

Of course, Swahn was a mere whipper-snapper in comparison with the 73 year-old John Copley, who also won a silver (in London in 1948) in the "mixed painting, engraving and etchings" category of the Art Competition. (Helpfully, the website from which I gleaned this information noted that this was "no longer recognised as a sport"). Art competitions were in the official programme for all Summer Olympics between 1912 and 1948 and, in the last year, medals were awarded in architecture, literature, music, painting and sculpture. In 1949, the International Olympic Committee decided that, in future, it would hold a non-competitive arts exhibition instead.

More realistically, for my generation, there remain open the age-group sporting events in which we can compete. Most of these might be modest in scope and standard, perhaps, but they still provide the opportunities to derive personal satisfaction and a sense of achievement. A couple of years ago, in one of our regular e-mail conversations, my good friend Andrew Carter – who is older than me by three days – reported that he had won a bottle of wine for being the first man over 60 to finish the Evesham 10k race: "Hardly the Olympics, but I feel like I've become a professional!". We are – both, hopefully – still a very long way from that distant point at which Dylan Thomas memorably instructed us to "not go gentle into that good night".

So what of the 1954 vintage? Which of my and Andrew's contemporaries scaled the domestic sporting heights?

The England cricketers with the most test caps are Allan Lamb (79) and Chris Tavaré (31) – both of whom were selected for my 1954 Test XI, as reported last month ("*The 1954 Vintage – Part 1*", 1ˢᵗ October 2020) – although only three other Englishmen make the list (with 5 caps in total). Lamb and Tavaré made 16 test match centuries between them (of which the latter contributed two), but the group as a whole took just two test wickets (one falling, rather improbably, to Lamb and the other to Arnie Sidebottom).

On the soccer field, the roll-call includes two prominent England internationals with nearly 100 caps between them: Trevor Francis, who was the first footballer transferred for £1 million when he moved from Birmingham City to Nottingham Forest in 1979 – a fact that really betrays the passage of time when we learned earlier this summer that Lionel Messi's contract with Barcelona reputedly included a buy-out clause of over 700 million euros – and Phil Thompson, the multi-trophy winning defender with Liverpool. There is also Sam Allardyce: an England manager, rather than player, albeit for only one match.

Given the demographics, it is no surprise that the 1980 British Lions rugby union tourists to South Africa included 5 players born in 1954. Of these, three were fly-halves – and all of them excellent players – David Richards of Wales and the Irishmen, Ollie Campbell and Tony Ward. I recall seeing Richards – then of Neath Grammar School – as the outstanding player in the Llanelli Schools Sevens tournament of 1972. In the league code, there have also been half a dozen Great Britain internationals, the most prominent of whom is probably the (Peebles-born) full-back George Fairbairn, who played 16 times for England as well as winning 17 GB caps between 1975 and 1982.

The overseas sporting Hall of Fame has some impressive members: Chris Evert, Bernard Hinault, Michael Holding (another 1954 Test XI selection), Marvin Hagler, Walter Payton *et al.* I must also include the distinguished Brazilian football captain (and qualified doctor) Brasileiro Sampaio de Souza Vieira de Oliveira – who was better known as Socrates – if only to reproduce an absolutely classical (pun intended) piece of John Motson commentary from Brazil's match with Italy at the 1982 World Cup: "And that was a goal by Socrates that sums up the philosophy of Brazilian football".

At this point, I shall go slightly *off piste* as far as sporting connections are concerned by noting that the 1954 cohort has also been prominent in other fields, notably feature film direction (James Cameron, Ron Howard, Joel Coen, Ang Lee, Jane Campion) and – especially – politics. The vintage can lay claim to Angela Merkel, Shinzo Abe and Condoleezza Rice as well as, er, Alex Salmond and Jean-Claude Juncker. I should note that this list includes presidents Recip Tayyip Erdogan of Turkey, Hugo Chávez of Venezuela and Alexander Lukashenko of Belarus, so perhaps I should move the discussion on elsewhere. How about contributors to popular culture: John Travolta, Matt Groening (the creator of *The Simpsons*) – and Adam Ant.

My first realisation, when watching an open-age sports event, that the players on the field in front of me were of roughly my age was at a Cambridge University First XV rugby match in 1974, as noted above. By that time – although I did not realise it until much later – I had already attended the first international sports event that featured a participant who was younger than I was. This was the England versus Luxembourg Ladies Volleyball match at the Leeds University sports hall in March 1973, when the home side included the 18 year-old Joan Quigley from the Kirkby club, who was already the veteran of 20 previous internationals.

In an idle moment, as I stared out of the window contemplating (yet again) the implications of the coronavirus – from tomorrow evening, given the new restrictions in Tier 4 Local Authority areas imposed by the Scottish Government, I will be breaking the law (repeat: breaking the law) if I travel outside East Dunbartonshire – I had considered conducting an enquiry of anorakian proportions. Which sporting contest had I attended – I wondered – that incorporated the highest level of 1954 representation? A moment's thought suggested that it would certainly have been the London Marathons – with their cast lists of thousands – that I went to see in the early 1980s, followed by the Wimbledon tennis and Open Championships fields of the same era.

Not very interesting. What about team sports? I suppose that an answer might have been found by trawling through my collection of match programmes – and focusing on those for the bigger events for rugby, soccer and cricket, in which the players' details were given – in order for me to pinpoint the fixture that included the highest number of my exact contemporaries. But life is too short, really. A glance at the programme for the Varsity Match of 1976 reveals that five of the participants had been born in 1954 (and that I was not one of them). That answer will suffice, I think.

And so the New State Pension age is reached and I arrive at another checkpoint on life's journey. It feels as if I were passing over the line across the road that marks the location of one of those intermediate sprints that feature part of the way along a mountainous Stage in the *Tour de France*. I trust that that is an appropriate analogy: a staging post at some considerable distance from the finishing line.

Let us hope that, in the years to come, we will be cheering the 80 year-old first-time novelist who wins the Booker Prize or the 90 year-old chemist being recognised by the Nobel Prize Committee. We of the 1954 vintage will look to follow them – albeit some distance behind – in heeding another of Dylan Thomas's commands: we will indeed "burn and rage at close of day/rage, rage against the dying of the light".[27]

www.anordinaryspectator.com/news-blog November 2020

Rugby League

# From Light Blue to the Red, White and Blue

Roundhay School in Leeds, which I attended between 1966 and 1973, has produced a number of fine rugby players over the years – including full and schools England internationals – albeit in the union code. However, it is the career of Keith Slater, who died last July at the age of 75, that really stands out.

As far as I am aware, Slater – whom I never met, unfortunately – is the only former pupil either to have won a Rugby Blue at Cambridge University (in 1964) or to have had a career in professional rugby league (for Wakefield Trinity between 1968 and 1972). This in itself would be striking enough within the narrow context of a school's rugby tradition. What is more interesting, I think, is that this career path – from Oxbridge Blue to the paid league ranks – is highly unusual. To the best of my knowledge – and I stand ready to be corrected – there have been only two other rugby players to have taken this route.

The details of Keith Slater's career have been admirably described in last summer's obituaries, notably on the Wakefield Trinity website and in the Autumn 2020 edition of this *Journal*. He had moved to Temple Moor GS (also in Leeds) by the time he was capped by England Schools in 1963. After representing Cambridge (and winning a Blue in his first year), he played on the wing for Headingley RUFC and then for Wakefield for four seasons.

Slater made 118 appearances for Trinity, scoring no fewer than 82 tries and also kicking 13 goals. The 7 tries he scored against Hunslet in a fixture in February 1971 equalled the record for a single match in Wakefield's colours created by Fred Smith in 1959. He represented Yorkshire at rugby league on four occasions.

Keith Slater features twice in my personal sports-spectating career. In April 1968, 6 months before he turned professional, he played for Headingley against Roundhay at Chandos Park in the first rugby union club game I ever attended. (This was over 6 years after my league debut watching my dad's beloved Hunslet at Parkside). In those days, Yorkshire club rugby union was not for the faint-hearted and I remember the game being ferociously tight and closely fought. My father and I later remarked that there was not much passing of the ball amongst the three-quarters – an understatement, there was only one try in the match – and, in retrospect, I doubt that Slater had much chance to show his paces.

The match programme for this game reveals that RM Lamb – one of six Headingley players behind the scrum to have an asterisk against his name to denote a Yorkshire county player – lined up in the centre; Mike Lamb later signed for Leeds and was to play with distinction for Bradford Northern, including in the 1973 Challenge Cup final, when he was on the losing side against Featherstone Rovers. At fly-half in the Headingley team was a certain I McGeechan – later an illustrious British Lions player and coach.

My stronger memory is of Slater playing for Wakefield at Parkside in November 1969. My father and I watched the game from the large covered stand at the Dewsbury Road end of the ground and we had a perfect view when, in the first half, the winger was put in the clear and sprinted down the touchline towards us. The Hunslet full-back was David Marshall – a very sound defensive player – who moved across to shepherd him towards the side of the pitch in the textbook manner. Slater feigned to cut inside, but then, as Marshall adjusted his balance, took the outside route to touch down in the corner without a finger being laid on him.

Even in the disappointment of our side conceding a try, dad and I recognised that we had just witnessed a piece of absolutely exquisite skill. Curiously, my other recollection of this incident is of when the other Hunslet players were taking their places behind the posts and Geoff Gunney walked over to the spot where Slater had rounded Marshall. He carefully replaced a large divot that the flurry of action had generated, ruefully shaking his head as he did so. What curious memories we retain after all these years.

I am pleased to report that the afternoon ended satisfactorily for the home support. Hunslet overturned a 0-7 half-time deficit to record a 10-7 win with Marshall's two goals supplementing tries by Barry Lee and Johnny Walker.

There is a single sufficient – and necessary – requirement to win a Rugby Blue at Oxford or Cambridge: you have to play in the Varsity Match. (I have known of players being in the side for the whole of the autumn – or Michaelmas – term and then not being selected for the big game: in which case, tough. Conversely, to their replacement: congratulations).

In the 1960s, the Varsity Match was by far the most significant club rugby union game of the English season. On the second Tuesday in December, 50-60,000 spectators would descend on Twickenham and there would be national coverage on BBC television. (I recall that, most years, I would be off school with a heavy cold that day).

Notwithstanding the inevitable turnover of players from one year to the next, the Oxford and Cambridge sides were consistently amongst the best – and certainly the best prepared – in the country. In the match programme for the first Varsity Match that I attended (in 1974), John Spencer – a Cambridge Blue for three years in the late 1960s – noted that "they are so organised as sides that [the players] will be disappointed with the organisation of every side in which they subsequently play". This from someone who was a former England captain and British Lion. The high standards were confirmed at the end of the decade when, in an (in)famous match played at Twickenham, Oxford University – captained by the All Black, Chris Laidlaw – defeated the touring South Africans.

It is not surprising, therefore, that when Keith Slater won his Blue in 1964, he was in very good company. I reckon that there were at least eight current or future internationals taking part that day, including two future British Lions: Mike Gibson of Ireland and Stewart Wilson of Scotland. One of the Oxford centres was Danny Hearn, a later England international, who tragically broke his neck three years later in a representative match against the All Blacks and was permanently paralysed. Opposite him, in the Cambridge centre, was Geoff Frankcom, who was identified in the match programme as the sole international in Headingley's team for the game at Roundhay in 1968. It's a small world.

Unfortunately, for the Light Blues, the afternoon was to end in disappointment as Oxford won convincingly by 19 points to 6. The following day's match report in *The Times* described the control exerted by the Oxford forwards and noted, in its annoyingly quaint style, that "it was seldom that the [Cambridge] wings looked like having a chance to gallop" although "Slater [mis-spelled as Salter] and Fleming each had a little canter" late in the game.

(A curious aside. One of the Cambridge scores – worth 3 points – was "a goal from a mark". In those days, a mark could be called anywhere on the pitch by digging the heel of the foot into the pitch when fielding a kick. If close enough to the posts, a place or drop kick for goal could be attempted. This was the first – and last – occasion on which it occurred in the Varsity Match. The move had been abolished in rugby league in 1922).

Although Slater continued to play for Cambridge University in the next two seasons, he was not selected for the Varsity Match in either year. However, in 1965, he was chosen to tour Argentina and Brazil with a combined Oxford and Cambridge side. In Argentina, he touched down three times in his five appearances. It's a fairly safe bet that there aren't too many rugby players who have scored tries in Córdoba and Rosario as well as Parkside and Belle Vue.

After Cambridge, Slater returned to Leeds where, as noted, he played rugby union for Headingley. This was Yorkshire's premier club, as determined – in the era before the meritocracy of a league structure – by the "quality" of its fixture list: Coventry, London Scottish, Richmond, *et al.* (Headingley declined to test themselves against local rivals in the Yorkshire Cup, not entering the competition in the half-century up to 1973). Then, in October 1968, he turned professional.

The enmity felt (and displayed) during this period by the senior officials in the Rugby Football Union (RFU) hierarchy towards its League counterpart – and towards those who chose to follow the path from the amateur game into the paid ranks – has been well documented. Wakefield Trinity's new signing might not have been a well-known international – thereby commanding the commensurate signing-on fee attained by the likes of David Watkins or Tom Brophy – but the club's capture of a Cambridge Blue would certainly have ruffled some Establishment feathers.

For many converts from union to league, there were also often difficulties at the receiving end, when the new team-mates compared the signing-on fee with what they themselves received when moving from amateur rugby league. In a later generation, the autobiographies of such as John Bentley and Adrian Hadley confirm the animosity that they detected on their respective arrivals in the home changing room.

It is interesting, however, that, at the time of signing Slater, Wakefield Trinity had had some recent experience of successfully recruiting from the union code to complement the usual league sources. The prop forward David Jeanes was already proving a powerful addition to their playing squad, having signed from Wakefield RFC the previous year, whilst, in the backs, Ken Batty also had a union background. Both had played in the 1968 Challenge Cup and Championship finals.

For the incoming player under these circumstances, the most effective response is to prove one's value on the pitch, particularly if teammates realise that the individual is contributing significantly to a successful team performance (and the achievement of winning pay). If there were any doubters at Trinity, they must surely have been dispelled by Slater's flying start: two tries against York on his debut followed by hat-tricks in the next couple of months against Warrington and Hull.

Nonetheless, it is clear that Wakefield Trinity had peaked in the 1967-68 season, as the following years proved to be a topsy-turvy ride: the club finished 12th in the 30-team league competition in 1968-69 followed by 21st in 1969-70, but then 5th in 1970-71, when Slater registered 31 tries for Trinity as the side reached the Championship semi-final before losing to Wigan.

There have been some "near misses" in terms of the Blue-to-League route. One was Mike Lamb – it's that small world again – whose move into rugby league a few weeks after Slater's was accompanied by much media coverage of his status as a Cambridge graduate. Earlier, in the 1950s, Colin Bell had represented Oxford University before changing codes to join Wakefield Trinity with whom he played for four years and enjoyed Yorkshire Cup success in 1956. Neither Lamb nor Bell appear in the lists of Old Blues, however.

The career paths of the other two players who did make the Blue-to-League transition both make fascinating stories. Harry Edgar has alerted me to that of Rheinallt Hugh (RH) Lloyd-Davies, who read Law at Trinity Hall, Cambridge, and won his Blue in the Varsity Match of 1947 when his two penalty goals gave his side a 6-0 win. His goal-kicking prowess impressed Barrow RLFC, which reportedly paid £1,000 for his services in 1950.

Harry has suggested that Lloyd-Davies might warrant a *Journal* article to himself and I can see why. After five matches for Barrow, he made himself scarce and headed for France. His Wikipedia entry, which draws heavily on an article written by Alan Watkins for *The Independent* in 1997, describes Lloyd-Davies's sad decline following his return to Britain. He was twice imprisoned – for fraud and theft – spent some time passing himself off as a colonel, was treated for alcoholism and was later homeless before dying in London in the 1980s. It is an extraordinary – and tragic – tale.

The second example post-dates the establishment of rugby league Varsity Match in 1981. In the following decade, Adrian (Ady) Spencer won Blues in both union and league before playing over 50 Super League matches for the London Broncos. His was something of a *cause célèbre* as, having also previously played for the capital's team in its London Crusaders guise (and without being paid, apparently), he was banned by the RFU after he participated in the 1994 union Varsity Match. (Rugby union was formally professionalised the following year). His case was taken up in Parliament by Doug Hoyle MP – later Baron Hoyle of Warrington – a long-standing supporter of the 13-a-side game and the father of Sir Lindsay Hoyle, the current Speaker of the House of Commons.

Back at Roundhay School, following Keith Slater's passing, the recollections by his contemporaries on the school's public Facebook site tell their own story of a well-liked classmate and a highly respected friend. These have been complemented by the fond personal memories of Wakefield Trinity supporters on their site. Such comments about Keith Slater the individual sit happily with his achievements on the rugby field in the light blue of Cambridge University and the red, white and blue of Wakefield Trinity.[28]

*The Rugby League Journal* Issue 73, Winter 2020

# Sport: General

# The Icing and the Cake

In the absence of watching any sport from the terrace or the boundary edge since the beginning of February, it might have been expected that I would have compensated by seeking out more sport on television. This has turned out not to be the case.

Since the Spring, the full catalogue of my television sport viewing has comprised:

- The BBC's evening highlights of England's Test match series against the West Indies and Pakistan (see "*Soul Limbo*", 10th July 2020);

- BBC Alba's coverage of the Glasgow City vs VfL Wolfsburg match in the UEFA Women's Champions League ("*Unfinished Business at Petershill Park*", 22nd August 2020);

- The respective finals of the rugby league Challenge Cup and rugby union's Heineken Champions League ("*Risks and Probable Outcomes*", 19th October 2020) plus a couple of games in the earlier rounds of the Challenge Cup;

- The weekly editions of the BBC's *The Super League Show* and *The NFL Show* (a review of the National [American] Football League) and Fox's *NRL Try Time* (the tries in Australia National Rugby League shown on a Sky terrestrial channel);

- The evening highlights of the major cycling tours of France, Spain and Italy (the *Tour de France* and *La Vuelta a Espana* on ITV4 and *La Giro d'Italia* on QUEST/Eurosport); and

- ITV's coverage of England's delayed Six Nations match against Italy (when the English half backs spent 80 minutes kicking the ball high into the early evening Rome sky).

For what it's worth, the programmes I have most looked forward to have been the ITV4 cycling highlights (with the excellent presentations by Gary Imlach and informed commentaries of Ned Boulting and David Millar) and *The NFL Show*.

The latter, in addition to the highlights of the week's key games, has included some revealing analysis by Jason Bell and Osi Umenyiora (both former NFL players) not only on the intricacies of individual plays on the field, but also some deep-rooted issues within the sport, including the "taking of the knee" and the psychological effect on the individual of long-term injury. The programme does have a laddish tendency, however, and the mid-season replacement of the reliable Mark Chapman by Dan Walker as its anchor is a step backwards. I am prepared to wince at some of the on-field hits that are shown, but Walker's comment that the Cincinnati Bengals' Joe Burrows "looked the most promising" of two young quarterbacks following an earlier "Me and Jason were wondering..." really did set the teeth on edge.

The overall choice of viewing has been constrained by the prescient cancellation of my Sky Sports subscription in 2019 but, even so, the above list is selective and not particularly long. There are no one-day cricket internationals or England soccer games (or, indeed, any soccer games apart from the Glasgow City/ FC Wolfsburg encounter) or any of England's recent rugby union internationals in the Autumn Nations Cup. There is no *Match of the Day* or golf or motor racing or athletics... Admittedly, some of these I probably wouldn't have watched in a "normal" year, but the fact still remains that the scope of my interest in the general sporting environment – and the specific outcomes within it – does appear to have narrowed.

I am not at all sure what the psychological roots of all this are, though I suspect that they are complex. I assume that underpinning it must be the continual process of revaluation of what is or is not important – prompted by the global impact of the coronavirus – that all of us must have undertaken in some form or another in recent months across many parts of our day-to-day lives.

I should acknowledge that – pre-coronavirus – I was already really not all that interested in watching the global multi-millionaires of the Manchester United and Arsenal brands battle it out in front of a capacity Old Trafford on *MOTD*. So it is not surprising that I have not had any more interest when the stadium is empty. However, it can't all be about the finances. My interest in *The NFL Show* has not been diminished by the reports of Patrick Mahomes – the quarterback of the Kansas City Chiefs – being awarded a contract worth $503 million over 10 years.

Perhaps some insight is given by looking back at the soccer games that I attended over the two years prior to last Spring. There was an international at Hampden Park, a Europa League tie at Celtic Park and Scottish Premiership fixtures in Kilmarnock and Edinburgh. But the other matches I watched were in Berwick, Alloa, Dumfries and Annan. Likewise, the rugby league venues included Workington and Millom as well as Huddersfield and Leeds and there was rugby union in Otley and shinty in Kingussie... It is not difficult to work out that, whilst I enjoy being an observer at a "major" event, I also like to attend the small-scale contest when there is a new place to visit and a local history to explore.

It was probably inevitable that the availability of television sports would not compensate for the absence of opportunities to watch local events. The sports on television are largely at the elite ends of their respective spectra – not at all surprisingly, given that broadcasters have hours of airtime to fill, the sponsors want value for money and the governing bodies and major clubs need to receive the finances for which they had budgeted.

Hence, for the rugby union authorities, the Autumn Nations Cup: on the one hand, a much-needed contribution to addressing a financial black hole; on the other, a quick-fix solution without any history, played in empty stadiums, the viewing rights for which were sold to the streaming arm of a global behemoth with no pedigree in the sport. Regrettably, for me, in the grand scheme of things, it just didn't seem that important.

The principal impacts of the coronavirus on sport have been below the elite levels. In Britain, the 2020 rugby league season was abandoned after a couple of games at all levels below the Super League. For the 2020-21 season, the Rugby Football Union has cancelled all matches below the top two divisions (and even the second tier – the Championship – has not yet started); Scottish Rugby followed suit for all matches in its league structure. The 2020 English cricket season saw the 18 First Class counties muddle through truncated versions of their 4-day and 1-day competitions, but the club-level programme was drastically curtailed. The recent lockdown in England ruled out amateur and grassroots team sports, whilst team sport in schools has also been severely affected.

And so the elite players are – if not thriving – keeping their heads above water. The multi-millionaire footballers and motor-racing drivers are still being paid. But the events in which they participate are – as they always have been – the icing on the cake. The difference now is that the icing is in danger of being all that is left. The cake itself is being hollowed out and is at risk of disappearing.

The Super League's governing body can probably feel satisfied that its competition succeeded in reaching the end of the season, which culminated in a pulsating Grand Final between St Helens and Wigan that was only decided in the final seconds of the match. However, in doing so, they would do well to remember that, amongst the players who took part in that encounter, were those that had begun their professional careers at lower league clubs such as Batley, Featherstone Rovers and Whitehaven. About a dozen others had aided their development via loan or dual registration experience with other teams in the lower divisions, including the North Wales Crusaders, Dewsbury Rams and Workington Town.

My concern is that, by the time that we reach the "new normal" of the post-pandemic world, there might be a generation of sports participants below the elite levels – especially players and coaches, but also administrators, volunteers and spectators – who will have moved on to other things, not to return. Where, then, will the elite players come from for the television sports of the future?

www.anordinaryspectator.com/news-blog December 2020

# Sport on Television

# Memorable Lines

As we move towards the end of the calendar year, let me refer back to a couple of the television sports programmes which I noted in the previous blog ("*The Icing and the Cake*", 10th December 2020).

They generated the occasional memorable line. Two examples.

The weekly *NRL Try Time* programme of Australian rugby league highlights produced by Fox was actually quite a hard watch. There was no introduction or summary and no context was given to the action in a match, for example by showing player dismissals or crucial drop goals. Instead, it was just an unrelenting diet of tries: perhaps 70 or 80 (plus replays) in 50 minutes of airtime.

In August, the build-up to one score was when James Tedesco, the Sydney Roosters full back, made a break down the centre of the field. As he was halted in a despairing tackle by his West Tigers opposite number, his shorts and jock strap were hauled down, thus exposing a bare backside. As the play continued, the commentator – uncredited, unfortunately – remarked: "That thing's broken... It's got a crack in it".

Absolutely brilliant. Moments later, a sweeping Roosters move produced a superb try in the right-hand corner for Brett Morris.

The second example – from Gary Imlach during ITV4's excellent coverage of the highlights of one of the days in the *La Vuelta a Espana* in November – was probably less spontaneous. In the usual way, at the individual time trial towards the end of the race, the day's current leader took his seat in a makeshift studio in front of a camera – with a backdrop of the sponsor's logo – until someone else finished the course in a faster time and moved in to take his place.

Imlach's commentary covered the moment when the time of the australian cyclist, Alex Edmondson, was beaten and he was about to leave the seat: "*he's about to vacate it for the next leader...[pause]... unless he refuses, of course*".

This was on the day of the US Presidential Election.

Finally, another line – not from a sports commentator, but from a poet: the Northern Irishman Derek Mahon, who died in October at the age of 78.

The obituaries referred to Mahon as "truculent" and "troubled" and the details of his personal life – estrangement from his parents, alcoholism, illness – make for sad reading. It might be expected, therefore, that in our present circumstances – approaching the depth of winter, dealing with the coronavirus and its various implications, wondering when the light might shine again – we would find little in Mahon's work to comfort us.

Not so. His reading of his short poem – *Everything Is Going To Be All Right* [29] – was broadcast by the Irish television channel RTE at the end of its news bulletin earlier in the year and this has been widely shared on the internet. The poem acknowledges that "There will be dying, there will be dying...", but goes on to state that "The sun rises in spite of everything..." and concludes with its title line "Everything is going to be all right".

I am determined to end the year on an upbeat note. Everything is going to be all right.

www.anordinaryspectator.com/news-blog December 2020

# Sport: General

# The Coronavirus: One Year On

It was on this weekend one year ago that I enjoyed a mini-tour of rugby-watching in and around Leeds. Four matches in three days: the rugby union encounters between Yorkshire Carnegie and Nottingham Rugby in the Championship (*"Arresting Decline"*, 5th February 2020) and Otley and Caldy in the National League Division 2 North (*"'Let's Keep It Up, Otley'"*, 6th February 2020) and the double-headed opener of the Super League season at Headingley, where the Castleford Tigers played the Toronto Wolfpack and the Leeds Rhinos took on Hull FC (*"The Return of Sonny Bill"*, 7th February 2020).

To date, this remains the most recent live action sport that I have watched in the flesh.

When we consider the events of the last year – and the pervasive impact of the coronavirus – it is tempting to think that much of the world has been put on hold. Foreign holidays have been cancelled, weddings postponed, concerts re-arranged for some future date... In the global sporting arena, the Olympic Games in Tokyo and the Euro 2020 football championships have been held over from last year to this. For the four rugby union teams noted above, their 2019-20 seasons were brought to a premature halt in March and, later, the 2020-21 season delayed until March at the earliest. And so on.

It was not quite so straightforward, of course. The combination of financial and broadcasting pressures meant that the truncated seasons were completed in the elite sports (*"The Icing and the Cake"*, 10th December 2020). Thus, an abbreviated rugby league Challenge Cup competition (involving only the 12 – later 11 – Super League clubs) was conducted (in empty stadiums) and reached a thrilling conclusion at Wembley in August, when Luke Gale's late drop goal gave Leeds a one-point victory over Salford in the final.

In the league, Leeds and Hull qualified for the Super League play-offs by finishing 5th and 6th, respectively, in the shortened 2019-20 season. (This itself represented the Super League authorities thinking on their feet, as the original plan had been for a top-four play-off). There was the possibility, therefore, of Hull FC lifting the title at the Grand Final having finished the regular season half-way down the division. In the event, although they impressively defeated the Warrington Wolves in their first match, they were then heavily beaten by the Wigan Warriors in the semi-final.

At this point, I should probably own up to one of my occasional "what do I know?" *mea culpa*s. In *"The Return of Sonny Bill"*, I remarked that Hull had invested heavily in some big, powerful forwards and that this looked to have been money well spent, given that Leeds had been overwhelmed by 30 points to 4. I noted that, as Hull could also draw on the evident firepower in their three-quarters and the accuracy of Marc Sneyd's kicking game, there was "much promise for their new Super League campaign". In the event, the club's almost immediate slump in form saw the coach, Lee Radford, lose his job in March and it was only a late-season rally that took them into the final play-off place.

Off the field, there has also been action. At the time of their match with Nottingham, Yorkshire Carnegie were hopelessly adrift at the bottom of their division, having taken only one point from their opening 10 matches. Nottingham added to their woes by winning by 62-10. Conversely, in their lower league, Caldy were striding away at the top of the table. The respective relegation and promotion of Yorkshire Carnegie (who have subsequently been re-branded as the Leeds Tykes) and Caldy were confirmed and, when the hostilities are eventually resumed, the two clubs will confront each other in National League 1.

In contrast with my expectations for Hull FC's prospects for the Super League season, I was more accurate in my assessment of the lower part of Otley's division. With three teams to be relegated, I did suggest that it would be a close-run affair, as Otley were then fourth-from-bottom and level on points with Luctonians. It did not turn out well. Otley had slipped down a place by the time the coronavirus-induced drawbridge was raised on the league season and, notwithstanding that they and the sides around them still had 5 matches left to play, the Rugby Football Union decided that Otley would join Preston Grasshoppers and Scunthorpe on the downward path to the North Premier Division.

In the Super League, the off-field events have certainly been significant. Toronto Wolfpack lost their 6 league matches before the season was halted in March. In July, the club announced that the "unexpected and overwhelming financial challenges" brought about by the pandemic meant that it would not fulfil the remainder of its fixtures once the league resumed in August. Toronto's 2020 results were expunged from the records, including the 10-28 loss to Castleford that I had witnessed in February. In November, a formal vote was held by the 11 remaining Super League clubs – plus the Rugby Football League and the

Super League Executive – on whether Toronto should be allowed to return to the competition in the 2021 season. The vote was 8-4 against with 1 abstention.

At present, there remain plans in place for a rugby league team from Ottawa to enter the National League 1 (the sport's third division in Britain) in 2022. Let's hope so. However, the huge uncertainty about any Toronto-based revival casts a long shadow over the development of regular transatlantic competition, notwithstanding that there are also eventual hopes for a New York-based team.[30]

The sense of events moving on applies in the wider world, of course, as well as in the narrower sporting context. One year ago, the US Senate was conducting the first impeachment trial of the former President Trump, whilst at the same time – on the Friday evening on my rugby-watching weekend, to be exact – the UK formally left the European Union and entered the transition phase for finalising the details of separation. This was to last for the remainder of the year, of course, the *denouement* only being revealed – like the stopping of the bomb's ticking clock at the end of a third-rate James Bond film – at the 11th hour.

And what of the predictions that were being made a year ago? The introductory paragraph of the February 1st 2020 edition of *The Economist* opened with the low-key statement that "[A] new coronavirus continued to spread rapidly in China". Jerome Powell, the chairman of the US Federal Reserve Bank was quoted as stating that the virus would probably cause "some disruption" to the global economy, though it was unclear how far that would extend. Powell, having drawn on the vast armoury of the Fed's analytical resources, is the winner of our Understatement of the Year Award.

By contrast, an editorial in the same newspaper referred to the "sparse data and conflicting reports" about a disease that was spreading exponentially. "The medical and economic cost will depend on governments slowing the disease's spread. The way to do this is by isolating cases as soon as they crop up and tracing and quarantining people that victims have been in contact with… If… that proves inadequate, they could shut schools, discourage travel and urge the cancellation of public events". For an early insight into how events would turn out in the UK, that was impressively accurate.

Likewise, in the section on US politics anticipating the first of the Democratic Party's presidential primaries (in Iowa later in the week), the publication suggested that, of all the major candidates on view (including Bernie Sanders and Elizabeth Warren), the one who would be the most likely to win the election against Trump was… Joe Biden.

I wonder if *The Economist* has views on Hull FC's likely performance in the 2021 Super League season.

www.anordinaryspectator.com/news-blog January 2021

# Cricket

# The Test Match World Title

Forgive me if I report on a piece of slightly anorakian historical cricket research. I blame it on the need to exercise the brain cells, in these continued strange times, as I await my invitation to receive the coronavirus vaccine.

The concept of my "Test Match World Title" is straightforward. It starts with the first series between Australia and England in 1876-77 and allows its winners to be judged as the first holders. As it happened, as the series was drawn 1-1 – thus giving us joint holders to begin with – it would appear that we would have to wait until the next series two years later (when Australia defeated England 1-0) to find our initial title holder. However, at this point, I will make the vital – and totally unilateral – executive decision that, in order to qualify for these purposes, a test matches series must have at least two games. Hence, the first holders of the title are indeed Australia, but only after their 2-0 series win in the 1881-82 series against England.

Thereafter, the rules of the game are analogous to that of a World Championship boxing title (or, indeed, the determination of the holders of the Ashes). Australia would retain the title until defeated in a series that had two or more matches – until 1884, in fact, when England won the series 1-0 with two matches drawn. And so on

This means that, in order to acquire the title, a side would not necessarily have had consistent excellence and success over a lengthy period of time (which is required to reach Number 1 in the International Cricket Council's rankings of test-playing countries). Rather, it is sufficient simply to have a single series win, at the opportune time, against the team that held the title.

[An aside. It might not have gone unnoticed that I have employed this historical approach on a previous occasion. *"And the Football World Title holders are..."* (7ᵗʰ January 2019) described the corresponding exercise in international football from 1872 to the end of 2018. The only difference in methodology was that individual match results, excluding Olympic Games, were considered. It was seen that the title was initially held jointly by England and Scotland (who drew the first encounter) and ended up with Holland. In 2019, the baton was subsequently passed to Germany and then back to Holland again. The current (end January 2021) holders of the Football World Title are Italy[31]].

Since England first relieved Australia of the Test Match World Title in 1884, it has changed hands on a further 55 occasions – most recently last year – which implies an average length of holding of 2½ years. Of course, until the West Indies, New Zealand and India entered the test match arena – in 1928, 1930 and 1932, respectively – there were only two (and then three) contenders for the crown, South Africa having (retrospectively) joined the party in 1889. Pakistan played its first test match in 1952 and Sri Lanka in 1982.

The relatively frequent turnover of the crown has occurred partly because of the frequency of teams winning a home series and then immediately losing a series on its next away tour: this has occurred on 21 occasions. The shortest duration for the title ownership is 22 days in the 1979-80 Australian season, when – highly unusually – the home side played concurrent series against England and West Indies. Australia took a decisive 2-0 lead to relieve England of the title on 8th January before going 0-2 down to the West Indies on 30th January, both series being of three matches.

England and Australia have held the title on 19 and 18 occasions, respectively, although the latter's total duration of ownership has been considerably longer, largely due to the long period of dominance that Australia had between 1934 and 1953. However, all the other countries noted above have had their turn: South Africa (on 4 occasions, initially in 1905-06), West Indies (3, including for 11 years following a series win over Australia in 1983-84), New Zealand (3), India (4, beginning with the 1971 series win in England), Pakistan (4) and Sri Lanka (2).

The comparison of each country's relative success in holding the Test Match World Title is perhaps most interesting in the period since (say) 1952, when the competitive environment has been such as to comprise at least 6 test match playing nations, rising to 7 with Sri Lanka's accession in 1982 and 8 with South Africa's return in 1992. (The total is now a round dozen with the inclusion of Zimbabwe, Bangladesh, Afghanistan and Ireland).

England have held the Test Match World Title on 12 occasions during this period. However, there was a long stretch – from 1982-83 (series loss in Australia) through to 2005 (home series win against the same opponents) – when the ownership of the title was held elsewhere. Moreover, no fewer than 8 of the 12 were examples of the short-duration "home series win, next away series lost" phenomenon that was noted earlier.

For England, the lengthier period of title ownership were from 1953 to 1958-59, 1967-68 to 1971 and 1977 to 1979-80. Each of these was part of longer runs of consecutive series – 14, 9 and 8, respectively – that were either won or drawn against all of the other test-playing nations (apart from the West Indies in the last of these periods). England's status as the Number 1 ranked test team for at least part of these times is a theme to which I shall return in a forthcoming blog.

The current holders of the Test Match World Title are England, following last summer's 1-0 win in the 3-match series against Pakistan, who themselves had taken the crown from Sri Lanka at the end of 2019. Having enjoyed another series win in Sri Lanka last month, England will resume their defence against India in Chennai tomorrow. A tough task awaits.[32]

**Note on data**

The details of every series of test match cricket to the end of 2019 are given in the *Wisden Cricketers' Almanack 2020*. The subsequent series (to January 2021) are given on the website of the International Cricket Council. The specific dates of individual series are available on Wikipedia.

The responsibility for any errors is mine. The results presented here are given in good faith.

www.anordinaryspectator.com/news-blog February 2021

# Cricket

# Edging Up and Down

The International Cricket Council (ICC) world rankings of test-playing countries are determined via a rigorous statistical process that takes account of all the test matches played over the previous 3-4 years. For a team to reach the Number 1 position requires, therefore, that it has consistent success over a significant period. Last month, it was announced that, following their latest series win over the West Indies, New Zealand had acquired this status.

Congratulations to them. They have three excellent seam bowlers (Trent Boult, Tim Southee and Neil Wagner), a fine wicketkeeper-batsman in BJ Watling and, in their captain Kane Williamson, the batsman currently rated as the best in the world. Moreover, they play the sport in what I (and many others, no doubt) consider to be the right spirit – hard and fair and with a smile on their collective face – to the great credit of Williamson and his predecessor, Brendon McCullum.

As it happened, the announcement coincided with my viewing of the excellent documentary *The Edge* (Noah Media Group, 2019), which charted the rise between 2009 and 2011 of the England team to be the ICC Number 1 side (having started at 7th) and then catalogued their subsequent decline. The documentary makes for fascinating (and, at times, difficult) viewing, particularly in revealing the tolls – physical and mental – that were exacted of the players in the England squad by the coach, Andy Flower, in the drive to reach the top of the tree.

Much of the material is not unexpected. It is likely that even the relatively casual follower of the England team would have been familiar with the personality traits of the likes of Alastair Cook, Tim Bresnan and Graeme Swann, as respectively described by the captain, Andrew Strauss: "doggedness, determination, resilience", "a solid, dependable person" and "chief joker, buffoon, pain the arse… invaluable". In this respect, it is reassuring that our expectations are confirmed.

*The Edge* spends a considerable length of time on the virtues and flaws of Kevin Pietersen: from his commanding presence and frequently superlative batting through to undermining his captain by texting his (Pietersen's) friends in the South African changing room during the Headingley test of 2012. There is a noticeably perceptive comment about him from Paul Collingwood: "When he first came into the England side, he needed England. As his career went on, the less he needed England, the harder he was to manage". However, it is Pietersen himself who, perhaps unwittingly, provides the most revealing insight, when referring to his need to take a break from the non-stop demands placed on him to play the various forms of the game: "As soon as you take your whites off, your value and your brand just … fall off the face of a cliff". I suspect that, with Pietersen, it was – and is – always about the brand.

We are probably also not surprised – though still made uncomfortable – by seeing the venomous hostility that exists in some test match confrontations, particularly those pitching England against Australia. The sledging appears to be vicious and unremitting with no prisoners taken. I happen to think that the spite-ridden comment made by the Australian captain, Michael Clarke, to James Anderson, as he came out to bat as England's last man to face the fearsome Mitchell Johnson in the Brisbane test of November 2013 – "get ready for a broken f...... arm" – ranks with the worst type of drugs-cheating in terms of being the antithesis of what international sport is supposed to represent.

[An aside. It appears that the boorish nonsense consistently brought to the game by New Zealand's neighbours across the Tasman Sea is not restricted to Ashes encounters. Australia's trite apologia following the exposure of the "Sandpaper-gate" scandal in South Africa in 2018 seems to have now bitten the dust, judging by their on-field behaviour in the recent (lost) home test series against India].

*The Edge*'s most revealing insights concern the emotional costs that were borne by some of the England players. Steven Finn refers to bursting into tears during a session with the team doctor, whilst Monty Panesar describes bingeing on junk food in the safe confinement of his hotel room.

However, the most painful – and poignant – viewing concerns the effects on Jonathan Trott who, in his own words, by the time of the same Brisbane test "…was really struggling internally… in tears on the field… [with] banging going on in my head". Not that his circumstances generated any sympathy from some of those paid to offer their supposedly expert analysis of the proceedings. "Pretty poor, pretty weak" opined David Warner, as Trott left the field after being dismissed.

My main grievance with *The Edge* is with the hype and inaccuracy attached to one of its core statements. There are several references to England not having reached the ICC's Number 1 position before – and, indeed, the DVD box states that they "[became] *the first and only English side to reach world number one*". To me, this did not sound quite right.

The ICC began ranking teams in 2003 and it is the case that England had not been in the Number 1 position in the period to 2011. But test cricket records date from 1877 – when Australia first hosted England at the Melbourne Cricket Ground – not 2003. In this respect, the documentary's retrospectively short-sighted presentation of test match history mirrors that of the media cheerleaders of the Super League, who often seem to view professional rugby league as having started in 1996 not 1895, or of soccer's Premiership, who forget that English football has had a top flight since 1888, not just from 1992.

To examine *The Edge*'s claims about England's historical Number 1 status (or the lack of it), let us consider the years from 1950 onwards. As noted in the previous blog (*The Test Match World Title*, 4th February 2021), this was a period in which there were at least 6 test match playing nations, rising to 8 by the time of South Africa's re-emergence into the international arena in 1991. It was also a period in which England enjoyed lengthy stretches when they either won or drew several consecutive series against all of the other test-playing nations: 14 between 1950-51 and 1958-59, 9 between 1966 and 1971 and 8 between 1976 and 1979-80 (the West Indies excepted in this last period). It is difficult to believe that England were not the Number 1 ranked team for at least part of these times.

And so it was the case. What *The Edge* did not report was that the ICC itself has retrospectively calculated its own test match rankings back to 1952 and that these are readily accessible. England were at Number 1 in four separate periods (covering a total of 106 months) over the subsequent half century, including for 33 months after June 1955 and 37 months after January 1970.

As noted, *The Edge* is an excellent documentary and it is recommended viewing for anyone with an interest in the sport. It's just a shame that it had to play fast and loose with test match cricket's historical record.

www.anordinaryspectator.com/news-blog February 2021

Family

# The Man Sitting Next To Me

My father – William (Bill) Rigg – features prominently during the many years of sports spectating that I have described in *An Ordinary Spectator*. It is appropriate that – today – I refer to him again.

In the book, I noted that, when he first took me to the Parkside ground in south Leeds to watch his beloved Hunslet play rugby league, there were three reasons why I would sit on his shoulders as he stood at the back of the stand: so that I could see over the heads of the other spectators; so that he could explain to me what was going on (the points tally, scrums, the referee's signals, and so on); and so that he could explain to me what was *really* going on, especially the different roles of the players (the speedy winger, the skilful half-back, the lonely full-back as the last line of defence…). I was six years old and I lapped it up.

My father's own induction to Parkside had occurred in the early 1930s, when he had been regularly taken to the ground by his maternal grandfather, a Scotsman called Peter McBride, and his uncle Willie McBride. Dad's father – my namesake, John Rigg – rarely attended, as his duties as a policeman meant that he had to work on most Saturdays.

We shared the enjoyment of Hunslet's success in the first half of the 1960s – a Yorkshire Cup, a Second Division championship, a Challenge Cup final appearance at Wembley – and then the pain of the club's precipitate decline in the years to 1973, when Parkside was sold for industrial warehousing and the club folded. Shortly afterwards, I left to go to university, but we made sure that, after the club had been resurrected as New Hunslet – when it initially endured a peripatetic existence playing at a number of venues, including both the greyhound and football stadiums on Elland Road, before settling permanently at the South Leeds Stadium in Middleton – we took in a fixture during my Christmas and Easter vacations. By that stage, mine was obviously a more distant attachment to the club, but Dad remained hopelessly optimistic: at one stage he endured a 12-month stretch without a home win.

My father was never one for shouting and hollering at the players and officials. He would naturally get excited at the creation of a scoring chance or a fine defensive tackle, but his preferred approach was as a more reflective observer with whom I would occasionally share a quiet observation about a team's tactics or a player's speed or a coach's options... The one (fairly) hard and fast rule we had was that the bag of sweets purchased for the occasion – usually toffees or mints – could not be breached until the first points had been scored.

Rather oddly, given that the Chandos Park ground of Roundhay RUFC was situated only about half a mile from home, it was some 7 years after my league spectating debut that we first attended a rugby union match: as it turned out, a full-blooded encounter between Roundhay and Headingley. We had watched the international fixtures on television, of course, but this was our initial live exposure to the "other" code. Afterwards, we wasted little time in analysing what we had seen – basically far more kicking and much less handling than in league – but that did not prevent us making further trips to both the Roundhay and Headingley grounds, the latter in particular to watch Yorkshire in the Northern Group of the County Championship.

I graduated to watching the bigger rugby league matches with my father at an early stage, beginning with the Great Britain vs Australia test match at Headingley in 1963. Subsequently, we regularly took in the Leeds-based league internationals against Australia or New Zealand. Then, for the 15 years or so from the mid-1980s, we made the annual pilgrimage to Wembley (him from Leeds, me from London and then Scotland, joined by my uncle Vic from Hampshire) for the Challenge Cup final, irrespective of who was playing in it. My father liked the spectacle of the big occasion, though I sense he was also drawn to the Wembley events by the attraction of our annual ritual and the repetition of the familiar.

And so to the cricket at Headingley, for which our first visits together even post-dated our joint venture into rugby union. I had been to see both Yorkshire and England play many times – either with friends or by myself – before my father and I started to attend the occasional match.

After all these years, it is astonishing what remains in the memory. I remember us watching Middlesex play at Headingley in 1972 and Dad being enthralled by the idiosyncratic run-up of John Price, who began each of his long journeys to the wicket by running directly towards us in our seats at long-off. A couple of years later, we saw Phil Carrick take some Surrey wickets one afternoon at Bradford Park Avenue. Then, in the August Bank Holiday Roses Match at Headingley in 1979, we watched Yorkshire complete a thrilling victory over Lancashire, the action being interrupted at one point by the sombre announcement over the loudspeaker that Lord Mountbatten had been killed in an explosion on his boat, followed by the gasps of shock from the spectators sitting around us. These were rare excursions, however: Dad was working during the week and I would be playing cricket at weekends.

Our joint visits to the soccer – all two of them – came later still, both Leeds United matches at Elland Road in 1981: a 1-1 cup-tie against Coventry City and a goalless league game against Liverpool. He said after the latter game that he had really enjoyed watching the skill of David Johnson and Kenny Dalglish in the Liverpool attack, but the truth was that he was simply not much of a soccer person. It was no surprise, of course, when he reminded me that his previous visit to Elland Road had been to watch Hunslet beat Leeds in the 1938 rugby league Championship final.

It was after my father had retired that we formed a more regular cricket-spectating partnership, notably for the second and third days of the Headingley test: the former in the lower tier of the Football Stand, the latter higher up in the balcony. He was the man sitting next to me as we watched the centuries being compiled (Gooch, Ponting, Steven Waugh), the five-fors hauled in (Reiffel, Waqar Younis, Mallender) and the ducks lined up in a row (Atherton, Flintoff, Cronje).

We only conversed infrequently during the actual play: just the occasional whispered comment about a change in the field or a dropped catch. Our discussions were primarily reserved for the lunch interval – my mother's sandwiches consumed in the seats on the other side of the stand, overlooking the rugby pitch – or, later, back at the parental home. We would compare notes on what we had observed: the trim neatness of Alec Stewart's appearance, the notable deceleration in Mike Smith's delivery stride (against Australia in 1997, his only test), the impressive urgency of the young Michael Vaughan's running between the wickets... We were invariably on the same wavelength.

The Indian tourists of 2002 produced a batting masterclass. In the gathering gloom of the Friday evening – as the lights on the scoreboard came on – Sourav Ganguly hit Ashley Giles over the old pavilion and Sachin Tendulkar deposited Andrew Caddick several rows back into the Members' seating in front of the old bowling green. 628 for 8 declared.

That was the last match that we watched together. Two years later, my father was claimed by mesothelioma.

Who knows whether I will be able to resume my rugby or cricket-watching this year. If the latter, it will not be for a test match – Ganguly and Tendulkar also provided my swansong – but perhaps a Championship or T20 fixture at Headingley. And, if so, it is fairly likely that at some point – probably to the slight discomfort of those in my immediate vicinity – I will find that I am muttering quietly. Nothing serious, just a hushed aside to my invisible neighbour about the altered field-setting or that latest missed chance.

I know that the man will be sitting next to me. And that we will compare notes again later.

Incidentally, he was born 100 years ago today.

William Alexander Rigg: born in Hunslet, Leeds, 16th March 1921; died in Moortown, Leeds, 2nd June 2004.

www.anordinaryspectator.com/news-blog March 2021

Rugby Union

# The First Rugby International

The first international rugby match was held 150 years ago today – 27<sup>th</sup> March 1871 – when Scotland defeated England at Raeburn Place in Edinburgh in front of about 4,000 spectators. Scotland scored two tries and a goal (a converted try) to England's single try. In modern scoring, that would be 17 points to 5 – decisive enough – and the following day's *Glasgow Herald* duly recognised "a result most satisfying to Scotland".

The respective compositions of the teams reflected the different initial paths that rugby football was taking in the two countries. Apart from one player from the West of Scotland club, the entire Scottish side played for either public school old boys clubs or the universities. Edinburgh Academicals – whose home ground Raeburn Place remains to this day – supplied 6 players. (West of Scotland FC, formed in 1865, were the only open club of the 8 who went on to form the Scottish Rugby Union (SRU) in 1873, two years after the first international).

By contrast, English rugby was already evolving around a locally based club system across the country. The Blackheath and Manchester clubs both supplied 4 players and Liverpool 3, whilst West Kent, The Gypsies and Ravenscourt Park provided 2 each. (None of the last 3 clubs survived the 1880s). Incidentally, for anyone counting heads, the first international was 20-a-side.

My own attendance at rugby union internationals covers a mere one-third of their total lifespan. I began with Wales versus England at Cardiff Arms Park in 1975 and, to date, the most recent is the Scotland versus New Zealand encounter at Murrayfield in the group stages of the 2007 World Cup. (On the latter occasion, I was less than impressed when, after I had stumped up £85 for a ticket in the West Stand, Scotland fielded a near-second XV, so that the first-choice players could avoid injury and be ready for the subsequent group match with Italy. The New Zealand captain, Richie McCaw, strolled over for a try in the first few minutes and the All Blacks cantered to a 40-0 win).

During this period, I accumulated a total of 27 spectating caps: 17 for England, two of which were against Scotland (including the latter's win at Twickenham in 1983, their last – until this year – on that ground) and a further 10 for Scotland against other countries. My success rate for England is low (6 wins in total or 35 per cent) and for Scotland even lower (4 out of 12, or 33 per cent). A total of seven visits to watch England in Cardiff or Paris has resulted in seven defeats.

Of course, my exposure to international rugby union had begun long before I attended a game. I watched games on television from an early age and stored some famous tries in my memory bank – Richard Sharp's classic fly-half's try against Scotland in 1963; Andy Hancock's length of the field effort for England, also against Scotland, in 1965; Keith Jarrett flashing on from the left of the screen to catch a bouncing ball and hare down the touchline in Cardiff to score for Wales against England in 1967. But my actual spectating debut was some 12 years after I had seen my first rugby league international when, as a 9 year-old, I was taken to the ferocious Great Britain/Australia test match at Headingley in 1963.

Whatever celebrations the SRU or Edinburgh Academicals had planned for today's anniversary have had to be put on hold, of course. How I would have liked to have taken the train from Milngavie to Edinburgh this lunchtime and gone to Raeburn Place either to watch a match or, if not, simply to have walked around the open space in which the historic encounter took place in 1871. Curse this blasted coronavirus pandemic. But I will carry out that mission at some stage in the future.

As the sport's overall governing body – World Rugby – celebrates 150 years of international competition, there is much with which it needs to engage if the future is to remain bright. The impact of repeated head trauma on the long-term health of players, the legal cases being prepared by some former players against the administrators for the alleged insufficient duty of care, the need to make the game more attractive for spectators to watch... These are all weighty issues.

My own *bête noir*, which I have noted before ("*Nationality*", 7th February 2018), is the ease with which international caps can be won by players whose links to the country are, at best, tenuous or opportunist via either the grandparent qualification or the three-year residency rules. (Of the 46 players in Scotland and Ireland's match squads for the opening round of this year Six Nations tournament, no fewer than 14 (30 per cent) had been born outside the country they were representing, including 9 (20 per cent) in either New Zealand or South Africa).

What will be guaranteed is the continued ability of the sport of rugby union to evolve. 150 years ago, we not only had 20 players a side... and the need to register a "goal" in order to win a match... and halves of 50 minutes in duration... We also had a different set of sartorial preferences.

The Scotland team played in brown shirts, adorned with a thistle, and white cricket flannels.

www.anordinaryspectator.com/news-blog March 2021

Cricket/Rugby League

# Shuffling into Retirement

In the UK, a restricted number of spectators are gradually being allowed back into stadia to watch the major sports events. 21,000 fans were permitted to attend yesterday's FA Cup Final between Chelsea and Leicester City in the Wembley Stadium that seats 90,000. It is expected that some spectators – predominantly on a Members-only basis – will watch some county cricket next month. "Gradually" and "expected" are implicit caveats, of course: it all depends on the Covid-19 statistics being favourable. The original plans for 600 fans to be allowed into Hampden Park to watch the Scottish Cup final between St Mirren and St Johnstone next weekend have been quashed following the outbreak of the Indian variant of the virus in Glasgow.

It is a statement of the obvious that a spectator sport needs the presence of spectators – usually, the more, the better – in order that its full character can be presented and experienced. Over the last year, we might have watched a Premier League soccer game or a Super League rugby match or a Six Nations international on our television screen and admired the fully competitive nature of the encounter being played out in front of us – complete with sound effects, as appropriate – but, deep down, we probably recognise that, without the crowd of engaged spectators in attendance, it is not really the full shilling.

In this essay, the theme I wish to explore is the relationship that is often built up – over time – between a club's spectators and an individual player and, as a consequence, the adverse effect that the requirements for dealing with Covid-19 have had on the acknowledgement of that relationship when it has come to an end. I am interested, in particular, in the examples of retirement from playing sport that have had to pass under the radar. I shall focus on two of the sports – cricket and rugby league – that should have had full seasons in the 2020 calendar year.

The new *Wisden Cricketers' Almanack*'s review of Warwickshire's 2020 season reports that "Ian Bell, Jeetan Patel and Tim Ambrose all shuffled into retirement without the farewell they deserved". The threesome had played a total of over 850 first-class matches (including over 150 test matches) and, across all forms of the game, Bell alone had represented his county on no fewer than 383 occasions over 20 seasons.

Elsewhere, those who also "shuffled" away included non-test playing county stalwarts such as Paul Horton (218 first-class matches over 18 years, including 15 with Lancashire), Ollie Rayner (151 matches over 14 seasons, principally with Middlesex) and Graham Wagg (164 matches over 19 seasons, including 10 with Glamorgan)

This contrasted with what had been possible 12 months earlier. Following his announcement in June 2019 that he would retire from professional cricket at the end of that season, Marcus Trescothick made one final on-field appearance as a substitute fielder in the final few minutes of Somerset's County Championship game against Essex at Taunton at the end of September. He was greeted with a standing ovation by the spectators and he left the field to a guard of honour from the opposition. Quite right too: it was a fitting tribute from those had watched him play over many years.

For some rugby league examples, I go back to the opening day of the 2020 Super League season and the Castleford Tigers vs Toronto Wolfpack and Hull FC vs Leeds Rhinos double header at Headingley ("*The Return of Sonny Bill*", 7th February, 2020). The eponymous Sonny Bill Williams (SBW) is one of those to have retired from the sport following the announcement that Toronto would not be able to fulfil last season's fixture schedule and his subsequent return to Australia where he played a further five games for the Sydney Roosters. His retirement could hardly be described as "under the radar", however, as it received widespread media coverage, including reports that he hoped to resume his professional boxing career.

The Toronto team at Headingley also fielded Jon Wilkin, who was in his second season with the club having previously played over 400 matches in his 16 years at St Helens. My summary of his side's defeat ("One senses that more will be required from both SBW and Wilkin if Toronto are to hold their own at this level") suggested – none too subtly, perhaps – that both players were somewhat off the pace in this game. Accordingly, it was no great surprise to me when Toronto's demise prompted Wilkin's retirement from playing although, unlike SBW's, this was a relatively low-key affair, given his impressive club and international career. Jon Wilkin has made a successful transfer into the BBC commentary team, where he is an informative and media-friendly analyst.

The end of the 2020 season saw other high-profile retirements from British rugby league, including James Graham at St Helens, Sean O'Loughlin at Wigan and Gareth Ellis at Hull FC. For the first pair, the final match was the dramatic Grand Final at the KCOM stadium in Hull, which St Helens won in the dying seconds of the game, so there was a significant media send-off, even if the ground itself was largely unpopulated. O'Loughlin is – for the modern era – the unusual case, as all his 450-plus club appearances were for his home-town club. But, as with Jon Wilkin, none of these retirements – Williams, Graham, *et al* – were major surprises, as the players were in their mid-thirties (apart from Ellis, who was 39).

It was a different story with one of the Leeds Rhinos team in the second match of the Headingley double-header – Stevie Ward – who left the field with concussion after half an hour. It was his last appearance on the rugby field, as 11 months later, in January this year, he announced that, due to the injury, he would be retiring at the age of 27. Ward had been a feature on the Rhinos scene for almost a decade – he had made his debut for the club as a teenager in 2012 – and, notwithstanding a series of injuries, had racked up over 130 appearances.

Retirements can be for many reasons, of course, of which age and injury are the most common. The point here is that, prior to the imposition of the Covid-19 restrictions on attendance, spectators had a known view of the playing universe – of who the participants were and which teams they represented. By contrast, when we (eventually) enter the post-restrictive "new normal" of watching live sport, a number of constituents of that universe will have been permanently removed. There will be a new "now" which will be devoid of some of the participants of the previous "then", whose departures we will only be able to mark long after they occurred.

It might be noted that it's not only retirement that will have been affected by Covid-19 in this way. In June last year, Tim Bresnan left Yorkshire CCC – for whom he had first played as an 18 year-old in 2003 – to join Warwickshire. He was a player regarded with great affection by the Yorkshire members and – as evident in many of the comments on the White Rose Forum supporters website – there was considerable disappointment that the absence of a traditional full-length season meant there was no occasion on which this could have been acknowledged publicly.

In the meantime, it is pleasing to know that there are some for whom the concept of retirement means something to be put on (semi)-permanent hold. In September 2019 – with his Kent career apparently approaching its termination – the then 43 year-old Darren Stevens scored 237 and took five second innings Yorkshire wickets in his county's huge championship win at Headingley. Last year, Stevens followed this up by easily being Kent's leading wicket taker – with 29 in 5 matches – in the truncated first-class programme. He duly opened his 2021 account with a century against Northamptonshire in the first championship match.

I do respect Darren Stevens's robust Augustinian approach to retirement: ie not just yet. When it does eventually come, I hope his many admirers are able to acknowledge it in the traditional ways.[33]

www.anordinaryspectator.com/news-blog May 2021

# Football

# An Ordinary Spectator Returns

Yesterday evening, Sweden played Ukraine at Hampden Park in the round of the Last 16 knock-out stage of the Euro 2020 tournament. It was the first sporting event I had seen for almost 17 months – or, to be precise, 513 days.

I had applied for a ticket at the end of 2019, when they were first put on sale. Although the sides for this particular contest were obviously not known at that stage – one of the attractions for me in seeking out the fixture – I was not successful in the initial allocation. However, I signalled my continued interest if and when a further tranche of tickets became available and I duly secured one at the beginning of last year. What I had not realised in my enthusiasm to land something was that I had inadvertently transferred my interest in one of the cheap(er) seats to a prime location in the front row of the upper tier of the North Stand. Still, needs must in my quest to participate (as a spectator) in one of 2020's premier sporting events.

That was pre-Covid, of course. After UEFA decided to postpone the tournament for a year, I was given the option of getting my money back or simply rolling things forward 12 months. Having chosen the latter, I then had to trust my luck in the ballot for seats, given the authorities' decision to restrict the overall attendance to 12,000 or just under 25 per cent of the ground's capacity.

As it happened, my luck was in and so, last night, there I was.

It might be noted that, having secured my place at the match, the accompanying baggage of entry requirements was substantial. I had been supplied with an electronic ticket, sent to my mobile phone; I had to wear a face mask, of course, and keep at least 1½ metres away from other fans; I had to bring ID; I could take no more snacks than would fill an A5 bag; I could not bring any drinks; I was not allowed any bags in excess of A4 size; I could not bring a brolly; I had to arrive at the ground within a designated 30 minute time slot (which turned out to be 1½-2 hours before the kick-off).

A reminder. This was for Sweden versus Ukraine at Hampden Park in front of a maximum of 12,000 supporters, though – to be fair to UEFA – these ground-rules were clearly set out in the various e-mails that they sent to me. (The official attendance turned out to be 9,221).

My wife would testify to my being unusually tense in the days leading up to the match. Part of that was due, no doubt, to my low-key technophobia: I would happily much rather settle for a paper ticket sent through the post than have to negotiate with the electronic accessory in my pocket. However, I think it might also have been explained by my prolonged – that is, over a period of nearly a year and a half – lack of experience of attending a major social event. I consider myself to be a reasonably rational and well-adjusted person but, until a two-day sojourn in Edinburgh last week, the farthest that we had ventured since the start of the first lockdown had been about 6 or 7 miles. I have no doubt that, for many people, the pervasive lagged effects of lockdown will be felt for some considerable time to come.

How grateful I was, therefore – notwithstanding the angst of the previous days (and weeks) in anticipation of the event – that the delayed Euro 2020 round of the Last 16 tie at Hampden Park had provided an invaluable staging post on my journey to whatever the eventual "new normal" will turn out to be.

Sweden were probably the favourites in the tie, having come top of Group E in the tournament's preliminary skirmishes (in which it had taken 36 matches to reduce the 24 teams that had reached the Finals down to the last 16). Ukraine had reached this stage by being one of the four best third-placed sides in the six groups, having finished behind the Netherlands and Austria in Group D. Sweden also had the higher (pre-tournament) placing in the FIFA world rankings: 18th, compared with Ukraine's 24th.

I was aware, however, that the earlier tournament performances and rankings probably counted for nothing: this was now a straight knock-out (and another reason for my selecting the tie in the first place). As it happened, by the end of the evening, when the full line-up of the 8 quarter-finalists was known, it transpired that 3 of them had come third in their respective groups and only another 3 had actually come top.

The national colours of the two teams were identical – yellow and azure blue – and so the visuals alone from my lofty vantage point did not provide an immediate sense of the relative sizes of support. I judged that it was about 50: 50 with the Swedes in their replica shirts and the Ukrainians much more inclined to favour being bedecked in their national flag. The latter – congregating in the seats below me to my left – certainly won the vocal contest, their continuous chanting seeming to be amplified by the acoustics of the stadium.

As expected, it was a closely fought match. In the opening exchanges, contested in the bright sunshine of an early summer Glasgow evening, neither side took any risks and each defended in depth; at one Sweden corner, Ukraine had 10 players in their own six-yard box with the other one on the penalty spot. However, the game came alive just before the half-hour mark when a sweeping Ukraine move was emphatically finished by the left-winger Oleksandr Zinchenko. Sweden's equaliser, just before half-time, had an element of fortune about it, as a shot from Emil Forsberg was deflected past the goalkeeper, Georgiy Bushchan. It was a due reward for Forsberg, however, who provided the Scandinavians' most potent attacking threat throughout the evening.

There were near misses in the second half: Ukraine hit the post and, at the other end, Forsberg had successive attempts that shaved the foot of a post and then rebounded from the cross-bar, but the 90 minutes petered out with a sense of inevitability about the arrival of extra time. The game slowed down further in this period, as fatigue and injuries took their toll. However, it contained a decisive moment when the Swedish defender, Marcus Danielson, who had played with some assurance throughout the evening, put in a reckless challenge on Artem Besedin. After a VAR review, his initial yellow card was upgraded to red.

Thereafter, as Ukraine sought to take advantage of their extra man advantage, I sensed that Sweden were hanging on for the penalty shoot-out. They nearly made it, but not quite. The stadium announcer had just stated that there would be 3 minutes of added time at the end of the second period of extra time, when Zinchenko sent in a tantalising cross from deep on the left wing and the substitute Artem Dovbyk headed the ball home.

Perhaps the Swedes were taken by surprise. For the previous two hours, Zinchenko had consistently declined to attempt to beat his man on the outside and centre the ball into the penalty area, preferring inside to double back and play a conservative pass to a nearby colleague. This time, perhaps sensing there was nothing to lose, he went for broke: a swift, out-swinging cross of pinpoint accuracy for his on-rushing colleague to exploit.

Cue unbridled celebration amongst the exuberant flag-wearers down below me. Zinchenko ran towards them and was engulfed. Meanwhile, on the pitch, at least half the Swedish team were prostrate on their backs.

And so my long-delayed evening at Euro 2020 came to a conclusion. Fervour, skill, endeavour, controversy, drama, winners and losers. In other words, sport. It has been a long time between drinks. But the Ordinary Spectator has returned to the well.

www.anordinaryspectator.com/news-blog June 2021

# Cricket

# A Day in Scarborough

*[In April 2021, I was contacted by Alastair Hignell, the former England rugby union international, about the work of Sporting Memories Foundation, of which he is a patron.*

*Sporting Memories uses the power of remembering and talking about sport – along with physical exercise – to assist in tackling dementia, depression and loneliness amongst older adults via online or community-based Clubs. Details of the charity's activities and effectiveness can be found at* www.sportingmemoriesnetwork.com/what-we-do.

*Amongst its resources is a collection of over 2,000 sporting memories – organised by sports and events – to enjoy or use. The collection, which is fully searchable, contains written memories, radio recordings, videos and photographs from sports fans, family members, players and writers.*

*Alastair, who had been alerted to my writings on sport by an old college friend, invited me to submit a piece. I was pleased to respond with some recollections of the Gillette Cup semi-final of 1969 (expanding on some content that had previously appeared in* An Ordinary Spectator*).*

*There is an extensive cricket component to the Sporting Memories collection, which can be accessed via the website address given below. A* Day Trip to Scarborough, *which was well received, was included in the section on memories relating to Yorkshire CCC in July 2021].*

In the summer of 1969, my friend Brian and I became expertly familiar with the bus and train routes that emanated from Leeds in order that we might follow the exploits of Yorkshire County Cricket Club on the county's various "out-grounds" – Harrogate, Huddersfield, Bradford Park Avenue *et al* – as well as at the headquarters at Headingley.

As the season wore on – and Yorkshire floundered in the lower reaches of the County Championship – it became evident that the key home fixture of the season would be the Gillette Cup semi-final against Nottinghamshire at North Marine Drive, Scarborough. A prize in the final at Lord's awaited. An added attraction was that Nottinghamshire were captained by the world's greatest all-rounder, Garfield Sobers.

In those days, the road journey from Leeds to the east coast was a slow one, with traffic hold ups guaranteed as the A64 wound its way through York and Malton. Brian and I caught a full bus at a ridiculously early hour from Leeds City bus station in the confident expectation that we would be at the ground well in time for the start. And so we were: we arrived an hour before play began. The trouble was, so did thousands of other people, who now formed a long queue from the entrance to the ground along the main road and around the neighbouring Trafalgar Square. There had been little in the way of pre-sold ticketing, even for a match as important as this. It was "first come, first served" and, after our long journey, there was a clear danger that we would not get in at all.

In the event, Brian and I must have got two of the last available places before the gates were closed. We queued for two hours and eventually entered the ground an hour after play had started. We saw immediately that the rumours circulating outside had been true: Geoff Boycott was already out (caught behind for a duck) and Yorkshire were struggling. We found some space on the grass on the far side of the ground near the big white marquees that served as refreshment tents.

It was a fantastic day's play and, after all these years, there are incidents from the match that I can recall with absolute clarity.

Yorkshire reached a reasonable score, though not an overwhelming one, thanks to some sensible batting by Phil Sharpe and Doug Padgett and a few big hits by the tailenders. One of these was a towering six from Don Wilson that I followed on its full trajectory, as it nearly disappeared into the sky and then, as gravity took its toll, plummeted to land somewhere between us and the refreshment tents. It was a magnificent strike, characteristic of Wilson's potential for dangerous hitting, when, as a tall left hander, he would plant his right leg down the wicket and look to free his arms in a full swing.

It is more than half a century ago and yet, in my mind's eye, I can readily transport myself back to a warm summer's day, when I am craning my neck back to watch the path of a cricket ball against a clear blue sky.

Thereafter the match hinged on whether Yorkshire could dismiss Sobers before he cut loose and won the game by himself. I watched entranced as Wilson bowled what appeared to be over after over at the great batsman, apparently tying him down for several minutes at a time with his accurate left arm spin, before Sobers would take advantage of a rare loose ball and send it crashing to the boundary. When Sobers was out – caught behind by Jimmy Binks off the bowling of the young Chris Old – I thought that the roar would probably have been heard back in Leeds. The other Nottinghamshire wickets fell steadily, one of which was to a running catch in the outfield by Old – another crystal-clear memory – and Yorkshire had won by the comfortable margin of 58 runs. I could not have imagined a more perfect day.

The date was 30th July 1969. It was 10 days after Neil Armstrong had become the first man to walk on the moon. I was 14 years old and the world was full of wonder.

https://cricket.sportingmemories.net July 2021

# Cricket

# Cricket-Watching Resumed – Part 1

To Yorkshire for a double-header of cricket-watching: my first for over two years. Last Thursday, Yorkshire versus Surrey in the Royal London One-Day Cup at Scarborough; two days later at Headingley, the Northern Superchargers versus the Welsh Fire in the England and Wales Cricket Board's "The Hundred" competition.

I selected the two matches in order to juxtapose the (fairly) old and the (very) new. The RL Cup is contested by the First Class counties over 50 overs per side; it is the latest variant on the one-day competitions that they have played since 1962 (when it was 65 overs each). Royal London have sponsored the tournament since 2014.

The Hundred is the ECB's brainchild (if that's the word) to attract new audiences to the sport. The then England director of cricket, Andrew Strauss, explained the thinking in an interview with BBC Radio Five Live's *Sportsweek* programme when the ECB revealed the format of the tournament in April 2018: *"What we're trying to do is appeal to… people that aren't traditional cricket fans. We want to make the game as simple as possible for them to understand"*.

The Hundred is a city-based tournament, hosted at test match grounds – Headingley being one of the eight chosen locations – the matches comprising 100 deliveries (in batches of 10 from each end) per side. The competition's first match – the women's fixture between the Oval Invincibles and the Manchester Originals – took place last Wednesday.

I will nail my colours to the mast. I am a traditionalist on matters cricket. However, I shall park my assessment of The Hundred for the time being and pick it up again in Part 2 of this essay with, hopefully, something approaching an open mind. First things first: the RL Cup.

Of course, whilst putting The Hundred to one side for a day or so, it was obviously the case that its shadow hung over the match at Scarborough. Yorkshire have supplied 11 players to the ECB's new competition – and Surrey 12 – so the teams on show comprised (for me) some familiar names and a significant number of unfamiliar ones, particularly in the visitors' ranks.

Surrey's comfortable victory was based on contributions from both the youthful and the experienced. In his first RL Cup match, the seam bowler Gus Atkinson took 4 for 43, including three of the first four wickets to fall. Later, the opener Mark Stoneman – a regular thorn in Yorkshire's flesh over the years – batted through the innings as Surrey reached the target of 166 for the loss of 5 wickets with over 10 overs to spare. That Yorkshire had been dismissed in only the 35th of their allocated 50 overs – and on a wicket that was far from spiteful – betrayed a collective misjudgement in the pacing of an innings. The 19 year-old Matthew Revis looked very promising, however, and it was a disappointment when a rash shot truncated his innings at 43.

In the long term, I will probably not recall the match for its detailed statistical outturn. I shall remember it – with affection – for constituting the resumption, after the long coronavirus hiatus, of my county cricket watching with all its quirks and skills: the circle drawn in the air by Yorkshire's off-spinning captain, Dom Bess, at the beginning of his run-up; the urgent skip into action by Surrey's left-arm spinner, Dan Moriarty, at the start of his; the brilliant diving catch by Jonny Tattersall; the neat efficiency of the two wicket-keepers, Jamie Smith and Harry Duke; the umpire Neil Mallender's acknowledgement to the section of the crowd that had signalled a 4 (rather than 6) when a lofted shot skirted the boundary rope; the wholehearted aggression of Yorkshire's South African fast-bowler Mat Pillans – released by Surrey in 2018 – who ended the day with 4 wickets; the skilful way in which the impressive Nico Reifer, another Surrey debutant, evaded a hostile delivery from Pillans by dropping his wrists and swaying out of the way… And so on. It was good to be back.

Indeed, my enjoyment of the occasion had begun even before play commenced. I arrived about an hour before the start and took my favourite place in the West Stand. (I was grateful to be sporting a wide hat in the warm sunshine). The familiar routines unfolded: my initial purchase of a coffee and flapjack; the idle chat amongst some of my near neighbours, some of whom had obviously not met for some time; the volunteer scorecard vendor selling his wares for £1 each; the players warming up on the outfield; the flags drifting in the breeze at the top of their poles; and, this being Scarborough, the seagulls above, circling and observing with a hint of menace. I confess to having felt a pang of emotion. We have all been through a lot and we are now – hopefully – coming out on the other side.

Down to my right stood the hospitality marquee, on the grass in front of which were the rows of deckchairs for the sponsors and their guests. I identified the rough acreage of grass – a couple of square metres at most – on which my friend and I had sat on another hot July day (in 1969) and watched Yorkshire's Gillette Cup semi-final win over the Gary Sobers-led Nottinghamshire. That had been my introduction to this – my favourite – cricket ground and I was mindful that it had been a long time ago.

After Surrey had completed their victory, I waited for a while before taking a couple of photographs and then making my way to the exit on the far side of the ground. By the time I got there, Mark Stoneman had already emerged from the changing room and, still in his kit, was talking to a couple of acquaintances by the boundary edge. Just along from him, a young boy – I would guess aged no older than 6 or 7 – was facing some under-arm deliveries thrown down to him from a few yards away by (I assume) his father. The boy played his shots with a correctly positioned left elbow and a perfectly straight bat.

As Stoneman started to walk past on his way back to the pavilion, the father stopped him to request a photo with his son. He agreed without any hesitation. A modern – very professional – cricketer with, perhaps, one for the future. It was a touching scene with which to end a very good day.

www.anordinaryspectator.com/news-blog July 2021

# Cricket

# Cricket-Watching Resumed – Part 2

It is difficult to exaggerate the general opprobrium with which "traditional" cricket supporters greeted the announcement in the Spring of 2018 by the England and Wales Cricket Board (ECB) of the format which its new "The Hundred" competition would have. (I acknowledge at the outset that, as things stand, I am also in this camp). The tournament – which had been scheduled to begin last year, but which commenced at The Oval last week – is being contested by 8 city-based sides playing matches of 100 deliveries per innings over a month in the middle of the summer.

The main difficulty I have with The Hundred concept is that it has been parachuted in from above. There is neither a sense of tradition nor of history – the emphasis is entirely on the "new". By design, there has been an abandonment of the county-based structure of the sport, in which a significant number of players come through local clubs and academies and where followers of the game can enjoy a sense of reflected pride when some of those players go on to the highest level. As a consequence, I was bound to wonder if there risked being only a fragile identification by The Hundred's spectators with their "local" side.

On the last of these points, the ECB – through its combination of an auction system and the central allocation of players – appears to have attempted to have things both ways. Hence, whilst the Northern Superchargers have 7 Yorkshire players and 4 from Durham in their 16-man squad, the two Yorkshiremen with currently the highest profile (Joe Root and Jonny Bairstow) have been allocated elsewhere (to the Trent Rockets and the Welsh Fire, respectively). Likewise, Ollie Pope (Surrey and England) finds himself in the Welsh Fire squad, the Lancashire captain Liam Livingstone is lining up with the Birmingham Phoenix, Steven Finn (a Middlesex player since 2005) is one of Manchester Originals and the Welsh Fire have a total of one Welshman in the whole of the men's playing squad. And so on. It all feels a bit arbitrary.

At a more general level, the traditionalist's ire is raised by The Hundred's domination of the central part of the summer, which further relegates the 4-day County Championship to the season's margins, diminishes the identity that has been established by the (successful) T20 competition and effectively reduces the Royal London One-Day Cup (played over 50 overs per side) to an under-nourished exercise for county Second XIs – or, at least county 1½ XIs. It's also reasonable to suggest, I think, that, given The Hundred's stated aim of reaching a new – and younger – cricketing audience, its overall image might not have been enhanced by one of its major sponsors being a firm of crisp manufacturers.

The cricket correspondents of (some of) the national media captured this overall perspective. In *The Guardian* (8th September 2019), Simon Burnton reported that "[the ECB] is convinced that cricket's fortunes will be transformed when the players are finally free to wear truly garish colours and the logo of a popular prawn cocktail-flavoured snack…". He was particular damning about what he had seen on the tournament's official website: "In particular, the final team names and the descriptions of their characteristics were so extraordinarily inane… Manchester Originals are "celebrating a global city of firsts" and "laughing in the face of limits". Birmingham Phoenix are "a celebration of the strength in diversity, because different is good"… [The] ECB, which had been repeatedly criticised for using ludicrous marketing-drivel during private meetings, had used even more ludicrous marketing-drivel in public".

The critical theme was picked up in the same newspaper the following month by Matthew Engel: "The ECB's strategy of forcing their new hyped-up contest…on an unwilling game is completely incoherent, staggeringly expensive and potentially disastrous… [The Hundred is] made-up teams playing a made-up game to sell junk food to children. Me, I hope it rains solidly for the next four Augusts".

This general stance continued through to the eve of this month's launch. George Dobell on *ESPNcricinfo* (15th July 2021) stated that "The [Hundred teams] have no pathways, no academies and no existing support base. They are parasites feeding on the players and supporters the county game has produced".

I reproduce these quotes here not for dramatic effect, but because their sources are amongst the most respected commentators on our national summer sport. Engel is a former editor of the *Wisden Cricketers' Almanack*. He and Dobell (and others) are writing about a game that they know about, care about – and fear for.

The effects of the global Covid-19 pandemic continue to be felt on the tournament, as the various travel and quarantine restrictions around the world have prevented the participation in this year's competition of many of the overseas stars who had initially signed up. This has noticeably applied to the Australian contingent: Steve Smith, David Warner, Mitchell Starc, Ellyse Perry *et al*. Their presence had been a significant feature of the organisers' initial hype, not least in the televised auction programme on *Sky Sports* which in style (according to Engel) "was aimed at the nine-year-olds who are the alleged target audience".

So much for the background context – as can be seen, generally critical from my perspective – in which I attended my first matches in The Hundred last Saturday: the women's and men's encounters between the Northern Superchargers and the Welsh Fire at Headingley. Of course, I recognise that the ECB would probably have been fairly indifferent to any pre-match suspicions (or, indeed, cynicism) that I might have had. As noted, I am a self-confessed cricket "traditionalist" and, accordingly, I am not in their "target demographic" (with apologies if that is not the correct marketing phrase). Nonetheless, I trust that I approached the event with an open mind in attempting to assess the validity of the whole concept.

The women's match was the first up and, accordingly, presented an interesting test. If the new target audience is genuinely being sought, this game clearly warranted some attention.

I reached the conclusion quite early on in this first game that The Hundred is T20 on speed. Not only are the innings obviously shorter – a maximum of 100 legitimate deliveries rather than 120 – but time is saved by changing ends every 10 deliveries (rather than every 6) and then only allowing 50 seconds for that changeover to be made. At the mid-point in the 10-ball batch, which is signalled by the umpire waving a white card, the fielding side can choose to change the bowler. The fielders do have the option of a two-minute "strategic time out" during the innings, but otherwise the general feeling is one of getting on with it, undoubtedly driven by the timetabling requirements of the television broadcasters.

The sense of urgency is complemented by the incessant noise. At the risk of stating the obvious, a match in The Hundred is not the place to go for a peaceful session of cricket-watching. Rather, at Headingley, the breaks between each batch of 10 deliveries – an "over" is not in the vocabulary, apparently – was marked by a update (in the respective first innings, at least) of the runs scored and balls bowled, the on-site DJ blasting out one of her clubland favourites (not all of which were known to me, I must confess) or one of the two roving MCs conducting (yet another) short interview with one of the 9 year-olds in the crowd. I felt that the MCs had a touch of the Butlins' Red Coats about them, as they led the communal countdown of the last 10 seconds before the first ball was bowled and, later, sought to find out if the spectators in the East Stand could shout louder than those on the Western Terrace (which was hardly a competition between equals, I thought).

In the respective second innings of the two matches, the main scoreboard went into reverse: runs required and deliveries remaining. It was here that the "make the game as simple as possible" mantra was fully revealed. Although the smaller scoreboard at the end of the Western Terrace gave slightly more detail, I could only see part of it because of my viewing position near the front of the Emerald Stand. The main scoreboard focused on runs and deliveries – not even total wickets, let alone the runs scored or conceded by individual players. The announcer did give the name of each new bowler but, when a player was dismissed, the attention was entirely on the incoming "batter" (sic) rather than any summary of the mode of dismissal or the runs he/she had scored.

I think this represented a significant gap in the presentation. Cricket is a game of several disciplines – batting, bowling, fielding, wicket-keeping – and it would have aided everyone's understanding of what was happening (including mine) if we had been told how many runs an individual had made or what the bowler's analysis was at the end of his/her maximum 20-delivery allocation or who had held the steepling catch on the boundary edge. If The Hundred's organisers were to take my advice, I would suggest that they look very hard at the excellence of the in-stadium commentaries undertaken in the National Football League or college American Football matches in the US: in my experience, these are fully informative, without being intrusive, and significantly assist the spectator.

While I am on the subject, I also think it was a mistake not to have had any form of match programme. I know that I am swimming against the tide here – many football clubs no longer produce such items – but, again thinking of the target audience, I do recall the pleasure which I derived from sport-related programmes and magazines when I was aged 9 or 10. If well-produced, they represent a well to which one can regularly return; if nothing else, they are a souvenir of the event. On this occasion, they might also have informed me who the umpires were in the two matches; I do not recall that their names were announced at any time.

The Welsh Fire batted first in both the women's and men's matches. In the former, I was particularly interested in seeing the visitors' wicket-keeper, Sarah Taylor. She is undoubtedly one of the most distinguished women cricketers that England has ever produced, her international career stretching from 2006 to 2019 and including 10 test matches as well as over 200 one-day or T20 internationals. She announced her arrival at the crease by reverse sweeping her second ball to the boundary and thereafter looking completely untroubled until she was stumped for 18, skilfully beaten in the flight by the left-arm spinner, Linsey Smith.

The Northern Superchargers looked to be making a bit of a hash of attempting to reach the victory target of 131, when they were reduced to 19 for 4 after 18 deliveries. However, their cause was rescued by a delightful innings of 92 not out by Jemimah Rodrigues, a 20 year-old who is already an experienced Indian international. She played a series of classic shots – drives through extra cover, deft cuts behind square on the off side, wristy whips to the vacant leg side boundary – and was a pleasure to watch. The Superchargers won with 15 balls to spare: a comfortable victory.

The Welsh Fire's men's side posted a higher total – 173 for 4 – than their female counterparts, having been given a predictably flying start by Jonny Bairstow (56 from 36 deliveries) with useful contributions from Ben Duckett and James Neesham.

The visitors' score proved to be just sufficient. Although the Northern Superchargers had fallen well behind the required rate at the half-way stage, they were brought back into contention by the Yorkshireman, Harry Brook, who struck 62 from 31 deliveries. 11 runs were required from the final 5 balls, but the bowler Jake Ball held his nerve impressively and, at 168 for 7, the hosts fell 5 runs short. As in the women's match, it was a 20 year-old – the Afghan leg-spinner Qais Ahmad, who took 4 wickets for the Welsh Fire – who was the "match hero" (or man-of-the-match in old-speak).

I will end by returning to an issue that I raised at the outset: the extent to which The Hundred's spectators would identify with their "local" side. I was given a clue about this when I was waiting outside the ground before the start of play. I chatted to a middle-aged woman from Durham who had come to the match with her teenage son. He was fully kitted out in a Northern Superchargers sweatshirt and he enthusiastically relayed to me the members of the squad who hailed from his neck of the woods. She explained that they were looking forward to supporting the side in their matches this week at Trent Bridge and Old Trafford. When I (rather presumptuously) asked if they were regular cricket-watchers, the woman replied that they were both season ticket holders at Durham CCC.

Inside the ground, the size of the crowd built up during the afternoon and early evening to reach something just over 10,000. For the vast majority, there was absolutely no doubt whom they were supporting, given the loud cheers that greeted the announcements of Ben Stokes and Adil Rashid in the hosts' line-up. As the men's match reached its climax – and the succession of Brook's 4s and 6s seemed to be leading the Northern Superchargers towards an improbable victory – the volume of home support was ratcheted up even further. The DJ's interventions in the breaks in play added to the vibrant party atmosphere. People were here to have a good time. And they did.

The questions remain, of course. How many spectators were attending their first cricket match, rather than temporarily amending their allegiance like the mother and son from Durham? How many will return next time? Or the time after that, when the likes of Ben Stokes have returned to the England test team? Or the time after that, when there might be a much colder evening than we had on Saturday? And, not least – over the medium to long term – what will be the effects of The Hundred on the playing standards of (and attendance levels watching) the England test match and 50 over sides? The jury is out.

## Postscript

Two days after I posted this blog, the England and Wales Cricket Board announced that Ben Stokes would "take an indefinite break from all cricket with immediate effect" and had withdrawn from England's Test squad for the series against India. It was stated that "the all-rounder will prioritise his mental wellbeing and rest his left index finger which has not fully healed".

www.anordinaryspectator.com/news-blog July 2021

# Rugby League

# A Fair Outcome

*"The rain pours down. But I do not care. I am hooked…*
*on the experience of the sporting event, viewed live and in the flesh".*

[*An Ordinary Spectator*, page ix]

On 19th August 1961, I attended my first live sports event. I sat on my father's shoulders at the back of the stand at the Parkside stadium in the industrial heart of south Leeds for the Northern Rugby League encounter between Hunslet and Whitehaven. The Preface to *An Ordinary Spectator* describes my recollection of the 6 year-old's experience.

It was 60 years ago today.

The Hunslet RLFC has played its home fixtures at the South Leeds Stadium in Middleton since 1995 and it was a visit there last month – for the Hunslet versus Keighley Cougars fixture – that I thought would be appropriate to mark the anniversary. More on that below.

60 years is a long time in any sport. In 1961, the Northern Rugby League comprised a single division of 30 teams, of which 16 were in Yorkshire, 12 in Lancashire and 2 in Cumberland. (This was before the major local government re-organisation of the 1970s, of course). Three of those clubs have folded (Bramley, Blackpool Borough and Liverpool City) and whilst others have come and gone in the meantime – Carlisle, Kent Invicta, Mansfield Marksmen *et al* – there are currently 36 teams in the three divisions of full-time and/or semi-professional British rugby league.

The geographical spread across the divisions is now more extensive with two clubs in each of France, Wales and London and other sides in Sheffield, Newcastle and Coventry. However, there has been a marked widening of the gap between rich and poor: at the extreme, between the wealth and resources that now underpin some of the Super League clubs such as Leeds and St Helens and the fragile existence of those at the lower end of League 1 (the third tier) that are reliant of attendances of a couple of hundred spectators and the determined efforts of local volunteers.

I couldn't resist looking at the rank order of the 30 clubs in the 1961-62 season (as determined by the end-of-season league table, given that August marked the beginning of the campaign) and the 36 clubs of the present day (as given by the league tables following last weekend's matches). Interestingly, of the current 12 Super League teams, only 7 finished in the top dozen of 60 years ago. Those that have now risen into the elite group are the Warrington Wolves, Hull FC, Salford Red Devils, Leigh Centurions and – of course – the Catalan Dragons, whilst the clubs that have fallen out of the old Top 12 are Featherstone Rovers, Widnes, Oldham, Swinton and Workington Town, the last of these by no fewer than 22 places.

For the statistically minded, it is possible to undertake a more formal analysis of the rank orders of the clubs in the two years (1961-62 and 2021) in order to examine whether there is a relationship between them. To do this, one can look at the two sets of ranks of the 27 clubs (or their successors in cases such as Hunslet and Bradford Northern/Bradford Bulls) that have survived since 1961 in order to calculate Spearman's Rank Correlation Co-efficient. (Charles Spearman, 1863-1945, was an English statistician and psychologist).

The range of possibilities for the Co-efficient lies between +1 (a perfect positive correlation) and -1 (a perfect negative correlation) and, by examining how far the figure is from zero for a given sample size – our sample is 27 – we are testing the "null hypothesis" that there is no correlation in the two rank orders.

In our case, the figure is +0.48. In other words, notwithstanding the shifts in fortune noted above, the clubs in the higher/middle/lower parts of the spectrum in 1961 tend also to be found in broadly the same positions today. Examples include Wigan (1st in 1961, currently 3rd), Halifax (14th and 13th) and Doncaster (26th and 24th). The positive figure is perhaps not surprising – I think I might have expected it to have been somewhat higher – and it allows the statistician to reject the null hypothesis in favour of the conclusion that there is a "moderate positive" correlation.

And so – our heads suitably cleared – to the immediate matter at hand: Hunslet versus Keighley in League 1. At the start of play, only one point separated the fourth-placed visitors from their seventh-placed hosts in the 10-team league table, although both teams were some distance from the competition's then pacesetters, Barrow. For Hunslet, it was a match of some significance as, in the previous month, they had not only lost their previous three games – which included an embarrassing collapse against the lowly-ranked Coventry Bears – but had parted company with their coach and then seen the resignation of the club chairman (although the latter decision has subsequently been reversed).

I watched the game in the company of Peter Todd, the former General Manager of the Hunslet club. He has a deep knowledge of rugby league, not only of the backgrounds of many of the players in action directly in front of us, but of the sport's history and its former participants. At various times, our conversation referenced an eclectic list of ex-professionals – Ken Rollin of Wakefield Trinity and Leeds, Colin Tyrer of Leigh and Wigan, Chris Joynt of St Helens – as well as covering current issues affecting the game, notably the decisions of the rugby league authorities in Australia and New Zealand not to participate in the (subsequently postponed) 2021 Rugby League World Cup. It was a very pleasant afternoon.

On the pitch, the teams were evenly matched. Keighley scored an early try and then, after half an hour, a second one to give them a 10-0 lead. However, Hunslet recovered well in the period before half-time and two short-range charges from the powerful prop forward, Jordan Andrade, produced a 12-10 interval lead. This had been extended to 20-10 until five minutes before the end, at which point the game looked secure for the home side. Not so. Two late Keighley tries, one of which was converted, produced a final score of 20-20.

Had this been a Super League fixture, there would have been "Golden Point" extra time, in which the teams played on until a winning score was achieved. However, in League 1, this does not occur: a drawn match is considered a legitimate result. And quite right too. Hunslet and Keighley had produced a whole-hearted and entertaining encounter that had swung back and forth. After 80 minutes play on a hot afternoon, there was nothing to separate them and both sides were out on their feet. The division of the spoils was a fair outcome.

www.anordinaryspectator.com/news-blog August 2021

# Women's Football

# A Commitment Made Good (Partly)

I reported last year (*"Unfinished Business at Petershill Park"*, 22nd August 2020) that the 2019-20 UEFA Women's Champions League quarter-final between Glasgow City and VfL Wolfsburg, which had originally been scheduled as a conventional two-legged affair the previous March, had been an early casualty of the coronavirus in the sports spectating itinerary that I had planned for 2020. (The match was eventually played 5 months later as a one-off fixture in San Sebastian, which the German side won 9-1). As its title suggested, I ended that particular blog with the acknowledgement that I had some unfinished business with the Glasgow City club and the hope that, at some future date, I could take in a match at its home ground at Petershill Park in Springburn.

I have now – partly at least – made good on that commitment. This season, Glasgow City have been playing their European fixtures at the Broadwood Stadium in Cumbernauld and yesterday afternoon I attended the club's 2nd round 2nd leg tie against the Swiss side, Servette FCCF *(Servette FC Chênois Féminin)*.

From my starting point in Milngavie, I knew from a previous visit – for the Clyde versus Stirling Albion fixture in the Scottish Professional Football League 2 in May 2016 – that it would be a train journey and then a bus ride to get to the stadium. The latter was provided at no cost to me, thanks to the largesse of the Scottish Government (and the UK taxpayer). Moreover, in order to attract a sizeable home support, the Glasgow City club had decided on a free entry policy for the tie. I was reasonably confident, therefore, that the afternoon's spectating would provide good value for money.

It was a very hot day and I was glad to take my place in the shade at the back of the main stand. The view beyond the stand on the opposite side of the ground gave me a sliver of Broadwood Loch to the left and, in the sun-drenched middle distance to the right, a lengthy stretch of the Kilsyth Hills.

To reach this stage, Glasgow City had had to play two first round matches – against Birkirkara FC of Malta and BIIL Shymkent of Kazakhstan – though the travel requirements had been relatively light: both matches were played at Broadwood last month.

There was all to play for in the Servette tie. The first leg had finished 1-1 and the reward for the winner would be a place in the group stage of the tournament's last 16. As Glasgow City are number 16 in the UEFA rankings, they would have been the favourites, given that Servette are at 71, though the latter rank is perhaps distorted by the Geneva-based side's relatively recent appearance on the European stage.

In the event, it was clear from an early stage that these were two evenly matched sides. In the first quarter of an hour, both teams kept their defensive shape and there was a competitive edge in midfield. It was something of a surprise, therefore, when a long clearance down the middle by the City goalkeeper, Lee Alexander, was flicked on by Niamh Farrelly and Priscila Chinchilla was able to take advantage of a clear run on the Servette goal and coolly register the first goal. "Route 1" it might have been, but with some skill attached.

The match was decided in the ten minutes on either side of half-time. Just before the break, Alexander – who otherwise had a fine game – lost concentration for a moment and picked up what the Dutch referee judged (correctly, in my view) was a back-pass from one of her defenders. The result was an indirect free-kick to Servette on the line of Glasgow City's six-yard box.

The whole of the City team took their places on the goal-line as the Servette players, Sandy Maendly and Jade Boho Sayo (who is generally known as Jade), stood over the ball. After one false start, in which a couple of City defenders prematurely charged from their line, Maendly tapped the ball forward and Jade drove it emphatically into the roof of the net. My immediate reaction was that this had been a well-rehearsed routine: the two Servette players had not rushed the opportunity, but had kept their cool and taken full advantage of the lifeline presented to their side.

The second – and decisive – Servette goal came three minutes after half time. After chasing what looked to have been a fairly innocuous-looking clearance down the right wing, the centre-forward Marta Peiró Giménez won the ball and released Amandine Soulard into space from which she delivered a cross to the far post, where it was attacked by Daina Bourma. Alexander made an excellent save but, unfortunately for City, the ball rebounded from the crossbar to the supporting Maendly, who headed it home.

These Servette players all gave impressive performances: Giménez played a tireless striker's role, on several occasions skilfully holding the ball up for her supporting colleagues; the right-back Soulard was a feisty competitor who, in front of her goal in the second half, produced a couple of timely defensive headers from threatening City crosses; in the midfield, Maendly delivered a series of well-weighted passes and, with one exception, a number of dangerous in-swinging corners from Servette's right-hand side, which the City defence consistently found difficult to deal with. Maendly would probably have been my choice as player-of-the-match, though it would have been a close-run contest with Chinchilla who, in addition to her well-taken goal, was a continual threat to the Servette defence with her close control and sharp acceleration.

The draining conditions did not prevent both sides from demonstrating the speed of their counter-attack. In the first half, after the visitors had made a hash of a short corner, Chinchilla won the ball and released the pacy Ode Fulutudilu for a long run on the Servette goal. It was defence-to-attack in a matter of seconds. It took a smart save from the goalkeeper, Ines Pereira, to prevent the scoreline reaching 2-0: a decisive moment, one feels, in retrospect. Near to the end, the roles were reversed and a run and pass by Jade led to Elodie Nakkach squandering a chance in front of a near-open goal. I had expected that the demanding conditions would mean that the overall pace of the game would slow dramatically in the second half, but this was not the case: a tribute to the players' fitness and the timing of their coaches' substitutions.

As with the men's counterpart, the players in the UEFA Women's Champions League are drawn from around the world. By my calculations, 15 different nationalities were represented in yesterday's two match-day squads. From the Glasgow City team, Chinchilla and Fulutudilu are Costa Rican and South African internationals, for example, whilst their opponents Pereira and Jade have represented Portugal and Equatorial Guinea, respectively. There was still room for domestically produced talent, however, with 4 Scots and 3 Swiss in the starting XIs.

One obvious area in which the men's and women's tournaments differ, of course, is in the financial rewards. *The Herald* reported yesterday that the winner of the Glasgow City-Servette tie could look forward to £345,000 in prizemoney for reaching the group stage. This might represent less than a week's wages for Cristiano Ronaldo at Manchester United, but it would have been a sizeable windfall for the budget of Glasgow City FC.

It was a very good afternoon's entertainment. The crowd – a few hundred perhaps – supported their team to the end, recognising the efforts and skills on show. We were a mixed group – male and female, of all ages – with a sufficient number of young girls for one to be confident that the groundwork is being laid for the next generation of women players. I also have to say – at the risk of appearing unduly prim and proper – that it was nice to attend a professional football match that was not accompanied, in the stand, by the usual tribalism, foul language and lack of respect for the opposition.

The focus of Glasgow City will now be on the domestic agenda and the attempt to qualify for next season's European competition. For these matches in the Scottish Women's Premier League, it will be back to Petershill Park.

www.anordinaryspectator.com/news-blog September 2021

# Cycling

# Queen's Drive

This year, I have been a regular viewer of the evening television highlights of cycling's three Grand Tours – *Giro d'Italia*, *Tour de France* and *Vuelta a España* – via the Eurosport, ITV4 and/or Quest channels. The quality of the respective presentations has varied – notably the editing and post-race analysis – but each event has been good to watch over its gruelling three-week duration. I am probably no nearer than I was at the beginning of the summer to donning the Lycra and sitting on a bike myself, but I do now know a little more than I did about the tactics of a breakaway or the timing of a sprint finish.

[An aside. When the various 2021 Sportsman of the Year accolades are being awarded, I suggest that those who decide these things look beyond the Olympic Games and Euro 2020 to consider the case for the Dutch cyclist, Fabio Jakobsen. Just over a year ago, he was near to death in a Polish hospital following a horrendous crash at the *Tour de Pologne*. The catalogue of the injuries he sustained makes for very grim reading. At this year's *Vuelta*, he won the Green Jersey for the race's overall points competition. A heroic and uplifting story].

ITV4 has been the broadcaster of the AJ Bell Tour of Britain, an eight-day race that ended today. (Another aside. My search on Google revealed that AJ Bell is a "public limited company that provides online investment platforms and stockbroker services"). It has to be acknowledged that the Tour does what it says on the tin – the start was in Penzance and the finale was in Aberdeen – albeit with some sizeable jumps between stages. Yesterday, the penultimate stage was of 195 kilometres from Hawick to Edinburgh and I duly took up a place to watch the final stretch down Queen's Drive at the foot of Arthur's Seat.

As with my journey to the football match in Cumbernauld earlier in the week ("*A Commitment Made Good (Partly)*", 9th September 2021), I drew on the resources of public transport to make the journey from Milngavie. This can be risky at weekends. I had known that there would be a replacement bus service at the start of the trip (though I hadn't anticipated that the driver would lose his way on the short journey between Bearsden and Westerton stations and start making his way back to Milngavie), but it was a surprise when I reached Queen's Street station in Glasgow and learned that the flagship train service to Edinburgh would also involve a replacement bus from Linlithgow.

As the bus crawled down the A8 through Corstorphine on the outskirts of the capital, I was anxiously looking at my watch and fearing that I would arrive at Queen's Drive to see the peloton disappearing into the distance. However, to my relief, it turned out that I had about 25 minutes to spare before the first riders came through.

My vantage point was just inside the last kilometre at the start of the final slight incline that led straight up towards the finishing line. This had been my intended spot: it enabled me to see the riders as they came around the long curve of Queen's Drive and then head into the distance. As if to recognise my neat bit of scheduling, the dark threatening clouds overhead started to be replaced by the bright sunshine that would last for the remainder of the afternoon.

I waited next to a couple in late middle age who were both cycling and walking enthusiasts. The man told me with some pride that the cottage they had hired as the base for a walking holiday in the Pyrenees had been on the route of this year's *Vuelta*. In common with some others around me, he had been following the progress of the day's stage on his mobile phone and he told me that the numbers in the breakaway had been whittled down to five, though none was in contention in the General Classification to win the overall Tour.

The leaders passed in an initial group of three – Matt Gibson, Yves Lampaert and Matteo Jorgenson – followed, after a few seconds, by Davide Ballerini and Pascal Eenkhoorn. The peloton swept by about a minute and a half later. (The Belgian, Lampaert, was the eventual winner). Whilst acknowledging that I was not witnessing a severe mountain climb or a frenetic sprint finish, I did think that there was something smooth and elegant about them all.

All the riders were greeted by warm and polite applause from the spectators behind the barriers on both sides of the road, the clapping seeming to complement the soft purr of tyre on road. This support was replicated for the stragglers who came in a little later – perhaps delayed by a crash or a "technical" (which, I understand, usually means a puncture) – including the young rider from the Great Britain team who, at the foot of the incline, inadvertently followed one of the support cars down the wrong road before being redirected on to the correct route.

Not surprisingly, many of the spectators – including whole families – were dressed for the part in their cycling gear, most of whom, in turn, had brought their own bicycles. It is not difficult to sense that this sport is healthy (in both senses) in Britain and one, moreover, that encourages participation as well as spectating.

Many of the spectators remained for some time after the race, hoping to catch a glimpse of the riders as they returned to the team buses, which were parked not far from where I had watched the race. The area was cordoned off to respect the current Covid-19 regulations, but this did not prevent Mark Cavendish – Britain's greatest sprint cyclist – from patiently working his way along the line for a series of selfies with his fans before he boarded the Deceuninck-Quick-Step bus. He did this for several minutes: an impressive effort, I thought, from someone who must have been close to exhaustion after another demanding 4½ hours in the saddle.

As with all cycling competitions on the road – and particularly the various Tours – there was a large entourage of accompanying vehicles: organisers' car, team directors' cars, cars racked with spare bicycles, police motorbikes, ambulance, and so on. In addition, the staffing requirements on the route are significant, of course, with each potentially dangerous item of street furniture requiring someone to man it and wave a warning flag. After the race, I passed the group of police outriders – is there are collective noun? – as they gathered together by their vehicles near the entrance to the Queen's Gallery of Holyrood Palace. From the north country English accents that I overheard, they were clearly drawn from across the country.

I waited for a few more minutes before crossing Queen's Drive to look back at the views. The team buses – their sponsors' names and riders' photographs prominently displayed on the outside and appropriately led by Jumbo-Visma – started to leave for Stonehaven in preparation for today's final stage of the Tour. I decided to re-cross the road and head for the Starbucks on the Royal Mile for (as it turned out) a flat white coffee and a slice of chocolate caramel shortbread. One of the officials in high-viz jackets was manning the crossing point. "You can cross now", he said, his back to the traffic. I waited. "You can cross now", he repeated, as if both surprised and impatient at my non-movement. "There's a bus coming, mate", I replied, as the vehicle containing the combined ranks of Deceuninck-Quick-Step – including Cavendish, no doubt – sped towards us.

Today's stage from Stonehaven to Aberdeen was won in a sprint finish by another Belgian, Wout van Aert of Jumbo-Visma. This gave him the overall victory in the 2021 Tour of Britain by six seconds from Britain's Ethan Hayter.

www.anordinaryspectator.com/news-blog September 2021

# Cricket

# Batsmen and Batters

Oh dear.

I fear that, for some, this essay might appear to have been written by an anti-woke curmudgeon who has no tolerance of progressive thinking. That has not been the intention.

Should I be fortunate enough – courtesy of good health and fine weather – to watch Adam Lyth and Gary Ballance in action for Yorkshire CCC next season, it will be the case that their principal roles in the team will have changed. This is because the Marylebone Cricket Club – the custodians of the Laws of Cricket – announced towards the end of last month that, with immediate effect, their skills will be employed not as batsmen, but as "batters".

It is the case, of course, that women's cricket is making rapid strides. This has been aided by the increased media coverage being given to international matches and, this year, the introduction of a women's competition in The Hundred that ran in parallel with that of the men. This is a healthy and hugely welcome development.

It is against this background that the MCC has decided that the term "batsman" represents an unacceptable gender-specific term that does not sit happily with the direction of travel of the game and of the wider society. Its official statement in announcing the change was that "MCC believes in cricket being a game for all and this move recognises the changing landscape of the game in modern times". Hence "batter", which has now been written in the laws applying to all forms of the game.

In her accompanying statement, Clare Connor – the new President of the MCC – drew on her experience as Director of Women's Cricket at the England and Wales Cricket Board: "Where the game is now, an eight year-old girl doesn't want to be a batsman, or a policeman, or a postman, or a fireman – why would she want to be anything that has the word man in?"

I think this is a mistaken approach – for three reasons.

First, although the word "batter" might sit happily with "bowler" and "fielder" (though, even then, "fieldsman" was commonly used until relatively recently), the word is unattractive, if not downright ugly. I know that it was formally employed in the promotion of The Hundred – and uniformly used in the consequent hype of the television coverage. However, I have to say that when its usage was then transferred to the BBC's evening test match highlights programme – especially by Michael Vaughan – it jarred horribly. As reportage on the highest level of the game, it was the equivalent of the fingernails being scraped down the blackboard.

It is here that the MCC's official statement is particularly revealing. It refers to the last redraft of the laws in 2017 when it was agreed, following consultation with key figures in women's cricket, that the terminology would remain as "batsman" and "batsmen". It then goes on to say that "[t]he changes announced today reflect the wider usage of the terms "batter" and "batters" which has occurred in cricketing circles in the intervening period". I am having difficulty interpreting this as anything other than The Hundred tail wagging the game as a whole's dog.

This leads to the second reason. The synonyms for "batter" include "bludgeon", "pummel", "abuse" and "clobber". Its all-embracing use in a cricketing sense is inappropriate. Ok, it might apply to Liam Livingstone hitting the ball over the Football Stand at Headingley, but there is surely far more to batting than that.

During my lifetime, the great batsmen have included Graeme Pollock, Tom Graveney and David Gower – to name but three. To my mind, they were not "batters". They played with elegance, grace and panache. They were craftsmen. They were batsmen. Kumar Sangakkara, VVS Laxman, Zaheer Abbas…

And so back through the earlier generations. To give the retrospective label of "batter" to Victor Trumper, KS Ranjitsinhji or Wally Hammond – and countless others – seems to me to reveal a disturbing lack of respect for the game's history. (And this from the MCC, let us not forget). Was Herbert Sutcliffe a batter? I don't think so. Besides, what do I now do with his *How to Become a First Class Batsman*, purchased when I was in short trousers for three shillings from his sports store in Leeds?

My third reason is a practical one. There are several sports – for example, tennis, triathlon, darts, show jumping and eventing – in which men and women compete for the same prize in the same arena. It makes sense for gender-neutral terminology to be applied in these spheres. But cricket is not one of these sports. The men's and women's games are separate, as emphatically demonstrated by The Hundred's double-headers.

Accordingly, I can see no reason why the nomenclature used in the laws of the game has to be exactly the same in both cases. Put simply, why not "batsman" and "batswoman" – to be used, as appropriate? The latter might initially seem a little clunky, no doubt, but that is surely a function of its unfamiliarity. (I note, incidentally, that, in American court and field sports, "linesman" and "lineswoman" are each widely recognised terms for the relevant officials).

I recognise that I am swimming against the tide with all this. In cricket, the "third man" fielding position and the tailender batting as a "nightwatchman" will surely be the next to go. Indeed, in the case of the former, I'm already surprised that it has survived the combination of Harry Lime selling adulterated penicillin in post-war Vienna and Kim Philby being denounced as the next in line of Soviet spies following the defection of Burgess and Maclean.

I also fully acknowledge that the interests of the "eight year-old girl" identified by Ms Connor should be taken into account. I would like as many eight year-old girls – and boys – as possible to take an active interest in the game. But this doesn't prevent me from putting forward a point of view from the perspective of a different member of the cricket family: the 60-something, who has followed the game for half a century and who played it for 20 years, but whose interest is now waning and/or moving elsewhere.

Of course, it's only a word. "Batter" for "batsman". So what? Nobody will die as a result of the change.

But, for me, it all represents another tear in the fabric. It's another (small) step in the current journey of English cricket that appears to be characterised by the search for transient populism, the abandonment of subtlety and tradition, and the easy recourse to dumbing down. And, after all this time, I'm afraid that it's also a further strain on my attachment to the game.

Still, here's hoping for 2022. I look forward to watching Adam Lyth and Garry Ballance at Headingley or Scarborough and being reminded that they are – that they remain – two really good batsmen.

www.anordinaryspectator.com/news-blog October 2021

Rugby League

# Same Time Next Year (Perhaps)

I had a ticket for the match scheduled for this evening – a good one too, Category B for £70.

Today should have seen the first semi-final of the 2021 Rugby League World Cup (RLWC) with, if the seedings had worked out correctly, Australia playing New Zealand at Elland Road in Leeds. However, following the withdrawal from the tournament of the two countries' rugby league authorities on 22nd July, the RLWC Board announced on 5th August that the event would be postponed for a year until the autumn of 2022.

The chairman of the Australian Rugby League Commission (ARLC), Peter V'landys, stated that: "[W]e must put the best interests of our players and officials first. Protecting them is our absolute priority. In the current environment, the risks to the safety, health and wellbeing of the players and officials travelling from Australia to participate in the tournament this year are insurmountable".

For some, the immediate reaction to the Australia/New Zealand announcement – apparently done by app to the RLWC organisers with a few minutes notice before a confirmation deadline – was one of apoplexy. The Chairman of the Rugby Football League, Simon Johnson, stated that it was "selfish, parochial and cowardly". One has to suppose that relations between the sport's principal international administrators will be more than a little strained for some time to come. However, with most of the dust now having settled, it is interesting to consider the overall circumstances of the postponement of RLWC 2021.

Mr Johnson – and others – were quick to point to the inconsistency with the approaches taken by other Australian sportsmen and women and their administrators. For example, it had been an Australian, Ashleigh Barty, who had won the Women's Singles Title at Wimbledon in July and both Australia and New Zealand were about to compete in the Olympic Games in Tokyo (where Australia would eventually come 6th in the medal table with 46 medals, including 17 golds).

The latter comparison is perhaps more easily defended, as the Olympic athletes were only in Japan for a relatively short time and obliged to leave within 48 hours of completing their event. More damning comparisons are with the Australian rugby union side, which has played Scotland and England at Murrayfield and Twickenham over the last two weekends and will meet Wales tomorrow, and the New Zealand All Blacks, who have included matches in Cardiff and Ireland on their autumn tour.

I was interested in the initial take on all this by Phil Gould – a respected and influential commentator on rugby league in Australia (and, formerly, a highly successful coach at club level and for New South Wales) – whose interview on Channel 9's *Wide World of Sports* programme the day after the Australians' withdrawal is accessible on YouTube. Gould referred to a daily infection rate of 30,000 new cases in the UK – it had actually averaged over 41,000 in the previous two weeks – and, in relation to the sport, the fact that a number of Super League matches had been cancelled in 2021 because of Covid-19 outbreaks within clubs.

Gould then noted that "[I]t will only back them [the players] up into next season. We had a short preparation for this season. We can't do it again. Just postpone it". He then expanded on this line of thought: "By the time they come back and quarantine and then they have 8 weeks break [part of the Collective Bargaining Agreement between the Australian authorities and players]… they don't start training until February. Can you imagine what that's going to look like next season… the quality of our competition?"

This is revealing, I think. It adds weight to the argument that, whilst there can be no doubt about the Australian authorities' desire to safeguard the health of the players under their jurisdiction, the impact of their country's Covid-19 restrictions on the pre-(2022) season preparations of the National Rugby League (NRL) clubs was also a key factor in the decision to withdraw. In its extreme form, this argument has been presented by some as Covid-19 being used as a smokescreen by the Australians to preserve the timetable of their domestic season. The Chief Executive of RLWC 2021, Jon Dutton, has referred to the "competing priorities from others" as a key reason for the postponement of the tournament.

In the period after the Australia/New Zealand announcement but before the RLWC 2021 was officially postponed, Dutton stated that the decision on whether or not the tournament would proceed this year was 50:50. At that point, it might have seemed that there were arguments for and against going ahead as scheduled; in reality, however, I suspect that the die had already been effectively cast.

One option might have been to plough on regardless. To say, in effect: ok, Australia and New Zealand are absent, so we will find two more teams instead (and make a virtue of the fact that it is a global competition). The next two teams in line might have been the United States and Serbia.

An alternative had been to field a team from the Australian and New Zealand players currently featuring in the Super League. At first, I was against the latter idea, thinking that the tournament should be for national teams only, but then I remembered that there is a good precedent. In the 2000 RLWC, my father and I had attended the match between Scotland and the Aotearoa Māori at the Firhill ground in Glasgow: a "good, hard-fought game" as I recorded in *An Ordinary Spectator* (which the Māori won by a single point).

In the event that RLWC 2021 had continued on schedule, England would have been the top seeds for the tournament. Had they then won it, the predictable response would have been "but Australia and New Zealand weren't there", to which an appropriate counter-reply might have been "whose decision was that?" However, there is little doubt that the absence of Australia and New Zealand would have hung over the tournament with consistent references to this being made in the media coverage. (Since Great Britain last won the World Cup in 1972, there have been 8 such tournaments. Australia have won 7 of them; the other – in 2008 – was won by New Zealand).

On the plus side, there would have been opportunities for the sport accruing from the fact that the absence of Australia and New Zealand would almost certainly have meant that two other countries would have reached the semi-finals that otherwise would not have done so. Let us suppose that one of those had been France, currently placed 8th in the world rankings. This would have given scope for a major promotional boost to rugby league in the country and something to supplement the recent successes of the Catalan Dragons in reaching the Super League Grand Final and the Toulouse Olympique XIII in winning promotion from the Championship.

Other factors might also have played into the thinking that the 2021 RLWC should have proceeded as planned. One was obviously the enormous amount of preparatory work that had been undertaken, not only for the Men's event but also for the Women's and Wheelchair tournaments. Moreover, unlike the Euro 2020 football tournament and the 2020 Olympic Games, the organisers were not certain that they could simply move things forward by 12 months without any great difficulty; some of the arrangements – the use of football grounds for the major matches, for example – were not guaranteed in a year's time. (In the event, only 5 of the planned 61 fixtures across the three tournaments have been affected in the re-scheduling for next year).

Related to this is the pride of place that the 2021 RLWC organisers had obtained within the television schedules; the BBC had signed up for extensive coverage of all three tournaments in a period in which there was relatively little competition from other sporting events. In 2022, the autumn sports schedule will be more crowded with the Commonwealth Games in Birmingham (which are scheduled to end on 8th August) and the FIFA World Cup in Qatar (which kicks off on 21$^{st}$ November). This has still provided a window for coverage of the postponed RLWC – the 3 tournament finals of which are now scheduled for a year today (19$^{th}$ November 2022) – but it is not yet clear that there will be the same amount of attention from the national broadcaster.

Against this background – and given the precise circumstances of the withdrawal by Australia/New Zealand – it must have been tempting for the 2021 RLWC organisers to have sought to confirm their pre-eminence in matters relating to the tournament, rather than seeming to have had its fate at least partly determined by the pre-season training schedules of the clubs in Australia's National Rugby League.

It was here that the matter was resolved, however. Yes, the NRL clubs hold the cards as far as the participation of the Australian and New Zealand national sides are concerned (via the NRL's obvious influence on the ARLC). But they are also the employers of the core of other national sides which, whilst they might still have entered the tournament, would have been substantially weakened if their NRL-based players had not been allowed to participate. It was the undermining of the full-strength sides from the Pacific Islands – Tonga, Fiji and Samoa – that, in addition to the complete absence of Australia and New Zealand, dealt the fatal blow to holding the RLWC this year. (There would also have been significant absences of players drawing on their heritage to represent Greece, Italy and the Lebanon). In the announcement of the postponement of the tournament, the RLWC organisers referred to the "non-release of up to 400 players, match officials and staff members from the NRL competition".

It is the case, of course, that any discussion of the postponement of the RLWC must acknowledge the vastly different approaches to dealing with the Covid-19 pandemic in the UK and Australia/New Zealand. The day before the official postponement of the tournament, the official number of deaths in the UK of those who had contracted Covid within the previous 28 days reached exactly 130,000; in Australia and New Zealand, the corresponding figures were 925 and 26, respectively. In contrast with the UK's apparently ever-changing set of regulations governing social distancing and (especially) overseas travel, Australia and New Zealand have attempted to maintain what have effectively been national bubbles – especially once the Delta variant of the virus took hold elsewhere – with, within that constraint, several strict lockdowns in the major cities.

Although it was the case that the UK initially saw much faster rates of take-up of first and second vaccinations, Australia and New Zealand have now caught up. As of yesterday, according to the three national statistics offices, the proportions of the populations aged 12 and over in the UK, Australia and New Zealand, who had had the second jab, stood at 80.1 per cent, 82.9 per cent and 82.1 per cent, respectively. In the meantime, the infection rate in the UK remains high: it averaged over 36,000 new cases each day in the first half of this month.

Who is to say that the Australian rugby league authorities did not make the correct decision?

It is clear from the world's near-two year experience of dealing with Covid-19 that making accurate predictions about its future incidence and mortality rates is very difficult. The RLWC has been postponed until the autumn of 2022, but, at this stage, we cannot be confident about what impact the pandemic will still be having on the state of global health in 12 months' time. More specifically, can anyone guarantee that the Australian and New Zealand rugby league authorities would still not be arguing that the risks to the health and safety of the players and officials travelling from Australia would be "insurmountable".

One final thought – and another regret – with regard to the postponement of the RLWC 2021. In the union code, the much-hyped event of the summer was the British Lions three-match test series in South Africa (which commenced a couple of days after the Australia/New Zealand withdrawal). It is generally agreed, even by the keenest supporters of the 15-man code, that, as spectacles, the first two matches in this series were absolutely awful, both sides seeming to rely entirely on kicking the ball to gain ground and compete for possession in the opponents' half of the field. The third match was little better. (The former Scotland coach, Matt Williams, spoke for many when he referred to "a horror series"). What a shame that the advocates of the league code have not had the opportunity to spotlight their sport this year by making the comparison with their brand of international competition and its much higher incidence of running with and passing the ball.

Let's hope that opportunity re-presents itself in a year's time.

www.anordinaryspectator.com/news-blog November 2021

# Badminton

# Twins' Success at the Emirates Arena

The Scottish Open Badminton Championship has a proud history. The tournament dates from 1907 and is the third-oldest in the world, the All-England Badminton Championship having been established in 1899. Yesterday, I attended this year's Finals Day at the Emirates Arena in Glasgow.

The early years of the tournament were dominated by the Englishman, George Alan Thomas (the 7th Baronet Thomas), who won a total of 28 titles – including the Men's Singles on 11 occasions – in the period to 1926. (He was also a British chess champion and a lawn tennis quarter-finalist at Wimbledon). The men's title did not leave England or Ireland until 1951, when Eddy B Choong of Malaysia was the first overseas winner.

The only Scottish winner of the Men's Singles has been Robert McCoig, who took the title 4 times in the 10 years to 1968. However, local success has been seen more recently in other events. The reigning Men's Doubles champions – from 2019, as last year's tournament was cancelled due to Covid-19 – were Alexander Dunn and Adam Hall, whilst Kirsty Gilmour won the Women's Singles in 2017 and 2018.

Although it is part of the European Tour, the Scottish Open does not have the scale of prize-money – and therefore drawing power – available to higher ranking tournaments around the world. However, this does not diminish the competitiveness – and unpredictability – of the tournament. In the Men's Singles event, in which two of the seeds dropped out before the tournament began, the other six had World Tour Rankings (WTR) between 28 and 63, but only two of these reached their allotted places in the quarter-finals and neither of these progressed any further. Across the 5 events as a whole, the 20 semi-final places were taken by 9 seeded and 11 unseeded competitors with 11 countries being represented.

The tournament took place over four days, the first two of which had crowded – and efficiently organised – itineraries. 176 matches were played on five adjacent courts on Thursday and Friday – from 9.00am until late in the evening – in order to reduce the 216 singles or doubles entrants in the 5 competitions down to the 40 who would contest Saturday's quarter-finals. (The Badminton World Federation website – www.bwfbadminton.com – was an excellent source of information on the tournament's progress and there was also full coverage on YouTube).

In the Women's Singles, the number 1 seed was Kirsty Gilmour – 19th in the WTR – but she dropped out of the event after only two points in her first-round tie. The beneficiary of her misfortune was Wen Chi Hsu of Chinese Taipei, who then did not drop a game on her way to taking the title, her win yesterday being over Line Højmark Kjærsfeld of Denmark, who was the number 2 seed (and 18th in the WTR).

The Men's Singles final was between two Malaysians – Ng Tze Yong and Soong Joo Ven – neither of whom had conceded a game in their four earlier matches. It was the former who, 70 years on, followed in the footsteps of his compatriot Eddy B Choong. I was struck by the powerful leaping smashes of both men, though the match lost some of its rhythm in the second game as a result of the frequent stoppages to sweep parts of the court following a stumble by one or other of the players. For some reason, this seemed to occur far more frequently in this match than any of the others.

There was domestic interest in two of the Doubles finals: the English pair Callum Hemming and Jessica Pugh were in the Mixed Doubles and the Glaswegian twins Christopher and Matthew Grimley in the Men's Doubles. Both pairings were successful. For the Scots, the decisive moment came when they saved a game point in their first game against the Malaysians Junaidi Arif and Haikal Muhammed; the next two points gave them the game 22-20 and a lead that they did not relinquish. (Unfortunately, *The Herald* – a national newspaper based in Glasgow – could not find room in today's 16-page sports section to report on the locals' success nor those of any of the other title winners).

Needless to say, the home victory was enthusiastically received by the spectators in the Arena (apart, perhaps, from the small group to our right displaying the Malaysian flag for the distant camera). Even in this match, however, the crowd was quietly respectful of the play on both sides of the net with the lengthy rallies prompting deserved rounds of polite applause interspersed with the occasional lone "Come on boys" directed at the home favourites.

None of the first 4 finals went to a third (and deciding) game and my reading of the form book – albeit as a badminton spectating novice – suggested that the Women's Doubles final might also only require two games. Not only were the Canadian pair of Rachel Honderich and Kristen Tsai the number 1 seeds, but they had been relatively untroubled in their four wins earlier in the event, registering their 168 points against only 89 conceded. This indeed turned out to be the case. Their opponents Anna Ching Yik Cheong and Teoh Mei Xing (also of Malaysia) put up a brave fight, but the Canadians were very impressive, both players showing both power – particularly the tall Honderich from the back of the court – and subtlety.

On the Saturday, the average duration of the quarter-final and semi-final matches (excluding one in which a competitor retired injured) was 41 minutes, the range extending from 22 minutes to one hour 8 minutes. There is little time for rest and recuperation – mainly a short break once 11 points had been scored in a game and a two-minute interval at the end of a game. The players must therefore combine the speed and agility required for the flurries of rapid action with the tactical nous to manoeuvre their opponents around the court and the stamina of middle-distance runners. (In the case of another Dane, Amalie Schulz, this might be long-distance runner: she played – and won – four matches on the Friday).

The high tempo with which the matches were conducted was firmly encouraged by the umpires. On one occasion, a player was stopped from going to the courtside to wipe his face with a towel and there were other instances when either the server or receiver was told to get ready more quickly. It was noticeable, however, that, on the few occasions when the players were unhappy with line calls, there was absolutely no dissent or disrespect shown towards the officials. The decisive calling and signalling of the line judges no doubt played a part in this.

As with all such occasions, the apprentice spectator quickly becomes familiar with the rituals and routines: the umpire's formal introduction of the players to the spectators; the short yells of some (though not all) of the doubles players – a call and response, it sometimes seemed to me – immediately before and/or after a point; the short lifespan (a few points usually) of the shuttlecocks prior to a player politely asking the umpire's permission to take a new one from the courtside stock…

To these could be added the ceremony of this particular Finals Day: the players' entrance into an arena temporarily cast in semi-darkness; the parade of the winners and runners-up (accompanied by *Scotland the Brave*) to collect their trophies and medals; and, poignantly in these Covid-related times, the finalists' presentations of those medals to themselves or each other.

About midway through the afternoon, on my return from a coffee break, I asked the friendly steward registering the number of spectators on her hand-counter what her current total was. The answer was just over 300. The day's events drew to a halt just before a quarter to five. As I left the Emirates Arena, I therefore joined the early leavers from the Celtic-Aberdeen soccer match that had kicked off at 3.00pm and was drawing to a close no more than 200 yards away at Celtic Park. I realised that the attendance at that game would have been over 50,000.

I knew that I had had an interesting and enjoyable afternoon; I hoped they had too.

Of course, we always need to be careful when interpreting headline numbers. The attendance inside the Emirates Arena might have been below the 500 or so that the organisers had perhaps been hoping for. But, as noted, the 2021 Scottish Open Badminton Finals Day is available in its entirety on YouTube. And by mid-day today – 24 hours after the start of the first match – it had registered 181,000 views.

www.anordinaryspectator.com/news-blog November 2021

# Rugby Union

# Reversal of Fortune

Having won all their first 11 fixtures, Lasswade RFC are the clear leaders of the Tennent's National League Division 3 – the fourth tier of amateur rugby union in Scotland – and are firm favourites to take the league title. The battle for the second promotion place is being closely fought, however, with four clubs – West of Scotland, Berwick, Howe of Fife and Hillhead-Jordanhill – currently in the mix. Yesterday, I went to Burnbrae to watch West of Scotland play Howe of Fife: second versus fourth at the start of play.

I had wondered about the sustainability of West's league position and not only because their nearest challengers all had games in hand. Some of their 7 wins had come in high-scoring matches, in which they had impressively come out on top (38-28, 31-24, 38-32), but their 4 defeats had been in matches against the other sides in the top 5, when they had conceded a total of 227 points. In the reverse fixture in September, Howe of Fife had beaten them 82-10.

In the re-match, West could not have made a better start. At the first ruck, a charged down kick led to a five-metre scrum from which the captain, Scott Cochrane, forced his way over the try-line. Howe responded with an impressive try of their own mid-way through the first half, courtesy of their skilful and speedy back division, but a second West try and a penalty goal gave the home side a 17-5 lead as the game entered its final quarter of an hour.

At that point, it looked as if the West pack had given them the upper hand. They had the advantage in the set scrums and, following the lead of Cochrane and his second-row partner Gareth Reid, were able consistently to make good ground with the well-rehearsed catch-and-drive at the line-out. These tactics were ideally suited to the conditions: the ground was heavy following a prolonged period of wet weather though, thankfully, the rain held off during the match itself.

However, the contest was then turned on its head. Howe registered two tries in five minutes – one of which was converted – to draw level at 17-17. Apart from the occasional dropped pass, the visitors' backs remained a significant threat, none more so than the teenage full-back, Gregor Smith – a consistently dangerous runner in broken field – whose 70-yard break ultimately led to his side's levelling score. The momentum of play running strongly in their favour, Howe must have sensed the win.

But it was not to be. The West forwards re-asserted their control and laid siege to the Howe try-line for most of the remainder of the game. The defence held out until the final play of the match – the electronic clock, showing that the 80 minutes were up, was shining brightly on the scoreboard – when a cynical offside in front of the Howe posts led to a yellow card for the perpetrator and a straightforward penalty kick for West to take the honours. A reversal of fortune, indeed, after events in September.

It turned out to have been a very good round of matches for West. The respective games involving Lasswade and Berwick were postponed and Hillhead-Jordanhill managed only a losing bonus point. West have consolidated their second place in the league table, therefore, though there is much of the season's rugby still to be played.

West of Scotland versus Howe of Fife was the first rugby union match I had been to see since Otley played Caldy 21 months ago (*"Let's Keep It Up, Otley"*, 6th February 2020). The weather was cold and damp, though there was a brief period when the late afternoon sun seemed to illuminate the trees down the main road to the left of the clubhouse. I had a full (and dry) view from the top of the main stand. The players were committed and disciplined, cheered on by their respective bands of supporters and guided by a sympathetic referee (Rob McHenry). It was an enjoyable afternoon of Scottish club rugby.

www.anordinaryspectator.com/news-blog December 2021

# Cricket

# Cricketing Role Model

Ray Illingworth, who died last Friday at the age of 89, was my most significant cricketing role model. Here, I draw on a couple of short passages from *An Ordinary Spectator* to describe the impact that he had on this impressionable young cricketer in his early teens.

At the time of the 1968 Headingley Roses match, I was thirteen:

> *"The match... followed a similar pattern to the corresponding game of two years earlier. Yorkshire bowled Lancashire out cheaply and then built up a big first innings lead, this time to win by an innings. For me, the striking thing about the Yorkshire innings was how, after a couple of the front-line batsmen had made big scores... the middle order also weighed in with some heavy scoring.*
>
> *Ray Illingworth was a key figure here: the test match off spinner who could come in at number eight, as he did on this occasion, and play shots like a number three or four. I had the same impressed reaction to his dual skills, with bat and ball, as I had had with Ken Taylor's ability to play more than one sport at a high level.*
>
> *Illingworth's case was closer to home, however: my position in the [school] under 13s team was as an off-spinning batsman who also captained the side. I was not to know at that time — although, like everybody else, I did not have long to wait — that Illingworth's prowess as a captain would also be revealed".*

*[Page 52]*

Illingworth's departure from Yorkshire to Leicestershire later that summer was given due prominence in the *Yorkshire Post*, which was apparently content to give near-equal weight to world geopolitics and the machinations of the county cricket club in presenting the main news stories. The front page headlines for the 21st August edition were "4.00am: Russians invade Czechoslovakia" and "Illingworth can go, says Mr Sellers". (The timing of the pronouncement by the chairman of the Yorkshire CCC selection committee was not given).

In August of the following summer, the 37 year-old Illingworth captained his new county against Yorkshire in a John Player Sunday League match at Scarborough.

> *"I watched Illingworth closely. He batted at number 7 and made a quickfire 30. He bowled when he thought it was the right time and the Yorkshire batsmen would not score heavily off him. He positioned himself in the field so that he was not called on to do any acrobatic fielding. He switched his other bowlers cleverly and moved his fielders around so that the favoured scoring shots of the Yorkshire batsmen were cut off.*
>
> *Through his leadership, Leicestershire were always in control of the match and they won without being seriously threatened. Illingworth was the epitome of a professional cricketer, schooled in the Bradford League and the hard Yorkshire changing room of the 1950s, and, to me looking on from the stand, it showed".*

*[Pages 76-77]*

Elsewhere in the book, when I report on my recollections of watching Bobby Moore play an immaculate game for West Ham United against Leeds United in a League Cup tie at Elland Road in October 1971, I note the parallel characteristics of the contemporary leaders in England's premier sports:

> *"…both captains of their country; both with a mastery of their respective sport's essential skills; both in full control on the field of play…"*

*[Pages 110-111]*

Ray Illingworth and Bobby Moore. Did we realise at the time how lucky we were? Raymond Illingworth CBE, 1932-2021. RIP

www.anordinaryspectator.com/news-blog December 2021

# Rugby League

# The Eagles and the Acorn

The first round of the 2022 Rugby League Challenge Cup – or the Betfred Challenge Cup, to reflect its gambling industry sponsorship – was played this weekend. 14 ties were contested, involving amateur clubs, with the winners joining 10 of the semi-professional League 1 sides in the next round. The Championship and Super League clubs will enter later in the competition with the final scheduled for the Tottenham Hotspur Stadium at the end of May.

The Edinburgh Eagles versus York Acorn RLC tie was played in the spacious grounds of the Royal High School in the suburb of Barnton in Scotland's capital city. Beforehand, I had wondered if it might be something of a mismatch. Whilst the Eagles had a distinguished pedigree of Challenge Cup participation, their qualification was through virtue of winning the 5-team Scottish National League in 2021. By contrast, the visitors will play this season in the highest tier of the amateur game in England – the Premier Division of the National Conference League – having won promotion last year.

The early passages of play suggested that my concerns were justified, as the Eagles were 0-10 down after 5 minutes. With their first set of possession, York engineered a three-man overlap on the right-hand side to run in a straightforward try. Then, when they next had the ball, some accurate passing and determined running produced a second try near the Eagles' posts. At that stage, it looked as if York had a clear advantage in the speed of their play-the-balls and the ease with which their confident passing was stretching the Eagles' defence.

However, the home side did not capitulate and indeed, for the remainder of the first half, the play was much more evenly balanced. A neat grubber kick by half-back Alex Williams led to confusion in the York rearguard and a try for Roserutabua Tawanayavulala, and it was only just before the interval that York scored again to give themselves some breathing space with a 16-6 half-time lead.

The match was watched by a few dozen spectators, mainly on the clubhouse side of the ground. I viewed the action from the grass bank than ran alongside the opposite touchline, on which I was able to move with the play as it ebbed and flowed. I did take a time-out to sit on a concrete step near one of the corner flags for my lunchtime snack – it had been a 1.30pm kick-off – and was rewarded when this third York try was registered right in front of me.

The game took an unexpected turn in the opening minutes of the second half, when the Eagles scored two converted tries to take the lead at 18-16. The first of these followed a sweeping move involving 5 or 6 players and then a long run by Orisi Waibuta over a combined distance of about 80 yards: a brilliant try, which I suspect won't be bettered by many others in this year's Challenge Cup competition.

As the try-scorers' names indicate, the Eagles' cause was aided by the presence in their match squad of several Fijians – members of the British Army, I was informed by one of the home officials – who brought a distinct physicality to their running and tackling. It seemed to me that, at that stage, the York side was somewhat rattled and, no doubt, also rather perplexed after the flying start that they had made to the game.

But it was now the visitors' turn to re-group. With the bustling prop forward Adam Endersby leading the way, they manoeuvred themselves into position to score a couple of short range tries against a tiring defence, aided by the Eagles conceding repeat sets of possession following a couple of needless penalties. This time, as the daylight faded, the lead that York Acorn built up was not to be overturned. They came away with a victory by 38 points to 24, the reward for which will be a home tie in the second round against the London-based Wests Warriors.

It was an afternoon well spent. The match was played without scrums (as a continued Covid precaution) and, given the considerable additional demands that this places on players' fitness, I thought that both sides did well to maintain their levels of energetic commitment for the game's full duration. It was soundly refereed, the official maintaining a zealous (but appropriate) approach to any tackle involving contact with the head. And it also seemed to be played in a good spirit, the only bout of brief fisticuffs occurring right at the very end, when, for some reason, the red mist seemed to descend on three or four players following the final tackle.

As noted, the journey's end for this season's Rugby League Challenge Cup – its 125th anniversary year, as it happens – will be at Tottenham, rather than the usual Wembley (where the final will return to in 2023). For most followers of the competition, that journey began – metaphorically at least – at the weekend at the grounds of amateur clubs across the heartlands of the sport: Leigh, Castleford, Hull *et al*. For a select few of us, it began at the Royal High School in Edinburgh.

www.anordinaryspectator.com/news-blog January 2022

# Wonderful Exploits in a Far-Away Land

In the autumn of 1962, when I was 7 years old, my father bought me a copy of the newly published *Windsors Rugby League Annual*.

I'm not sure whether, at that age, I was too concerned about the missing apostrophe in the title. However, I did quickly realise that it was a fascinating booklet and that my dad's expenditure of two shillings and sixpence had been money well spent. Its cover measured only 6 inches by 4, but the paperback comprised over 140 pages glued together on a flimsy spine that was eventually to disintegrate through my continual reading.

The sponsor was Jim Windsor, the Managing Director of Windsors (Sporting Investments) Ltd – i.e. a bookmaker – based in Leeds. He provided the Preface to a publication that clearly had official endorsement from the Rugby Football League. There was a Foreword from Lord Derby as well as "personal messages" from Wilf Spaven and Bill Fallowfield, respectively the President, Chairman and Secretary of the RFL. The contents were compiled and edited by Ken J Adams.

The Annual's contents ranged from a reminiscence of the famous "Rorke's Drift" Test match in Sydney of 1914 by one of its survivors – Frank Williams of Halifax and Wales – through to the views of John Bapty of the *Yorkshire Evening Post* on the imminent introduction of the two-divisional league structure. There was also a full fixture list for the upcoming 1962-63 season, which was to begin with the short-lived Eastern and Western Championships.

However, the feature that really grabbed my attention was the lengthy description by Phil King of *The People* of the recently completed British Lions tour of Australasia. Actually, "grabbed my attention" is a considerable understatement: I was absolutely captivated. The article took up 34 pages and included a couple of dozen action photographs. There was also a complementary – and shorter – "Australian View of the Tour" by Tom Goodman of the *Sydney Morning Herald*.

The *Rugby League Journal* makes frequent reference to the successes of the 1970 Lions: rightly so, of course, given their revered status as the last Ashes-winning squad to depart from these shores. However, in this Diamond Jubilee year, it is appropriate to mark the achievements of their illustrious predecessors of 1962.

The exploits of these tourists in Australia are now firmly part of the historical record: convincing wins in the first two Tests (by 31-12 and 17-10) to retain the Ashes that had been in Great Britain's possession since 1956; narrow defeat in the third Test by 17-18, courtesy of the last-minute touchline conversion of a disputed Australian try; victory over St George, Australia's premier club side, by 33 points to 5; a five-point winning margin over New South Wales in a match that saw six players (including all four wingers) sent off...

The basis of the Lions' success in Australia was "the storming work of their really great Test pack", which Phil King described with some relish. The pattern was established in the first Test in Sydney: "McTigue was magnificent... The balding Wigan prop pugnaciously bounced off four high-tackling Australians before he sent skipper Ashton over...". Likewise, "second-rowers Huddart and Edgar continually crashed and buffeted their way into Australian territory and they were superbly prompted by mobile Herbert and dashing Turner". King's narrative continued in like vein as the tourists progressed through NSW, Queensland and the Northern Territories.

The 7 year-old reader lapped all this up. I was transported to this magical country in which rugby league was apparently played on sun-drenched afternoons on bone-hard pitches. In Sydney and Brisbane, this was in front of huge crowds – over a quarter of a million spectators watched the five games noted above – though the tourists also had fixtures in exotic-sounding locations such as Toowoomba and Wollongong and Wagga Wagga. Australia even had its own Newcastle. I devoured my extra-curricular geography lessons with relish.

I also could not get enough of King's scene-setting: "the rail journey on the Newcastle Flyer over the picturesque Hawkesbury river is one of the best sightseeing trips of the tour"; in Brisbane, "the first floor of the 93 year-old Australian Hotel, where the team stayed, still looks like part of a Wild West film set"; later, the tourists "began their second Test preparation at Surfers' Paradise on Queensland's glamorous Gold Coast". This was clearly an exciting and exotic land – and some distance from my more familiar suburban north Leeds.

King made the most of his position inside the Great Britain tent. He reported on the saving of "tanners" that was made when "Mick Sullivan found 'a certain lever' at the back of the juke box" at a hotel party in Brisbane. Earlier, in Sydney, he had seen the six dismissed players from the NSW match waiting together outside the disciplinary room: "they reminded me of naughty schoolboys". One of these was Sullivan, who was with the Australian winger, Mike Cleary, "laughing and joking like long lost pals. On the field they had been fighting like tigers".

The tourists' pre-match preparations were slightly more relaxed than might be the case for any modern-day counterparts. On one occasion, there was an exhibition of boomerang and spear-throwing, which was just about safe enough. However, in Cairns – on the morning of the match against Far North Queensland – virtually the whole team went on a 16-mile sea trip and several players were "very, very ill" with sea-sickness. The match was won thanks to a last-minute try by Gerry Round.

The 1961-62 Championship season had been dominated by Wigan and Wakefield Trinity, who finished 8 points clear of third-placed Featherstone Rovers and 13 points above fourth-placed Huddersfield in the final league table. It was perhaps no surprise, therefore, that these two sides supplied almost half of the players – 12 out of 26 – in the Great Britain tour party. The remaining 14 players came from 8 clubs with Workington Town and St Helens providing 3 each. Huddersfield – the Championship winners following the Top-4 play offs – had a sole representative in their prop forward, Ken Noble. Eric Ashton of Wigan was the tour captain.

At the time, I probably didn't pay much attention to the length of the tour, as its long and exhausting duration was the norm in those days. The 1962 tourists played 30 matches in 86 days in Australia and New Zealand (and some of them didn't finish there, as noted below). What did strike me, however, was the rapidity with which some games followed on from the match before.

In Australia, there were 7 occasions on which matches were played on consecutive days, including the days after first two Tests. So it was that Billy Boston followed up his two tries in the second Test in Brisbane with another five the following day in the huge win over Wide Bay-Burnett in Maryborough (having survived the earlier boomerang and spear-throwing exhibition).

Perhaps not surprisingly, there are occasions when Phil King's description of the tour reads as much that of a fervent Great Britain supporter than an objective reporter. Hence, part of the explanation for Great Britain's two-point defeat to Newcastle (which was played only two days after the NSW encounter) was "some almost laughable refereeing in Newcastle's favour". It is instructive, therefore, to be able also to draw on Tom Goodman's more detached perspective.

Goodman was clearly impressed by several of the British players, notably Ashton ("a grand field captain – poised, resourceful"), Derek Turner ("a loose forward of all-round power"), Alex Murphy ("among the great halves of all time with his glittering speed and lovely footwork") and, interestingly, Laurie Gilfedder, whose versatility at centre and second-row, combined with his goal-kicking, made him "a superb stand-by player".

Where Goodman took issue with the conventional wisdom was in his assessment of the second-row forward Dick Huddart for whom "the lavish praise...

was rather flattering because his spectacular success... was aided by much poor tackling". I would guess that this *Journal*'s editor would have something to say about that view of the Cumbrian great, not least because – drawing on the well-worn sporting truism/cliché – you can only play what's in front of you.

Tom Goodman ended his review of the tour with an Australian's generous summary: "You sent us a grand team. We are grateful and we hope to profit from what we saw". They did, of course. It was only a little over a year to the beginning of the Australians' 1963 tour of Britain, when the Ashes pendulum would swing back again.

These days, of course, when reflecting on the 1962 tour, we can supplement the contemporary sources with the material now available on DVD – I recommend *Rugby League: 1962 and 1963 Ashes Tours*, available from the *Journal*'s shop – and YouTube.

As if immediately to undermine Tom Goodman's assessment of Dick Huddart's performances, the first action shot on the DVD is of the latter ripping the ball from an opponent and making a 50-yard dash downfield. There are another half-dozen such rampaging charges by the St Helens star shown in the clips from the first two tests, including his long-range try in the opening encounter in Sydney.

The other highlights come thick and fast on the DVD: McTigue's ball-handling skills to set up skipper Ashton's two tries in the first test; Boston shrugging off tacklers on his powerful surge to the line in Brisbane; Murphy's brilliant 45-yard run from the base of a scrum for a try on the return to Sydney; a wonderful try-saving tackle by full-back Round on the Australian winger Eddie Lumsden... Viewing these action shots serves to confirm the mental images that I had derived reading Phil King's descriptions in Jim Windsor's publication all those years ago.

As the tour progressed, the combination of draining itinerary and serious injury began to take its toll. Don Fox was the first to leave the tour, after the match in Cairns, and, by the end of the long Australian leg – in which 18 of the 21 matches had been won – injuries had also ruled out Ashton and Murphy for the rest of the trip. Several other players carried injuries across the Tasman Sea where the Kiwis – who had already shown what they could do by defeating Great Britain convincingly at Headingley the previous year – were lying in wait.

The tourists won 6 of their 9 matches in New Zealand, racking up half-century scores in 3 of them (including 81 points against Bay of Plenty in Rotorua). But the two Test matches were different affairs, the home side winning both convincingly. Having used only 15 players in the whole series in Australia (including 11 who played in all three matches), the tourists drew more fully from the whole squad for the internationals against New Zealand. Only 4 players

– Gerry Round, Neil Fox, Brian McTigue and Dick Huddart – played in all the tour's 5 Test matches.

Phil King's article devotes only two pages to the New Zealand leg of the tour, about which there is a distinct sense of anti-climax – "the injury-ridden tourists… became dispirited and disinterested" – with the final match resulting in a heavy defeat to Auckland.

*Windsors Rugby League Annual* did not report on the postscript to Great Britain's 1962 Australasian tour, which was the short visit by a reduced party to South Africa, where three matches were played. As AN Gaulton dryly recorded in his *The Encyclopaedia of Rugby League Football* (1968), the total of 219 points registered by the teams in these matches – Great Britain won all three – "do not suggest that there was any serious defensive play".

The overall playing record of the 1962 Great Britain tourists does not match that of their 1970 counterparts. In addition to winning their Ashes series, the latter won all three of their Test matches in New Zealand and suffered only one defeat on their entire 24-match trip. By contrast, as we have seen, the 1962 tourists won only two of their five Tests.

And yet, the 1962 vintage will always have a place in my affections. In the years that followed, whenever the players turned out for their clubs against my dad's team, Hunslet, at Parkside – Harold Poynton for Wakefield Trinity, Peter Small for Castleford, Gary Cooper for Featherstone Rovers *et al* – I would recall the 7 year-old's excitement at reading in *Windsors Rugby League Annual* of their wonderful exploits in a far-away land.

The Diamond Jubilee of the British Lions 1962 Australasian tour is a reminder of just how important such tours used to be in Rugby League. The abandonment of this wonderful tradition represents a sad loss to the sport.

Has anyone seen a missing apostrophe?

*The Rugby League Journal* Issue 78, Spring 2022

# Boxing

# Southpaws

I had had some previous experience of being a sports spectator at boxing events – the Oxford versus Cambridge Varsity Boxing Matches of 1977 and 1979 to be precise, as reported in *An Ordinary Spectator* – but that had been a long time ago and, of course, those contests featured amateur combatants. Last Saturday evening was somewhat different: Josh Taylor versus Jack Catterall at the OVO Hydro in Glasgow.

This was a fight for the Super Lightweight World Championship with Taylor's WBC, WBA, IBF and WBO titles – acquired at various times over the last three years – all on the line. In other words – cutting through the alphabet soup – the winner would be the undisputed world champion at the weight limit of 140 pounds (10 stones or 63.5 kg). It was the first time that all 4 versions of a championship title had been at stake at a fight in Britain.

Although Catterall was the more experienced professional boxer – and unbeaten in 26 fights over 10 years – Taylor was the clear pre-bout favourite. On the morning of the fight, the bookmakers' odds on his win were 14 to 1 *on*, compared with the challenger's price of 13 to 2 against: a marked difference for a two-horse race. Moreover, Taylor – also undefeated in an 18-bout professional career since winning a gold medal (in the Hydro) at the 2014 Commonwealth Games – had the anticipated advantage of a vociferous home support, given his Prestonpans birthplace. Catterall, from Chorley in Lancashire, knew that he was entering hostile territory.

The Taylor-Catterall fight was one of no fewer than 11 on the card. The first bout was in the early evening, but the main protagonists were not scheduled to "ringwalk" until 10pm – as determined by the satellite television schedule, of course. Moreover, in what I gather is the normal way, the final details of the running order on the undercard were not announced until Saturday morning, apart from the Featherweight contest between Roseisy Ramirez of Cuba and the Irishman, Eric Donovan.

I took up my seat – an excellent view from the front row of the second tier – at about half past five, by which time the first fight had already taken place. Although there were perhaps only a couple of hundred spectators in the arena at that time – like me, no doubt, determined to get full value for money (in my case for a £60 ticket and £22.44 in other charges) – it was noticeable that the noise level was already high, principally in support of the Irish Super Welterweight, Keiron Molloy, who won his first professional fight in the second round. I asked myself what the volume would be like for the main contest, when the Hydro's full 11,000+ capacity – many lubricated by a lengthy session of beer consumption – was in place.

The *dramatis personae* of the undercard performed in front of us: a combination of the inexperienced taking their first steps on the professional ladder and the occasional journeyman pugilist. This contrast was evident in the Cruiserweight contest between Scott Forest, also in his first professional fight, and Erik Nazaryan, a veteran from Georgia with a 49 per cent success rate from 57 previous contests: the former won when his opponent retired in the second round.

There was certainly a variety in the fights on offer. There were impressive wins for Bilal Fawaz and John Docherty, respectively a Middleweight and Super Middleweight, the latter with the only straight knock-out of the evening in overcoming Jordan Grant. In the only women's contest, Ebonie Jones, in her second professional fight, and the 40 year-old Effy Kathopouli stood toe-to-toe and slogged it out for 6 rounds: the draw was a fair result, I thought.

Later, two Glaswegians, Nick Campbell and Jay McFarlane, disputed the Scottish Heavyweight title that had lain vacant for over 70 years. Campbell seemed to take control in the 6th round with a succession of head shots that, somehow, McFarlane – at just under 20 stones and attired in a kilt – managed to walk through. McFarlane then launched a spirited counter-attack to the accompanying support of the growing numbers in the crowd. However, when Campbell launched another fusillade in the next round – and McFarlane again remained upright – the referee stepped in to end the contest. The general consensus around me was that this had not been before time.

The main supporting bout was the Ramirez/Donovan contest. The Cuban is highly regarded as a candidate for further honours and, after an evenly fought start, the fight ended with a technical knock-out in the third round, when the Irishman was pinned on the ropes and succumbed to a crushing body punch. This was the second occasion on which a shot to the body – rather than the head – had ended the fight. The Czech boxer Jaroslav Hriadel suffered the same fate against the well-supported Kurt Walker from Northern Ireland and was clearly in some pain afterwards.

All major sporting occasions have their own rituals and, of course, Saturday evening's events at the Hydro were no exception. The arena was in constant darkness – I couldn't read my notes in front of me – but the ring was clearly illuminated by the overhead lighting with other beams of light flashing across the ringside seats. The boxers made their individual entrances down the walkway to the ring accompanied by the music of their choice. Not surprisingly, *Eye of the Tiger* (from *Rocky III*) featured a couple of times, though I was more impressed by Ebonie Jones's choice of Nancy Sinatra singing *These Boots are Made for Walking*.

All the contestants on the undercard seemed to adhere to the sport's acknowledged codes of conduct. There was a uniform touching of gloves at the start of each fight and, occasionally, at the end of a round. The defeated boxers congratulated their victorious opponents. Of course, the vanquished were then faced with the return journey back up the walkway to the changing room: a lonely walk with their own thoughts, I would guess, though each was chaperoned by a member of the security staff. Thankfully, on this occasion, all were able to walk back unaided, albeit with clouded heads (Grant and McFarlane) or aching ribs (Donovan and Hriadel).

I made an effort to focus on each of the undercard's defeated fighters as they made their way back up the walkway. I wondered about the circumstances of the individual journeys that had brought Malam Varela from Portugal, Miroslav Serban from Kromeriz in the Czech Republic and Damian Esquisabel from Santander in Spain – amongst others – to this place at this time. All three of these particular fighters are now in their early 30s. In their preparation for their appearance at the Hydro – and their casual dismissal by a chattering crowd impatient for the main event – they had endured the training, the sacrifices and the pain of a brutal and unforgiving sport. With their stars apparently on the wane, what would their futures bring?

The arena was nearly full by the time of the Ramirez/Donovan contest. When this finished earlier than scheduled, there were about 25 minutes to fill before the Taylor/Catterall showdown. It was not wasted. This was party time in Saturday evening Glasgow and the house DJ knew his market: Neil Diamond's *Sweet Caroline*, the 1970s Euro disco *Yes Sir, I can Boogie* (now appropriated by the Tartan Army of Scottish football supporters) and Queen's *Radio Ga Ga* as well as a couple of club anthems with which, I must confess, I was not entirely familiar. Interestingly, he also played the Oasis track *Don't Look Back in Anger*, which I thought might have been deemed provocative, given the band's shared regional roots with Josh Taylor's challenger. But that was looking for subtleties that didn't exist. The singing and dancing revellers belted out the song with gusto.

The musical interlude ended with Amy Macdonald leading a rousing rendition of *Flower of Scotland*. Again, I wondered about the subtext. I'm sure I was not the only one to register that to have "sent him homeward tae think again" might be applied more immediately to Jack Catterall and his supporters, rather than a long-dead English king. I have to say, though, that – aside from the occasional isolated exhortation for Taylor to smash the English bastard – there was no great sense of a Scotland/England conflict, and nor had there been in the week-long pre-match hype on the television sports news channel. One of my neighbours told me that Taylor has a sizeable support base in England.

And so to the main event. Catterall entered the arena to widespread – and predictable – booing, apart from the cheers of a group of supporters on the far side from me. Taylor was preceded by an entourage that proudly hoisted the four championship belts that he possessed. My earlier question was answered shortly afterwards. When the MC came to make the formal announcement of Taylor's name to the crowd, his words were drowned out by the huge roar.

Here – as an aside – I must own up to another confession. When I was very young and occasionally watching the boxing highlights on television, I did wonder for some time why so many boxers came from Southport. Perhaps it was Harry Carpenter's diction in presenting the action on the BBC's *Sportsview*. The word is southpaw, of course, and it refers to the fighter leading with his right hand and with his right foot forward. I had a wry smile when I saw both Taylor and Catterall take up this stance.

It was evident from the first bell that, contrary to what was implied by the pre-match odds, these were two evenly matched fighters. Whatever his status as the underdog, Catterall was certainly not intimidated by either his opponent or his surroundings. Neither man gained control in the early rounds as the contest regressed into a scrappy affair with little fluid movement and a great deal of holding and grappling. I thought that Catterall decisively took the 6th round, the end of which marked the mid-point of the bout's scheduled duration. I also sensed that Taylor's supporters around me were becoming worried at his lack of clear dominance and the prospect of an adverse outcome. This concern was then amplified in the 7th when Taylor was cut below the right eye and the following round, when he was temporarily floored.

Both boxers incurred the wrath of the referee: Catterall was publicly warned for excessive holding in the 10th round and then, at the end of the 11th, Taylor was similarly penalised for striking his opponent after the bell. At the end of contest, both my immediate neighbours – a middle-aged man attending with his adult daughter and a younger man celebrating a mate's birthday – were distinctly pessimistic about Taylor's chances of getting the judges' verdict.

It was a split decision – 2-1 – which, in his announc ement of the result, the MC knew how to exploit for its full dramatic effect. The first scorecard was read out in Catterall's favour and the second for Taylor. The marks of the third judge were announced, followed by "… and still undisputed…". As at the beginning, so at the end: the crowd's roar drowned out the rest of the MC's proclamation.

It was a roar of triumph, but also – I suspect – an expression of relief. As it turned out, my neighbours' assessments had been fully in tune with most independent analysts, including those who had maintained their running blogs throughout the contest. The Sky Sports blog stated that Taylor had been "outskilled and outmanoeuvred by Catterall, who has been relentlessly good" and that the judges' verdict was "unbelievable" and "absolutely staggering" and the *MainOnline* called it "a truly shocking decision", whilst the *Irish Times* diplomatically suggested that "not everyone will be happy with that result".

The furore has continued since the end of the fight. Yesterday, Sir Lindsay Hoyle tweeted his opinion that "it was a disgraceful decision… the result is a travesty of justice".

I was aware that Sir Lindsay is a keen follower of sport (notably rugby league), but I did wonder why the Speaker of the House of Commons – no less – should take such a public interest in the judges' controversial decision. However, it did not take me long to determine why he should move away from his usual position of strict neutrality. Sir Lindsay Hoyle has been the Member of Parliament for Chorley since 1997.

www.anordinaryspectator.com/news-blog February 2022

# Plan B

It had been some time since I had seen a match in the Scottish Professional Football League (Annan Athletic vs Elgin City in January 2020) and even longer since a game in the Scottish Premiership (Hearts vs St Mirren in November 2019), so on Saturday I travelled to Easter Road in Edinburgh for the encounter between two clubs – Hibernian and St Johnstone – that I had not previously viewed in the flesh.

The Scottish league season is three-quarters of the way through. At the start of play, Hibs were in 5th place in the league table and one of no fewer than six teams covered by only four points between 4th and 9th. With only 4 matches to play before the "split" into the top and bottom 6s (for the last 5 games), there was clearly an intense battle to secure a place in the upper tier and, possibly, a qualification for one of next season's European competitions.

St Johnstone were not part of that group. Following last year's success in securing both the Scottish Cup and the Scottish League Cup, this season has been a disappointment. The side began the day second from bottom in the table, some 7 points adrift of third-from-bottom Aberdeen. Their main objective for the remainder of the season would appear to be avoiding ending up right at the foot of the table (in the place occupied by Dundee, one point behind with a game in hand), which would bring automatic relegation. Second-from-bottom would secure a hazardous play-off tie against one of the Championship sides.

On the train journey across from Glasgow to Edinburgh, the other seats at my table and all four seats at the one across the aisle were taken by a group of St Johnstone supporters: young lads, perhaps aged 15 to 17 or 18. Their chosen beverages included alcoholic and energy drinks and they were loud and, at times, uncouth, but the aggression of the main protagonists was directed at others within the group, rather than outsiders such as me. Towards the end of the journey, when I engaged those seated at my table in conversation, we had a pleasant chat about football and sport in general. The lad opposite me said that he didn't know much about cricket, but was aware that a famous cricketer (Shane Warne) had died the day before. He was also impressed that Hibernian had priced his ticket at just £5: good for the club, I agreed, if it were seeking to boost attendance by younger supporters.

My intention had been to secure my entrance to the match at a visit to the ticket office just outside the ground. To my surprise, it was locked when I tried the door. On enquiring with a nearby steward, I was told that the game had sold out. It was not just the Under 18s who were paying £5 for a ticket; apart from those in the hospitality boxes, everybody was. After walking to the other end of the ground, I asked another steward whether there were any returned tickets on sale. "You could try the ticket office", she replied. I knew then that my anticipated afternoon of watching Hibernian vs St Johnstone would have to wait for another day.

Of course, I do have a track record for attempted sports-watching that has gone slightly awry. The washed-out days at cricket matches are understandable. Less so, perhaps, attempting to watch a rugby union fixture in Bristol at the wrong ground, with the game already having been postponed, and with the added bonus of risking life and limb to cross a busy highway in the process (as reported in *Still An Ordinary Spectator*).

Fortunately, on Saturday, there was still time for a Plan B. And a good one it was too. A £10 taxi ride took me across the city from Easter Road to Inverleith in plenty of time before the match between Edinburgh Academical and the Currie Chieftains in the Scottish Premiership – rugby union (sponsored by Tennent's) rather than football (sponsored by Cinch).

I had been meaning to visit Raeburn Place for some time. As I have reported before – "*The First Rugby International*", 27th March 2021 – the ground has a unique place in the history of the sport as it was the venue for the Scotland vs England encounter in 1871 that commenced the 150-plus years of international rugby. I had previously been informed that there was a stone monument in the grounds to commemorate the event. What better opportunity to seek it out.

I made enquiries about this in the clubhouse before the game when I button-holed one of the club's members, who turned out to be Paul Arnold, the captain of the Third XV. He introduced me to the club secretary, John Wright. Like me, John is an exiled Yorkshireman – in his case, from Bradford – and we had a great discussion about the fierce club rugby that was played in that county in the 1970s. Paul told me that he wasn't exactly sure where the monument was, but, from our vantage point on the balcony of the impressive clubhouse, he pointed out the general area on the far side of the grounds that he thought to be the most likely.

I have to say that, although both Paul and John were in demand from other club members in the remaining minutes before the kick-off, they were both hugely supportive in their responses to the slightly odd request made by a complete stranger. I was left with the strong impression of a welcoming and friendly rugby club.

For both sides, the match was the last one in the regular Premiership season prior to the Top-4 play-offs. As Currie had already emphatically secured the top spot and, likewise, the home side were already guaranteed of at least 4th position, it might have been supposed that this was something of a dead rubber.

That was certainly not the case. There was a full commitment from both teams with the visitors taking the early initiative, when a powerful forward surge brought a try for Gregor Nelson. The Accies responded when a long flat pass from fly-half Vincent Hart put the second-row forward Struan Whittaker on a try-scoring run, only for Currie to retake the lead and head into half-time up by 12-7. Thereafter, Currie were always in control of the match, taking leads of 19-7 and 24-10 before two late home tries narrowed the final score to 24-20. The forward battle was an interesting one: Currie had by far the better of the line-outs until late in the game, whereas the Accies' ascendancy in the scrum became more pronounced as the second half progressed. I thought that the game's most influential player was the Currie flank forward and captain Fergus Scott who, in addition to his tackling stint, provided regular examples of skilful link play in his handling of the ball.

I must admit to having missed Currie's third try early in the second half. At that stage, I was some distance from the pitch on the far side of the Edinburgh Academical sports ground searching for a stone monument in the general area that Paul Arnold had suggested. I met with success. The writing – in upper case – on the stone is not easy to discern, but I can confirm that it reads:

1871      1971

TO COMMEMORATE THE FIRST
INTERNATIONAL MATCH IN THE
WORLD UNDER RUGBY RULES
PLAYED AT RAEBURN PLACE
EDINBURGH IN 1871 BETWEEN
SCOTLAND & ENGLAND

The monument is currently at the edge of a large pile of rubble on which, on this occasion, a group of small children were playing. I do hope that, at some stage, it might be recovered and given its proper prominence nearer to the clubhouse so that the Raeburn Place site can combine the modernity of its splendid clubhouse with this reference to its rich history.

The result of the Edinburgh Academical-Currie match means that the final placings of the (rugby union) Premiership's Top-4 have been decided. One of the semi-finals in three weeks' time will be hosted by Currie at their Malleny Park home ground in Balerno – when the visitors will be Edinburgh Academical FC.

Meanwhile, as the rugby match was coming to a close, Hibernian and

St Johnstone were playing out a 0-0 draw at Easter Road. The lads from Perth would probably have been pleased with the outcome, although Dundee's draw at Motherwell means that it is *status quo* at the foot of the (football) Premiership table.

www.anordinaryspectator.com/news-blog March 2022

Cricket

# Shane Warne at Headingley

*"We returned to our seats just as the Australians were taking the field for the afternoon session. They did so through a guard of honour made at the boundary edge by a group of disabled cricketers, dressed in their whites, who had given a demonstration of their skills on the outfield during the break. This was a courageous group – including some blind and some with missing limbs – and they formed two lines to welcome the Australians as Gilchrist led his team on to the ground.*

*Most of the Australians jogged or walked straight through the disabled players' tunnel, clearly focusing on their immediate tasks when play resumed, though Gilchrist held out a large wicketkeeping glove to the player at the end of one of the lines. The last player out was Shane Warne, who stopped and went slowly along one of the lines, shaking hands with everyone in it. I found this incredibly moving. Good on you, mate, I thought".*

[*An Ordinary Spectator*, page 295]

Shane Warne died on Friday at the age of 52. I saw him play for Australia at Headingley in the Ashes Test matches of 1993, 1997 and 2001 and in a World Cup group match against South Africa in 1999.

In *An Ordinary Spectator*, I noted that, in the one-day match, South Africa's sizeable total would have been even larger had it not been for Warne's "impressively tight and controlled bowling" in the middle of the innings – he took 2 for 33 from 10 overs, by far the most economical bowling on the day. Australia had to win the match to stay in the competition, which they duly did thanks to a century by the captain Steve Waugh (and an infamous dropped catch by Herschelle Gibbs). Australia won the World Cup by defeating Pakistan at Lord's a week later.

It's probably true to say that Headingley was not Warne's happiest Test match hunting ground. He took a total of 3 wickets there – which was 3 more than the runs he scored in his two innings. No matter. The 2001 Test is principally remembered for Mark Butcher's match-winning innings of 173 not out for England on the final day. However, for me, the most striking memory from this match – noted above – is from the end of the lunch break on the Saturday.

145 Test Matches. 708 Test Match Wickets. 3,145 Test Match Runs. 125 Test Match Catches.

Shane Warne 1969–2022. RIP.

www.anordinaryspectator.com/news-blog March 2022

# Cricket

# Five Steps to WG Grace

In my student summers of the mid-1970s, I played three half-seasons for Saltaire CC in the Bradford League. In the first of these, when we were in the First Division, I opened the batting in the away fixture at Bowling Old Lane CC.

The opposition's opening bowler was Harold Rhodes – ex Derbyshire and England – by then in his late 30s, but still a formidable proposition. It was a seamer's wicket. I battled for an hour and made 12; it is one of the innings of which I am most proud.

Although Rhodes had made his first-class debut in 1953, it was three years later that he took his maiden "five-for" in Yorkshire's second innings at Chesterfield to snatch a 6-run victory for the home side. The Yorkshire captain that season was Mr WHH Sutcliffe – son of the great Herbert – the penultimate amateur skipper of the White Rose county.

Billy Sutcliffe averaged a modest 26 runs per innings in his 10 year first-class career, but he did make a big hundred – 181 – against Kent at Canterbury in 1952. His partner in a 201-run stand for the fourth wicket was someone whose career average turned out to be somewhat higher, aided by his own score of 120 in Yorkshire's innings victory: Len Hutton.

Hutton made his debut for Yorkshire as a 17 year-old in 1934. In July of that year, against Gloucestershire at Bristol, he made 39 in the first innings and was run out for nought in the second (a fate he had also suffered in his very first match at Fenner's against Cambridge University two months earlier). In the opposition's ranks was the 51 year-old Charlie Parker, who retired the following year as Gloucestershire's all-time wicket-taker – a record he still holds – his left-arm spin claiming 3,170 victims at under 20 apiece over 32 years. Parker took five of these wickets in Yorkshire's second innings to set his side up for a nine-wicket win.

Over 30 years earlier – in 1903 – when Parker played for Gloucestershire in a first-class match against London County at the Crystal Palace Park, he was unable to prevent one of the opposition batsmen scoring 150 in the first innings, the same player having earlier taken six Gloucestershire wickets. This was WG Grace no less – then aged 54 – who, not surprisingly, was the central figure (secretary, manager and captain) in the London set-up during its short lifespan as a first-class entity (from 1900 to 1904).

Grace began his career with Gloucestershire in 1870. Six years later, he registered 318 not out against Yorkshire at Cheltenham College. Until 2004 (when it was overhauled by Craig Spearman), this stood as the highest individual score for the county. It remains the highest against their opponents.

The daisy chain reaches from the mid-1970s to the mid-1870s. My journey back to WG Grace has taken five steps. It has picked up a club cricketer, a county stalwart, amateur captain(s), test-match players, all-time greats...

It is a history of the game.

www.anordinaryspectator.com/news-blog April 2022

Cricket/Rugby League

# Dual Sportsmen

When my father introduced me to the game of cricket in the early 1960s, the Yorkshire team was full of fascinating characters: Trueman, Illingworth, Boycott *et al*. However, at that stage, it was another player – Ken Taylor – who particularly interested me. Not only did he play cricket for Yorkshire – indeed, he also represented England three times – but in the winter he played football for Huddersfield Town.

I thought this was amazing. What a way to earn your living: playing more than one sport all the year around. It also provided reassuring confirmation that my own ambitions to represent my country at both rugby league and cricket (and at rugby union and football as well, come to that) – sadly and mysteriously unfulfilled, as it turned out – were not entirely out of the question.

I was to learn that the cricket/football combination was not uncommon amongst the Tykes. Brian Close had been on the books at Leeds United and Arsenal and had played half a dozen games for Bradford City, whilst Chris Balderstone (later of Leicestershire and England) also played for Huddersfield Town before enjoying a long career at Carlisle United. Later, Arnie Sidebottom, who featured in 16 games for Manchester United before joining the conveyer belt to Huddersfield, represented England in an Ashes test match at Trent Bridge.

The cricket/rugby union linkages were even stronger. The 1964 England cricket captain – MJK Smith of Warwickshire – had also played rugby union for England, winning a cap against Wales in 1956. In the following decade, first class cricket was played by no fewer than 5 England rugby players, including Peter Squires (Yorkshire) and Alastair Hignell (Cambridge University and Gloucestershire).

The obvious question arises. Where were the rugby league players in these examples of dual sporting excellence with the summer game?

At the time of my introduction to the sport, there seemed to be only one name ever mentioned when this question was asked. The Maesteg fly-half Alan

Rees signed for Leeds after playing three times for Wales in 1962. He was at the club for three years, though injury restricted the number of his appearances to a couple of dozen or so. However, this was more than enough for him to qualify as a dual sportsman, as he had been playing first class cricket since 1955. Rees played in 216 such matches for Glamorgan up to 1968, top-scoring with 111 not out against Lancashire in 1964. His place in *Wisden* is guaranteed – somewhat ironically as a rugby player – thanks to his entry in the "Unusual Dismissals" section: he was given out "handled the ball" at Lord's in 1965.

In the following decade, two other players could be said to have combined rugby league and first class cricket. One was Keith Jarrett, who had starred for Wales against England at Cardiff Arms Park in 1967, three months after leaving school, and then won another nine caps before signing for Barrow in 1969. His league career was cruelly cut short when he suffered a stroke in 1973. In the same year as his dramatic entry on to the rugby union stage, Jarrett played two matches for Glamorgan, his top score being a modest 18 not out.

A similar story was presented by John Gray, who played rugby union for Coventry before signing for Wigan in 1973. This superb player won 11 rugby league caps for England and Great Britain before emigrating to Australia and enjoying huge success with North Sydney and Manly-Warringah. His sporting roots in the Midlands included 7 appearances for Warwickshire in first class cricket, when he took 21 wickets with his left-arm medium pace. His best bowling performance was a remarkable 5 for 2 against Scotland in his first match in 1968.

There is one other – more recent – name to be added to this (short) list dating from the 1960s. Having previously played rugby union for the Cardiff Blues and Newcastle Falcons, Liam Botham's career in rugby league comprised 28 matches with the Leeds Rhinos, London Broncos and Wigan Warriors over the three seasons to 2005. Whilst not quite emulating the cricketing achievements of his father, Ian, the younger Botham did play in three first class matches for Hampshire in 1996, taking 5 wickets in his first game. His dual participation in top level rugby league and cricket is no small feat in the modern era.

We have to go back to the 1940s for the British rugby league player who reached the highest level as a cricketer. This was Alan Wharton, who played in the three-quarters for Salford. He played over 480 first class cricket matches, mainly for Lancashire, scoring no fewer than 31 centuries as an attacking left-handed batsman. He won his solitary test cap against New Zealand at Headingley in 1949 in an England side that included Len Hutton and Denis Compton.

It can be seen that the rugby league/first class cricket combination has been relatively rare within the home nations. Since the 1960s, Alan Rees is the only example of someone having parallel careers in the two sports, as Jarrett, Gray and Botham had all completed their main cricketing exploits by the time they played professional rugby league. Moreover, it is noticeable that all four of these players had played top level rugby union before performing on the league stage.

It goes without saying that, in every generation of rugby league players, there have been very many skilled in other ball games, including a good club standard of cricket – from Wakefield Trinity's Ted Bateson (who also played for Lancashire 2nd XI) in the 1920s through to the great Willie Horne in the 1950s and Phil Cookson of Leeds twenty years later, to name but three. But appearances at the county cricket level have been few and far between.

The reasons for this are no doubt complex, but it is likely that – even for those with the required ability – the practicalities of wage-earning would have been a significant part of the explanation. For part-time rugby league players holding down full-time jobs – more often than not in heavy industrial occupations – there simply weren't the opportunities to take the summers off to play county cricket.

The rugby league/cricket combination has been more prevalent in Australia and New Zealand. Here, pride of place must go to the Auckland centre three-quarter (and opening batsman), Verdun Scott, who was selected for tours of England at both rugby league (1939) and cricket (1949). The first of these was abandoned after two matches – truncated by the outbreak of the Second World War – but Scott was to play in all 4 test matches a decade later, taking his place at the top of the batting order with Bert Sutcliffe. (At Headingley, his opponents included the English debutant, Alan Wharton). In total, Scott played on 10 occasions for New Zealand, his top score being 84 against the West Indies in 1952.

Three other players – John Ackland, Sel Belsham and Charles Finlayson – have donned the colours of the New Zealand rugby league team as well as turning out for either the Auckland or Wellington sides in first class cricket. Ackland's solitary cap was against Papua New Guinea in 1983, following a season's stint in the Second Division with Hunslet and a contribution towards his adopted club's famous first-round Challenge Cup win over Hull Kingston Rovers, who at that time were the First Division's highest flyers. His cricketing skills brought him 10 wickets in 6 first class matches for Auckland. Belsham also played in half a dozen games for Auckland, as a wicketkeeper. His rugby league test career was longer, however: 10 consecutive matches from 1955, including the 1957 World Cup in Australia.

Finlayson went one better in terms of cricketing matches for Auckland and Wellington though, remarkably, his 7 appearances as a left-handed all-rounder were stretched over the 21 years from 1910. At that time, first class cricketers in New Zealand were unpaid (just like its rugby league players) and it was on the basis of his club form that Finlayson was selected to play against Australia in 1928. He does not count as a test match cricketer, however, as New Zealand's first match with this status did not take place until 1930. His single appearance as a Kiwi rugby player occurred in a heavy defeat to New South Wales in 1913.

The number of dual top-level rugby league players and first class cricketers from Australia runs into double figures. Perhaps the most remarkable achievement was that of Bill Farnsworth, who achieved this feat (just) in both Australia and England. He played one first class cricket match for both New South Wales and Lancashire CCC, but is better known for his rugby exploits, winning four caps and touring Britain (with his brother Viv) in 1911-12; he also played for Oldham before and after the First World War.

On the next tour in 1921-22 – although he did not play in a test match – was Rex Norman, who had previously played 7 matches for the NSW cricket side, taking a handy 31 wickets with his left-arm medium pace. In the post-Second World War period, the half-back Johnny Brown won his solitary Kangaroo cap in 1970, his rugby league appearances for Queensland (eight) just outnumbering those at cricket (six).

Some of the Australian dual sportsmen unequivocally had cricket as their first sport. One was Herbie Collins, who played in the 1911 off-season for Eastern Suburbs in the New South Wales Rugby League, but later captained Australia 11 times in a cricketing career that included a century on his test debut in 1920 and a place on the 1926 tour of England. However, the most famous was the great fast bowler Ray Lindwall, who played at full back for St George in the NSWRL between 1940 and 1946, although he lost three of these years to war service. His compatriot "Jock" Livingston played for South Sydney in the same competition during the war years, later taking his left-handed batting skills to Northamptonshire CCC where he played for eight seasons in the 1950s.

For Arthur Clues, the primary sport was rugby league, of course. He did not reach first class standard as a cricketer, but I cannot omit him from this round-up, given his marvellous claim – to which Harry Edgar has drawn my attention – that he scored both a try hat-trick and a century at Headingley (albeit on different pitches).

One final observation from the cricket field. Jock Livingston was an outstanding cover point fieldsman. The same was true of at least a couple of the other names given above – Alan Rees and Ken Taylor – at a time when general fielding standards were far inferior to what they are today.

I wonder if this further illustration of the multi-faceted skills of these sportsmen helps to explain their interest to us, both at the time and as we look back with fond memory.

When we were growing up and playing with our friends after school – touch rugby or soccer under the streetlights and then, in the longer evenings, cricket in the park – we aspired to be the likes of Geoff Shelton or Bobby Charlton in one season *and* Geoff Boycott or Freddie Trueman in the next. It was the talented all-round games-players – with their ability to play at the top level in both the winter and the summer – who offered the hope that this might be possible.

*The Rugby League Journal* Summer 2022

# Cricket

# Insult to Injury[34]

It was only well after I had stopped playing cricket that I realised how fortunate I had been. For much of the 20-year period that I had enjoyed participating in the game, I had been an opening batsman. And I had managed to avoid serious injury.

In my early days, the batting protection consisted of a box and gloves (my own) and pads from the school's kit bag. The gloves were basically useless: thin material with those inadequate green spiky prongs to cover the knuckles. I later graduated with relief to the "sausage" variety.

At first, I wore the regular bruising around my thigh and hip as a badge of honour: after all, I was brought up in Yorkshire, where the Brian Close philosophy of taking the blow and not rubbing the wound was *de rigueur*. It was my mother who saw sense. She fashioned a long thigh pad that covered my hip and the top of my leg and this served me well for many years.

As for helmets, they were nowhere in sight. Even after Mike Brearley led the way with his skull-cap and the first-class cricketers started to wear what appeared to be different versions of grilled motorcycle helmet, they did not feature at my level; indeed, I don't recall ever playing in a match in which one was worn. This was obviously not particularly helpful when struck on the head (see below).

Of course, I was not continually faced with a diet of speedsters bowling at 90 mph on bouncy pitches. But some bowlers were quick enough, thank you very much. Moreover, like all club cricketers, I was regularly playing on pitches that had what is euphemistically called "variable" bounce. It was on one of these, in a club match in Surrey, that I realised that I had lost the flight of the ball after it had pitched and reared. There followed that split second in which the emotion flashes from surprise to apprehension to terror as one waits to be struck. I still do not know how that particular delivery missed me.

As for being struck on the head, that occurred at school in a house match. The ball reared up from a length (from a medium-paced trundler, thankfully) to

354

hit me on the shoulder before glancing off the side of my head – fairly firmly, I have to say – into the waiting hands of the short-leg fieldsman. In a different sporting arena, Geoff Hurst or Alan Gilzean would have been proud of the effort.

My shock and discomfort were relieved – temporarily – when I heard short-leg appeal for the catch. "You cheeky fellow", I thought (or words to that effect). "Do you really think that the impact of the ball on the side of my head sounds like ball-on-willow?" After a brief pause, I looked down the wicket at the umpire. He was nodding his head up and down, his finger confidently raised.

Insult to injury.

*The Nightwatchman: Wisden Cricket Quarterly* June 2022

# Match Programmes

*"We might easily scoff at the naivety or crassness of some of the adverting lines and programme notes of half a century ago. That is not my intention... Rather, it is to make the serious point that the match programmes of the 1960s were products of their times. They reflected – and were influenced by – the cultural norms of the era".*

[*The Rugby League Journal,* Issue 47, Summer 2014, reproduced in *Still An Ordinary Spectator,* page 70]

It is now exactly one year since I resumed my sports-watching career – at the Ukraine versus Sweden Euro2020 match at Hampden Park in Glasgow – following the various lockdowns and cancellations necessitated by the Covid-19 pandemic. During this time, I have been to about a dozen different types of event. These have ranged from the relatively small scale (amateur rugby league and women's football) through to national tournaments (cycling and badminton) and international competition (World Championship Boxing as well as Euro2020).

One noticeable feature of the spectator "experience" over this period has struck me: the reduced availability of printed match programmes.

The paper-based souvenir of the event has not been totally absent: a traditional scorecard at the Yorkshire/Surrey 50-over One Day Cup cricket match; the 1-page typed team sheets at the Hunslet/Keighley and Edinburgh Eagles/York Acorn rugby league games and the 4-page summary sheet of teams, fixtures and Club President's welcome for the West of Scotland/Howe of Fife rugby union fixture. There was also a Euro2020 tournament brochure available at Hampden.

But that's all. There were no printed match or tournament programmes available at the much-hyped Northern Superchargers/Welsh Fire cricket encounters (men's and women's) in "The Hundred" at Headingley, the Glasgow City/Servette match in the UEFA Women's Champions League at the Broadwood Stadium in Cumbernauld, the Scottish Open Badminton tournament at the Emirates Arena in Glasgow, the world title boxing bout between Josh Taylor and Jack Catterall at the OVO Hydro or the Edinburgh Academical/Currie Chieftains rugby union match at Raeburn Place in the Scottish Premiership.

I can understand some of the reasons for this. In the period immediately following the relaxation of Covid-19 rules, there was an understandable reluctance amongst many to be exposed to the handling of materials with which they were not familiar. This was – and, to some extent, still is – the era of hand-sanitising and the reluctance to touch.

Another factor is that the technology has continued to move on apace: a growing proportion of us – though not everyone, it has to be said – satisfy our immediate information requirements by accessing the phone or the tablet or the watch. Interestingly, when I enquired about match programmes at both the Scottish Open Badminton tournament and the Edinburgh/Currie rugby match, I was referred to the screens on the walls inside the Emirates Arena and the clubhouse at Raeburn Place, respectively.

In addition, the absence of paper match programmes is consistent with the powerful *zeitgeist* of reducing the consumption of the earth's resources, albeit that wood-based products are not finite as the raw material can be harvested. And, not least, not having to produce programmes represents a saving in the costs and time required in the preparation for the match or tournament by the hosts.

Of these reasons, the post-Covid rationale is obviously a new factor that was not present before the pandemic. The others represent the continuation of underlying trends that had been evident for some time. Still, I think the reduced availability of the match programme is a shame – again for several reasons.

First of all – notwithstanding the technical alternatives – it is a readily accessible source of information. When attending a sports fixture, I like to know the names of the individual participants in front of me – even the one-page team-sheet will suffice in that respect – and if this is supplemented by some background material (biographical details, a league table, a fixture list...) so much the better.

The provision of information is principally an immediate requirement: something I need on the day. The second benefit of the match programme is of a medium or longer-term nature: it provides (along with the paper match ticket, another disappearing feature) a souvenir for future reference.

It is here that I think the promotors of sports events are missing a trick, particularly for those events at which they are seeking to attract "new" audiences. Two of those listed above stand out: the Hundred cricket fixtures at Headingley (which, as noted, included a women's match) and the UEFA Women's Champions League game in Cumbernauld. These events will have been witnessed by a significant number of spectators who were attending such fixtures for the first time – and who, from my casual observation of both these occasions, will have enjoyed the experience – but who had nothing to show for it afterwards (unless they were persuaded to invest in a highly priced replica shirt, of course).

This second reason merges over time into a third, which is more specialised and about which I have written before (*"Match Programmes: Windows Into the Past"* and *"The Parksider"* in the Summer 2014 and Summer 2019 editions, respectively, of the *Rugby League Journal*). It is the value of match programmes as social records in their own right: as reference points for future cultural historians.

In the former article, I noted the naïve request in the Bradford Northern Supporters Club Notes in a match programme for a fixture in 1966: "We are appealing once again for young ladies to put forward their names for Miss Bradford Northern. Last season the entries were very disappointing to say the least". A year earlier, the Warrington programme welcomed the two Hull wingers: "Barry and Clive Sullivan are coloured boys from Cardiff's Tiger Bay". [It should actually have been "Brian and Clive Sullivan…"]. There are other examples on which I could draw, but the key point – emphasised in the quote at the beginning of this essay – is that they reflected the cultural norms of the era and stand as part of the record of that time.

The final reason is a more personal one, indeed more selfish. It reflects the interest of the sports participant himself or herself by recognising that there is a pleasure to be gained by seeing one's own name in the printed list of the players on show.

In my case, the modesty of my playing career(s) has produced a relatively small sample – a schools' rugby fixture and a few club cricket games – but the relevant match programmes are dutifully (and proudly) stored with the remainder of my collection. Not that the details were always correct. One of the scorecards for a Saltaire CC match in the Bradford League in 1975 refers to one "Jack Rigg". No-one had ever called me by that name up to that point – but "Jack" it was for my team-mates for the rest of the season.

I readily acknowledge – not for the first time – that I am heading against the general direction of travel. It's partly a generational thing, I suspect: a realisation that that which was comfortable and familiar in the days (and years) past is now falling prey to the changes – technological, social, economic – that govern the world around us. Indeed, I have been here relatively recently on a related theme (*"Batsmen and Batters"*, October 2021).

In the case of match programmes, there is perhaps one consolation. The great writer Mark Twain is supposed to have said: "Buy land. They're not making it anymore". As far as I am aware, Twain was not a trained economist, but he was canny enough to recognise that, when the supply of a commodity is fixed or reduced, a rise in demand will lead to an increased price. Who knows what will happen to the demand for old match programmes – as investments or as historical records – as general wear and tear (and casual disposal) reduces the stock and the supply of replacements dries up? I would be wise to hang on to my collection, I think.

www.anordinaryspectator.com/news-blog June 2022

# Cricket

# 959 Runs

I have no doubt that the ECB will be basking in the reflected glory of England's successful Test Match series against New Zealand.

I might have missed it, but I haven't seen its acknowledgement of the YCCC coaching and mentoring system that guided the development from young ages of the 3 batsmen in England's top 5 (with another on standby) who produced a total of 959 runs for the national team over the course of the three matches.

Make no mistake – I have no truck at all with bullying or racism. And I have viewed the Club's abysmal handling of Azeem Rafiq's complaints with a combination of embarrassment and disdain.

I also acknowledge that the batting skills of Messrs Root, Bairstow and Lees (and Brook) will have been honed by several coaches and advisers – in Yorkshire and elsewhere – over the years. However, it is clear that, in the early stages of these batsmen's development, some of the coaching staff within the Club were getting on with their jobs and doing them properly.

I hope that they are now drawing some satisfaction from seeing their efforts being rewarded in their *protégés'* performances on the highest stage.

The White Rose Forum June 2022

# Cricket

# A More-than-useful Outfit

*"New Zealand were too streetwise and professional and, quite clearly, more skilful. Scotland batted first and made a modest total and New Zealand easily reached the target by mid-afternoon. It was a pleasant half day in the sunshine in the company of a couple of friends from Milngavie, but the result was never in doubt and, by tea time, we were in one of the pubs near Haymarket station watching the soccer play-off match from Wembley between Watford and Bolton Wanderers, from which the former emerged to take that season's final promotion place into the Premiership".*

[*An Ordinary Spectator,* page 272]

These are difficult times for Cricket Scotland, the sport's governing body north of the border. Last Sunday, its Board resigned *en masse* in advance of the publication the following day of an independent report, commissioned by Sports Scotland, which concluded that the body was "institutionally racist". This was an unfortunate prelude to my long-anticipated visit – with friends – to the attractive Grange cricket ground in Edinburgh yesterday for the second of two T20 games between Scotland and New Zealand. However, this is likely to be my only attendance at a cricket match this year and so I shall concentrate on the action on the field.

The two encounters are of some significance for both sides, given their participation in the T20 World Cup in Australia in October/November. New Zealand's preparation for the tournament has already included the three matches played in Ireland last week (along with three 50-over One Day Internationals) with more to come in the Netherlands and the West Indies next month before they host a T20 Tri-Series involving Pakistan and Bangladesh.

For Scotland, the build-up to the World Cup has been somewhat different. The matches against New Zealand constitute this year's only games in this format prior to meeting the West Indies in their opening Group B fixture of the tournament in Hobart. Instead, their efforts have been focused on the 7-team ICC Cricket World Cup League 2 – a long drawn-out competition played over 3½ years – from which the top three sides will go through to the (50 over) 2023 World Cup Qualifier tournament in Zimbabwe next summer. (Scotland are currently well-placed at second in the table behind Oman with a large number of games in hand).

I had seen Scotland play New Zealand at the Grange before. The extract from *An Ordinary Spectator* – given above – reported on the Group fixture in the 1999 World Cup. Given the sides' current rankings in T20 cricket – New Zealand 5th, Scotland 16th – there was obviously some risk of a similar mismatch. (New Zealand had won the first fixture on Wednesday by 68 runs).

And, indeed, this is what transpired. New Zealand registered 103 in their first 10 overs and 151 in their second to post a total of 254 for 5, their record score in a T20 fixture. The core of the innings was an impressive 83 by Mark Chapman, which was supplemented by a series of belligerent innings from the middle-order, notably Michael Bracewell, whose 61 from 25 deliveries came after he had been dropped – a straightforward chance – before he had opened his account.

The Scotland captain, Richie Berrington, marshalled his troops with some imagination, changing the bowling after virtually every over, and Mark Watt took three fine catches in the outfield. However, the dominant features of the New Zealand innings were the cleanliness of the batsmen's striking – there were a total of 18 sixes in the innings, most of which cleared the boundaries by some margin – allied to the skilful placement of the strokes along the ground.

Incidentally, the T20 format of the game does seem to have dispensed with the traditional concept of a batsman "playing himself in". Finn Allen, the New Zealand opener who had scored a century in the previous fixture, deposited his first ball into the trees behind us at long-on (though he was dismissed four deliveries later).

The Scotland supporters' spirits were raised when George Munsey struck three fine off-side boundaries in the first over of the reply. However, he was out shortly afterwards, one of two wickets in the over bowled by Jimmy Neesham, whom I had seen playing in my last cricket-spectating encounter – for the Welsh Fire in "The Hundred" at Headingley last summer (*"Cricket-Watching Resumed: Part 2"*, 28th July 2021). When a run out then reduced Scotland to 37 for 4 in the fifth over, the game was effectively done and dusted. There was some resistance from Chris Greaves, who made 37, but the Scotland innings drifted to its conclusion at 152 for 9. A win for New Zealand by 102 runs.

I trust that Cricket Scotland will have judged that the occasion had been a success. An entertaining match had been watched by a capacity crowd – a diverse capacity crowd, note – that had fully respected the efforts of both sides. I sensed that, whilst most might have been disappointed at the margin of Scotland's defeat, they would also have recognised that their opponents were a more-than-useful outfit (which will be strengthened even further for the World Cup by the likes of Kane Williamson, Martin Guptill and Trent Boult).

Afterwards, we walked along the path next to the Water of Leith and then up into the city centre. Our conversation drifted – the attractiveness of the housing in this formerly industrial part of town, the health of another of our friends, the short-listed candidates for the Conservative Party leadership… Normal life, really – in which an afternoon in the warm sunshine watching the cricket had been a very pleasant part.

www.anordinaryspectator.com/news-blog July 2022

# Rugby League

# Even Longer Times Between Visits – Part 1

*"On my first (and only) visit to what was then called Wheldon Road, I was both mystified and disconcerted by what seemed to be a huge expanse of soap bubbles stretching out by the side of one of the neighbouring roads, the locals either ignoring it or walking through and around it. Looking back, I assume that it was something to do with the discharges from one of the local chemical or other industrial sites: at the time, it was something from another – and harsher – world than the boy from suburban north Leeds was used to".*

[*An Ordinary Spectator*, page 58]

In *"A Long Time Between Visits"* (15ᵗʰ July 2018), I reported on going to watch a Keighley Cougars home rugby league match with the Oldham Roughyeds. I noted that it was my first visit to that particular ground – named the Cougar Stadium since 1991, but known before that as Lawkholme Lane – since September 1965, a gap of 52 years and 10 months. 52 years and 298 days to be precise.

Last Friday evening, I beat that record, when I attended the Castleford Tigers versus Catalan Dragons Super League encounter at what is now called The Mend-a-Hose Jungle in Castleford. On the occasion of my only previous visit – in April 1965 for a Top 16 Championship play-off match between Castleford and Hunslet – the ground had again been known simply by its location: Wheldon Road. That was 57 years and 110 days ago. (For clarity, this is not just the period that has elapsed since my first visit to the ground; it is also the length of time since my last visit).

My excursions in the mid-1960s to watch Hunslet's away fixtures took place within a relatively narrow window of a couple of years. In addition to the matches in Keighley and Castleford, there were trips to Belle Vue, Fartown and Craven Park – the home grounds of Wakefield Trinity, Huddersfield and Hull Kingston Rovers, respectively. In addition, there were the local fixtures at Bramley and Leeds and, not least, a Challenge Cup tie in February 1964 at the Mount Pleasant ground of Batley (of which more tomorrow).

This was a period in which my Uncle Bob – a keen motorist and a fearless navigator in foreign parts – shared my father's support for the Hunslet team with some enthusiasm and adopted the role of more-than-willing chauffeur. (My father and I also saw a fixture at the Blackpool Borough ground in August 1967, when we happened – by coincidence, I'm sure – to be on the west coast for a family holiday). It was a relatively short-lived phase, however, though not from any diminution of interest on my uncle's part. By the autumn of 1966, I had entered grammar school and selection for the Under 13s XV – rugby union, of course – limited my availability for sports spectating on Saturday afternoons.

As noted above, my principal recollection of the first trip to Castleford was the disconcerting sight of the "huge expanse of soap bubbles" that was evident in some of the streets in the town itself, about which the local inhabitants appeared to be totally indifferent. I was subsequently to learn that this was not an uncommon sight in the Castleford of that time and resulted from the volume of detergents that the local industrial processes had deposited into the town's River Aire.

I do not recollect much about the 1965 match itself other than that the visitors gave a below-par performance and that Castleford won quite easily – by 18-7, as the records show. (It would have been understandable, perhaps, if the Hunslet team had had half an eye on their forthcoming Wembley appearance – two weeks later – in the Challenge Cup final against Wigan). However, I do recall that we were seated in the upper tier of the Main Stand and that my views of the pitch were hindered by the series of horizontal metal bars that were placed on the tier's balcony at the foot of each of the rows of steps that led further back into the stand.

On Friday, my walk from the railway station to the ground took me through Henry Moore Square – named after the town's most famous son. The square is dominated by the solid red-brick building of the former Castleford and Allerton Mutual Industrial Society – "Established 1871" – from which a series of large colourful flags proudly denoted both the modern town and its origins as a Roman army settlement, Lagentium. On the other side of the road are a couple of desperate box buildings from the 1960s or 1970s: sad intrusions in a public space named in honour of a creative genius.

It was a warm evening, following several days on which the temperature had hovered around the 30 degree mark, but this didn't seem to dissuade the customers ordering their burgers and chips from one of the temporary retail outlets lined up in the busy area behind the Main Stand. At the end of the row, in the beer tent, an informal panel discussion featured three Castleford players from the 1980s and 1990s – Lee Crooks, Bob Beardmore and Graham Steadman – who, between them, represented the club on over 750 occasions. I listened for a while before returning to the burger van and ordering a tea.

"You want a what?" responded the girl behind the counter with an undisguised – and apparently genuine – incredulity. "In this weather?"

I replied that drinking tea could help you to cool down. (I could have mentioned the afternoon rituals of the British in India, but didn't). The girl was not persuaded.

The Castleford-Catalan match had promised to be a close affair, as the previous occasion on which the sides had met at the Jungle, earlier in the season, had only been decided in Castleford's favour by a single-point drop-goal in sudden-death extra time. At the start of the evening, I judged that, at fourth place in the league table, Catalan were fairly safe in securing a top 6 play-off place in the quest for the Super League title. However, Castleford, although only one place behind the visitors, were six points adrift of them and in a scrap with four other sides for the two remaining play-off berths.

It was predictably hard-fought game. Both sides scored two tries, but the Castleford goal-kicker, Gareth O'Brien, added three penalties to his two conversions, whereas the Catalan touchdowns went unconverted. I thought that the home side's victory owed much to the controlled aggression of their defensive effort: there were three occasions in the first half when the impact of the tackle legitimately dislodged the ball from the Catalan attacker's grasp close to the Castleford try-line and, again, after the interval, their defensive systems remained resilient in the face of sustained pressure from the visitors. 18-8 was the final outcome.[35]

I could be confident that my seat for the match on Friday was on the same side of the ground as it had been in 1965 as the Main Stand is the only one with seating. I had an old-fashioned solid wooden tip-up seat in the lower tier – about six rows from the front near the half-way line behind the visitors' dug-out – and it gave an excellent view of proceedings, particularly after the setting sun had fallen below the junction of the roofs of the stands in the far corner. (I was aware that this lower tier had not been a seating area in 1965: Trevor Delaney's *The Grounds of Rugby League,* published in 1991, notes that it had been a standing room paddock with the seats not being installed until 1970).

After the game, I went up into the upper tier, where the seating is now of the modern plastic tip-up variety. The horizontal metal bars – their supports embedded in a wooden base – are still there. For confirmation, I asked an elderly steward – who had earlier kindly escorted me all the way to my seat – how long he thought the bars might have been in place: "decades" was his reply. I cast my eye along the rows of seats three or four places back and, with a frisson of recognition, pictured my 10 year-old self looking out on to the pitch and watching Alan Hardisty and Geoff Gunney in action.

Trevor Delaney refers to the "comprehensive improvements" that were made at Wheldon Road in the period after my first visit. But his authoritative work was published over 30 years ago, of course, and time has moved on. An article in the August 2022 edition of the excellent *Roar* – the Castleford Tigers' official monthly magazine – quotes Mark Grattan, the club's Managing Director: "It has long been recognised that Wheldon Road needs a serious upgrade".

Plans are in place. Currently, there is a formal consultation process on the proposals for a comprehensive overhaul of the stadium, the club's planning application for which (to Wakefield Council) is – crucially – in partnership with a firm of real estate developers which also seeks permission for a separate "new employment development" at the Castleford junction of the M62.

I doubt that the wooden tip-ups seats or the metal bars will survive the overhaul. But, having enjoyed my visit to Wheldon Road on Friday, I hope that, in seeking to meet Mr Grattan's wish "to significantly improve the experience for supporters", the re-designed ground also maintains the intimate atmosphere of the current version.

I walked back through Henry Moore Square to the railway station in the knowledge that the Wheldon Road ground/The Mend-a-Hose Jungle of Castleford Tigers RLFC had attained a new (strictly personal) record: 57 years and 110 days.

And then, on Sunday, I went to Batley.

www.anordinaryspectator.com/news-blog August 2022

# Rugby League

# Even Longer Times Between Visits – Part 2

In the previous blog (*"Even Longer Times Between Visits – Part 1"*, 17th August 2022), I reported on my attendance at last Friday's Super League encounter between the Castleford Tigers and Catalan Dragons at The Mend-a-Hose Jungle. The 57 years and 110 days since my previous visit to the ground – when it was simply called Wheldon Road – for the Castleford versus Hunslet fixture in April 1965 represented a personal record for the longest period between visits to the same sports venue.

On Sunday afternoon, I beat the record again.

My visit to what is still generally called Mount Pleasant (although the sponsors would certainly prefer the Fox's Biscuit Stadium) – for the Championship match between the Batley Bulldogs and Barrow Raiders – took place 58 years and 167 days after I had seen Hunslet defeat Batley on that ground in a second-round Challenge Cup tie in February 1964.

Batley's association with Mount Pleasant makes Castleford's presence at Wheldon Road (where they have played since 1927) seem like a recently arranged tenancy. It dates from 1880, some 15 years before the "Great Split" within English rugby and the formation of what was initially called the Northern Rugby Football Union, of which the club – then affectionately known as the "Gallant Youths" rather than the Bulldogs – was a founder member. It was those early years of the Northern Union that provided Batley with its richest haul of silverware; the club won the first Challenge Cup final in 1897 and landed the trophy twice more in the next four years.

I arrived at the Batley bus station (from Leeds via a circuitous route through Morley) with plenty of time before the kick-off. I was fairly sure of the route to the ground, but I decided to check with a middle-aged man wearing a Batley replica rugby shirt, who was standing near the station exit. "Through the Market Place, left at Fox's Biscuits and then right, up that bloody great hill". His directions were spot on.

The Market Place is an impressive public space. Its principal buildings – notably Batley Town Hall and the former Carnegie Library (now the Batley Library and Art Gallery) – date from Edwardian times. These are complemented by the Methodist Church at the bottom of the square, next to which is the neat three-storeyed Jo Cox House, part of the Yorkshire Children's Centre and named in honour of the town's former MP, who was murdered in 2016. The external façade of an Italian restaurant is presented in sympathy with the surrounding architecture.

I still have the match programmes for the 1964 fixture – purchased for the princely sum of three old pence – the contents of which neatly captured the vastly different hold on the public's attention that the early rounds of the Challenge Cup had in that era, compared with today. The introductory paragraph opened with: "The day which has been eagerly anticipated by thousands of sports fans for some time has dawned at last". I remember that the attendance was indeed sizeable – 11,500, a figure that has not subsequently been surpassed for a Batley home fixture.

As with my visit to Castleford a year later (reported yesterday), I have a clear memory (I think) of where I was in the ground. My recollection is that, in order to see the action – as a 9-year old boy of below average height – I stood near the touchline behind a fence or railing, with my father and uncle some distance behind me up the crowded banking. I also recall that the playing surface was raised slightly, compared with where I was standing, so that, when the action was in front of me, I was looking up at the players. (For completeness, Hunslet won the match 14-6).

In the last two decades, the Batley Bulldogs have been a solid presence in the Championship – the professional game's second tier – and this consistency has been maintained this season, as they began Sunday's match in fourth place in the league table. With Barrow occupying sixth position, the game – as with the Super League encounter two days earlier – was of some significance for the end-of-season play-offs (which apply to the top 5 in the Championship[36]).

By the close of play, Batley were still fourth in the league table, but Barrow had moved up into fifth – only one point behind – thanks to a convincing 30-12 win. The visitors made an impressive start and were 14-0 up after 20 minutes, thanks to two tries by full-back Luke Cresswell. At half-time, the visitors' lead was 18-6 and the key question was whether, with the ground's noticeable slope now in their favour, Batley could turn round the deficit in the hot, draining conditions. The answer was given emphatically in the first ten minutes of the second half, when two sweeping tries ensured that the lead of the impressive Barrow side became unassailable.

It was a good game, keenly contested – but also fairly, as far as I could see – and well refereed by Robert Hicks. Even though the game was beyond them, the Batley players kept going to the end, defending their line resolutely in the closing minutes. It was also a tribute to the fitness of both sets of players that there was no real diminution of tempo on an afternoon when the reading on the thermometer breached 30 degrees. [37]

After the match, I engaged an elderly man in conversation at the corner of the ground. I asked him if he had been coming to watch Batley for a long time and he replied that he had, as he was now aged 78. His recollection was that there had been banking along one touchline before the construction of what is now called the Glen Tomlinson Stand (in which I had spent most of the afternoon before watching the closing stages from the terraces behind the posts near the entrance to the ground). His memory might be faulty – as might mine – but I was content that his testimony meant that I could mentally re-visit my vantage point of 58-plus years ago.

I walked back down the hill to the bus station. There, also waiting for the Leeds bus, was the Batley supporter who had given me the instructions for reaching the ground. He said that he had been disappointed with his team's performance, but – as had the elderly man at the ground – he paid due tribute to the Barrow side's all-round excellence.

We enjoyed a pleasant conversation on the return journey. I suggested that Batley seemed to be a well-run club and he agreed. I learned that the club owned the ground and did not have any debt. There was also a longstanding tradition of the board not to dismiss the coach when results did not go well: a contract might not be renewed, but there was no dismissal. We shook hands when he departed from the bus in Hunslet. Not for the first time, I reflected on the innate capacity of the casual sports watcher – the Ordinary Spectator, whether at the cricket at Headingley, soccer at Tynecastle, rugby league in Batley, high school American Football in San Antonio *et al* – to compare notes in a (temporary) connection with a like-minded enthusiast.

And so, 58-plus years. I am bound to ask myself: does re-visiting a venue after all this time actually mean anything? Or does it simply represent the passage of a very long period in which my attention has been elsewhere? Or again, to present these questions in a slightly different way, what would I say to the friend I had at age 9 if we were next to meet aged 67?

My sense – for what it's worth – is that there is something there. That there is a sense of closing a circle – of tidying up a loose end that my father and uncle had unwittingly, but lovingly, created all those years ago.

If that's the case, another question arises. Can the record for the longest unbroken gap between my visits to a sports ground – now held by Mount Pleasant/ the Fox's Biscuits Stadium in Batley – be beaten?

The answer is yes. On the rugby league circuit, Wakefield Trinity offers a possibility. Assuming that the club does not move from what is now called the Belle Vue Stadium (where, as with Batley, it has been since before the establishment of the Northern Union) – and given that my previous visit to the venue was in October 1966 – I would need to attend a match there some time after 24$^{th}$ March 2025 (though not before).

Unlikely, but not impossible.

Other sports venues might also provide possibilities. The next cab in the rank is the Welford Road Stadium of the Leicester Tigers rugby union club (which was the Leicester Football Club when it hosted the England/France Schools rugby international that I went to see on a school trip in April 1967). This would require a trip to Leicester sometime after 19$^{th}$ September 2025.

As far as football or cricket are concerned, the contenders are some considerable time after that – Bramall Lane (courtesy of my detour to watch Sheffield United play West Ham United in March 1975 when visiting friends at the university) and Old Trafford (Lancashire versus Yorkshire in August 1976) – for which the relevant future dates would be 6$^{th}$ September 2033 and 14$^{th}$ February 2035, respectively. (I realise that this is all somewhat anorakian and, moreover, that I am encroaching into territory usually occupied by the astronomer. For example, the path of Halley's Comet will next take it closest to Earth on 29$^{th}$ July 2062).

The Bramall Lane and Old Trafford outcomes assume, of course, that I hadn't visited either the Belle Vue Stadium in Wakefield nor the Welford Road Stadium in Leicester in the meantime (after their relevant dates) and set the bar even higher. This would be taking me into my 10$^{th}$ decade.

Even more unlikely, therefore, even allowing for the quirky madness of the Ordinary Spectator. Though still more likely than seeing Halley's Comet pass by.

www.anordinaryspectator.com/news-blog August 2022

# Football

# Welcome to Glasgow[38]

In 1992, I moved from London to take up a new job in Glasgow. Although I had a long-deceased grandmother who had been born in the city, any family connections had been lost in that part of the world. For me, it was a strange and unfamiliar place.

My new office colleagues had a range of soccer interests, which included, in one case, going down to Manchester every fortnight to watch United. When they learned that I hailed from Leeds, they revealed an impressive knowledge of the Elland Road sides of old. This was not surprising, given the number of Scots who had featured prominently in the Leeds teams of our formative soccer-watching years – Bremner, Lorimer, the Gray brothers, Harvey, McQueen, Jordan *et al*.

And then, in October, Glasgow Rangers met Leeds United in a two-legged tie in the European Cup.

In those days, it was only a country's champion side that competed for European club football's top prize. Rangers had lifted the Scottish title the previous year for the fourth consecutive time (in the unbroken run that would eventually end at nine). Leeds had taken the last of the (pre-Premier League) English First Division honours, heading off my colleague's Old Trafford favourites by four points in the final league table of 1991-92.

Looking back from today's perspective of the hugely bloated Champions League, it seems mildly incredible that one of these sides – both of which had lifted European silverware in their time – should face elimination in the season's autumn. However, by this second round stage, there were only 16 teams left in the competition. (If I have understood the chronology correctly, it was at this season's group stage that the rebranding to the UEFA Champions League took over).

The stage was set for the "Battle of Britain". (Or perhaps *another* "BOB", given that I recalled that the nomenclature had also been used for the epic Glasgow Celtic-Leeds United European Cup semi-final of 1970). And – after all this time,

I'm still not at all sure how – someone in the office acquired the tickets for a group us all to go to the first leg, which was to be played at Ibrox Stadium.

Of course, in addition to having impressive European pedigrees, the two clubs had other – less savoury – reputational baggage, not least the presence of their hardcore hooligan elements. For this reason – plus the recognition that there would be an overwhelming demand for tickets for both games – it was decided that visiting supporters would not be allowed to attend either match.

We sat in the Govan Stand with its excellent view across the pitch. In the minutes leading up the kick-off, with the ground full – and no away support to disturb the proceedings – the intensity of the crowd's expectations reached a fever pitch. This was no doubt partly due to the importance of the fixture. More pertinently, however, the fact was that over 43,000 Rangers supporters were gathered in the one place. The roar was absolutely deafening – one of the loudest I have ever heard at a sports stadium. *The Sash* and *Billy Boys* – the latter with reference to being "up to our knees in Fenian blood" – rang out around the ground.

I watched – and heard – all this with a bewildered astonishment. And I realised that my understanding of the city of Glasgow – or, at least, of one half of it – was increasing apace.

More drama followed immediately. Within a minute of the kick off, on their first attack, the visitors won a corner on their right. The ball came into the Rangers penalty area and was headed out to the Leeds captain, Gary McAllister, who was lurking at the angle of the penalty area, also on the right-hand side. In a textbook demonstration of the skill – angling his body, taking his weight on his non-striking leg and keeping his head over the ball – McAllister volleyed the ball into the top far corner of the Rangers net.

In its own right, it was undoubtedly one of the best goals I had ever seen. However, in the context of the occasion, it was – literally – breath-taking. (In *An Ordinary Spectator*, I listed the McAllister goal amongst my "First XI of Sporting Nano-dramas" that I had witnessed during half a century of sports spectating).

The Leeds players mobbed McAllister to the sound of the proverbial pin dropping somewhere in the ground. Or, at least, it would have been, had not the goal elicited a joyful response from a small knot of Leeds United supporters – probably no more than a dozen altogether – further down the stand on my right-hand side.

This only added to the home supporters' grief. Not only had their side fallen behind before the opening skirmishes had been properly engaged – and conceded a precious away goal into the bargain – but the sanctity of the ground had been invaded by those who were not welcome. There was a rising chorus of vitriolic hostility towards the Leeds supporters, who, after obviously concealing their identity in order to gain entrance to the ground, were now completely open in their allegiance. I thought it wise to keep my counsel: not a hard decision, if I'm honest.

To their credit, Rangers kept their composure and recovered well. They had a fair sprinkling of big match players – Richard Gough, Ally McCoist, Mark Hateley – who, after the early setback, did not panic, but calmly and professionally set about trying to turn things around. They were aided by Ian Durrant – the best player on the pitch – who shaded his midfield duel with the aggressive David Batty and, most noticeably, consistently used the possession that came his way intelligently and efficiently. The action around him was frenetic, but he did not waste a pass.

Roared on by the home support, Rangers had taken the lead by half-time, courtesy of a John Lukic own-goal and a timely demonstration of McCoist's close-range predatory instincts. As there were no further goals in the second half – a fiercely contested affair conducted against an unrelenting cacophony of sound, the noise seemingly amplified by the acoustics of the stadium – the tie was left tantalisingly poised – at 2-1 to Rangers – in advance of the Elland Road re-match two weeks later.

In the event, the Glasgow side progressed into the next stage of the competition with something to spare. Hateley scored an early goal from long range in the second leg and, on the hour mark, laid on another for McCoist, leaving Leeds well beaten. The Elland Road faithful had to settle for a late consolation goal by Eric Cantona (who, three weeks later, became a Manchester United player).

Following the completion of the tie, back in the office, I took it like a man. My half-hearted protestations – "I'm more a rugby follower, really" – cut no ice at all with the McCoist and Durrant supporters. Meanwhile, the Celtic contingent amongst my colleagues kept their counsel whilst, I sensed, at the same time being seriously aggrieved that Leeds had not done them the obvious favour.

The 1992 "Battle of Britain" really did feature some of the best British players of the era. In addition to the names already checked, the contest involved Trevor Steven and Gordon Strachan, Andy Goram and Gary Speed, Stuart McCall and David Rocastle… Only Cantona and the Rangers substitute, Pieter Huistra, were foreign internationals. In this respect – as with the concurrent farewells to both the old-style European Cup and the English First Division – the match does now seem to represent the end of an era.

I am bound to fall back on a reference I have used before (most recently in "*The Coronavirus provides a reminder*", 2nd May 2020) from H.G. Bissinger's *Friday Night Lights*. The author reflects on an incongruous visit made to a high school (American) football game in Marshall, Texas, by a delegation of Russians who had been visiting a nearby US Air Force base: "[T]hey don't understand a lick of football, but… their understanding of America by the end of the game will be absolute whether they realise it or not".

By the time I got home that evening, my understanding of Glasgow – and Scotland – had certainly been enhanced.

October 21st 1992. Thirty years ago today.

www.anordinaryspectator.com/news-blog October 2022

# Rugby League

# "Nos illuc in fine"

If and when I am eventually raised to the House of Lords, I shall arrange for the motto of my coat of arms to read *"Nos illuc in fine"*. We get there in the end.

I suspect that there are many participants in the current Rugby League World Cup – players, coaches, administrators, spectators – who would recognise the sentiment. The tournament was originally scheduled for the Autumn of 2021, but was postponed midst much controversy and (between some) ill-feeling – see *"Same Time Next Year (Perhaps)"*, 19th November 2021. It has now completed the semi-final stage with Australia and Samoa scheduled to meet next Saturday at Old Trafford to decide the winners. (I shall focus here on the men's tournament; there have been separate women's and wheelchair events).

I wonder if, in retrospect, the tournament organisers might wonder if having 16 sides in the competition might have been too many. At the elite level, the sport's talent is spread fairly thinly, notwithstanding the scope for "heritage" players in Australia and England opting to represent the countries of a parent or grandparent.

In the group stage of the tournament, there were a number of very one-sided matches. England racked up 94 points against Greece, whilst Tonga scored 92 against the Cook Islands and Australia 84 against Scotland. The sides at the bottom of the 4 groups played (and lost) a total of 12 games in the process of which they registered a total of 76 points, but conceded no fewer than 618: an average score-line of 6-51.

(I am prepared to acknowledge that there is a counter-argument suggesting that the countries in which the fledgling sport of rugby league has scope to grow and prosper might need to go through these painful rites of passage. In the group stage of the 1995 Rugby Union World Cup, played in South Africa, New Zealand defeated Japan by 145 points to 17. Whilst it is claimed by some that this result held back the development of the sport in Japan by many years, it was nonetheless the case that, by the time of the 2019 tournament (which Japan hosted), the home side had reached the standard at which it could defeat both Ireland and Scotland in the group stage and progress to the quarter-final).

As far as the current Rugby League World Cup is concerned, most pundits would have predicted Australia and New Zealand to take their places in the semi-final and this was indeed how it transpired. On Friday evening, I went to Elland Road in Leeds to watch these teams face off.

In advance of the match, I did wonder if Australia's relatively trouble-free passage to this stage might act against them. In their four games (including the quarter-final against the Lebanon), they had registered 240 points – including 43 tries – and conceded only 18. By contrast, New Zealand had been battle-hardened in their compelling quarter-final match with Fiji, in which they only took the lead for the first time within the last 10 minutes.

I mentioned this when I fell into conversation with a middle-aged man wearing an Australian rugby shirt as we walked towards the ground before the match. "Do you fancy your chances?" I asked him. "I think Australia will win", he replied in a broad Yorkshire accent. "New Zealand were a bit clunky in their last match".

In the event, Australia were fully engaged from the opening kick-off and New Zealand were far from clunky. The tone was set in the latter's *haka*, the amplified sound of which swept through the stands. Thereafter, from beginning to end, it was an absolutely pulsating encounter of unremitting action, high skill and physical confrontation. New Zealand took the lead after 10 minutes with Dylan Brown's smartly judged cross-kick to the try-line, which Joseph Manu leapt to catch and pass back for Jahrome Hughes to gather and score.

We waited for the inevitable Kangaroo response. It came a few minutes later and was a try of absolute brilliance. The half-back-cum-hooker Ben Hunt sent a high 50 yard punt spiralling deep into New Zealand territory which Josh Addo-Carr, having sprinted down the left wing, caught on the full at full speed without breaking stride on his way to the try line. The kick was inch-perfect and Addo-Carr timed his arrival to meet it with absolute precision. As the winger walked back to take his place for the New Zealand re-start, I wondered how many long hours on the training field had been invested – by both kicker and recipient – in order to generate such a breath-taking outcome.

Both sides added tries before half-time, when New Zealand led 14-10. In the second half, the battle continued unabated with, on several occasions, the spectators around me gasping (or perhaps wincing) in astonishment – and admiration – at some of the physical challenges they were witnessing.

It was perhaps somewhat ironic, therefore, that Australia's winning try was a relatively soft affair. Having been awarded what I thought was a contentious penalty 10 yards from the New Zealand line, the Australian captain, James

Tedesco, instructed the playmaker Nathan Cleary to take a tap kick rather than an attempt at goal. Cleary duly did so and passed the ball to Cameron Murray, who charged through a couple of would-be tacklers to score under the posts. At the time, it seemed to have been an unexpected breach of the New Zealand defensive line; looking at the television replay later, it was clear that Tedesco, with a clinical assessment of the state of play, had sensed a vulnerability in his tiring opponents which his side could ruthlessly exploit. Cleary's conversion made it 16-14 and, even though there were still over 25 minutes left to play, that turned out to be the final score.

In contrast with the *ersatz* Australian I had met earlier, the majority of the local supporters seemed to favour the New Zealanders. A chant of "Kiwi, Kiwi" rang round the ground in the closing minutes as the "neutral" locals realised that the players' diminishing reserves of energy were approaching complete exhaustion. Australia held on, however, despite a couple of late scares, their status as tournament favourites vindicated.

It being 11th November, the traditional colours of the two sides' shirts – green and gold, and black and white – were supplemented with the design of a poppy, in Australia's case on one of the sleeves and for New Zealand on the chest. As it happened, earlier in the day, along with a couple of hundred other people – including the whole of the Kangaroos' squad of players and staff – I had attended the short Remembrance Day service in Victoria Square, where the Leeds War Memorial is situated.

James Tedesco's day had begun with him laying a wreath at the ceremony. By the end of the evening, he had led his side into the Rugby League World Cup final.[39]

www.anordinaryspectator.com/news-blog November 2022

# Football

## Splendid Dribbling Skills

*"The modest Scotland total was knocked off by Yorkshire without the loss of a wicket, thanks to the captain Martyn Moxon and a promising young player called Michael Vaughan".*

[*An Ordinary Spectator*, page 272].

Initially, all 211 member football associations were eligible to attempt qualification for the 22$^{nd}$ edition of the FIFA World Cup, although half a dozen subsequently fell by the wayside for non-football reasons, including North Korea (due to safety concerns about Covid-19) and Russia (disqualified following the invasion of Ukraine). 32 teams duly qualified for the multi-billion dollar tournament in Qatar, the group stage of which is currently approaching its conclusion. In 18 days time, the final will be contested in the 80,000 capacity Lusail Iconic Stadium.

It is all something of a far cry from the first official international football (soccer) international, which was played between Scotland and England at the West of Scotland Cricket Club ground in Partick, Glasgow, on 30$^{th}$ November 1872: 150 years ago today. The match – watched by 4,000 spectators, some (though not all) of whom paid one shilling each – finished in a 0-0 draw.

An important word here is "official". Football historians will point to five other England-Scotland matches that had taken place from 1870, but these had all been in London with, crucially, the Scotland teams entirely comprised of players based in England. For the November 1872 encounter, the England team crossed the border to take on a side whose players were all based in Scotland. (It would appear that the organisers set out to present this match as the first official international at a very early stage).

Indeed, the Scotland team was not only drawn from domestically-based players. It was drawn from the members of a single club – Queen's Park, the pioneers of the development of the skills and tactics of the "association" version of football in the British Isles (and, therefore, the world). By contrast, the England team had players from 9 different clubs, of which Notts County, Sheffield Wednesday and Crystal Palace are instantly recognisable to the modern supporter. Other representatives came from both Oxford and Cambridge Universities, Harrow Chequers and the 1ˢᵗ Surrey Rifles.

For the contemporary newspaper accounts of the match, I consulted the *Leeds Mercury* and the *Yorkshire Post and Leeds Intelligentsia* for 2ⁿᵈ December 1872, both of which allocated one paragraph to the game, the latter in its "Sporting News" section after its reports on steeple-chasing, coursing and hunting.

The reports suggest that there were several things with which the football supporter of a century and a half later can readily identify. Most obviously, the contest was 11-a-side (in contrast with the first rugby international, played in March 1871 at Raeburn Place in Edinburgh, in which Scotland and England had each fielded 20 players – see *"Plan B"*, 7ᵗʰ March 2022). In addition, both sides were commended for their splendid dribbling skills, although passing moves seem to have been in short supply. Moreover, Scotland wore dark blue shirts with an embroidered thistle and England white shirts, although – less frequently observed these days – the English also wore caps and the Scots red cowls. The closest that either side came to scoring a goal was when the ball narrowly – and, to some, disputedly – cleared the tape that was used to represent the England crossbar. (Where was VAR when it was needed?)

Prior to today, my only previous visit to the West of Scotland CC ground had been in May 1995, when I watched Scotland play Yorkshire in a group match in the Benson and Hedges Trophy. Jim Love, with whom I had played in the Yorkshire Cricket Federation (i.e. Under 19) side of 1974, was the Scotland captain. He scored a half-century but, as noted above, it was a one-sided affair, the visitors winning by 10 wickets. My reference to the venue in *An Ordinary Spectator* opined "[T]hat more is not made of the fact that this was the location for the first-ever soccer international… is something of a minor mystery to me".

The significance of the ground (for football) is now indicated by two plaques that have been placed on the clubhouse wall in the period since my initial visit. The upper one reads:

"The World's first international football match
was played between Scotland and England
at the West of Scotland Cricket Ground,
Hamilton Crescent, Glasgow, on St Andrew's
Day, the 30ᵗʰ November, 1872.

Presented by Mr John C McGinn,
President of the Scottish Football Association,
30ᵗʰ November 2002."

The plaque is neatly presented, albeit with its wooden frame showing some signs of wear after two decades of west of Scotland weather. It is also unobtrusive. Indeed – to the casual observer – it is dominated by the second plaque placed just below it (in 2018), which commemorates the first appearance of Rangers Football Club in a Scottish Cup Final: a match (and its replay) against Vale of Leven on the same ground in 1877.

The inscription on the latter states triumphantly that: "[T]hese games were to change the course of Rangers history". As a symbolic representation of the hegemonic role that the Old Firm of Rangers and Celtic play in Scottish football, the dual-plaque display says a great deal, I think.

The Scottish Football Association has maintained a low-key approach to this latest anniversary, apart from announcing a commemorative Scotland-England fixture at Hampden Park in September next year. (The SFA website gives far more prominence to the 50th anniversary of the inaugural women's international in 1972). This appears to follow the lead of Scottish Rugby. I noted that in *Plan B* that there was nothing at the Edinburgh Academical sports ground at Raeburn Place to mark the 150th anniversary of rugby union's first international, whilst the stone monument commemorating the centenary in 1971 is currently at the edge of a large pile of rubble on the far side of the field.

Accordingly, when I took the train into Partick this morning to visit the cricket ground, I expected that I might be largely alone, perhaps to walk around the boundary edge and take a couple of photographs before wandering back to Dumbarton Road in search of a coffee shop. How wrong I was. It was not long before I learned that The Hampden Collection – a group of volunteers celebrating the pioneering role Scotland played at the dawn of association football – had spent some considerable time with the West of Scotland CC and others preparing for the 150th anniversary.

By one o'clock, a sizeable number had gathered on the terracing of the clubhouse – boosted by a substantial media presence – as two teams of primary school footballers attired in the respective kits of 1872 (though without the caps and cowls) replayed the inaugural fixture. There was only limited space for 11-a-side on the truncated pitch, but there was no little skill shown – the England goalkeeper made a splendid first-half save – as well as sound positional awareness. There was also some bravery; the teams were both comprised of boys and girls and one of the latter, having inadvertently taken the ball full in the face, continued on as if nothing had happened (though I did notice that the referee kept an eye on her to check she was ok).

The day's event closed with a short ceremony at 2.15pm when there was a "kick-off" involving two of the great grandsons of Joseph Taylor, one of that first Scotland team.

During the course of the day, I spoke at length on separate occasions to three of the volunteers, beginning with Will Moffat of the Hampden Bowling Club, with whom I had an enjoyable chat on entering the ground. Each in turn demonstrated their informed enthusiasm for the group's work and their detailed knowledge of the first international. Thus, I was able to supplement that which I had previously acquired from Wikipedia with the information that the pitch had run north-south (the Scots playing downhill in the first half towards the imposing façade of Partick Burgh Hall, which had been completed earlier that year) and that the kick-off had been delayed from its 2.00pm scheduled start due to the sheer numbers of spectators.

My interests are not only in watching sport in the present day and in reflecting on the sport that I have watched in the course of my lifetime. I am also drawn to the circumstances surrounding those defining occasions – and the associated venues – in the history of sport that have been the key milestones on the long journey of sports spectating (and playing) that has brought us into modern times. In terms of international football, this is a journey that has – to date – run from the West of Scotland CC in Scotland 1872 to the Lusail Iconic Stadium in Qatar in 2022.

And the result of the primary school pupils' soccer match? Not quite the exact replication of the goalless draw of 150 years ago. A late goal gave victory to England: 1-0.

[For completeness, I did later find my coffee shop on the Dumbarton Road. The excellent Caffé Monza on my way back to Partick Station].

www.anordinaryspectator.com/news-blog November 2022

Valediction

# The Flame

The slim candle – about two inches in length – stands on a tiny brass plinth in the corner of a small shallow box. Behind the box, which is placed on the top shelf of a bookcase, is the letter rack that I purchased from the *beriozka* in Moscow in 1980, a souvenir of the Olympic Games that had taken place a few weeks before my visit. The rack contains a miscellany of bookmarks and used theatre tickets and (very) old golf scorecards and – with pride of place, I think – the card and envelope ("*Dear Stanta*" (sic)) that my (then) infant daughter wrote to Father Christmas all those years ago.

After I bring a match to the candle and turn off the room's electric light, the flame provides the only illumination. I take my seat, so that my eyes – spectacles removed and placed within reach next to me – are level with the flame at a distance of about two feet. The back of the bookcase is tightly adjacent to one of the softly painted walls of the room.

At first it seems as if the flame won't take. There is a hesitation at the end of the wick, as if the fragility of the beginning of life will bring about its immediate termination. But then the flame grows stronger and I know that it will run for its full duration. 20 minutes are promised in which "to pause and reflect", although, as it later transpires, the actual lifespan is shorter by a couple of minutes.

The flame dances slightly. There is no obvious draught in the room and the expulsion of $CO_2$ from my light breathing does not extend across the full range between us but, nonetheless, there is a delicate movement in the flame as if, once lit, it can never stand perfectly still, but must always be in motion.

The flame grows taller and stronger. The face of the letter rack becomes brightly illuminated in stark contrast to the surrounding darkness – is it too much to compare this immediate scene with part of a masterpiece by Caravaggio or Joseph Wright of Derby? Equally striking is the sharpness of the silhouette generated by the rack and its contents on the wall: a clear definition of grey-black against the light of the background surface. Briefly, I turn around and see my own silhouette – a distant hulking grey – on the wall behind me. It is a question of position and perspective: there will be a variety of silhouettes around the room, depending on the surrounding architecture and the place of the viewer.

My thoughts are temporarily dominated by this perspective of cause and effect. I am the flame. The letter rack and its contents represent the events of my life – family, sport, culture, travel – and the silhouette is the totality of the wider impacts that have been left behind: on the lives of those I have loved and on the lives of those I have never known. I realise that this analogy is both painful and sad, for when the flame expires so will these broader impacts.

The flame flourishes. After a while, its length matches that of the remaining wax in the candle and then it exceeds it – double the length, triple the length… I find that if I screw my eyes up tightly, there appears to be a long beam of light that extends from well above the candle and through its length and then down towards the floor. At the two ends of the beam, the light seems to widen and split, as if attempting to replicate Newton's experiment of pure white light refracting in a prism.

For a few moments, I replace my spectacles. Not surprisingly, the flame is much more sharply defined – I am short-sighted – with its sharper edges and clearer shape. But I prefer the softer, vaguer version, so I remove my glasses once again. Inside the flame, the wick appears to lean to one side, as if tiring from the effort of remaining upright. Its tip glows red, whilst the base of the flame shows blue.

The end of the flame's life is action-packed. Its size diminishes slightly, as if prefacing a steady reduction in scope and brightness. But no, it recovers, attempting to restore its former grandeur. Then it declines again, this time without a recovery to its previous glory. For a while, it holds on again, before reducing in size once more. These variations in its life force are reflected instantaneously in changes in the brightness of the letter rack and the sharpness of the silhouette on the wall. In the flame's inexorable decline, there is a constant shift in the subject's breathing: heavy gasps followed by light exhalation.

The fullness of the flame is lost for the first time. There is still some light, however – or rather a collection of lights: small pinpricks of different colours, not dissimilar to the illuminations on the tiniest of Christmas trees. Amazingly, a small, short-lived full flame re-appears and then is lost again. The pinpricks re-appear. Finally, they also are extinguished. It takes me a few seconds to realise that I am staring into a darkness that, this time, will not be relieved.

I follow my instructions and continue to pause and reflect for another couple of minutes. Then, after getting up to switch on the room light, I return to the bookcase and examine the box. I see that part of its corner has been burnt away leaving a small open semi-circle, where the thin card had previously been.

The flame had left a permanent impact after all.

www.anordinaryspectator.com/news-blog December 2022

# Notes

## The Wrong Ground – But a Good Game Nonetheless

1    The Hunslet Club Parkside and Hunslet Warriors clubs merged in November 2022 to form Hunslet ARLFC.

## Good Company and Chance Encounters

2    Essex won the 2017 County Championship by a sizeable margin, their 248 points in the final table comfortably exceeding second-placed Lancashire's 176. Yorkshire finished in joint 4th place with 148 points, though this was only two points above the total registered by Middlesex, who were 7th and therefore took one of the two relegation places.

## A Keen Contest on a Dreich Afternoon

3    Another of my less than successful sporting predictions, as it turned out. Including the Peebles match, West of Scotland lost all their last 8 league games conceding 325 points in the process. Critically, they also had 3 points deducted in the league table for failing to fulfil a fixture due to being unable to field a team. At the end of the season, this put the club level on points in the table with Whitecraigs and, with the inferior points difference, West were relegated. In the final match away at Kirkcaldy, the divisional champions, West were denied a losing bonus point (for defeat by a 7-point margin or less) when their opponents kicked a 40-metre penalty goal in the third minute of injury time.

## 700-Plus Years After Edward I – A Two-All Draw

4    Dennis McCleary, the football secretary of Berwick Rangers FC, was kind enough to arrange for the reproduction of this blog in the club's match programme – The Black and the Gold – for the subsequent home fixture against Edinburgh City.

## Even Better Times at Rugby Park

5    Ross County were relegated at the end of the 2017-18 season. The following season, they won the Scottish Championship and were thus promoted back to the Scottish Premiership. Kilmarnock were relegated to the Championship at the end of the 2020-21 season, but promoted back to the Premiership a year later.

## The Conductor of the Orchestra

6    Scarlets lost the final of the 2017-18 Guinness Pro14 to Leinster by 32-40 in Dublin.

## Below Average

7    Yorkshire did win their three remaining fixtures in the North group and went on to defeat Essex in the quarter-final at Chelmsford. They were beaten by Hampshire in the semi-final at Southampton.

## Geoff Gunney MBE

[8]  An edited version of this blog was published as the obituary to Geoff Gunney in the *Forty-20* rugby league magazine in July 2018.

[9]  From "Into my heart an air that kills", part of *A Shropshire Lad* written in 1896.

## A Long Time Between Visits

[10]  In 2020, it was announced that, following a bidding process, the location of the Rugby League Museum would be in the George Hotel in Huddersfield. However, in 2022, Kirklees Council stated that the museum would be sited elsewhere in the town. This has put the whole project on hold with press reports (in July 2022) suggesting that some of the earlier bidders – including in Wigan and Leeds – would seek to resurrect their bids should the process go back out to tender.

## Another Tough Pool

[11]  Saracens won all 6 matches in the group and were seeded at number 1 for the quarter-finals. Glasgow Warriors also qualified for the knock-out stage – as number 8 seed – having been one of the best-placed group runners-up and the two sides met again in the quarter-final. Saracens won 56-27 and went on to lift the trophy, defeating Leinster in the final.

## Recreation Park

[12]  Alloa Athletic were 2-1 up at St Mirren with 5 minutes left to play. The home side then scored two goals to win 3-2.

## And the World Football Title Holders Are…

[13]  From the beginning of 2019, the Title was passed from the Netherlands to Italy, Spain, France, Denmark and Croatia, the last of which held it at the start of the 2022 FIFA World Cup. In that tournament, Croatia were defeated by Argentina, who then beat France in the final on penalties. Thus, Argentina were the World Football Title Holders at the beginning of 2023.

## Tests of Skill and Character

[14]  Valencia won the second leg 1-0.

## Ebbs and Flows

[15]  Judd Trump won the 2019 World Snooker Championship defeating John Higgins 18-9 in the final.

## Kings, Queens and Poets

[16]  Queen of the South's 5-0 home win in the second leg of their play-off against Montrose gave them a 6-2 aggregate victory. Stephen Dobbie scored three goals to break the club's record for goals in a season. The subsequent 3-1 aggregate win over Raith Rovers preserved Queen of the South's status as a Championship club for the 2019-20 season.

## The Circle of Cricketing Life

[17]  Essex won the 2019 County Championship; Somerset were runners-up.

## A Local Rivalry

[18]  Kingussie Camanachd Club won the 2019 Mowi Premiership; Newtonmore Camanachd Club finished fifth in the table.

## Lest We Forget

[19]  The 2019-20 Scottish football season was suspended in March 2020 due to the Covid-19 pandemic. In May, it was decided that the average points per game would be used to determine final league positions. As a result, Celtic were awarded a 9th consecutive Premiership title, whilst Hearts were relegated to the Championship, a decision which prompted the Edinburgh-based club to (unsuccessfully) pursue legal action.

## Degrees of Latitude

[20]  In April 2020, following the suspension of all football in Scotland the previous month due to the Covid-19 pandemic, it was decided that the league placings at that point should stand in determining promotion from the Championship, League 1 and League 2 and relegation from the Championship and League 1. Cove Rangers were promoted from League 2 and Stranraer were relegated from League 1 (thus re-establishing the Elgin City-Stranraer fixture for the 2020-21 season).

## Arresting Decline

[21]  The Yorkshire Carnegie rugby club was re-branded as the Leeds Tykes in September 2020.

## "Let's Keep It Up, Otley"

[22]  Caldy had secured promotion to National League 1 prior to the English rugby union season being suspended in March 2020 due to the Covid-19 pandemic. Scunthorpe already having been relegated, the other two relegation places were determined by a "best playing record formula" adopted by the Rugby Football Union. Otley were duly relegated to the Northern Premier league – see the later "One Year On" (January 2021).

## The Coronavirus: Economics, Questions and Priorities

[23]  Published in November 1986 (ISBN 0-906577-74-8).

## The Football Stand

[24]  Emerald Publishing terminated its sponsorship deal with Yorkshire CCC at the height of the club's racism scandal in November 2021. In April 2022, it was announced that Clean Slate Studio, an Indian media firm, would take over as principal sponsor at Headingley on a two-year agreement.

## The Coronavirus Provides a Reminder

[25]  From "If", written about 1895 and first published in 1910.

## Unfinished Business at Petershill Park

26  VfL Wolfsburg were defeated 3-1 by Olympique Lyonnais Féminin in the final of the 2019-20 Women's Champions League, the French side winning the title for the fifth successive year. A few days later, Pernille Harder was transferred to Chelsea FC Women for a fee reported to be £250,000.

## The 1954 Vintage – Part 2

27  From "Do not go gentle into that good night" in *The Collected Poems of Dylan Thomas*, New Directions, 1953.

## From Light Blue to the Red, White and Blue

28  My article about Keith Slater in the Winter 2020 edition of the *Rugby League Journal* prompted some very interesting feedback.

Thankfully, I had stated that I was ready to be corrected – on my suggestion that Slater had been one of only three Rugby Blues from Cambridge University to have played professional rugby league and that he had also been the only ex-pupil of Roundhay School in Leeds (my alma mater) to have had a career in the league code – and I duly was (on both counts) by alert *Journal* subscribers.

Richard Lowther informed me that Jonathan Griffiths played for the Paris St Germain club in the inaugural Super League season of 1996, making his debut against the Leeds Rhinos at Headingley. Previously a flank forward with the Wakefield rugby union club and England Under 21s, he played in the centre for PSG. He went on to be a dual Rugby Blue at Cambridge at union and league. (He is not to be confused with his namesake, the former Welsh union international scrum half, who signed for St Helens in 1989 and represented Wales and Great Britain at league).

Likewise, Steven Boothroyd reported that Roundhay School can lay claim to Phil Hasty, who had a distinguished league career with the Hunslet Hawks, Hull KR, York City Knights and Rochdale Hornets between 2002 and 2008. The speedy half-back was the National League 2 Player of the Season in 2003, when he also featured in the Hawks's famous Challenge Cup win over the Super League's Huddersfield Giants.

I was pleased to include this information in a Postscript to the article, which was published in the Spring 2021 edition of the *Journal*.

## Memorable Lines

29  Derek Mahon, *Selected Poems*, Viking, 1991.

## The Coronavirus: One Year On

30  The proposed entry of the Ottawa Aces into the Rugby Football League was based on the acquisition by a Canadian consortium of the RFL membership previously held by Hemel Stags. Subsequently, this membership was transferred to Cornwall RLFC, which entered League 1 in 2022.

## The Test Match World Title

[31] See Endnote 13 above.

[32] India won the 2021 series 3-1. In the subsequent series in England later in the year, India led 2-1 when the fifth and final game was postponed and re-arranged for July 2022. (England won this match to draw the series 2-2). By that time, India had played further series against New Zealand at home (won 1-0 with one draw) and South Africa away (lost 1-2), after which South Africa lost 1-2 in England. England remained the holders of the Test Match World Title at the beginning of 2023 having won 3-0 in Pakistan in December 2022.

## Shuffling Into Retirement

[33] This particular blog was referenced in Brian Carpenter's "Cricket and Blogs 2021" article in the *Wisden Cricketers' Almanack 2022*.

## Insult to Injury

[34] "Insult to Injury" was one of my entries in the *Wisden Cricketers' Almanack 2021*'s Writing Competition. It was published as one of the 12 commended runners-up in the Summer 2022 edition of *The Nightwatchman: The Wisden Cricket Quarterly*.

## Even Longer Times Between Visits – Part 1

[35] The Castleford Tigers finished in 7th place in the Super League table and did not qualify for the play-offs. The Catalan Dragons did qualify, but were defeated by the Leeds Rhinos in the first round.

## Even Longer Times Between Visits – Part 2

[36] An error on my part. The top 6 teams contested the play-offs in the 2022 Rugby League Championship division.

[37] The Batley Bulldogs finished 5th in the 2022 Championship table and played the Barrow Raiders (who finished 4th) again – away from home – in the first round of the play-offs. They won by 18 points to 8 and then went on to defeat the second-placed Featherstone Rovers 32-28 in the play-off semi-final. Batley were defeated by the Leigh Centurions in the final, the latter thereby gaining promotion to the 2023 Super League.

## Welcome to Glasgow

[38] This essay was also published in Issue 83 of the retro football magazine *Backpass* in January 2023.

## Nos illuc in fine

[39] Australia defeated Samoa 30-10 in the final.

# Acknowledgements

I begin by replicating the Acknowledgements made in *An Ordinary Spectator: 50 Years of Sport* and *Still An Ordinary Spectator: Five More Years of Watching Sport*. This is by recognising that sports spectating is a communal activity and that my thanks are due to all those – organisers, administrators, players, officials and coaches as well as fellow spectators – with whom I have shared the various sporting events described in this book. The opportunity to attend the events covered in this volume – large and small – has been dependent on the efforts of many other people.

As with the previous two publications, the team at SilverWood Books has produced the book with great professionalism. In particular, the Publishing Director Helen Hart has again provided consistent encouragement and constructive advice and has overseen the page layouts with considerable care and skill. The final design of the cover perfectly complements those used for the earlier books.

All the photographs in the book have been taken by or on behalf of the author. I am grateful to the positive feedback received on the respective photographs of their clubs' grounds from David Warren, Secretary of Millom RLFC, and Colin T Adamson, Honorary Secretary of Scarborough CC. All reasonable efforts have been made to contact copyright owners. If anyone feels that their copyright has been breached, I should be very happy to address that in any future reprint.

Finally – and, again, as before – the members of my family have, at various times, provided valued feedback on the drafts of many of the essays and articles that appear in this book. (Any errors that remain are entirely my responsibility). More generally, they have continued to support and sustain me with their love and affection. *An Ordinary Spectator Returns: Watching Sport Again* is dedicated to Angela, Tom and Katie.

# Bibliography

## Books and Booklets
### Sport

Ken J Adams ed., *Windsors Rugby League Annual,* Windsors (Sporting Investments) Ltd, 1962.

Eric Ashton, *Glory in the Centre Spot,* Scratching Shed Publishing Ltd, 2009.

Maurice Bamford, *Play to Win: Rugby League Heroes,* London League Publications Ltd, 2005.

John Bentley, *John Bentley: My Story,* Andre Deutesch Limited, 1999.

HG Bissinger, *Friday Night Lights,* Da Capo Press, 25th Anniversary Edition, 2015.

Lawrence Booth ed., *Wisden Cricketers' Almanack,* John Wisden & Co. Ltd., 2019, 2020, 2022.

Tony Collins, *Rugby's Great Split: Class, Culture and the Origins of Rugby League Football,* Frank Cass Publishers, 1998.

Harry Edgar, *Rugby League Memories: Volume Two,* Rugby League Journal Publishing, 2016.

Gareth Davies and Ian Garland, *Who's Who of Welsh International Soccer Players,* Bridge Books, 1991.

Paul Gallico, *Farewell to Sport,* First Nebraska (paperback edition), 2008.

AN Gaulton, *The Encyclopaedia of Rugby League Football,* Robert Hale Limited, 1968.

Dave Hadfield, *Up and Over: A Trek Through Rugby League Land,* Mainstream Publishing, 2004.

Les Hoole and Mike Green, *The Parksiders: A Brief History of Hunslet RLFC, 1883-1973,* Mike Green, 1988.

Les Hoole and Mike Green, *Parkside Memories,* Mike Green, 1989.

Michael Joyce, *Football League Players Records, 1988 to 1939,* Tony Brown, 2002.

Keith Macklin, *The Rugby League Game,* Stanley Paul & Co. Ltd, 1967.

Douglas Middleton, *Heriot's! A Centenary History of George Heriot's School Former Pupils Rugby Club,* Sportsprint, 1990.

Bennet Omalu, *Truth Doesn't Have a Side: My Alarming Discovery about the Danger of Contact Sports,* Zondervan, 2017.

Ronald Reng, *A Life Too Short: The Tragedy of Robert Enke,* Yellow Jersey Press, 2011.

John Rigg, *An Ordinary Spectator: 50 Years of Watching Sport,* SilverWood Books, 2012.

John Rigg, *Still An Ordinary Spectator: Five More Years of Watching Sport*, SilverWood Books, 2017.

Gordon Ross ed., *Playfair Cricket Annual, 1971*, Playfair.

Herbert Sutcliffe, *How to Become a First Class Batsman*, Herbert Sutcliffe Ltd publisher, 1949.

## Other

*Guinness World Records*, Guinness Media Inc., 2005.

Diarmaid MacCulloch, *A History of Christianity*, Allen Lane, 2009.

HCG Matthew and Brian Harrison eds., *Oxford Dictionary of National Biography*, Oxford University Press, 2004.


## DVD

*Rugby League. 1962 & 1963 Ashes Tours.*

*Rugby League. 1965 Challenge Cup Final.*


## Film

*Concussion*, Columbia Pictures, 2015.

*Jaws*, Zanuck/Brown Company, 1975.

*This Sporting Life*, Independent Artists Productions, 1963.


## Literature and Music

Robert Burns, *"To a Mouse"* in *The Complete Poems and Songs of Robert Burns*, Waverley Books, 2011.

AE Houseman, *"A Shropshire Lad"* in *A Shropshire Lad and Other Poems, The Collected Poems of AE Housman*, Penguin Classics, 2010.

Derek Mahon, *"Everything Is Going To Be All Right"* in *Selected Poems*, Viking, 1991.

Rudyard Kipling, *"If"* in *Rudyard Kipling: 100 Poems, Old and New*, Cambridge University Press, 2018.

William Shakespeare, *Julius Caesar*, in *The Arden Shakespeare Complete Works*, The Arden Shakespeare, 2000.

John Suchet and Darren Henly, *The Friendly Guide to Beethoven*, Hodder Arnold, 2006.

Dylan Thomas, *"Do not go gentle into that good night"* in *The Collected Poems of Dylan Thomas*, New Directions, 1953.

## Magazines and Journals

*Backpass; Football League Review; Forbes; Forty-20; The Nightwatchman: Wisden Cricket Quarterly; Radio Times; Roar [Castleford RLFC]; The Rugby League Journal; Rugby World; Sports Illustrated.*

## Newspapers (various editions)

*Bolton Evening News; The Economist; The Guardian; The Herald [Glasgow]; The Independent; Lancashire Evening Post; Leeds Mercury; Leigh Chronicle; Manchester Courier and Lancashire General Advertiser; New York Daily News; Newcastle Morning Herald and Miners' Advocate [Australia]; The People; Racing Post; The Scotsman; Sydney Morning Herald; The Times; Toronto Star; Yorkshire Evening Post; Yorkshire Post.*

## Radio

*Sportsweek*, Radio Five Live, BBC, 2018.
*Test Match Special*, BBC, 1957 to present.

## Television
### Sport

*Alan Shearer: Dementia, Football and Me*, BBC, 2017.
*Clwb Rygbi* , BBC Wales, 2019.
*Concussion: The Impact of Sport*, Sky Sports, 2017.
*The Edge*, Noah Media Group, 2019.
*La Giro d'Italia*, QUEST and Eurosport, 2020.
*Grandstand*, BBC, 1958-2007.
*The NFL Show*, BBC, 2020.
*NRL Try Time*, Fox [Australia], 2020.
*Pot Black*, BBC, 1969-1986, 1991-1993, 2005-2007.
*Rugby League's Legendary Watersplash Final*, BBC, *2018*.
*Sports Personality of the Year*, BBC, 2019.
*Sportsview*, BBC, 1954-1968.
*The Super League Show*, BBC, 2020.
*Tour de France*, ITV4, 2020.
*La Vuelta a Espana*, ITV4, 2020.
*Wide World of Sports*, Channel 9 [Australia], 2020.

## Other

*Edge of Darkness*, BBC Television, 1985.

## Websites

### Statistical sources

www.ESPNcricinfo.com.
www.worldfootball.net.


## Other

www.anordinaryspectator.com. John Rigg's website for *An Ordinary Spectator: 50 Years of Watching Sport*, *Still An Ordinary Spectator: Five More Years of Watching Sport* and *An Ordinary Spectator Returns: Watching Sport Again*.
www.ayr-racecourse.co.uk. Ayr Racecourse.
www.bwfbadminton.com. Badminton World Federation.
www.blackandambers.co.uk. Newport RFC.
www.sportingmemoriesnetwork.com. Sporting Memories Foundation.
www.swintonlionsrlc.co.uk. Swinton Lions Supporters Trust.
www.tapatalk.com/groups/whiteroseforum. Followers of Yorkshire CCC.

# Index

Ingram Content Group UK Ltd.
Milton Keynes UK
UKHW031801040723
424524UK00008B/151